KENTUCKY COURT AND OTHER RECORDS
VOLUME II

✣

From Original Court Entries

✣

WILLS, DEEDS, ORDERS, SUITS, CHURCH MINUTES, MARRIAGES, OLD BIBLES AND TOMBSTONE INSCRIPTIONS

Records From

Fayette, Jefferson, and Lincoln (first three great counties), Bath, Bourbon, Bracken, Clark, Fleming, Harrison, Hardin, Jessamine, Mason, Madison, Montgomery, Nicholas, Oldham, Scott, Woodford, Warren

✣

Compiled By

MRS. WILLIAM BRECKENRIDGE ARDERY

SOUTHERN HISTORICAL PRESS, INC.

Book Publishers

Please direct all correspondence and orders to:

www.southernhistoricalpress.com
or
SOUTHERN HISTORICAL PRESS, Inc.
PO BOX 1267
375 West Broad Street
Greenville, SC   29601
southernhistoricalpress@gmail.com

Originally published: Lexington, KY 1932
Reprinted by:
Southern Historical Press, Inc.
Greenville, SC
ISBN #0-89308-782-3
All rights Reserved.
Printed in the United States of America

DEDICATION

✣

To My Mother

LOUISE PENDLETON SPENCER

who gave encouragement to this work and inspiration to my life, I lovingly dedicate this book, Kentucky Court and Other Records, Volume II.

Julia Spencer Ardery.

KENTUCKY

In the year 1772 Fincastle County became the frontier county of Virginia, extending to the Mississippi it embraced all of what is now Kentucky, and a part of Southwestern Virginia. The county of Fincastle was dissolved by legislative enactment of the State of Virginia December 31, 1776 at which time a portion of it became Kentucky County, Virginia. In May, 1780, Kentucky County was subdivided into three counties: Fayette, Jefferson Lincoln.

Fayette County embraced all of that part of the present State of Kentucky east and north of the Kentucky River and its Middle Fork. The bounds of Jefferson County were "that part of the south side of the Kentucky River which lies west and north of a line beginning at the mouth of Benson's Big Creek, and running up the same and its main fork to the head; thence south to the nearest waters of Hammond's Creek, and down the same to its junction with the Town Fork of Salt River, thence south to the Green River, and down the same to its junction with the Ohio."

Lincoln County included all of what is now the State of Kentucky not embraced in the counties of Fayette and Jefferson.

Nelson County was formed from a portion of Jefferson in 1784, and was the fourth county formed in the state.

On May 1, 1785, Fayette County was divided into two counties, the northern portion being called Bourbon, and the southern portion retaining the name Fayette. Bourbon was the fifth county.

Mercer County was established by the State of Virginia in 1785 and was cut from Lincoln County. It was the sixth county formed in the state.

Madison County was the seventh county and was carved from Lincoln County and established in 1785.

On May 1, 1788, Mason County was formed out of territory taken from Bourbon. The new county embraced all of the territory in Eastern Kentucky, and Northern Kentucky to the mouth of the Licking River. It was the eighth county formed by Virginia.

Woodford County was set up by Virginia from territory taken from Fayette in 1788. It was the last of nine counties of Kentucky established by the State of Virginia.

FORMATION OF COUNTIES

	New Counties	Old Counties Out of Which Formed	Year
Counties Formed by State of Virginia	1. Jefferson____Kentucky		1780
	2. Fayette_____Kentucky		1780
	3. Lincoln_____Kentucky		1780
	4. Nelson_____Jefferson		1784
	5. Bourbon____Fayette		1785
	6. Mercer_____Lincoln		1785
	7. Madison____Lincoln		1785
	8. Mason_____Bourbon		1788
	9. Woodford___Fayette		1788
	10. Washington_____Nelson		1792
	11. Scott_____Woodford		1792

BATH COUNTY
(Formed from Montgomery County, 1811)

WILLS FROM BOOK A

ATCHISON, WM.—To wife, Sarah, at death, division among hrs.; two youngest sons, Henry and Elijah. Written July 20, 1811. Probated June 15, 1814. Wts.: Wm. Lowe, Sam'l Willson.

BRACKEN, MATHEW—To wife, Nancy, for schooling children. Extr.: Thos. Arnett. Aug. 26, 1813. Wts.: Jno. Arnett, Thos. Arnett.

BRECKENRIDGE, ROBERT—To wife, Mary; son, Alexander if he returns; sons, Francis, Preston and John Doke (Doak); son, James; dau., Anne Breckenridge; dau., Polly Caldwell; son, Alexander, if living. Jan. 26, 1814. Wts.: Jas. M. Graham, Robt. Mitchell, Mathew Mitchell, Allen Godgell (?).

BRISTOL, JOHN—To wife, Sarah; son, Ezra; to Dove Walker, his sister's dau., property and Bible. Extrix.: wife; Extr.: Jas. M. Graham. Written Apr. 8, 1813. Probated June 14, 1813. Wts.: Rowland Richards, Alex. Tavis.

COSHOW, BENONI—To son, John; dau., Elizabeth Cemmons; dau., Sarah Taylor; dau., Esther Scott; son, Wm.; dau., Agnes D. Cannon; dau., Jenny Cannon; dau., Hannah Maice as long as she remains single; wife, Agnes; granddau., Elizabeth Scott. Extrs.: son, John and John Taylor. Estate sold and divided among all aforesaid hrs. Two grandsons, Benoni Taylor and Benoni Scott. Written Aug. 20, 1809. Probated Sept. 23, 1811. Wts.: Richard Stamper, John Arnett, John Stamper.

DAYE, JOHN—To wife, Caty (Caby) and at her death between chdn. viz: Elijah, Elizabeth, Geo., Abigail, Rhoda, Saythorn and unborn child. Extrs.: Wm. Morgan, Jeremiah Jackson. Written Feb. 16, 1814. Probated Apr. 11, 1814. Wts.: Richard Ross, Martha Butcher, Margaret Dougherty.

HARRISON, CARLISLE—"Enlisted in the U. S. Army." Property to bro., Joseph Harrison. Written July 11, 1813, Maysville. Probated Oct. 11, 1814. Wt.: A. Bryson.

HICKLIN, HUGH—"Of Harrison Co., Ky." Extrs.: John McNab of Montgomery Co., Henry McDaniel of Fayette Co., and Levi Covvell of Harrison Co., Names wife, Elizabeth; dau., Ann; dau., Margaret; dau., Jane; son, John; dau., Ruth's chdn. when of age; property in hands of Jno. McNab; son, Hugh to have great Bible, etc.; dau., Sarah; dau., Martha; dau., Mary; grandson, Chas. Hicklin. Written March 21, 1811. Probated Sept. 1811. Wts.: Alexander McDonnel, Isaac Rice, Richard Harcourt, Peter R. Gill, Reubin Randolph, Mahlon Hall, John Richey.

JEWIT, (JOUETT) CAPTAIN JOHN—Inventory, pg. 295—March 25, 1822. Appraisers: Geo. Coleman, Robt. B. Crooks, Jas. Wade.

Note: The above is the inventory of the famous patriot and Revolutionary soldier of Virginia who rode from Cuckoo to warn Jefferson and the Virginia Legislature of the approach of Tarlton.

LONSDALE, JAMES — Mentions his father, William Lonsdale; two chdn., Elizabeth and Jacob; wife, Ester; father-in-law, John Warner. and Dr. Jno. Stevens, Extrs. Written Nov. 19, 1819. Probated Dec., 1819.

LONSDALE, JOHN—Appoints father, Wm. Lonsdale, his heir-at-law of all estate; joiners tools to David Hindman, Isaac Trumbo. Written Oct. 19, 1813. Probated June 13, 1814. Wts.: Zacheriah Green, John Crow.

LONSDALE, WM.—nuncupative will—Admitted by Jas. Lonsdale, proved by Thos. Fletcher and John Jones and Mary Hawkins. To son, James, all estate of John Lonsdale, decd., except joiners tools to David Heneman, they being left by will of John Lonsdale; balance to Wm. F. Hawkins and David T. Hawkins, sons of Mary Hawkins. Francis Lonsdale one of the heirs-at-law and Richard Menefee who intermarried with Polly Lonsdale, another of the heirs-at-law, appeared in court and made objections.

MAPPIN, SARAH—To chdn.: John Mappin, Jas. Mappin (decd?), Hannah Williams, Joseph Mappin, Sarah Rogers, dau., Elizabeth Bracken; son-in-law, Sam'l Rogers. Written June 27, 1814. Probated Oct. 10, 1814. Wts.: I. (or J.) Harrison, Henry Kiphart.

McCORMACK, WM.—To wife, for the bringing up of his family; when chdn. come of age to have property, and when youngest comes of age all to be sold and they be made equal with others. Written Jan. 16, 1814. Probated Apr. 11, 1814. Wts.: Hugh Wiley, Jas. Dean.

NAYLOR, PAUL—To wife for life to rear chdn., and at her death or marriage, division to be made. May 1, 1814. Probated July 11, 1814. Wts.: Geo. Linch, Geo. Berry.

OAKLEY, THOMAS—nuncupative will—Geo. Pugh and Wm. Manly on the 9th of Feb., 1813, at camp at the foot of the Miami Rapids, heard Thos. Oakley, a private in said Pugh's Company say he had no hope of recovery from sickness and wished his property deposed of as follows: to Joel Parker, a note he held on Jas. Johnson, etc.; debts paid Jno. Jones and Mrs. Boyd; a sorrel colt given little Billy Oakley not to be taken from him; desired Capt. Pugh to write an order for Joel Parker and David Allen. Probated Aug. 12, 1813.

POWERS, JAMES—To wife, Elenor; to boys; daus. to be made equal with sons. Extrs.: Thos. Fletcher, son, Jeremiah Power. Written May 4, 1814. Probated June, 1814. Wts.: Thos. Peony, Thos. Sinclair.

ROGERS, SAMUEL—To wife, Martha, for bringing up and schooling chdn.; oldest boys, John and James. Written Feb. 16, 1814. Probated June 15, 1814. Wts.: Sam'l Wilson, Elijah Atchison.

SCHROFFE, (SHROFFE) JOHN ADAM—To friend, Samuel Poor; friend, Joseph Harrison. Written Apr. 13, 1814. Probated June 13, 1814. Wts.: Jacob Trumbo, Thos. Owings.

SINCLAIR, AMOS—To wife, Mary; chdn.: John, Thos., Mary Snelling, Susannah Brown; grandson, Amos Sinclair, son of Thos. Extr.: son, Thos. Sinclair. Written July 16, 1813. Probated Sept. 13, 1813. Wts.: Jas. Young, Nathl. W. Ralls.

ATKENSON, MARYANN—Widow of Thos. Atkenson, dower. Oct. 12, 1812.

HAMILTON, ELIZABETH—Dower, late Elizabeth Elliott, widow of John Elliott, decd. Jan. 29, 1812.

LONSDALE, SARAH—Widow of Wm. Lonsdale, dower. Sept. 12, 1814.

INVENTORIES AND ESTATES APPRAISED

Names appearing in this index are not included in General Index

Thoa. Atkenson, 1812.

Mary Blair, 1812.

Joseph Cann, (Conn), 1814.
Jas. Carr, 1814.
Wm. Cantrill, 1812.
Zedoc Clavell, 1812.

John Day, 1814.
Wm. Donaldson, 1814.
Thos. Fletcher, 1814.

Presley Gill, 1812.

Frederick Hawes, 1814.

Wm. Higgins, 1814.

Wm. Ledford, 1814.

Mathew Miller, 1814.
Wm. McCormack, 1814.

Wm. Perrin, 1813.
Wm. Powers, 1814.

Sanders, Searcy, 1814.
Adam Schrofe, 1814.
Casper Shrout, 1812.
Josiah Strausberry, 1814.
Benj. Stringfield, 1813.

BOURBON COUNTY

(Formed from Fayette County, 1785)

Abstracts by Jane Clay Kenney

WILLS FROM BOOKS A, B, C, AND D

BRANHAM, MARGARET—Nuncupative will—About ten days before her death, Oct. 19, 1847, stated to Margaret A. Scott at her home, her intention to leave estate in hands of James Lindsay for support of Jacob Lindsay; said James to be reasonably compensated for acting as trustee; also made this statement to Maria L. Rogers. Sworn to by Margaret A. Scott, Oct. 1847. Further stated to James Lindsay she owed her son, Jacob Lindsay a dividend from her estate, having paid her other children and intended giving him all, to be placed in the hands of Isaac Skinner for his use. Sworn to by Jas. Lindsay, Nov. 1, 1847. Proved Nov. 1847. Note: The above Margaret Branham was formerly the widow of Thomas Lindsay of Culpeper County, Va., and was half-sister of Thomas Hutchcraft (Revolutionary soldier). Thomas Lindsay, according to a letter written by his granddaughter, was a merchant, and, after the Revolutionary War, went into the Carolinas to trade and was lost there. His widow married James Branham in Culpeper County, Va., 1806 anl soon thereafter moved to Kentucky. Issue of Thomas and Margaret Lindsay as given in the above mentioned letter: Jacob; Reubin; Thomas married Elizabeth Elkin; Nimrod Long married 1817 Lavinia Garrard Grimes and died Sept. 2, 1840, his wife died Sept. 14, 1840; Margaret A.; Charles born Nov. 27, 1795; Nancy married Mr. Todd; Elizabeth and Jane.

DAWSON, SAMUEL—Will Book C, page 316—Names: wife, Martha; sons, Thos., John, Samuel Jones Dawson; daughters, Priscilla Jones and Martha Clay. Dated Oct. 4, 1807.–Nov. 1807 Wts.: Walter Buel, Abrm. Irvine, Robert Walker, Wm. F. Lock.

DICKEY, DAVID—Will Book D, page 268—Names: sons, Milus, Fielding, John Lawson, lots in Port William and Alexander; daughters, Amy, Polly, Eby. Executors: James Houston Wm. Rogers. Witnesses—John Winn, Samuel and Levi Houston. July 10, 1811. July court, 1812.

DONNELL, JAMES—Will Book D, page 527—Wife, Polly; sons, James, Thomas, Samuel; daughters, Ellen, Eliza. Dec. 16, 1813. November, 1814. Witnesses—Jas. Donnell and James Quiett.

DOUGLAS, SAMUEL—Will Book B, page 52—Names—wife, Hannah; brother, Wm. Douglas and his children; nephew, John Mccullough, sister's son; Samuel Douglas, brother's son; niece, Hannah Drake, sister's daughter. July 23, 1799. Sept., 1799. Witnesses—Moses Bledsoe, James Stark, Abel Headington. To Eliz. Wilson, 5 lbs.

DUFFIELD, ROBT.—Will Book A, page 285—Son, Abraham, Robt., and Benjamin, Thos., Isaac and John; wife, Isabella. Dec. 25, 1795. Jan., 1796. Witnesses—Benj. Radcliff, and Christianna Radcliff.

DUNLAP, JOHN (of Lancaster County, South Carolina)—Will Book A, page 127—Wife, Elizabeth daughter, Jane, Scinthia Kid; sisters, Isabell Howe and Jane Howe's children; nephew, John Howe—, Jane's son . . . brother, Thomas. Feb. 2, 1791. No probate date. Witnesses—John Howe, Wm. Dunlap, Wm. Taylor.

EDWARDS, HADEN—Will Book B, page 201—Wife, Penelope; sons, Benjamin, Sandford, George, John; daughters, Penelope Pope, Nancy Williams, Betsy Chanulor; granddaughter, Penelope Edwards, lands in Henderson County. Roger Williams, an extr. Nov. 10, 1802. August, 1803. Reuben Field, Wm. Stamps, and Zely Reno, witnesses.

FIELD, ANNA—B, 224—Sons, Larkin, and John; dau., Mary Slaughter,

Anna Roberts. Aug. 28, 1799-March, 1804. Wts: Polly Field, Wm. McGee, Philip Field.

FIELD, JOHN—D, 132—Wife, Diannah; sons Henry, Curtis, Harry Ezekiel, and John; daus: Nancy Morrow, Judah Field, Lucindia Field, and Polly Smith. Aug. 12, 1810-Dec. 1810. Wts.: Wm. S. Bryan, and Larkin Field.

FORMAN, JOHN—C, 468—Wife, Mary; sons, Williams, Aaron; daus., Catherine Landers, Elizabeth Hannah, Nancy Boyce, Polly Evans, Margaret Strode. Oct. 6, 1808-Jan. 1809. John Shortridge, Isaac Clinkenbeard, John Scott, and Simon Taylor, Wts.

FRAKES, NATHAN—C, 312—Sons, Nathan and John, and other children not named. Sept. 22, 1807-Oct. 1807. Wts. Wilson Alexander, etc.

FORQUERAN, PETER, SR.—B, 29—Wife, Joice; sons, John, Peter, Jr.; daus: Betty Hall; 2 gd sons: Peter and Jas. Mastin, and gd. dau. Jenny Branch; children of dau. Betty by a former husband; son-in-law, Caleb Hall. Wts. Samuel and Abraham Woodward. Dated May 27, 1784. Probated June, 1798.

FEARN, JOHN—B, 49—Little nephew, Geo. Fearn; my bro. Samuel Fearn, 280 acres; my sister, Mary Bagbey, 640 acres, my bro. and I bought of Wm. Cannon of Va. my sister Mary Bagby. Apr. 4, 1799-July, 1799. Wm. Bagby, Samuel Donell, Samuel Fearn, extrs. Leven Riley, Reason Francis, Wm. Beshaw, wts.

FULTIN, JAMES—C, 191—Wife, Polly; sons, John and James; dau., Peggy. Nov. 11, 1806-Dec. 1806. Wts.: Ninian Steele, George King.

GARRARD, DANIEL—D, 469—Wife, Elizabeth; sons, Thomas and Wm. daus., Rosannah, wife of Waran Bates; Frances Humphreys, wife of Geo. H.; Lucy, wife of Joseph L. Stevens; gd. children, Elizabeth and Sarah Hughes and Ralph, Dan'l and Wm. Hughes, children of Elizabeth, wife of George Hughes. Mar. 8, 1812-Jan. 1814. Wts.: Thos. A. Thomson, Laban and Eliz. Shipp, etc.

GROOMS, WM.—D, 163—Wife, Elizabeth; sons, Aaron, Jacob, Moses, and Isaac; all chdn. Mar. 10, 1811-Apr. 1811. Samuel Call, Moses Badders, etc., Wts.

GARRARD, GEORGE—C, 296—Brothers, Wm. and Thos.; sisters Frances Humphreys, Sally Grimes, Lucy Stephens, Rosannah Bates, Sept. 1807-Oct. 1807.

GALLOWAY, WILLIAM—A, 174—Wife, Rebenah; children to be schooled; oldest son George Galloway, son William (150 acres) sons John & James, (tract of land that James Galloway and Kilbreath are now on), youngest son Joseph G., (when of age), their sisters, Mary, Ann and Rebecca Galloway (3 sisters). Wife, Wm. Mitchell, and John Hamilton, extrs. Jan. 20, 1794-May 1794. Wts. John and Jas. Galloway, and Alex. Breckenridge.

GLASGOW, JOHN—A, 202—Wife, Anna; dau., Polly (her mother's

clothes, silver buckles, etc., that were her mother's); dau., Jenny; my bro., Nathaniel Glasgow; wife Ann to rear and school my children, Polly and Jenny. Aug 15, 1794-Dec. 1794. John, Alex. & Jas. Thomson, Wts.

HALL, JOHN—C, 461—Sons, Theophilus and John; dau., Hannah Hutchinson; her daus., Polly Hall and Deborah. Oct. 20, 1807-Jan. 1809. Joseph and Geo. Case, etc., Wts.

HITT, WILLIAM—D, 1—Sisters, Agnes Hitt, and Sally Hitt. Aug. 23, 1809-Sept. 1809. Wts.: John Carter, Martin Hitt, Dan. Ayers.

HILLIS, WM.—C, 86—Mentions wife and children, but not named, land in Green County, Ohio. Mar. 10, 1804-Mar. 1806. Wife, Peggy, later married James Dykes (see C, 89). Wm. Hillis, John Boyd, etc. Wts.

HALL, MOSES—C, 152—Names wife, Hannah; sons, Wm., Edward, Moses, Alexander, John and Aaron; daus., Martha Hook, Mary Femster; mentions three g. sons named Moses. Extrs.: Wm. Milligan and Aaron Hall. Sept. 6, 1802-July, 1806. Wts.: John Porter, Jesse Fitzgerald, Arthur Scott, etc.

HENDERSON, ALEX.—A, 324—Sons, Robert, Samuel and James Henderson; sons: Joseph, Alexander, David and Daniel Henderson; dau. Florence Henderson, son George H.; gd. son, Alex. Henderson (son of my son, John H.); my dau., Jane Beatty. Extrs.: Samuel and David H. Oct. 30, 1791-Oct. 1796. Wts. Samuel Henderson, Josias McClure, Elizabeth Henderson.

HUFFSTUTER, ULERICK—B, 149—Wife, Mary; daus., Mary, Ruth, Susanna, and Ann; sons, John, James, Mathew, and George. Peter McIntosh, Bethuel Baxter of Madison county mentioned. Sept. 28, 1801-Apr. 1802. Edmund Baxter, Wt.

HUMBLE, CONROD—A, 57—Wife, Hannah and son, Uriah (200 acres on Licking R.); son, Noah (100 acres he lives on); to son-in-law, John Fitzwater; son-in-law, Richard Custer (250 acres in Jefferson county); dau Rachel (250 acres in Jeff. Co.); my bro. Michael Humble to deed 825 acres below mouth of Ky. on Ohio river to Jas. Johnston, my bro-in-law. Jan. 5, 1791. No probate date.

HAND, ELIZABETH—B, 20—To Edward Fugate; to son, John; son, Robert Hand, son Henry Hand. To Ann Trussel and Milly White (furniture) all rest between Mary Fugate and Henry Hand. Capt. Robt. Johnson and Edw. Fugate, extrs. July 1797-Nov. 1798. Wts. Darky and Thos. Thomas. Note: Polly Hand mar. Thos. Thomas.

HAMBLETON, (HAMILTON) WM.—B, 112—Sons, Alexander, Thos., Robt., and Samuel; daus., Nelly Blair, Ibby Hinman; wife, Isabella. Mar. 29, 1800-Jan. 1801. John Hopkins, John Wagner, Sam. Donnell, Wts.

HORNBACK, SIMON—B, 114—Sons, Abraham, Michael, George, John, Isaac, Jacob and Simon; daus., Polly Susie, Peggy Barbara; wife, Margaret; bro., Michael. Dec. 17, 1800-Jan. 1801. A. and Martha Trumbo, wts.

HUGHES, JAMES—D, 281—Wife, Barsheba; sons, George, Enoch, John, Mason; dau., Nancy; bro., John. Jan. 15, 1812-Sept. 1812. Wts.: Ralph, Wm. and Elizabeth Hughes.

HIBLER, WM.—D, 494—Wife, Mary, nee Screachfield; sons, Daniel, Wm., Joseph, Wm.; daus., Mary Ammerman, Eliz. Ammerman, Lena Hornbaker, Cathy Sellers, Nancy Sellars, Susannah Kepinger. Oct. 9, 1812-Feb. 1814. David Jameson, Wt.

HARNEY, SELBY—D, 528—Son, Gilbert, (other children, but names not given). Extrs.: Samuel A. Harney and John Hopkins. Wts.: Esther Hopkins, Sally Wagner and John Hopkins. Feb. 2, 1814-Mar. 1814.

JACOBY, HENRY—B, 118—Mentions children of his bro., Francis Jacoby; Adam Jacoby; mentions parents. May 9, 1798-Mar. 1801. Eliz. Watts, John Butler, Wts.

JONES, JOHN—A, 37—Wife, Susanna; sons, John, Jacob, Benamin; daus., Christiana, Betsy, Susanna, Catherine. Aug. 17, 1790-Dec. 1790. Sus. and Christopher Keiser, Hervy Speaks, Jas. Green, Wts.

JONES, SUSANNAH—Nunc. A, 98—Margaret Swanck testifies that Mrs. Jones wanted her oldest dau., (lame) to have all. June 15, 1791-Dec. 1791. Barbary Jones, Wt.

JAMESON, SAMUEL—A, 149—My oldest bro., Wm. Jameson's eldest son, Chas; to Samuel Robinson (living with me); my only wife, Rebekah, at her death, land to go to bro., David Jameson's son, Samuel. Robt. Finley and Jas. Kirkpatrick, Extrs. Oct. 29, 1793-Dec. 1793. David Jameson, Geo. Wilson, Wm. Robinson, Wts.

JACOBY, FRANCIS LUCIEN—A, 7—May 7, 1788-July 15, 1788. Wife, Frederica, "my small children," all, viz: Katrina, Eliz., Butler, Susannah, Ralph, Gladinglug (?), Frank, Henry, Fred, Daniel, Betsy, Jacob, John and Adam (when of age). Wts.: John Grant, Wm. Butler, Cath E. Butler.

JONES, JOHN—A, 37—Aug. 17, 1790. Wife, Susannah; son, John, 200 acres on Mill Cr., (when 21); sons, Benj. and Jacob (when 21); my 4 daus., Christiana, Betsy, Susanna and Catherine Jones; my bro., Jacob Jones. Dec. 1790.

JONES, CHAS—D, 339—Wife, Nancy Jones; sons, Isaac, Edward, Walter, Catesby, Chas., David, William. July 20, 1812-Mar. 1813. Wts.: Wm. and Sarah Arrasmith.

JONES, THOS.—D, 382—Wife, Affia; sons, James W., Thos., Garrard, daus., Sally, Jane, Betsy, Irvine, Alesanna Brown. Oct. 4 1811-July, 1813. Wts.: Jas. Hickman, Lott Trimble. Sons and Thos. Mitchell, Andrew H. Wright and Nichalos Talbott, Extrs.

JENKINS, WM.—D, 376—Extrs., Edward Stoker, David Jameson. To Sam'l Jamison; to Hannah, wife of David Jamison; to Sarah, dau., of David Jamison. Wts.: John Jameson, Hannah Jameson, John H. Cotton. June 10, 1813-July, 1813.

KELLY, NANCY—C, 448—Late Nancy Webb, and Wm. Kelly in right of his wife as widow of Wm. E. Webb, deceased. Oct. 1808.

KIRBY, THOS—D, 97—Wife, Nancy; children, names not given. Apr. 29, 1810-Sept. 1810. Wts.: John M. Allen, Jno. Keiser, Sr. Extrs.: wife and bro.-in-law, Jno. Kiser.

KINKEAD, JOSEPH—A, 226—Wife, Jane, all. Aug. 31, 1795-Nov. 1795. Wts.: Wm. Martin, Water Caldwell.

KINKEAD, DAVID—A, 234—Eldest dau., Mary; son, Thos.; dau., Nancy; dau., Elizabeth; son, David; son, Joseph; youngest son, Samuel. Dau., Nancy and son-in-law, John Davidson, Extrs. Wts.: Michael Fisher, Joseph Petty. Dec. 1795. Probate not dated.

KUYKENDALL, HENRY—A, 298—Son, Jacob K., 2 sons, Henry and John K.; dau., Rebecca; my gd. children, Henry and John Kuykendall and Rebecca Shanton's children. Sons Extrs. Wts.: Jas. Green, Wm. McCune. Nov. 27, 1795-July, 1796.

HARMON, PETER—D, 46—Wife; sons, Peter, Jasper, Jonas; daus., Elizabeth Ashford, Sally Board, Polly Hyzer. Aug. 22, 1809. Wts.: Philip Hyzer, John McCann, Jas. Ross. Probated Jan. 1810.

KEITH, GEORGE—C, 89—Sons, Richard, Garrett, Edward, George, James (deceased); daus., Eliz. Green, Mary Robinson, Joannah Kerico (Carrico?), Monica Dougherty. Mar. 16, 1806-Apr. 1806. Wts.: John Hand, Jas. Brown.

KEMP, REUBEN—C, 227—Wife, Jenny; sons, Chas., Edward, Reuben, James. Mar. 29, 1807-Apr. 1807. Wts.: John Talbott, James Clevenger.

KENNEBROOK, JOHN—B, 188—Beloved friend, Thos. Simpson. Jan. 5, 1803-Mar. 1803. John Boyd, Jas. McCoune, Wts.

LAIL, GEORGE—A, 133—Wife, Margaret; son, John; to Catarinah Lail, dau. of Peter Lail, deceased, when 18; sons, George and John, the plantation after my wife's death; (if George ever comes and applies for land); rest to be divided eq. between Eliz. Frabks and Margaret Simmolt and Eveleas Casner and George and John Lail (to my four above named children, if George doesn't apply. Wife and Casper Carsner and Andrew Simmolt, Extrs. July 2, 1793. No probate date.

LAIR, ELIZABETH—B, 206—Mother; brother, John Lair; Geo. Smiser, Extr. Mar. 18, 1803-June, 1803. Michael Smith, Katherine Keese, Wts.

LAMY, (LANEY?) WM.—A, 73—Brothers, Robt. and Alexander; to Patrick Griffy and Wm. Ardery, (Penn. money); to Mrs. Nesbit, wife of Wm. Nesbit; to Jas. Miller. Jno. Ardery and Wm. Nesbit, Extrs. June 18, 1791-Oct. 1791. Jas. and Isaac Egnew, Wts.

LIGHTER, HENRY—C, 403—Wife, Catherine; son, Henry; dau., Mary; other children not named. July 4, 1804-Sept. 1808. Michael and Mathias Bever, Wts.

LONGMORE, HUGH—D, 82—Wife, Sarah; sons, William and George. Feb. 7, 1810-Mar. 1810. Benj. Mills, David A. Graves, Wts.

LAIR, ELIZABETH—C, 93—Sons, Chas., John, Wm., Joseph and Matthias; dau., Sarah; Elizabeth Smiser, dau. of Geo. Smiser. Jan. 30, 1806-Apr. 1806. Geo. Reading, Catherine Kees, Wts.

LYON, JOHN—C, 309—Wife and children, but names not given. Mar. 23, 1791-Sept. 1807.

LYDICK, ANDREW—C, 320—Wife, Elizabeth. Nov. 5, 1807-Dec. 1807. Rich Biddle, Wt.

LAUGHLIN, (McCLAUGHLIN?) JAMES—A, 128—Son, George McLaughlin; dau., Ealis McL., both Extrs. George to choose gdn. till 21. Mar. 14, 1791-Aug. 1793.

LYNE, EDMUND—A, 96—Friend, Harry Innis, Extr. Slaves to be freed. Nov. 26, 1791-Dec. 1791. Thos. West, Extr.

LEVENS, ANN—A, 169—Dec. 24, 1793-Mar. 1794. Oldest son, Henry Levens; daus., Patience Mash (Wash?), Rebecca Selvy; 3rd son, Nicholas Levens; 2nd son, Richard Levens; dau., Ann McCrary; youngest son, Jas. Levens. Henry Delay, Wm. Sparks, Wts.

McCLELLAND, WM.—D, 327—Wife, Martha; sons, Alexander, Elijah, Robert (the eldest), James, Elisha, son Wm's heir, Patty Harris Mc.; daus., Jane, wife of Robt. Miller, Martha, wife of Joseph McKim; gd.dau., Patty Orr Mc., dau. of Jas. Nov. 10, 1812-Jan. 1813. Thos. Talbott, Wt.

McCLANAHAN, WM.—D, 360—Mother, Eliz. McClanahan; brother, Thos. McC. Mar. 26, 1813-June, 1813. Wm. Love, Wm. Markham, R. Williams, Wts.

McCLURE, JAMES—D, 454—Wife, Margaret; son, James; daus., Jean, Elizabeth Culberson, Mary, wife of John Nisbet, Margaret, wife of John Moore; gd. daus., Peggy and Suffroney McClanahan; gd. son, Jno. McClanahan. Aug. 3, 1813-Nov. 1813.

McCOY, JOHN—D, 459—Wife, Elizabeth; sons, Martin, Daniel, Duncan, James, William; daus., Nancy, Sarah, Mary, Eliz. Fight. Sept. 14, 1813-Dec. 1813. Wm. and Benj. Coolin, Chas. Porter, Wts.

McCLURE, ANDREW—A, 151—Wife, Rebeckah; sons, James Allin and Andrew; two little daus., Ellinor Wright McClure and Polly McClure; two little sons . . . (plantation on Howards Creek in Clarke County and Fayette). Bros., Samuel and John McClure, Extrs. Aug. 15, 1793-Dec. 1793.

McCLURE, WILLIAM—A, 194—June 20, 1794. Wife, Elizabeth; oldest dau., Lucy; son, John; 2nd dau., Jain; youngest dau., Aliner. Son, John and Samuel Wilson, Extrs.

McNAY, AGNES—A, 165—Dau., Isabella; son, John (2nd child); Nancy, Joseph; dau., Sarah; dau., Margaret; son, James, my right of any part that fell to me at the last adm. made by my son James . . . my son-in-law, James Little. Probated July, 1793.

McCANN, JOHN—A, 221—Wife, Nancy and children. Sept. 8, 1795-Oct. 1795. Children to be schooled. Capt. Thos. Rule, Extr.

McCLANAHAN, THOS.—C, 476—Son, Wm., decd., his widow, Elizabeth; g. son, Thos. McClanahan; g. son, Wm. McClanahan; Wm. Brown and wife, Lucy; John Harrison and wife, Elizabeth; Jas. Pullin and wife, Aggy, g. dau.; Sally McClanahan, Polly McClanahan aforesaid, my daus., and widow of Wm., decd.; son, Thomas, my Military survey; son-in-law, David Hickman and wife, Clary; Robt. Johnstone and wife, Peggy; g. sons, Wm. Johnston and Maurice Langhorne; to Samuel Elgin and wife, Aggy; to Thos. Ashford and wife, Sally and Isaiah Elkins and wife, Ann, land in Woodford Co. Extr.: son, Thomas. Written May 4, 1807. Probated Feb. 1809. Wts.: Elizemon Basey, Wm. Love, Alfred Bayse. Codicil: two sons of son, Wm., decd., viz: Thos. and Wm. trustees named for Agatha Pullin; g. dau., Peggy Dudley, wife of Robt. W. Dudley; six daus., of Elizabeth McClanahan, widow of William, two of whom the above Agatha Pullin and Peggy Dudley. Feb. 1809.

McDANIEL, ENEAS—B, 165—Wife, Isabella; sons, Alexander, John, Rowland, Robert and Francis; dau., Jane Devore; Geo. Givens, Benj. Kendrick and Chas. Smith, Jr., mentioned. Aug. 20, 1802-Sept. 1802. John and Chas. Clarkson, Wm. Kendrick, Wts.

McCLINTOCK, DANIEL—B, 25—Wife, Frances, (Penn. currency); children to be schooled, viz: Elizabeth, Thos., Joseph, Margaret and Alex. Bros., Wm. Nisbet with Joseph and Wm. McClintock, Extrs. Oct. 20, 1798-Jan.1799. Wts.: John Ardery, John Hickman.

MASON, GEORGE—A, 3—Nuncupative will—"Shot by Indians in Lower Blue Licks, Sept. 5th, 1787"—he desired Mr. Denit to pay his debts, and residue to go to Jas. Taylor, son of Joseph Taylor, deceased, of Fairfax Co., near Alexandria to be divided among his brothers and sisters, except the wearing apparel to go to Wm. Johnson and his sister. Wts.: Wm. W. Flyn and Edw. Lyne. Tues., Oct. 16, 1787.

MOORE, JACOB—A, 39—Deed of gift to loving sisters, Nancy Funk, Eliz. Alkire and also Philip Moore, a bond upon Joseph Bunion of County of Hardy, on So. Fork. Sept. 6, 1790-Dec. 1790. Jno. Alkire, Wt.

METHENY, THOS.—A, 146—The 50 acres John Slagle lives on to my nephew, Thos. Slagle, the son of my sister, Ann; to sisters, Ann and Sarah. My father, Extr. Nov. 8, 1793-Nov. 1793.

MOORE, THOS.—A, 193—Wife, Mary; 7 children, (one unborn) when of age; Thos., John, Andrew, Peter, George and Frederick. July 7, 1794-Aug. 1794.

MATHENY, DANIEL—B, 217—Son-in-law, Daniel Turney; sons, Moses, Andrew; daus., Ellender, Anna, Sarah, Elizabeth, Mary, Judah; wife, Judah. Apr. 6, 1803-Jan. 1804. Sally Mays, John Neal, Wts.

MARNEY, ROBT.—B, 264—Grandchildren, John Batson Mary Drummonds, entire estate; sons, John, James, Amos, Daniel, Jonathan; daus., Rachel and Rebecca. Extrs.: James Drummond and Mordecai Batson. Jan. 24, 1805-Mar. 1805. Wts.: Robt. and Wm. Battson.

MITCHELL, SAMUEL—C, 148—Bros., Joseph and John Mitchell (both young). Oct. 2, 1795-July, 1806. Isaac Orchard, Wt.

MOORE, McCLANAHAN—C, 279—Children mentioned, but only one named, Sibby. Willis Field, Extr. Aug. 21, 1807-Sept. 1807.

MITCHELL, ALEX.—C—Wife, Jean; sons, Joseph and John; daus., Patsy and Hannah. Oct. 9, 1808-Mar. 1809. Thos. Mitchell, Wt.

MOUNTJOY, GEORGE—D, 389—Wife, Sarah; sons, Edmund and George. Extr.: Alvin Mountjoy. Jan. 5, 1810-Sept. 1813.

NESBIT, JEREMIAH—A, 281—Mar. 23, 1796. Wife, Sarah; my children when youngest comes of age; Mary, Rachel, Margaret, Robert, Sarah, Eliz., Jeremiah, Samuel, Wm., and Jean Nesbit, (when Samuel and Wm. are 16). Bro., Wm. Nesbit and John Morrow, Extrs. Wts.: Wm. McClintock, Geo. Mountjoy, Robt. Morrow. May, 1796.

NESBIT, WM.—C, 29—Sons, John, Joseph, Jeremiah; dau., Elizabeth, wife, Nancy. July 11, 1805-Sept. 1805. Joseph and Thos. Patton, Wts.

NORTHCUTT, JEREMIAH—C,341—Wife, Mary; sons, Hosea, William, Benjamin, John and George; daus., Anna, Mary, Nancy. Nov. 9, 1807-Mar.1808. Wts.: Wm. Chamblin, John Bridges, Wm. Phillips.

NELSON, CHARLES—B, 158—Wife, Eleanor; sons, Isaac, John, Elias, Levi and James; daus., Elizabeth, Sarah, Caty; mentions Jonathan Crouch. Sept. 9, 1802-Sept. 1802. Wts.: Jno. Musick, Peter Hendricks, Jane Sharrah.

OWINGS, JOHN COCKY—D, 215—Of Baltimore Co., Md., wife, Colegate Deye; daus., Mary, wife of Alex. Nesbit, Chaveilla, Penelope, D. Price, Fanny, and Charlotte; sons, John Cockey, Thomas. Jan. 1, 1810-Feb. 17, 1810. Md., Dec. Court, 1811, Ky. Wts.: Thos. Love, W. Price, A. Ogden.

PALMER, JOHN—A—Wife, Jane; two sons, John and George; 4 sons; sons, Wm. and Thos.; each of my children now single; property to be sold and divided among all. Wife, sons and Chas. Smith, Extrs. Mar. 3, 1796-Mar. 1796. Wts.: Robt. McDonel, John Wells, Dorothy Wells.

PARISH, WM.—D, 361—Wife, Sebina; dau., Rebecca. Extr.: Samuel Keith. Apr. 20, 1813-June, 1813. Test: James Lamme, Everett Palmer, Peyton Palmer.

PARISH, NATHANIEL—D, 136—"Son of Joel Parish of Louisa Co., Va." Sons, Joel, Zachariah, Nathaniel; daus., Betsy Dykes, Polly Parish; Polly Thomason of N. C., gd. mother to the above children; wife, Martha; sons, Thos., Calloway, Ansel, Ezekiel; daus., Sophia, Nancy, Permelia, Kitty, Eliza. Apr. 13, 1810-Dec. 1810. Test.: John Payne, Rebecca Payne, Augustin Eastin.

PATTON, WM.—A, 165—Sons, Joseph, Thos., John, William; daus., Mary, Resannah, Elizabeth, Martha, Rebecca, Sarah and Anna;

BOURBON COUNTY ESTATES 21

bound boy, Alex. Patton Irvin; son-in-law, Joseph McClintock.
July 31, 1794-May, 1795. Test.: Joseph and Wm. McClintock and
James Lea (Rea?).

PAYNE, JOSEPH—A, 275—Wife, Peggy; son, Thos.; daus., Molly,
Betsy, Nancy, Amey; bro., Wayford. Jan. 3, 1796-March, 1796.
Wts.: Joseph and Benjamin Penn, Chichester Chinn. (See Wood-
ford County and Anderson for Wayford (Wafer) Payne).

PEYTON, TIMOTHY—A, 17—"Of Prince William Co., Va." Wife,
Sarah; my children, Sitha Ann, Ann Thornton, Frances Elizabeth, Valentine Smallwood and unborn child; pre-emption land in
Fayette County; my son, Valentine Smallwood, 4000 acres I hold
as heir to my bro., Valentine Peyton; my bro.-in-law, Jas. Matson
and children. John McMillian, Extr. Sept. 5, 1782-Jan. 16, 1788.
Wts.: Jesse Davis, John Davis, Geo. Jackson, Thos. Calvert.

PILCHER, JOHN—D, 418—Nephew, Merrit Pilcher; bro., Moses Pilcher. Probated Oct. 1813. Wts.: Hiram Shaw, Joshua C. Livingston, Valentine Shaley.

PORTER, JOHN—D, 19—"From Virginia." Land bought in Va., by
Wm. Porter, mentions Richmond and Westmoreland Cos., Sugget's
Point, near Bowlers Ferry, Va.; bro., Edward, decd., sons, Luellen
(born 1796); John (born Feb. 19, 1806); son, Austin (born
1809); dau., Lucretia (born 1804); Sept. 10, 1809-Dec. 1809. Wts.:
N. C. Standiford, C. B. Garrard, James Metcalfe.

POSTON, ELIJAH—D, 201—Wife, Susanna; sons, Samuel, Wm., John,
dau., Sally. Sept. 13, 1811-Oct. 1811. Wts.: Thos. Clendennin,
John Shortridge, Jesse White.

PROTZMAN, JOHN—C, 336—"Washington County, Maryland." Wife,
Mary; sons, John, Nancy, Henry; daus., Nelly Kitty, Polly Mc-
Kinnan?. June 29, 1807-Dec. 1808. Test.: Leonard Shuford,
Nich. Parrott, David Schadley.

PULLEN, JEDEDIAH—D, 176—Wife, Betsy; sons, John, James,
Thomas; daus., Sinah Clinkenbeard, wife of Isaac C.; Betsy Smart,
wife of Richard Smart, Polly Foster, wife of Asa Foster, Sarah
Fegan, wife of Zacharia Fegan. Nov. 1809-July, 1811. Wts.: Geo.
Case, Wm. Pullen, Samuel Levescue.

PRYOR, JOSEPH—D, 330—Wife, Mary; sons, Joseph, Samuel, William, Richard, Thornton, Edward; daus., Ann Duvall, Polly, Nancy,
Prudence Hall; g. son, Duke Pryor; g. dau., Nancy, dau. of Thornton Pryor; bro., Luke Pryor, decd., son, John. Dec. 13, 1812-Feb.
1813. Test.: John Trimble, Isaac Allen.

QUIET, JAMES—B, 132—Wife; son, James; daus., Nellie Baird, Peggy
Hopkins, Hannah Donnell, Martha Blair, Polly and Catherine. Oct.
31, 1800-Oct. 1801. Wts.: David Knox, I Ervin.

RAWLINGS, JOSHUA—B, 133—Son, Loyd; daus., Susannah, Anna;
2nd wife, Sophia; son, Lee; daus., Sisley and Dorcas. Aug. 25,
1801-Sept. 1801. Test.: Jas. Fleming, Jas. Campbell, Stephen Rad-
cliffe.

RAINE, JOHN—C, 81—Son, Henry; dau., Polly; gd. dau., Katy Raine.

Sept. 29, 1804-Mar. 1806.   Daniel Irvin, John Sites, John Walls, Wts.

READING, GEORGE—A, 123—"In 67th year." To son, George Reading, eldest son, Samuel Reading, ½ of 1760 acres on Benson Creek, Kentucky River (Anthony Foster, Jr. survey); son, John Mullen Reading (400 acres which Simon Kenton surveyed for me on Fleming Creek, Licking River): my son, Wm. Reading; 3 sons, 3000 acres (agreement in hands of Wm. Logwood and with Geo. Stoval Smith); 1000 acres on Benson Big Creek, etc. Written June 23, 1792. Probated _____. (Note: This George Reading is father of several Revolutionary soldiers who came into Franklin County where this land is located).

REDMON, GEORGE—A, 35—Bro.-in-law, William Bruce; wife, Nancy; daus., Elizabeth, Mary, Margaret, Sarah; sons, Thos., Chas., George Win and John. 9 chdn. Dec. 31, 1789-Nov. 1796. John Cook, Samuel Cook, Martha Redman, Wts. "If a silent yet unborn." Bro., Wm. Redman, Extr.

RITCHEY, WM.—A, 207—Son, Gilbert R.; 2 daus., 10£ each; 6 sons, Abram, Wm., John, Gilbert and Isaac. Dec. 22, 1794—Jan. 1795 Peter and Geo. Snapp, Wts.

REYNOLDS, THOS.—B, 142—Mentions Jeory Hull, Rachel Hull, Archibald Hull and Richard Hull and James Anderson. These Extrs. Oct. 22, 1801-Dec. 1801.

RUDDLES, ISAAC—A, 239—Wife, Elizabeth; sons, Steven, Abram, Cornelius; daus., Betsy Mulhering, Mary Daniel (?). Mar. 6, 1806-Feb. 1812. Thos. A Thomson, Jesse Daugherty, Wm. Thomson, Wts.

RANKIN, REUBEN—D, 241—Wife, Isabella; sons, Reuben, James, Benjamin, Robert; gd. children, Reuben and Isabella, heirs of dau., Peggy Hall, decd. Jan. 13, 1810-Mar. 1812. Abraham Buford, Wt.

RULE, SARAH—B, 242—Sons, Thomas, Andrew, (deceased), John, three other sons mentioned but not named; dau., Meary Rule; Elizabeth Edwards; Sarah Rule. Mar. 13, 1804-July, 1804. Wm. Kennett, Jonathan Dazey, Joseph Wharton, Wts.

RUBY, HENRY—C, 359—Wife, Rachel ;sons, Henry, Reuben; son-in-law, Michael Matheny; other children, but names not given. Nov. 3, 1807-April, 1808. Wts.: Willis Field, Larkin Field, John Field, Sr.

SCONCE, JOHN—A, 189—Sons, Robt., Thomas, John; wife, Margaret; bro., James. Jan. 3, 1794-July, 1794. Wts.: Samuel Slack, Jas. Briton, Thos. Sconce. Children to have guardian and schooling.

SCONCE, THOS.—A, 219—"Aged 29." Wife, Isbel, bond due from Wm. McCon; each of my nephews; my bro., Samuel Sconce; bro., Robt. Sept. 19, 1795-Oct. 1795.

SMITH, JOHN—A, 187—Wife, Caterine. Extrs.: Jas. Ardery, John

Mitchell. Feb. 2, 1794-July, 1794. Samuel and Stephen Peyton, John Davidson, Wts.

SMELZER, PETER—A, 229—Wife, Barbara; sons, Peter, John, Jacob, daus., Barbara, wife of Philip Doubenspeck, Catherine, wife to Melcha Koutzmann, Mary Elizabeth, John, Annamaria, Eve Elizabeth and Margaret and Jacob, my youngest son, lands I bought of John South, 400 acres; youngest son, Jacob, under age; my children; Mary Elizabeth, etc.; 600 acres in Mason County; Peter, S., my eldest son, etc. Oct. 21, 1795-Dec. 1795.

STROTHER, THOS.—A, 364—Wife, Nelly Strother; to Thos. Benson, son of Wm., 150 acres in Fayette County that Zach. Benson now lives on—stud kept by Wm. Markham; to Wm. and Thos. McClanahan, sons of Thos. McClanahan, Jr., (slaves); to Peggy, Polly, Anney and Mariah, daus. of aforesaid Thos. McClanahan (under age) 200£ each. Wife and Thos. McClanahan, Jr., Extrs. Apr. 3, 1798-June, 1798.

SMITH, JOHN—A, 187—Wife, Catrina who had left him; Wm. McCann. Extrs.: Jas. Ardery, John Mitchell. Feb. 2, 1794-July, 1794.

SPEARS, CHRISTIAN—D, 188—Wife, Ann Mary; sons, John, Adam, Henry; other children, names not given. July 19, 1811. Jacob Spears, Wt.

SCONCE, ROBT.—C, 465—Wife, Mary Sconce; sons, Robt., James and Samuel; dau., Polly; gd. dau., Cinthy Berry Sconce; Rebecca Adams, dau. of Wm. Adams. Nov. 29, 1808-Jan. 1809. Jane Champ, Wt.

SMITH, THOS.—C, 68—Dau., Betsy Smith, to have entire estate—if she die without issue, to be divided among John Smith, Margaret Hitt, Eliz. Howard, Ann Hitt, Rebecca Smith and Robt. Smith. Sept. 12, 1805-Dec. 1805. Hugh Larrimore, Wt.

SELF, VINCENT—C, 250—Daus., Eliz. and Sarah. Nov. 4, 1806-Jan. 1807. Robt. Porter and John Rule, Wts.

STOKES, JOHN—B, 74—Wife, Ann; sons, Benjamin, John, Thos.; daus., Katrun, Polly, Nancy. Apr. 7, 1788-June, 1800. Wts.: Benj. Snodgrass, David Crouch, John Crouch.

SUMMERS, JOHN—B, 154—Wife, Agness; sons, John, Joseph, (land in Madison Co.); daus., Agness, Hanna, Sarah; mentions Jas. Robinson; son-in-law, Robt. Barns. May 13, 1802-Aug. 1802. Jas. Carnahan, Benj. Deckard, Wm. McClure, Wts.

SMITH, JOHN—B, 242—Daus., Knelley Kasi E.; sons, Wm. Enoch, Medleton. Extrs.: Zadock Smith and Cassandra Edmends. June 10, 1804-July, 1804. Test.: Samuel Clay, Thos. West, Ann Clay.

SMITH, THOS.—B, 222—Wife, Elizabeth; sons, John, Thos., Robert; daus., Margarett Hitt, Elizabeth Howard, Rebecca Ann Hitt. Nov. 23, 1803-Mar. 1804. Wts.: John Carter, Robt. Champ, Sarah Ross.

TILLETT, JOHN—D, 300—Wife, Jane; sons, James, William, John,

Giles; g. dau., Sarah, dau. of George, decd.; daus., Nancy Cotten, Jane Reed, Elizabeth Boggess, Mary Spencer, Susanna Warren. Mar. 27, 1810-Sept. 1812. Wts.: M. and Samuel Talbott, Jas Ford.

TUCKER, ALEX.—D, 220—Wife, Eleanor; sons, Greenberry, Aquilla; daus., Priscilla, Nancy, Rebecca. Nov. 15, 1811-Dec. 1811. Wts.: Solomon Hoggins, John McDaniel.

THORNTON, CHAS, TALIFERRO—D, 182—Wife, Ann Walker; children, names not given; unborn child. Extrs.: bro., Anthony Thornton and bro.-in-law, Walker Buckner. Apr. 12, 1811-July, 1811. Wts.: Anthony and Walker Thornton.

TODD, JOHN, SR.—D, 48—Wife, Mary; daus., Peggy and Sophia; Susannah Hamilton; Elizabeth Ashbrook, John Todd, Jr., Rutha Greathouse, Rebecca Morris, Sintha Todd. Oct. 14, 1809-Jan. 1810. Wts.: Wm. Morris, John Clark, Nathan Frakes, Wm. McClanahan.

THURMAN, JOSHUA—A, 274—My sister, Mary Smith's dau., Betsy Smith, land in Hanover County, Va.; my sister, Lucy Ward's dau., Betsy Ward, slaves; my bro., John Thurman's dau., Sally Thurman, young mare on Green River; my bro., John Thurman's son, Thos., a rifle. Dec. 27, 1794-July, 1795. Wts.: John Jones, Thos. Endicott, John Jones, Jr., Barzilla Endicott. My bro., Richard Thurman's children.

TRIMBLE, DAVID—A, 46—Son, George; dau., Nancy King; son, Isaac; to son Isaac's son, David; my children to wit: James, John, and Nancy King, heirs of Jas. Elliott, deceased; Thomas, David, Wm., George, John McKinney, Isaac and Forgus Grayham; my son, Wm and George Trimble, John McKinney and Isaac Trimble, also, Forgus Graham and their heirs; three daus. Nancy King, Polly McKinney and Betsy Graham. Sept. 6, 1798-June, 1799. Wts.: John McKinney, John Boyd.

THORNHILL, JOHN—B, 124—Sons, John and Reuben; all chdn. not named; daus., Sarah and Susie. Mar. 17, 1801-Apr. 1801. Wts.: John Barns, John Blain, Wm. Butler.

TUCKER, JONATHAN—B, 236—"Late of County of Montgomery and State of Maryland," now of County of Bourbon. Wife, Patsy Tucker; sons, Leonard, Edward, Thos. Lindsey Tucker, Jonathan Garroway Tucker, Jeremiah; daus., Milley Hoggin, wife of Solomon Hoggin, Lettice, Henrietta, Kesiah, Betsy, Patsy; mentions hrs. of Jeremiah Godman; Solomon Simpson, Solomon Davis, Benj. Neale; gd. son, Horatio Warren, and gd. dau., Levinia (both in Maryland). Mar. 20, 1804-Apr. 1804. Wts.: Thos. Goddard, Chas. Smith.

TULL, ISAAC—D, 378—Names wife, Betsey; son, John Rankin Tull; adopted dau., Eliza Tull Simpson; chdn. of Nancy Pollitt, wife of Thos. of Md. ____ 1812-July, 1813. Wts.: Wm. Forman, etc.

TROTTER, JOSEPH—C, 522—Wife, Nancy; sons, Joseph, William, James; daus., Mary, Sally, Nancy; gd. daus., Betsy Mills and Peggy Mitchell; gd. son, James Purvine. Sept. 5, 1808-Apr. 1809. Wts.: Josiah Collins, John Collins, Henry Hall.

TIMBERLAKE, RICHARD—C, 292—Wife, Mary; son, Henry; daus., Mary Duncan, Nancy Trimble, Rebecca Findley, Betsy. Oct. 1807. Wts.: John Walton, Thos. Walton, Wm. Clarke. Son, Henry and son-in-law, Robt. Trimble, Extrs.

THOMPSON, JOSEPH—A, 177—Wife, Jean (till youngest son, John is of age); all rest to be supported. John Moore, Extr. Oct. 30, 1793-May, 1794.

THOMAS, JAMES—A, 342—Wife, Sarah; son, David (200 acres on Grays Run); son, James (deed from Edw. Trabue); son, Thos; dau., Rebecca Thomas (unmarried); dau., Ann Jones. Aug 30, 1794-Apr. 1797. Wts.: John Beggs, Conrod Custer, Arnnell Custer.

WALLER, EDWARD—A, 100—My mother to have my part of my father's estate due me, also profits of lands in Stafford County during her life and then returning to my estate; my wife, Sally; education of my children; my 2 daus., Mariam and Betsy Waller; unborn child; my bro., Thos. Waller; my several sisters; John Waller and others in partnership with my lands. June 15, 1791-Jan. 1792. Col. John Edwards, Extr., and guardian to my children.

WARD, ISAAC—A, 147—Sons, John and James Ward; wife, Elizabeth; when son Isaac arrives to maturity; dau., Nancy. June 1, 1793-Nov. 1793. Wts.: Samuel and Mary Nisbet, Nathan Rawlings.

WALLACE, JOSEPH—C, 276—Wife, Elizabeth; sons, Andrew, Joseph, William; daus., Isabella, Jane, Elizabth, Margaret; bro., Stephen Wallace; Thos. Rogers. May 20, 1807-Sept. 1807. Wts.: Stephen Wallis, David Jameson.

WALLICE, MARGARET—B, 225— Aged 51; unmarried bro., Stephenson Wallice; Andrew Wallice, decd.; Joseph Wallice; mother, Jean Wallace; nieces, Margaret Jonson and Mary Hambleton. July 20, 1802-March, 1804. Wts.: Wm. and Samuel McConnell, Alex. Mitchell.

WASON, (WASSON) JAMES—A, 366— Estate, Jan. 9, 1798, wife; 4 boys, orphans, "oldest 17 years old and youngest is 8," bonds in Penna.

WEAKLIN, WM. COOK—A, 135—Wife, Mary; son, Boyles Weaklin, (200 acres); to Turner Rogers, (200 acres); to Betsy Weaklin, Charles Weaklin, Wm. Canady Weaklin, (500 acres on Ohio, being balance I let W. Bowles have to be equally divided). Son, Bowles, Extr. Dec. 29, 1792-May, 1793.

WEBB, JAMES—Nuncupative will—A, 41—"Killed by Indians," proved by oath of Master Ogden, Stephen Boyle, and Robt. Ellison. James Webb was killed by the Indians in last expedition against the Maumees, made immediately as he started on the expedition. He was leaving the house of Stephen Boyle where he had for some months resided. He took his horse by the bridle and gave it to an orphan child, Thos. Allin, who resided with said Stephen, and said it was his desire that his brother Benjamin Webb should have his clothes, and Stephen Boyle should have his crops they tended together, and settle his affairs. Nov. 1790-Dec. court, 1790.

WEBB, WINNEY—G, 110—My bro., Isaac Webb; nephew, James Webb; nephew, Isaac Webb; nephew Cuthbert Webb; nephew, John Webb (son of bro. Isaac); niece, Winney Scott, also her son, Isaac and her dau., Winney; my niece Lucy Scott; niece, Mary Nicholson; niece, Elizabeth Webb; nephew, Chas. Webb; nephew, John Webb (son of bro. Chas.); niece, Winney Webb; nephew, George Harrison and his dau., Winney; nephew, John Ball; niece, Frances Fauntleroy, and her dau., Winney, her dau., Elizabeth; my niece, Frances Jones (during her widowhood, a house in which she resides); Matthew T. Scott shall pay her $30.00 a year; to Amanda and Louisa Jones, daus., of my niece, Frances Jones; to Thos. Conn, son of my niece, Kitty Conn; to Mrs. Lucy Webb, my brother's wife; to Williamson Jones, son of my niece, Fanny Jones (a horse). Extrs.: Matthew T. Scott, George Ware. May 10, 1823. Wts.: Wm. H. Ramey and Wm. H. Richardson. Codicil: Winney Fauntleroy, lately deceased. Aug 29, 1823-Prob. Sept. 1823.

WELCH, MICHAEL—B, 71—Wife, Mary; sons, Abraham, John; daus., Abial, Margaret, Catherine, Mary. Mar. 12, 1796-Apr. 1800. Wts.: John Steel, John Smith, Wm. Miller.

WEST, JOHN—A, 74—Wife, Rachel; son, John West; my 4 children, Margaret, Martha, John and Roger West, dau., Sarah Eades. Nov. 23, 1791-Dec. 1791. Robert Eades mentioned. Wt.: John Allen.

WILSON, GEORGE—D, 471—Wife, Elizabeth; sons, Hamilton, William and John, land in Henry Co.; five daus., names not given. Nov. 1, 1813-Dec. 1813. Wts.: Joshua H. Philips, Henry F. Wilson, Joseph Perkins.

WHITLEDGE, JOHN—A, 13—Wife, Alcey, equal between my orphans; to son, John; to Susannah Whiledge; son, Lina Whitledge; to Ursula; to son, Thomas Whitledge, (my above mentioned 5 children); my bro., Thos. W. Oct. 5, 1788-Nov. 18, 1788.

WHITE, JOHN—D, 44—Wife, Susannah; sons, John, Thomas; daus., Sally and Polly. July 9, 1804-Oct. 1809. Wts.: P. Smartwelders, James Davis, Robt. W. Findley, John Watson.

WHEELER, RUTH—C, 327—Son, Wm. Jackson; daus., Elizabeth Lamar, Unity Wheeler, Susan Meredith, wife of Thos. Meredith; Mary Crammer (Cranmer?), gd. dau., Ruth Meredith. Dec. 18, 1807-Jan. 1808.

WILLIAMS, JOHN—B, 171—Wife, Elizabeth. Mention Wm. Mark, Extr. July 26, 1802-Sept. 1802.

WILLIAMS, CHARLES—D, 239—Sons, Pope and Sanford; dau., Jane; "other children," names not given. Jan. 29, 1812-Feb. 1, 1812. Wts.: George Fishback, Joseph Pugh, Wise Hitch.

WILSON, JOHN—A, 217—Son-in-law, Jas. Burns, all. Mar. 12, 1795-Oct. 1795. Wts.: John Beggs, Conrad Custer, John Hinkston. David Wilson, Extr.

WRIGHT, WILLIAM—C, 149—Wife, Martha; sons, Robt., John, Hugh, James, William, Samuel, Thos.; daus., Hannah Melvin, Mary Steward, Margaret Hendrix, Eliz. Leer, Sally Hannah, Jean Champ; son-in-law, David Leer; Joseph Hannah. Oct. 17, 1802-July, 1806. Wts.: Samuel Black, Tilghman Hickman, Wm. Black.

YOUNG, SAMUEL, DR.—A, 1—All to John Dawson, medicine, etc. June 4, 1786-June 20, 1786. Wts.: Benj. Harrison, John Trimble, John Farlow.

BOYLE COUNTY

(Formed 1842 from Mercer and Lincoln)

Note: the following persons did not all leave wills. It is, however, a copy of the index to Will Book A, and exactly as it appears in this first will book of Boyle County, Kentucky.

INDEX TO WILL BOOK A

Names appearing in this index are not included in General Index

Fitton, Edward
Fisher, Jesh.
Fields, Jas. Jr.
Fields, Susan
Funk, Fanny C.

Gray, Robert
Grant, John
Gaines, Ezekiel F.
Gaines, Elmira T.
Grant's Deed of Trust to Harlons
Garr, Larence
Gray, Jas.
Graves, Jas.
Graham, Theresa M.
Gray, Jane

Harrod, Ann
Harlan, Elijah
Henderson, Elizabeth
Hope, Michael
Harlan, Davis C.
Hamner, Sarah
Hurley, Leah
Harmon, Wm.
Harlan, Mary
Hedgeman, Dennis
Humble, Mary S.
Hawkins, Ann
Hays, I. R.
Harlan, Henry
Hall, John
Hocker, Samuel
Harlan, J. G.
Harrison, Thos. H.
Hurley, Enoch
Heron, Sam.
Henderson, Chas.

Isom, Jas.
Irvine, Abram L.
Irvine, John H.

Jackson, Anthony

Kirkland, Chas.
Knox, Robt.
Knox, Isabella
King, John W.
Kerr, Patrick
Kerr, Pricella

Laws, Jeremiah
Lackley, Gabriel
Lay, Martin
Long, Jacob
Lind, Margaret St. Clair Clark

Meaux, Jno. G.
Moore, Margaret
McGinnis, Jesse
Moore, Samuel S., Sr.
Montgomery, Isaac
Mays, Jas. W.
McDowell, Sarah
McGrath, Wm. R.
McIntosh, George S.
McCann, Wm.
McClanahan, Thos.
Martin, Mrs. Jane
McGinnis, Mary
Mock, R.
McDowell, Col. Joseph
Meaux, Walter
Marrs, Jas.
Moore, Lawson
McClane, Elizabeth
McKay, J. C.
McGinnis, Samuel
Moreland, John
Maury, M. F.
Morrow, Margaret
Mock, J. J.

Nield, Geo. R.
Neff, Francis

Owens, Mason
Owsley, Wm.

Prewitt, Martha A.
Prall, Benj.
Parks, Elizabeth (marriage contract with E. Rogers).
Potts, Samuel
Prewitt, Elizabeth
Pipes, Wm.
Prewitt, Thos.
Procter, Benj.
Pipes, Nathl.

Rogers, Evan (marriage contract with Elizabeth Parks).
Rogers, Elizabeth
Raines, Jas.
Rochester, Sarah
Ripperdan, Frederick
Robertson, Duncan F.
Reed, F.
Rogers, E.
Reed, Thos.
Reed, Isabella
Robards, Robert
Robinson, Thomas
Read, Ann
Russell, D. A.

Ramsey, Jane C.

South, John
Smith, Jesse
Sparrow, Dennis
Street, Nathl.
Spears, John F.
Smith, Henry
Smith, Ephriam A.
Sevier, Isaac
Sutton, Sarah
Stewart, Wm.
Spears, Geo. C.

Taylor, Wm.
Tadlock, Carter
Tewmey, Wm.
Tucker, Jas. L.
Tompsins, John
Tarkington, Thos. F.

Vanarsdale, Isaac

Wade, Jeremiah
Wade, Wm.
Wade, Leneca W.
Witherspoon, Sarah W.
Wilhoite, Nickolas
Walker, Robt.
Walker, Mrs. E. M.
Wilhoit, Rody
Wallace, C. B.
Wingate, Esther
Williams, Fanny R.
Walker, Mary

Yeager, Frederick
Yeager, Joseph
Yankee, Jacob
Young, Jno. C.

Zimmerman, Jas. F.

BRACKEN COUNTY

(Formed from Mason and Campbell Counties, 1796)

Contributed by Hattie Scott, Frankfort, Ky.

INDEX TO FIRST WILLS

Names appearing in this index are not included in General Index

Alexander, Wm.
Ackworth, Henry
Alexander, Mary
Alexander, Wm.

Bonwell, Smith
Baker, Jno.
Blassingamms, Jas.
Bennett, Jas.
Black, Jas.
Black, John
Barkley, Jas.
Bowman, Caspar
Buckner, Philip
Barker, Jos.
Bonwell, Thos.

Collins, Ambrose
Case, Shadrack

Donovan, Dan'l
Donovan, Jacob

Elliott, Wm.

Fee, John

Graymoyer, Fred'k

Harmon, Michael
Hamilton, John, Sr.
Hutchison, Sam'l Sr.
Heck, Jacob
Houston, Levi

Insko, Jos.

Jenkins, Jno.

Keighler, Lewis
Moore, Levi, Sr.
Morrow, Andrew
Miranda, Jas.
Mitchell, Nath'l
Martin, George

Newland, George
Newland, Rachel

Ogden, Wm.
Osborn, Susan

Perkins, Levi
Poe, Edw.
Patterson, Wm.

Reynolds, Jas.

Soward, Elijah
Sellers, Leonard

Taliaferro, Mch.
Tutt, Richard
Taliaferro, Geo. C.

Walton, Simion
Wells, James
Woodward, Wm.
Wood, Sam'l
Wilson, Wm. A.

Young Barly

BRACKEN COUNTY WILLS

ALEXANDER, WILLIAM—Bk. A, pg. 287—"Of Lexington, Rock-bridge Co., Va.," Bro., Archibald; sister, Jane and bro., Sam's child; dau., Phoebe; son, John; son, Archibald; son-in-law, Edward Graham; wife, Nancy; single daus., Betsy, Nancy, Patsy, until 21 yrs. old; son, Andrew; dau., Peggy, Sally, Phebe, Betsy, Nancy, Patsy. Extrs.: son, Andrew, son-in-law, Samuel L. Campbell. Written Apr. 15, 1797. Wts.: Timothy Donovan, Rockbridge Co., Va. Probated June 6, 1797.

BAKER, JOHN—Bk. A, pg. 14—Sons, Aron and Abraham; daus., Elizabeth Sheperd, Mary Tatmean, Hannah Tatman, Rachel Love, Otillia Baker and Peggy's dau., Catherine. Extrs.: sons, Aron and Abraham. Written Apr. 2, 1808. Wts.: John Miller, Isaac Reese. Probated Sept. 1808.

BLASINGAME, JAMES—Bk. A, pg. 260—Wife, Mary; three sons, viz: Buckley, Jas. Harry and Thos.. C.; daus., Nancy Holton, Frances Taliferro, Ursulla Taunehill (?), Caty Anderson. Written Aug. 29, 1811. Probated Sept. 1812.

BENNETT, JAMES—Bk. A, pg. 404—To wife, Sarah; three chdn., Abner, Susannah Bennett and Chesley Bennett. Uncle, David Chiles, Extr. Written Aug. 21, 1815. Wts.: Reuben Bennett, John Bennett. Probated Jan. 1816.

HARMON, MICHAEL—Bk. A, pg. 137—To my two eldest sons, Samuel and John, land in Clermont Co., Ohio; son, Valentine; oldest dau., Mary Swigert; to Elizabeth Humlong; to Cathren Bier; Margaret Moore, dau. of Susannah Moore, decd., and Harmon and Asa Moore, sons of same; wife, Margaret; grandchdn. Sons, John and Valentine, Extrs. Written Aug. 5, 1807. Probated Dec. 1807.

McDOWELL, JOHN—Estate appraised May, 1816. Among purchasers at sale: Thomas McDowell, Nancy McDowell, Jane McDowell, Polly McDowell, Lewis Linville, John McDowell, Joseph McDowell. June 1816 Settlement—Commissioners: Robt. Walton, Wm. Field. Mentions payment to Lewis Linville, Thos. McDowell, I. McDowell and J. W. McDowell.

DOWNING HRS. to McDOWELL HRS—Deed Bk. H, pg. 44—April 27, 1826. By decree of Circuit Court, July term, 1821, suit in chancery therein depending where in Joseph McDowell, Thomas Morgan and wife, Susannah, late McDowell, Jane McDowell, Thomas McDowell, Benjamin McDowell and wife, Mary, John Cobler and wife, Rebecca, late McDowell, John McDowell, Lavinia McDowell, Elizabeth McDowell, Nancy McDowell and Edmund McDowell were complainants, said court decreed, that defendants, Downing heirs, viz: Wm. Kinney and wife, Susan, James Hooten and wife, Nancy, Robert Thompson and wife, Elizabeth, John Tucker and wife, Sarah, Josephus Mitchell and wife, Mary, Thomas Gano and wife, Priscilla, Rebecca Downing, Jane Downing and Robert Downing convey before Nov. 1st, next, to complainants residue of land not heretofore conveyed by John H. Rudd and Hugh B. Payne, Commissioners. (Note: Thos. McDowell m. 12-25-1814, Isabella Hooten (Hutton), m. 5-15-1851 Lumilla Shoales).

ELLIOTT, WM., SR.—Bk. C, pg. 185—Son, Wm. Elliott, Jr., Extr. Wife, Elizabeth; son, William; chdn., Elijah, Reuben, Sally Mc-Clanahan, Elizabeth Bartlett, Nancy Field, Isaac Elliott and their chdn. Written Feb. 9, 1828. Probated May, 1828.

ARTUS, MATTHEW—Bk. C, pg. 92—To dau., Brittania Pepper; son, James; son, John; son, Joseph; son, Samuel; son, Bazel; dau., ____ Artus; dau., Lydia Artus. Wife, Elizabeth and son, Joseph, Extrs. Written Feb. 24, 1826. Probated Aug. 1826.

BUCKNER, PHILIP—Bk. B, pg. 233—To son, Samuel; grandson, Coleman Buckner when 21; his father, Samuel Buckner; dau., Betsy Blanchard; dau., Polly Hord; son, William Buckner; dau., Fanny Morris; dau., Sally Pickett; son, Thomas; wife, Tabbie and four chdn. rest. Samuel Sukee Talibetto (Taliferro?), John and Thos. Buckner, Wts. Written Feb. 28, 1817. Probated Dec. 1820.

POE, EDWARD—Bk. B, pg. 22—To oldest dau., Abigail Day, wife of John Day; oldest son, Joseph; son, John; son, Patrick; dau., Martha Hurst, wife of John Hurst; wife Catherine; son, Samuel. Written July 30, 1806. Probated May, 1816. Wts.: Isaac Day, Geo. Lee, Matthew Patteson.

DEVAR, MICHAEL—To five first chdn., Margaret, Sarah Ragsdale, James, Susan and William Devar, their grandmother, Mary Silk; third and second wife's chdn., Mary, George and Mazy Ann Devar, land in Harrison Co., where Mazy Ann Bailey now lives; land owned by widow of Benj. Brumly, decd; four last chdn., Benjamin, Rebeccah, Louisa and Matilda; wife, Mary. Written April 28, 1842. Probated June 27, 1842.

RICE, PHILIP RUSSELL—Bk. D, pg. 503—To wife, Martha; three sons, Hudson M., John V., and Wm. S., "all my chdn."; Malinda's two sons; dau., Ann; son, Russell. Written Aug. 17, 1840. Probated Sept. 27, 1841.

CLARK COUNTY

(Formed from Fayette and Bourbon Counties, 1792)

INDEX TO WILL BOOK A

Abbreviations: w-will; i-inventory; a-appraisement; set.-settlement; d-dower; div.-division; gdn.-guardian; s-sale; admr.-administrator.

Names appearing in this index are not included in General Index

Downey, Martha—w., i., set.
Davis, Solomon—i., s.
Daniel, Vivian—w.
Daniel, Nancy—d.
Davenport, Stephens—i.

Emmet, Sarah—w., i.
Embry, Jacob—w., i.
Embree, Wm.—i., s.
Edmondson, Archibald—w.
Eubank, Thos.—i., set., gdn., set.

Florah, Wm.—i.

Gordon, Jno.—w., i. (Goochland Co., Va.)

Harrow, Dan'l—w. i.
Hazelrigg, Elijah—
Harris, Thos.—w., i.
Hukil, Henry—w., i.
Hazelrig, Chas.—w., i., s.
Hays, Wm.—acct., admr., set.

Ireland, Nelly—d.

Jacobs, Catherine—d.
Johnson, Martha—(late Oliver) d.
Johnson, Wm—i.

Ledgewood, Wm.—w.
Lewis, Robt.—w., i., s.
Linville, Wm.—i.
Luske, Sam'l—i.

McCafere, Wm.—i.
McMurray, Sam'l—i.
McMannas, Thos.—i.
Morgan, Jesse—i.
McCreary, Robt.—i. set.
McCreary, Mary—d.
McFeaters, Jno.—w.
Morton, Jno.—i.
McClure, Andrew—w., i.
McMillan, Jas.—w., i.
McDaniel, Wm.—i., set., s.

Martin, David—(act. with Buckner) i.
McCreery, Jno.—gdn., set.
McGuire, Frances—w.

Noe, Peter—w., i.

O'Harrow, Patrick—w.
O'Harrow, Daniel—w., i.
Olliver, Jno.—i., gdn., set.
Plummer, Ann—d.
Payton, Timothy—i.
Parris, Timothy—set. with Joe Ellis, orphan of Jno. Ellis.
Patton, Matthew—w., i.

Rulon, Nathaniel—i.
Richardson, Wm—w.
Roy, Benj.—i.
Rhea. Jas.—i.
Ramey, Nancy—d. (late Nancy Smith, in estate of Joseph Smith, decd.)
Richardson, Robt.—i.
Richie, Jane—w., i.
Ray, Benj—set.

Smith, Joseph—w., i., div., gdn., set.
Swany, Daniel—w.
Sanford, Derrett—a.
Scott, Baptist—w., i.
Staples—gdn., set.

Townsin, Jas.—w., i.
Tinsley, David—i.
Taylor, Jonathan—w.

Woolmar, Jno.—i.
Wills, W. Frederick—w., i., set., gdn. set.
Wilson, Joseph—i.
Winn, Thos.—i
Wills, Fanny—d.
Waddle, Geo.—w.
Watson, Patrick—i.
White, Landie—i.
White, Jonathan—w., i.

Note: Wills from Book A published in Kentucky Court and Pioneer Records.

WILL BOOK B

ALRIDGE, (ALRIDG) WILLIAM—pg. 296—To wife, Mary Alridg, money due from son, Nicholas; son Nicholas' eldest dau. Sarah;

son William's son, William; to Thos. Bolware's son, William; to Mary Woosley, wife of Thos. Woosley; to Rebecca Cook, dau. of dau. Mary Bolware. Extr., David Hampton. Written Aug. 12, 1807—probated Dec. 28, 1807. Wts.: Nathan Tucker, Freeman Cottershell, Archibald Cooper.

ALEXANDER, JOHN—will, pg. 301—To son, Andrew Alexander; two daus., Prudence Todd and Polly Alexander; property previously advanced to other chdn.; to Mary McCoy; to John Alexander, son of Samuel Alexander; to John Alexander McCoy, son of John and Mary McCoy when of age; to three chdn.; Andrew Alexander, Prudence Todd and Polly Alexander; Wm. Sharp to live on place where now living two yrs. after lease expires. Extrs.: Stephen Trigg and Jno. Oldham. Written Sept. 29, 1807—probated Dec. 28, 1807. Wts.: Jno. Kelly, Jas. M. Moore, Thos. Tribble.

ARNETT, THOS—will, pg. 353—To son, Jacob; dau. Nancy; to Rachel and Polly Arnett when of age or marry, daus. of son Abijah Arnett, decd., land if it can be obtained from heirs of Wm. Canaday, decd. which land on Turkey Creek, branch of Stoner, is dower of widow of said Abijah; wife, Sarah, all money due from Mathew Anderson; sons, Thos., Samuel, John; daus., Elizabeth and Sally. Extrs.: sons, Thos. and John. Written July 9, 1807—probated May 23, 1808. Wts.: Thos. Wornall, Jacob Dawson, Abijah Dawson.

BODKINS, JAS.—will, pg. 6—To wife, Delilah, land bought of Col. John Payne; son, Geo. Bodkins; sons, John, Thos. Wm., and James, property formerly given them; daus., Margaret Bensten, Sarah Barnor, Rachel Duglas and Betsey Mary Ginna, Ann Wise, property formerly given them. Extr.: son, George. Written Aug. 8, 1804—codicil dated Aug. 8, 1804, mentions Richard Wise—probated Aug. 27, 1804. Wts.: Wm. Morris, Matthew Patton, Jno. Patton.

BRISTON, JAMES—will, pg. 261—To son, John; son, Gedeon; son, James; son, Archibald; wife, Margaret. Dated Mar. 12, 1804. Wts.: Thos. Wornall, Jno. Donaldson, Thos. Gist.

BOYLE, JOHN—Inv. dated Jan. 28, 1808, sale dated Feb. 11, 1808—Those listed in sale bill: Jno. Ashley, Abijah Brooks, Daniel Cummins, John Boyle, James Boyle, Jane Boyle, Maxamilian Bordin, Alphred Boram, Wiley Brasfield, Gabrail Chisholm, Christopher Commins, Jno. Commins, Jno. Danally, Joseph Duncan, Armsted Hughs, Jas. Hubank, Benj. Gordin, Wm. Dawson, Jno. Dawson, Wm. Foreman, Wm. Sander, Jno. Gansucy, David Scott, Jno. Matthews, John Rountree, Robt. Richards, Zechd. Ridgmay, Stephen Strode, Jacob Fodery, Thos. Vivian, Mary Strode, John Strode, Jas. McDonald, Samuel Constable, Wm. Poston, Thos. Lafferty, Jno. Bean, Jno. Spau. Admrs.: Wm. Forman, Jas. Boyle.

BON, JAMES—will—To stepson, Wm. Boyle; step-dau. Prudy Snethan; wife, Mary; son, Mend. Written Sept. 21, 1806—probated March 28, 1808. Wts.: David McGee, Joseph King.

CLARKE, ROBT., JR.—will, pg. 220—To wife, Betsy; dau. Patsey Gist, land purchased of Col. James McMillan to be assigned her by Capt. Dillard Collins and John Sympson; dau., Polly Clarke, land purchased of Col. Wm. McMillan, Extrs. to pay her tuition and board at school; son, Robert, he to be kept at school until 20 yrs. of age, bro. James Clarke his gdn.; if wife have child after my decease, this child to be given in proportion to others; all chdn. viz: Susan Puckett, Nancy Irwin, Patsy Gist, Polly Clarke, Robt. Clarke, Patterson Clarke. Extrix.: wife, Extrs.: Wm. Smith, Jas. Clarke. Written Dec. 13, 1806—probated Jan. 26, 1807.

CHEATHAM, JAS.—gdn. set.—John Cheatham, infant orphan of Jas. Cheatham and legatee in will.

CROSTHWAIT, JACOB—will, pg. 303—To son, Samuel, "land run off for me by Josiah Hart;" to Jno. Ireland and Elinor, his wife, on account of Aaron Crosthwait, decd., her former husband; to wife; chdn. and grandchdn, viz: Brockman Crosthwait, Elizabeth Crosthwait, Asa Crosthwait and Aaron Crosthwait. Extrs.: Elijah Crosthwait and Jacob Coons. Written March 18, 1803—probated Dec. 28, 1807. Wts.: Jas. Sympson, Ellis Spillman.

CHRISTY, JULIUS—will, pg. 357—Sons, John, Ambrose; dau. Elizabeth Glass; dau. Ann Lindsay; dau. Frances Carr (?); dau. Sarah Davis; dau. Agatha Kirtley; son, George; son, James; son, Samuel. Extr.: son, Ambrose. Written Dec. 5, 1805—probated July 25, 1808. Wts.: N. Murphy, Mary Murphy, Sarah Day.

COATS, MARY M.—will, pg. 418—To sister, Ann Elgin; bro. Walter Sotherland's son, Thomas; bro. Walter, bond on Thos. Crews of Madison Co.; to daus. of bros. Frederick, Walter, John, David, Enos and sister, Ann Elgin's daus.; to Sarah Sotherland, wife of bro. Walter. Extr.: bro. John. Written March 7, 1809—probated April 24, 1809. Wts.: Thos. Constant, John Constant.

DALE, NANCY—Late Nancy Richardson, widow of Wm. Richardson, dower—Aug. 3, 1804.

DANIELS, CHAS.—will, pg. 86—To 3 chdn., Amel, Dillard and Polly and another, if born to wife, Nancy. Chdn. to be educated. Extr.: bro. Jesse Daniels. Written Nov. 24, 1805—probated Dec. 23, 1805. Wts.: Henry Daniel, Jas. Daniel, Jr., Lewis Bleasoe.

DENNIS, JOHN—Gdn. Set., pg. 235—John Rountree, gdn., to Polly Dennis, now Polly Gordan, infant orphan of John Dennis, deceased, 1801.

ELLIS, JOHN—Orphans' Gdn. Set.—Timothy Parish set. with Timothy and Joel Ellis, July 4, 1804.

EWING, SAMUEL—will, pg. 35—To wife, Eleanor, for life then division between Mary Holsey, dau. of bro. Wm. Ewing, decd., Patrick Gellaspe, son of Wm. Gellespe, Eleanor and Nancy Nunely, daus. of _____ Nunely, decd. Extrs.: Wm. Gelaspe and Wm. Robinson, Jr. Written Sept. 27, 1804—probated Feb. 24, 1805. Wts.: Jno. Lyle, Jas. Kinney.

EVANS, RICHARD—will, pg. 45—To sons and daus., viz: Mabery Evens, Mary Waddell, Elizabeth Stinson, Susannah Waddell, Jas. Evens and Ann Bell, dau. Sarah Evens (youngest dau.); wife, Mary Evens and dau. Sarah, Extrix. Written Feb. 27, 1797—probated May 27, 1805. Wts.: Paul Huls, Robert Walker, John Huls.

EUBANKS, THOS.—Gdn. Set. pg 102—Jas. Eubank, gdn. of Jas., Geo., Harrison, Sally and Caroline. Dec. 21, 1805.

HAGGARD, NATHANIEL—will, pg. 200—To wife, Elizabeth; son, Nathaniel made equal with rest of chdn.; to Hennery Hazelrigg and son, John; dau., Mary Kindred; sons, Jas. and David; Bartlett Haggard; Jane Gentry; Elizabeth Kindred, my chdn. Wife, Elizabeth and sons, Etrs. Written July 16, 1800—probated Aug. 25, 1806. Wts.: Allen Neel, Robt. Elkin..

HOCKADAY—EDMUND—will, pg. 294—To wife, Martha; dau. Betsey Irvine; son, Isaac; dau. Martha Shackleford; son, Edmund; son, John after wife's death; property to be divided between three oldest chdn., viz: Betsey Irvine, Isaac Hockaday and Martha Shackleford. Extrs.: son-in-law, Wm. Irvine, Isaac Hockaday and Geo. Shackleford. Written Oct. 6, 1807—probated Dec. 28, 1807. Wts.: Robt. Didlake.

HAYDEN, GEO.—Sale and Div. pg. 457—Admr. Jeremiah Hayden—9 Legatees: Jeremiah G. Hayden; Amy Hayden, who married Jno. Hutchison of Va.; Jas. Hayden; Wm. Hayden; Elizabeth Hayden who married Thos. Halsel; Jane Hayden; John Hayden; Ann Hayden; Joseph Hayden.

HILL, JOHN—will, pg. 376—To wife, Elizabeth; son, John; son-in-law, Richard Empson; son-in-law, Nathan Martin; son-in-law, Josiah Ashley; son, Wm.; dau. Lucy; son, Garland; other six chdn. before mentioned. Extrix.: wife; Extr.: son, John. Written Aug. 21, 1804 —probated Oct. 24, 1808. Wts.: Jas. Sympson, John McClure, Peter Clawson.

JANES, WM.—will, pg. 442—To wife, Polly; son, Elijah, under age; dau. Lucy Janes; son, Wm.; grandson, Alexander Janes. Extrix.: wife, Polly; son, Wm. and Jacob Fishback Extrs. Written May 8, 1809—probated Aug. 28, 1809. Wts.: Wm. Wayman, Jacob Fishback, Phoebe Fishback.

MARTIN, THOS.—will, pg. 40—To sister, Mary Ann Taylor, ½ tract in Ohio given him by father some yrs. previous; to bro. Geo. M. Martin, other half said tract; sister Eliza C. Martin, negroes given him by father some yrs. previous; mother, Elizabeth Martin. Written Dec. 24, 1804—probated May 27, 1805. Wts.: Jacob Fishback, Samuel Lyon, Jno. Summers.

McGUIRE, JNO.—will, pg. 326—To son, Wm.; two sons, Willis and Edward; dau. Betsy McGuire; grandau., Betsy Taylor; to Polly Baxter for support of two chdn., land entered in name of Benj. Berry; money coming from father's estate to pay off daus. Betsy and Polly Baxter. Extrs.: sons, Wm. and Edward. Written Dec. 30, 1807—probated Feb. 22, 1808. Wts.: Thos. Berry, Sr., Jno. Rankins, Thos. Berry, Jr.

NEEL, ALLEN—will, pg. 126—To wife, Nancy; division to be made among chdn.; son, Wm. Extrs.: wife, son, Wm. and Zachariah Elkin. Written Jan. 4, 1806—probated June 23, 1806. Wts.: Robt. McMillion, Robt. Elkin, Thos. Burris.

OLIVER, JOHN—Gdn. Set. pg. 270—Allotment of dower to Martha

Oliver (1799) now Martha Johnson, Nicholas Oliver, Kitty Oliver, Tabitha Oliver, decd. and John Oliver.

OUSLEY, SARAH—will, pg. 380—To dau., Mary Ousley and her child, Curtha (Martha?), when of age. Dau. Nancy Extrix. Written Aug. 5, 1808—probated Oct. 24, 1808. Wts.: D. Bullock, Jas. P. Bulock, Ann Brooks.

PETTY, WM.—will, pg. 41—To wife, Lettys; youngest son, Thos; son, Francis; dau. Rhoda Cast; rest of chdn.: Elizabeth Dodson, Rachel Russel, Hannah Ward, Zachariah, Wm. Randdell, John, James, Sarah Stevens, Lias. Extrs.: Wife and son, Thos. Written May 1, 1804—probated May 27, 1805. Wts.: Chas. Tracey, Sarah Tracey.

PATTON, MATTHEW—Set. pg. 54—John and Wm. Patton, sons of Matthew Patton, decd. land on Paint Creek, in Ohio given them 1797, in instrument of estimation of land, dated April 28, 1806.

PARRISH, WM.—will, pg 298—To wife, Susanna, she to maintain and school chdn., and at her death property divided among whole of chdn. or descendants; Extr. to sell Ohio lands on Darbey Creek, 1000 acres on Tradewater; Edmund Hockaday, Sr. and Robt. Didlake and Isaac Hockaday and son, Jas. Parrish of Madison Co., when said James becomes of age, Extrs. Written Mar. 29, 1805—probated Dec. 28, 1807.

PATRICK, THOS.—will, pg. 440—Bond on Jno. Baker of Clark Co.; wife, Sally for life, then to Livina Frazer, and then to her dau. Peggy Frazer; son, Byron; balance between chdn. viz: Wm. Enoch, Polly, John, Thos., Byron, Patrick. Written Apr. 22, 1809—probated Aug. 28, 1809. Wts.: Peter Goosey, Jr., Isaac Oliver.

RAMSEY, DANIEL—will, pg. 123—Wife, Rachel to make chdn. who are under age equal with married chdn. when she thinks best; son, James; Daniel Wood; son, John; grandson, James, son of Daniel Ramsey; place whereon son, Daniel formerly lived to be in possession of his widow. Extrix.: wife, Extr. David Hampton, Jr. Written Jan. 23, 1806—probated March 24, 1806. Wts.: Elizabeth Haggard, Alex. Anderson, Samuel Reed.

RICHARDSON, LANDIE—will, pg. 188—Makes friend, Wm. Roberts of Jessamine Co., atty. to investigate title to land in that county entered in name of Hiram Harrison by Lewis Craig which warrants were originally his own and signed to Hiram Harrison without consent and conveyed to him by said Hiram Harrison, conveyance burnt in Fayette Co.; to grandson, James Richardson, son of Wm. decd., place whereon said Wm. lived and died; son, Francis; dau. Nancy W. Payne, wife of Jesse Payne; dau. Martha Biggers; son, James, land on Red River, reserving portion for heirs of Edward Cory, decd. for locating; dau. Sarah Harrison and chdn. free from interest of Hiram Harrison; grandson, Landre Richardson, son of Robt. decd., tract whereon his mother, Mary Richardson now lives. Extrs.: wife and son, Francis. Written Feb. 7, 1805—probated Sept. 22, 1806. Wts.: Stephen Dooley, Wm. Rolgton (Ralston), Jas. Wells.

RICHARDSON, JOHN—will, pg. 374—To wife, Betsey and at her death to five young chdn. Extrs.: wife and Nathaniel Vin, (?). Written

March 21, 1808—probated Aug. 22, 1808. Wts.: W. W. Poer, Wm. Richardson, Polly Richardson.

RITCHIE, VILOTTE—will, pg. 445—(Nuncupative). Alex. Thompson, Extr. bro. George; sister's dau. Vilott Thompson; bro. Alex. Ritchie's son, George; Jno. Gelaspie. Oct. 1809.

STRODE, JOHN, SR.—will, pg. 57—To wife, Molly (Mary) and at her death to dau. Nelly Lafferty; balance equally divided among all chdn. Extrs.: son, John and Thos. Lafferty. Written Apr. 23, 1805 —probated Aug. 26, 1806. Wts.: James Sympson, Jno. Warren, Maximillian Bowren.

STRODE, MARY—dower, pg. 132—In estate of late husband, John Strode, decd.; personal property and tract whereon her husband latey resided to Abijah Brooks' corner, etc.

STAPLES, WM.—Orphans' Gdn., pg. 39—John Jackson, gdn. Betsey Dance Staples, infant orphan of Wm. Staples, decd; Shadrack Staples and Joshua Staples. July 31, 1806.

TAYLOR, ANN—will, pg. 402—To daus., Sally and Betsey; son Neddy M. Taylor; son, Gibson; son, George; son, Samuel; property by deceased husband's will. Extrs.: sons, Wm. and George Taylor. Written Sept. 1, 1808—probated Feb. 27, 1809. Wts.: Jacob Fishback, Ed. Calloway, N. Taylor.

TUTTLE, JOHN—will, pg. 405—To wife; sons, John James, Wm. Benj. and Henry; daus. Clarkey, Elizabeth, Sarah. Extrs.: John Newland and wife, Clarky Tuttle. Written Dec. 5, 1808—probated Feb. 27, 1808. Wts.: Peter Goosey, Sally Goosey.

WRIGHT (RIGHT), JOSEPH—will, pg. 1—To wife, Frances, during widowhood, then to son, John; dau. Nancy Johnson; dau. Frances Hazelrigg; son, Wm.; son, Francis; dau. Elizabeth Penill; dau. Isbel Miller; remainder divided among all chdn. Extrs.: wife and Joshuay Hazelrig and son, John. Written May 16, 1804—probated Aug. 27, 1804. Wts.: D. Hampton, Samuel Reed, Joseph Reed.

WILLS, WM., SR.—will, pg. 63—"Very far advanced in years"; wife, Elizabeth, and at her death, to her dau. Margaret's heirs; eldest son, John; son, Wm.; dau. Mary Baldwin; dau. Margaret; dau. Jane Dunlap; son, Jas.; son, Matthew. Extrs.: sons, Jas. and Matthew. Written June 13, 1803—probated Sept. 23, 1805. Wts.: Jno. Quisenberry, Jas. Keys, Aaron Quisenberry.

WRIGHT, JONATHAN—will, pg. 110—To wife, Elizabeth; to Gunmenia Waterman; to grandson, Jonathan Waterman; dau., Amy Pool, and her 4 chdn. Extrix.: wife. Written June 8, 1803—probated Jan. 27, 1806. Wts.: Wm. Morris, Harrison Jacob.

WOODY, SARAH—allotment dower—Late Sarah Ramey, widow of Dan'l Ramey (Ramsey), decd. Nov. 28, 1808.

WELLS (WILLS), FREDERICK—Gdn. Set., pg. 454—To Fanny Wells, gdn. of Durrett, Nancy, Isaach and Thornton Wills.

CLARK COUNTY INVENTORIES—BOOK B

Names appearing in this index are not included in General Index

Bernard, Wm.—Inv.
Brandenburg, Matthew—Inv.
Bullock, Paterson—Inv.

Clark's—Inv., Dow.
Clay's—Inv.
Culbertson, John—Inv. pg. 344
Conkright, Herculis—Inv.

Davenport, Stephen
Davis, Solomon—Set.

Edwards, Humphrey—Inv. Set.

Flinn, Michael—Inv.

Gordon, John—Set. dated 1805.
Ganes, (Geans) Wm.—Inv. pg. 450.

Huff, Paul—Inv. pg. 24.
Hazelrigg, Wm.—Inv. Set. pg. 153.
Harris, John—Inv. pg. 351.
Henderson, John—Inv. pg. 356.

Jacobs, Henry—Gdn.

Lusk, Samuel—Admr. Set. pg. 107.
Leforce, Wm.—Inv. pg. 413.

Mullin, Geo.—Inv. pg. 39.

Perkins, Julius.
Prewitt, Elias—Inv. pg. 146.
Perkins, Wm. Inv.

Richardson, Wm.—Admr. Appt.

Swinney, James—Inv.
Smith, Robert—Inv.
Starr, Jno.
Swiney, Wm.—Inv. pg. 195.

Trimble, Wm.—Inv. pg. 184.
Tanner, John—Inv. pg. 396.

Winnings, (Wining) James—Sale.

FRANKLIN COUNTY

(Formed from Mercer, Shelby, Woodford, 1794)

WILL BOOK A.

LLOYD, THOMAS—"Of Woodford County, Va." (later Ky.)—To dau. Mary, wife of Jas. Tate; wife, Araminta Julianna; granddau. Martha Floyd Cox, if she dies before she marries or becomes 21 yrs. of age, property to wife; to Thos. Cox. Extrs.: wife and friends and neighbors, Nathaniel Saunders and Wm. Monthomery (Montgomery). Written Aug. 10, 1792. Wts.: Caleb Wallace, Edward Austin, Elisha English. Probated Aug. 1795.

WARE, JAS.—"Of Woodford Co."—To three sons, James, William and Edmund; all my chdn. viz: John, Nicholas' hrs., James, Clary Sale, William and Edmund. Extrs.: three sons. Written ____ 25, 1790. Wts.: Wm. Hickman, Thos. Sullenger. Probated April, 1796.

COLQUIT, SARAH—To son, William; dau., Ann Garnett's chdn. (she deceased) when Walter Garnett comes to age of eighteen; son-in-law, John Garnett; dau. Sally Gibson until William Gibson comes of age, then to him, and if he die to Sally Gibson's surviving chdn. Extrs.: Edmund Vaughan, John Brown, Earnest Martinie, John Brown. Written Feb. 15, 1796. Wts.: Wm. Ware, Wm. Ballard, Susanna Martinie. Probated June 22, 1796.

ROBINSON, ALEXANDER—To mother; sister, Rachel Campbell's two daus. Martha and Izbel; bro. Robert's dau. Polly Robinson; bro. John Robinson's son, Alexander. Extrs.: two bros., John and William. Written Sept. 24, 1796. Wts.: Robt. Blackwell, Izbel Robinson. Probated Nov. 15, 1796.

PERRY, JOHN—To wife, Elizabeth: chdn. Santford, Nancy and Robert. Extrs.: Robt. Perry, Rodrick Perry, John Rennick. Probated Nov. 1796.

POINDEXTER—THOMAS—To son, Jas.; son, Robt.; son, Richard; son, George; dau. Elizabeth Jones Cammack; dau. Lucy, chdn.: Gabriel Thos., Robt., Jas., Richard, Geo.,; dau. Molly Cosby's hrs.: Stithe, Nicholas, Francis, Betsy and Garland Cosby; daus. Elizabeth Jones Cammack and Lucy; to Garland Cosby's sons, Stith, Nicholas, Francis, Garland. Extrs.: sons, Thos., Jas. P., and Garland Cosby. Written Jan. 15, 1796. Wts.: Joseph Adams, Jno. Perry, Robt. Perry. Probated July, 1796.

ARBUCKLE, JOHN—To Geo. Peyton; to wife, Hannah; dau. Betty Arbuckle. Written Oct. 13, 1796. Wts.: John David, Thos. Douthit, Samuel Arbuckle. Probated Feb. 21, 1797.

MURRAYS, WM.—"Of District of Villa Gayoso in Government of Natchez"; property in Louisianna to be unsold during life of wife, Martha Murray with the express purpose that her son, James McIntyre not live with her; to Anna Marion Rumsey; son, Wm. Murray, whether in the U. S. or elsewhere, reserving to his mother all her rights provided by law; to son, William, "my seal bearing my arms." Extrs.: friends, Wm. Dunbar, of Lecond (?) Creek and John Smith of Villa Gayoso, respecting interests in this country, and son, Wm. Extr. of other part of will. Written Sept. 7, 1794. Wts.: Thos. M. Green, Everard Green, Roger Dixon, Bernard Isenhootz, Jacob G. Katell, Wm. Smith, Frederick Katell. Probated in Philadelphia, Pa., March, 1797 and Franklin Co., Ky., Apr., 1797.

MONTGOMERY, SAMUEL—To sons, John and Joseph and they to give to Samuel Montgomery; property divided among Samuel, John and Joseph. Written June 1, 1797. Test.: Robt. Montgomery, Wm. Montgomery. Probated Nov. 21, 1797.

COOK, MARGARET—To Wm. Cook, to Seth Cook, sons of son, Jesse Cook, decd; to Hosea Cook, son of Hosea Cook, decd., paid them when of age; rest of property divided between nine chdn., viz: Rachael Murphey, Barthsheba Dunn, Helen Bohannon, Rhoda Jamison, Wm. Cook, Seth Cook, Margaret Hacket, Abraham Cook and Unice Miles; at Barsheba Dunn's death, to her chdn., her husband, Wm. Dunn. Extrs.: sons, Wm. and Seth. Written March 11, 1797. Wts.: Joseph Lewis, John Miles, John Buchannon. Probated Feb. 1798.

COUCHMAN, JONATHAN—To Virgil Poe; to friend, Capt. Wm. Fenwick; wife, Dicey and my infant son. Extrs.: Wm. Fenwick, Wm. Manning. Written Nov. 15, 1798. Wts.: Jno. M. Scott, Jas. Benham, David Carson. Probated Dec. 1798.

GRAHAM, JAMES—To wife, step-dau., Mary Canada and "my own three chdn.: Margaret, Ellender and John"; money due in Lancaster Co., Penn. Extrs.: Jamy Tate, Henry Hockersmith. Written Mar.

13, 1799. Wts.: Thos Settle, Gilbert Christian, Arthur McGaughey, Geo. Widenn (?). Probated Apr. 1799.

BROWN, SAMUEL MONTGOMERY—"About to take a lengthy voyage to unhealthy climate." To wife, Mary Brown; nephew, Robert Brown Jamison. Extrix.: wife, Mary with Harris Innis and Daniel Weisegar to advise. Written Apr. 2, 1798. Wts.: John Raitton, Thos. Baker. Probated Dec. 1799.

WILSON, JOHN—To dau. Nancy Wilson; son, Thos.; other chdn.: Sally Wilson, Mary Clark, John Wilson and Rachel Wilson. Etr.: friend. Thos. Gist. Written Mar. 16, 1797. Wts.: Robt. Fenwick, Thos. Palmer, Codicil appts. son, John Extr. Probated Feb. 1800.

McBRAYERS, JAMES, "GENT."—To son, William; grandson, Jas. Mc-Brayers, son of son, Wm., land in Jefferson Co.; son James, part same tract; son, Hugh, land in Jefferson; to first male heir of son, John; youngest son, Andrew (unmarried); son, Wm., money to be recovered of Absolom Watkins. Extrs.: Samuel McAffee and son, Wm. Wts.: Robt. Blackwell, Wm. McBrayers. Written Aug. 2, 1800—probated Jan. 1801.

GILSON, HENRY—To wife, Sary; dau. Polly; son, James, he to be Extr.; son John; Elizabeth Graham and Jean Graham given property previously. Written Jan. 19, 1801. Wts.: Jas. Fogg, Jas. Hatton, Jno. Nitchey. Probated Feb. 1801.

McFADDING, HUGH—Property previously given Mary Fields, James McFadding, Elizabeth Lawson, Jane Ledgewood, Rebecca Blackford; son, Wm.; wife, Elizabeth. Extrs.: wife and James Ledgewood. Written Jan. 25, 1801. Wts.: Jas. Hutton, Jas. Fogg, Jas. Ledgewood. Probated Apr. 1801.

HOLLOWAY, CHAS.—Wife, Hannah; "my chdn."; to bro. Geo. Holloway in Va. Extrs.: Jesse Vawter, Richard Shipp. Wts.: Jno. D. Graves, Hannah Musick, John Bell. Probated Jan. 17, 1803.

BOYD, JAS.—To wife, Rebeckah; mother; bro., Wm. Boyd and mother, Jane Boyd, Extrs. Wts.: Elisha Herndon, Aaron Dooley, Wm. Boyd. Probated Dec. 1803.

HARRIS, HANNAH—To son, John Harris; daus., Ann Innis, Elizabeth Todd, Sarah Smith, Mary Hanna, Rachel and Hannah Harris. Extrs.: son, John, and sons-in-law, Thos. Todd, Harry Innis. Written June 29, 1802. Wts.: Lewis Arnold, Ann Innis, Virginia Amoreux. (?).

THOMAS, EDMUND—Wife, Ann; sons, and daus. when 21 yrs. old. Extrs.: Thos. Wallace, Henry Clay, Culthbert Banks, Walter Chiles, Geo. Madison, Thos. Todd, Christopher Greenup. Written Dec. 4, 1803. Wts.: Isaac Gano, Jno. Crutchfield, Barnabus McHenry. Probated Dec. 1803.

GANO, REV. JOHN—To wife, Sarah, all property she possessed at the time of marriage, use of mansion tract of land, should she choose to remove to Carolinas, she to be furnished with choice of horses, etc.; chdn.: Daniel, Margaret, Stephen, John, Sarah, Isaac, Richard Susanna. Narrative of my life to be completed by my son, Stephen.

Extrix.: wife, Extrs.: Daniel Gano, Col. Baker Ewing and Gov. Jas. Garrard. Written Dec. 29, 1798—probated Jan. 1805. Wts.: Turner Richardson, John Hunt, Margaret Hunt. (Note: Rev. John Gano said to have baptized George Washington).

TRACY, SAMUEL—To son, John; dau., Polly Fought; rest to Betsey Parant, Jas. Tracy and Peggy Tracy. Extrs.: Thos. Quidy, Jas. Smart, Wm. Payne, Thos. McCrary. Written Feb. 20, 1804. Wts.: Thos. McQuady, Thos. Pareant, Dan'l Weiseger. Probated June 1805.

BENNERS, ELIZABETH— To dau., Ann Elizabeth Instone and at her death, to her chdn., because she has more need thereof than rest of my family and connections. Friend Christopher Greenup, Trustee and Extr. Written Sept. 29, 1804. Wts.: Thos. C. Lewis, Jas. Witherold, Jno. Stiles. Probated Aug. 1805.

GRAVES, WM.—To wife, Mary. Extrs.: wife and Jno. Arnold, Jr. Written Aug. 7, 1804. Wts.: Thos. Withers, Scott Brown, Rebeca Withers. Probated Dec. 1805.

ARNOLD, JEAN—To Jenny Arnold for Benj. Arnold when of age; to Jenny Arnold, dau. to Abigal Arnold; son, John Arnold. Written Nov. 2, 1798. Wts.: Wm. McBrayers, Robt. Walker, Jennet McBrayers. Probated Jan. 1806.

BROWN, JOHN—Wife, Nancy; son, Wm. and in case he never returns from army, to dau., Abediance Brown; dau., Polly Brown; son, Daniel. Admrs.: bro. Jesse Brown, Daniel Brown, Wm. Montgomery. Wts.: Wm. Hickman, Moses Hickman, Rich. Roberts. Probated Sept. 25, 1805.

SLAUGHTER,EDGECOMB S.—To sister, Martha Slaughter. Written Apr. 21, 1791. Wts.: Fras. B. Slaughter, Philip Buckner, Patc. Joyes. Probated Nov. 1799.

LOWRY, THOS.—To Catharine Harris Shiell and Maria Knot Innis. Extr.: Harry Innis, he to adjust my demand as ass'nee of Isaac Hicks agst. Goforth of Ohio. Written Aug. 24, 1803. Wts.: Jno. Morris, Wm. Owen. Probated Nov. 1803.

CRUTCHER, HENRY—To wife, Martha; chdn., Joanna Sacra, Isaac, Elizabeth Pemberton and Catherine Cook; sons, Henry and Reubin; whereas by death of Mrs. Ann Beasley of Caroline Co., Va., and will of her decd. husband, Wm. Beasley, entitled by marriage with said wife, Martha, to portion of estate of decd., division to be made among sons, Henry and Reubin; son-in-law, Wm. Cook and Jas. Secra and Jesse Brown and Edmund Beasley, Extrs. Written Sept. 12, 1806. Wts.: Will Samuel, Jas. Porter, Achilles Sneed, D. E. Brown. Probated March, 1807.

FENWICK, BALINDA—To be buried agreeable to ceremonies of Holy Roman Apostolic Catholic Church; dau., Elizabeth Culhoon; son, Joseph Fenwick, his miniature; son, Joseph's chdn.; son, Enock Fenwick; son, Henry; Rev. Edward D. Fenwick; son, Ignatius M. Fenwick; Right Honorable Dr. Carroll, Bishop of Baltimore; son, Ignatius Fenwick, Extr. Written May 28, 1808. Wts.: I. Tywman, John M. Scott, Sukey Wyngate, Levin Twyman. Probated June 20, 1808.

FRANKLIN COUNTY INVENTORIES AND APPRAISEMENTS THROUGH 1810

Names appearing in this index are not included in General Index

Richie Boulware, Aug. 18, 1795.
Thos. Lloyds, March 24, 1796.
Sarah Colquit, July 2, 1796.
Thos. Poindexter, Nov. 25, 1796.
Alex. Robinson, 1796 (?).
Peter Samuel, Jan. 17, 1797.
Margaret Cook, Aug. 15, 1797.
Wm. McGren, Dec. 19, 1797.
Thos. Jackson, Jan. 29, 1799.
Richard Pemberton, Nov. 27, 1798.
Jas. Graham, Aug. 27, 1799.
Thos. Wilson, Jan. 1800.
Smith Wingate, Aug. 27, 1799.
Samuel Montgomery Brown, Feb. 28, 1800.
Geo. Smith, Oct. 27, 1800.
Jas. Bledsoe, Nov. 25, 1800.
Robt. Woolridge, June 18, 1801.
Jno. Byrne, Jan. 16, 1800 (or 1).
Thos. Nickols, Aug. 22, 1802
Turner Richardson, Dec. 27, 1802.
Jas. Fogg, Feb. 1803.
Reubin Ware, May, 1803.
Chas. Holloway, Aug. 15, 1803.
Joshua Jackson, Apr. 20, 1804.
Edmund Turner, Feb. 1804.
Wm. Tracy, Feb. 9, 1804.
Otho Beaty, March 17, 1804.
Robt. Holton, Sept. 1804.
Jno. Gano, Sept. 16, 1805.
Felix McAlister, Apr. 12, 1806.
Jno. Brown, Nov. 19, 1806.
Jno. Black, Nov. 1806.
Wm. James, Nov. 22, 1806.
Chas. Patterson of Buckingham Co., Va., Mar. 25, 1805.
Hugh Burne, March 16, 1807.
Henry Crutcher, March 27, 1807.
John Colson, June 1, 1805.

Jas. Monday. Dec. 3, 1807.
Nathaniel Saunders, Dec. 2, 1807.
John Logan, Oct. 1807.
Wm. Hensley, Feb. 13, 1808.
Jane Brown, Nov. 1807.
John Erdington, May, 1808.
Thos. Reed, May, 1808.
Philip Bush, June 20, 1808.
Isaac Sacrey, May 14, 1808.
Philip Rowzee, Aug. 10, 1808.
Jno. Major, Aug. 10, 1808.
Susannah Lightfoot, part of estate in hands of Dan'l Ragins, Va.
Henry Gibson, Apr. 1801.
Burton Loftus, June 20, 1805.
Thos. Hicklin, Jan. 1805.
Owen Powell, June, 1809.
Benj. Head, Jan. 16, 1809.
Isaac Ward, July 31, 1809.
Jno. McDowell, Dec. 1809.
Capt. Francis Graham, Dec. 1809.
Jas. Tracy, Jan. 1810.
James Arnold, Apr. 1810.
Stephen Arnold, March, 1810.
Elzy L. James, May, 1810.
Ambrose Graham, May, 1810.
Henry Turnstall, June, 1810.
Wm. Marshall, June, 1810.
Henry Thompson, June, 1810.
David Zook, June, 1810.
Soloman Zook (Sook), June, 1810.
Thos. Turnstall, Aug. 1810.
Andrew Bourn, May, 1810.
Caleb Hall, Aug. 1810.
Daniel Stephens, Nov. 24, 1810.
Thos. Carneal, June, 1811.

HARDIN COUNTY
(Formed from Nelson County, 1792)

Contributed by Miss Hattie Scott, Frankfort, Ky.

INDEX TO WILL BOOK A

Names appearing in this index are not included in General Index

Ashley, (Ashby?) Bladen, Inv.
Ashcraft, Jediah, will, wife and children named.

Barnett, Joseph, Inv.

Baird, (Beard) James, will, (spelled both ways) number chdn.
Beaden, Aaron, Inv.
Bell, Peter, deposition.

Berry, Enoch, will, wife and chdn. named.

Braddock, General and wife, Rebecca.

Bradley, (Brady) James, will, spelled both ways; names wife and many children.

Brady, Morris, will, names wife and many children.

Brady, Jonathan, will, names wife and children.

Brashear, Nicholas R.: Inv.

Brown, James: Inv.

Bryant, Ignatius: Inv.

Burns, Eleanor: deceased, Inv. Dec. 7, 1799.

Bush, Isaac: constable.

Clous, George, Jr.: will, names father and mother, 1794.

Clous, John: Inv.

Close, George, Sr.: Inv. (Clous?).

Crow, John: Inv.

Carr, John: Inv.

Crawford, Robt.: will, names wife, children and grand children.

Cooper, Job: Inv.

Crafton, Joseph: Inv.

Cotes, Catherine: Inv.

Caldhoon, Hugh: Inv.

Dorsey, Thos.:will, refers to wife and children and his lost fortune.

Dye, Isaac: will, names wife and children, 1796.

Dodge, Isaiah, (Josiah): Inv., wife's dower.

Dougherty, Rich.: Inv.

Ewin, Ervin, Ewen, Erven, (?) John, Sr.: will, names his home county in Va., mother, brother, wife and children.

Elder, Joseph: Inv., widow.

Enlow, Mordecai: Inv.

Friend, Banner: will, names sister and brother, 1793.

Frakes, Henry: will, names wife and children.

Frakes, Hannah:

F——, John

Farguson, (Ferguson?) Usher: Inv.

Glen, Wm.: heir to Thos. Glen.

Goodwin, Abraham: Inv.

Greenwall, Joseph: will, names wife, children and grand children. (Greenwalt?).

Gum, Jehu: Inv.

Gum, Rhoda: deposition.

Helm, Benj.: Inv.

Highbough, George: Inv.

Hinch, George: deceased.

Hodgen, Robt.: bond.

Howell, Jacob: Inv.

Hughes, George: Inv.

Jaggers, Daniel, Sr.: will, names wife and many children.

Kennedy, Robt.: Inv.

Kimberlin, Jacob: Inv.

Kermickle, Peter: will, children. (Carmichael?)

Kerkendall, (Kykendall) Jacob: will, names wife and children. (This is more often spelled "Kuykendall" and is today).

LaRue, John: Inv.

LaRue, Peter: appts. attorney.

LaRue, Jas. and Jabez: appts. attorney.

Lee, Chas.: Inv.

Larue, Isaac:

Lucas, Wm.: will, names wife and children.

McClain, John: inv.

McComas, Nathaniel: Inv., Mar., 1795.

McGovern, Chas.: Inv.

McGovern, Eliz.:

McIntire, Thos.: Inv.

McDowell, (McDole in index) Robt.: will, names mother and brother.

McKinsey, Enoch: will, names wife. (Spelled McKensey in will).

Madison, Gabriel: appts. Taylor, attorney.

May, David: Inv.

Melingor, Wm.: Inv.

Miller, Christopher: will, names wife and children.

Miller, Earnest: Inv.

Morrison, David: Inv.

Morrison, Isaac: will, names wife and number of children.

Paul, John: Inv.
Pairtree, John: will.
Pearpoint, Francis, Sr.: will, names wife, son, grand son, and wife's sister.
Pearpoint, Francis, Jr.: Inv.
Pearpoint, Mary:
Portwood, Page: Inv.
Purtle, Jacob: Inv.
Phebus, John: will, wife named, children.

Rawlings, Edmund: will, wife and married children named.
Redman, Jno.: Inv.
Redman, Thos.: Inv., 1799, widow.
Richardson, Robt. and Mary: deceased, Inv.
Ruder, Asher: Inv. (Reeder?).

Sheare, Wm.: Inv.
Skaggs, Sarah: deposition.
Stater, (Slater?) Adam: Inv.
Slater, Adam: Inv.
Strunk, Abraham: will, names brothers and sisters, all in Va.

Stuart, Wm.: Inv.
Swank, John: Inv.
Swearing, John: Inv.

Thomas, Henry: Inv.
Truman, Edward: will, names wife and married children.
Trunk, Abram: Inv.

Vanmetre, Jacob: will. names wife and large family.
Vertrees, John: will, names wife and large family, including stepchildren.

Watts, George: will, names wife and children.
Wiley, Walter: will, names number of children. (Wylie).
Williams, Jacob: Inv.
Winters, Samuel: Inv.
Withers, Wm.: will, names many children, locates lands in Va.
Wright, Benj.: frees a slave.

Young, Adam: Inv.

JEFFERSON COUNTY
(Formed 1790)

Copied by members of the John Marshall Chapter, D. A. R.

Note: Wills from Will Book 1 have been published in National Genealogical Quarterly, beginning Vol. VI.

WILL BOOK 2

THOMPSON, JOHN—Gives to wife, Elizabeth Thompson for her life time and after her death equally to his children. His wife to be Executrix. Jan. 1, 1804. In codicil: his sons, with his wife are appointed Executors. July 24, 1805. Probated June 13, 1813.

STAFFORD, THOMAS—Gives to his wife, Eve; and to John, Benj., Elizabeth Bishop and Susanna Purry, children to share and share alike. To Sarah Ward's children, certain property when they come of age. Children: Benjamin, Elizabeth Bishop, Sarah Ward, Mary Newkirk, Margaret Sliger, Thomas Stafford, Martha Young and Susanna Purry. His sons are Executors. Oct. 11, 1809. Probated Oct. 11, 1813.

EDWARDS, FREDRICK—Gives to his wife, Mary Edwards, for her life; to his son, Joseph; to his granddaughters, Polly C. Bartlett, Nancy Bartlett; to his grandson, Pendleton Strother; to his grandson, Robert Edwards, son of Robert Edwards, killed at River Raison.

Should the above heirs die, the property is to be divided among Wm. Edwards, John Edwards and James Montgomery Edwards and Elizabeth Bartlett. Ex.: William Edwards and John Edwards. Made March 6, 1813. Probated Oct. 11, 1813.

WEEMS, JOHN—To his wife, Mary S. Weems and to his children: James, Elizabeth M. Weems, Kitty Weems, Alice Weems, George Weems, Martha Weems, Julia N. Weems and David Weems. Aug. 29, 1813. Probated Oct. 11, 1813.

COLLINS, JOHN—Gives to his wife the property she had at their marriage. Betsy Collins, wife to Dr. James C. Johnson, his stock of Medicine. Should I inherit any part of my father's estate, that is to be divided between my brother Daniel and sister Esther. Sept. 2, 1813. Ex.: James C. Johnson. Dec. 13, 1813.

MYRTLE, JOHN—Gives to his wife, Phoebe Myrtle and his children Phoebe Myrtle, Ex. July 7, 1801. Probated Dec. 13, 1813.

MARTIN, JOHN—Gives Joseph Martin, Joseph Fleming in trust for his sister, Marcy Walker; to Joseph Martin in trust for Priscilla Green; to James Overstreet and William Farker, in trust for Nancy Misner; to cousins, Mary McGimes, Ephya Ray; to his sister, Elizabeth Fleming; to his half-sister, Polly Campbell; and to his half-brother, Alexander Thompson. Aug 29, 1813. Ex.: Archibald Allen, Gen. Rob. Breckenridge, Richard C. Anderson. Probated Jan. 10, 1814.

JONES, ALICE—Gives to son, John; to daughter, Anna Dashiel; to grandson, William Scarborough Jones; to grandson, William Ward Jones; to daughter, Elinor Smith Jones. Ex.: John Jones. July 8, 1812. Probated March 14, 1814.

LAWRENCE, BENJAMIN—Gives to son, Samuel; Levin; to his grandchildren: Benjamin Winchester, Lavina Snowden, Olivia Winchester, Amanda Winchester, Polly D. Winchester, Louisa Winchester, William Chambers Winchester; to granddaughter, Polly Chambers; to daughter, Susanna Williamson; to daughter, Elizabeth Hynes; to daughter, Rebecca Winchester; to granddaughter, Polly Hobb; to granddaughter, Matilda L. Dorsey; grandson, Elias Dorsey; Levin L. Dorsey; Benjamin L. Dorsey; Mathew Brown; Eliza Lawrence; Levin Hynes; Polly D. Hynes. Ex.: Levin Lawrence, William R. Hynes. June 12, 1812. Probated March 14, 1814.

REED, ABRAM—Gives to his mother, Mary Reed; to his sister, Rebecca Reed; brother, John Reed; brother, Joseph and brother, James. Ex.: James Reed. March 3, 1814. Probated May 9, 1814.

WHIPP, GEO.—To his son, John, to keep the property together during the lifetime of his wife, Susanna; to his son, Ruben; son, George Denton; to his daughter, Susan; daughter, Rebecca; to son, Wesley; to three children, Betsy, Joshua and Samuel; to Susana support during life. Ex.: John Whips. June 16, 1810. Probated May 9, 1814.

DUNCAN, HENRY—Gives to his children and wife. Ex.: Nancy Duncan and Coleman Duncan. June 4, 1814. Probated June 13, 1814,

SPRADLING, WILLIAM—To a colored woman and her four children. Ex.: David L. Ward, Wm. Pope, Jr., and John Speed. Probated Sept, 12, 1814.

McCONNEL, JAMES L.—To wife, Malinda; to sister, Elizabeth. Ex.: Richard Fenley, Wm. Pope, John Bustard. Nov. 5, 1814. Probated March 13, 1815.

WILHOYTE, JOHN—To wife, Elizabeth and children, including Aaron. Ex.: Elizabeth Wilhoyte. Dec. 3, 1814. Probated March 3, 1815.

BOHANON, RICHARD—To wife, Deborah; sons, Pierce, William, Henry and to daughter, Elizabeth Jane and Ambrose; to his son, Larkin and to sons, George and Julius. Ex.: wife, Deborah and sons, George and Julius. Oct. 7, 1814. Probated Mar. 13, 1815.

DOUGHERTY, WILLIAM—To wife, Elizabeth and children; daughter, Patsy William. Ex.: wife, Elizabeth Dougherty. Dec. 8, 1814. Probated Mar. 14, 1815.

HEMPHILL, SAMUEL To his mother. Ex.: Mother. Feb. 22, 1815. Probated May 15, 1815.

JOHNSON, GABRIEL I.—To wife, Enfield and son, Gabriel J. Johnson; son, Benjamin William Johnson; son, Thos. Johnson. Ex.: Wife, Enfield, Thos. Prather and Gabriel Johnson. April 6, 1815. Probated May 8, 1815.

FILLICE, GRIFFIN—To Wm. Rose; to Henson Hobbs; John Rose; Polly Rose; Elizabeth Rose; to Elisha Freeman. Ex.: John Rose. April 6, 1815. Probated June 12, 1815.

PORTER, WILLIAM—To his children: Jane Shawbridge, Elinor Whittington, Elizabeth, Henry, Julia Ann. Ex.: Dr. James Porter. July 9, 1815. Probated Aug. 14, 1815.

HOLLIS, JOHN—To son, Joshua W. Hollis; to wife, Ruth Hollis; Calvin Luther Agin. Ex.: _____. Mar. 4, 1815. Probated Aug. 14, 1815.

McCOLLOCH, CHRISTOPHER—To wife and children, Daniel, Rachel Alexander. Ex.: Patrick Taggert, Alex. Pope, Abner Field. Sept. 5, 1815. Probated Sept. 11, 1815.

ZARING, HENRY—To sister, Catherine and brother, John Phillip and Benjamin Jacob. Mar. 15, 1815. Probated Oct. 9, 1815.

RICHARD, SAMUEL—To friend, William Dunn and Mary, his wife. Nov. 6, 1815. Probated Jan. 8, 1816.

PATTON, JAMES—To wife, Phoebe and daughter Polly and to son, George. Ex.: Phoebe Patton, Wordon Pope. Dec. 20, 1815. Probated Jan. 8, 1816.

SHIPP, EDMUD (EDMUND)—To daughter, Nancy; to daughter, Sallie G. Howell; to daughter, Betsy; daughter, Lucy; son, Thomas; son, Edmond; son, Ewell; granddaughter, Minerva L. Lampton; Fannie L. Lampton; Edmond S. Lampton; to his wife, Tabitha for life. Ex.: Tabitha Ship, Dan. S. Howell, Edmund Ship. Jan. 5, 1816. Probated Mar. 11, 1816.

MILLER, EDWARDS—To wife, Hannah; son, Thos. B. Miller; son, Robert; daughter, Hannah. Ex.: Robert Miller, Isaac W. Dabney. Jan. 26, 1816. Probated Mar. 7, 1816.

REYNOLD, RICHARD—To his wife, Mary and son, Richard; to granddaughter, Ann Smith and other children. Exrs.: Andrew Steele and Wordon Pope. Oct. 1, 1808. Probated Mar. 11, 1816.

BULLITT, ALEXANDER SCOTT—To wife, Mary; to sons, Cuthbert, William Christian, Thos., James; to daughter, Anna C.; to son, Wm. C.; to daughter, Mary; Hellen Massie. Ex.: Mary Bullitt, Henry Massie, sons, Cuthbert and William. Aug. 26, 1815. Probated May 13, 1816.

STOWERS, NICHOLAS—To wife, Fanny; son, William; daughter, Barbara Farnsley; son, Patrick; daughter, Polly Banks; daughter, Elizabeth Nossington; daughters, Lucy, Libby, Matilda. Ex.: Patrick Stowers, Thomas _____, Thomas Prine, M. Lewis and Hancock Taylor. Mar. 5, 1816. Probated May 13, 1816.

NEWMAN, OBEDIAH—Everything to his wife, Martha W. Newman. Jan. 24, 1811. Probated Aug. 12, 1816.

SHANNONHOUSE, ABEL—Andrew Valley and Joseph Laton, present before his death, declare that he wished his wife, Mary to have all his property. July 15, 1816. Aug. 12, 1816.

THEOBALD, THOMAS—Wishes his niece, Nancy Pendegrass, to have his property. July 25, 1816. Probated Aug. 13, 1816.

BUCKNER, AMBROSE—To wife, Rebecca Buckner. Ex.: Rebecca Buckner. Feb. 6, 1816. Probated Oct. 14, 1816.

BROWN, JOHN—To his wife, Susanna P. Brown and children; children of deceased daughter, Elizabeth Smith. Ex.: Susanna Brown, John Brown, Dr. John Miller. Dec. 22, 1816. Probated Jan. 13, 1817.

FORWOOD, WILLIAM—To his wife, Hannah; to son, Samuel; to George Pomeroy's four children by first Sarah Forwood: Polly, Hannah, William, Elizabeth. Ex.: Samuel Forword. Dec. 6, 1816. Probated Jan. 13, 1817.

HOLLIS, NANCY—For support of colored girl, Celia. Ex.: Richard Phillipps, Frederick Henderliter. Dec. 13, 1816. Probated Jan. 13, 1817.

ARTEBURN, WILLIAM—To his granddaughter, Lidia McKie and to his wife, Nancy, for life; then to Elijah, William, Samuel, Presley, Betsy Pomwell and Lidia Saffer. Ex. William and Presley Arterburn. Sept. 19, 1815. Probated Oct. 14, 1816.

VEACH, JOHN—To daughter, Frances Bealty Brooky; son, Alexander; daughter, Elizabeth; daughter, Sarah; to Rev. Robert N. Bishop. Ex.: Hancock Taylor. Apr. 17, 1817. Probated May 12, 1817.

LUCKETT, ELIZABETH—To granddaughters, Elizabeth Jane, Love Luckett; granddaughter, Sarah Luckett; to son, Lawson; to sister,

Molly Ann Luckett; remainder to son, Thomas H. Luckett. Ex.: Thomas H. Luckett. Feb. 20, 1817. Probated May 12, 1817.

MERRIWETHER, JAMES—To son, Robert; to his wife, Elizabeth Merriwether, interest in Ky., to sons, David, James, William, Thomas, John, Robert. Land in Louisiana to his wife for life. Lancelott Minor, Hawood Goodburn and David Bullock in trust for daughter, Ann; to granddaughter, Sallie Merriwether. Ex.: Col. William D. Callis, Capt. Jas. Winston, Capt. John Poindexter. Oct. 10, 1800. Probated ____ 13, 1801. Louisa Co., Va., probated Aug. 11, 1817.

BULLITT, MARY—To daughter, Eliza C. Prather; to Samuel Churchill, in trust for William Churchill; rest for Minor Thos. Bullitt and Thomas James Bullitt. Ex.: Samuel Churchill. Sept. 11, 1817. Probated Oct. 13, 1817.

FUNSTALL, JAMES N.—To brother, Edmund and brother George William; to sisters, Maria S. Funstall, Lucinda Jane W. Funstall. Ex.: Thomas Funstall, Brooks Hill. Oct. 13, 1817. Probated Oct. 16, 1817.

FERGUSON, SAMUEL—To his wife, Ann; to son, Benjamin; sons, Samuel William and George; to his granddaughter, Mary Ferguson. Ex.: Ann Ferguson, wife, and John Ferguson and Benjamin Ferguson, sons. Jan. 13, 1816. Probated Dec. 8, 1817.

COLEMAN, ROBERT—To his Bettie, his estate. Ex.: Bettie Coleman. Mar. 5, 1812. Probated Dec. 8, 1817.

KELLER, WILLIAM—To wife and sons, Abraham and John and to daughter, Elizabeth. Ex.: Wife, son, Abraham Keller, son-in-law, Abraham Keller. Aug. 5, 1811. Probated Dec. 9, 1817.

QUICK, JACOB—To wife, Elinor; to children: Doris Jones, John Gray Moore, James Isiah, Elizabeth Jane. Ex.: Elinor Quick, wife, Samuel Quick, brother. Feb. 14, 1818. Probated March 9, 1818.

FUNSTALL, JOSEPH and his wife, JANE—Indenture to son, Joseph F. Funstall, right to property against any or all other heirs. July 3, 1817.

MILLER, ANTHONY—To his brothers, Buckner and Robert; to Thomas Miller, nephew; William Miller, nephew; to his Lavina Miller; niece, Doratha Jane; James Buckner Bright, nephew; Anthony Miller, nephew; William Thomas Winlock, nephew; Doratha Ann Pomeroy, niece. Ex.: Brothers, Buckner and Robert Miller. Mar. 12, 1818. Probated June 8, 1818.

TRIGG, THOMAS—To his wife, Mary; to his children. Ex.: William Duerson and William Edwards. Oct. 25 1811. Probated June 8, 1818.

KAYE, FREDERICK AUGUSTUS—To his wife, Mary Dorothy; sons, Frederick Augustus, William and Henry; to sons, John and Francis Jacob; to daughters, Catherine, wife of Wm. Reed, Mary, wife of John Shiving, Elizabeth, wife of Coleman Daniel. Ex.: Wm. Reed, John Shiving. Jan, 10, 1818. Probated June 8, 1818.

NORTON, MATHEW—To friend, Katherine W. Huston and residue to brother Robert. Ex.: William Scott and John Lynn. Dec. 10, 1817. Probated June 9, 1818.

WILLIAMS, JEREMIAH—To his wife, Martha; son, Moses, daughter, Eveline; to sons, Joseph and Jeremiah; to daughter, Patsy; daughter, Nancy; daughter, Eliza, daughter, Amelia, to son Washington; to daughter, Phoebe; son, John; daughter, Katherine Andkins. Ex.: Martha Williams, wife. Probated June 9, 1818.

PITTS, ROBERT—To his wife, Charlotte; after her Rosamund Julia Ann, Clarin, Felix, Ellen and Washington Pitts, children of Archibald Pitts; Thomas, Polly, Sally, Kitty, Charlotte, children of Thomas Pitts; to his half-sister, Elinor Aull. Ex.: Charlotte Pitts, wife. June 8, 1818. Probated Aug. 11, 1818.

SKIDMORE, PAUL—To wife, Frances Matilda; son, John; daughters, Eliza Bethea, Sarah Ann, Ann Clarke Jones. Ex.: Frances Matilda Skidmore, wife, John Gaffney. Dec. 4, 1817. Probated Aug. 12, 1818.

ROSS, LAWRENCE—To wife, Susanna; to son, Presley N. Ross; son, Shapley; daughter, Polly Peyton; daughter, Betsy Phillips; daughter Nancy White; daughter, Sukey Love; daughter, Sally Sullivan; daughter, Ann Prinz; daughter, Milly Carter; daughter, Fannie Oldham, married Conway Oldham. Ex.: Susanna Ross, wife, Shapley Ross, Presley Ross. Mar. 2, 1818. Probated Sept. 15, 1818.

BROOKS, JOSEPH—To his wife, Nancy, to son, Squire; to son-in-law, Elisha Standiford and to Nancy, his wife. What is left to Joseph Anderson Brooks; to son-in-law, Solomon Neill and his wife, Margaret; daughter, Mary Pendegrass, Margaret America Pendegrass. Ex.: Joseph Anderson Brooks, Solomon Neill and Elisha Standiford. Sept. 10, 1818. Probated Oct. 12, 1818.

BECKWITH, UPTON—To his wife, Betsy Beckwith, should infant child die, then to his brothers and sisters. Ex.: John, brother and nephew, John P. Summers. Probated Jan. 11, 1819.

HALL, E.—To his wife, Fanny; to Bessie Webster; and to wife's children. Ex.: Fanny Hall, wife and R. Hall, son. Probated Mar. 8, 1819.

STAFFORD, EVE.—To son, Benjamin; son, Thomas; son, John; daughter Sarah Polly Newkirk; son-in-law, David Sliger; daughter, Elizabeth, Peggy, Martha and Susan. Ex.: Job Harryman, David Sliger. July 14, 1815. Probated Mar. 8, 1819.

KELLER, JOSEPH—To his wife, Sarah and to children, Eliza, Isaac, Abraham, Rebecca and Sarah. April 6, 1818. Ex.: Geo. Hikes, Sr., Richard Barbour. Probated Oct. 12, 1818.

RICHARDSON, WILLIAM F.—Gives to his mother, brother Stanhope, friend, Richard A. Green, to Aunt Nancy, sister, Mary. Ex.: Thos. Boswell. Oct. 23, 1818. Probated Mar. 8, 1819.

BUCHNER, (BUCKNER) HALEY—To wife, Lillian; to sons, Henry S., Patterson C., Presley B.; daughter, Keziah; divides remainder among children, including Samuel P. and Avery M. Ex.: Avery M. Buchner, Henry S. Buchner. Feb. 6, 1816. Probated May 10, 1819.

WHITE, GEO—Gives to Anne and son, George Rowley for their education and divides estate among his children. Ex.: William G. White, Lee White, William D. White, Lawrence Young. Mar. 20, 1819. Probated May 10, 1819.

SKIMERHORN, ANN S.—Gives to son, James Francis, two dollars, the remainder, Conrad Rush and son, Jacob Skimerhorn. Ex.: Conrad Rush. May 7, 1819. Probated June 14, 1819.

WATSON, WILLIAM—Gives to wife, Anna and to children, Margaret, Sarah, Thomas, Samuel, William, Anna, Narcissa, Narvel James Ryan. Witnesses: Jacob Oglesby, John Watson, William Kyle. Mar. 11, 1819. Probated June 14, 1819.

MERCER, JOHN—Of Fredericksburg, Va., gives to Hugh Mercer and heirs forever, except his picture to his sister, Mrs. Patton. Ex.: Hugh Mercer. Jan. 3, 1815. Probated Aug. 9, 1819.

MERCER, HUGH—Gives to wife, Isabella, estate in King George Co., Va., to children who may survive her. Ex.: Isabella Mercer, Col. George Weedon, Dr. John Tennant, James Duncanson. Mar. 20, 1776. Probated Aug. 9, 1819.

HOUSTON, ELI—Gives to wife, Lucy Ann. Ex.: James Houston of Bourbon Co., and Lawrence Clore of Jefferson Co. Mar. 20, 1819. Probated Sept. 13, 1819.

BERTHAND, JAMES—Gives to his wife, Mary Ann Julia, after her death to Nicholas Berthand, his son. Ex.: Thos. Prather, Fortunatus Cosby. Dec. 15, 1812. Probated Sept. 13, 1819.

WHEELER, JOHN HANSON—Gives to wife, Deborah; to daughters, Polly Rose, Mahala Rose, Ann H. Chaplin; to children, daughter Elizabeth Miller, deceased; to sons, John and Josiah, Elias Hardin Wheeler; to daughters, Sarah, Emily; to Matilda and Henrietta, Priscilla; son, Albert Perry Wheeler; sons, Truman White Wheeler, Eulisses Henson Wheeler. Ex.: Deborah Wheeler, wife, John Wheeler, son. June 19, 1819. Probated Oct. 12, 1819.

KELLER, SARAH—Gives to brother, Isaac Estill, money due to him; to Rebecca Keller, Betsy Evans and Sarah Keller, nieces. Ex.: Richard Barbour. Oct. 2, 1819. Probated Oct. 12, 1819.

FUNK, JACOB—To wife, Mary, after her death, to step-daughter and to his children, Julia Susan, Eliza Temperance, Teracy Luisa; sons, Thompson Taylor; Joseph Perry. Ex.: Nathan Taylor, brother-in-law, Mary Taylor, wife. Oct. 6, 1819. Probated Dec. 13, 1819.

GARRY, BENNETT—To wife, Charity, after her death to Margaret Garry and Rebecca Smith. Ex.: Charity Garry, wife. Nov. 16, 1819. Probated Dec. 13, 1819.

BRADSHAW, JOHN—Gives Major Thomas Doyle all his property except for purchase of ring for wife of Dr. Allison, also for wife of H. H. Breckinridge. Ex.: Thomas Doyle, H. H. Breckinridge. May 21, 1794. Probated Mar. 9, 1819.

HEADINGTON, JOSHUA—Gives to son, Elliott Headington and daughter, Caroline Matild Headington; to his wife, Maria Headington. Ex.: Maria Headington, wife. Oct. 6, 1818. Probated June 12, 1820.

MAPLE, JOHN—Gives to sons, Samuel, John, George, Peter, daughters, Hannah, Polly, Sarah Pegga, Rebecca, Nancy Ann, Elizabeth; to Arthur Maple and to wife, Sarah for life or widowhoood, the estate Ex.: Sarah Maple, wife, Samuel Maple, son. July 11, 1820. Probated Aug. 4, 1820.

HARDING, JOSIAH—Gives to wife and her heirs property which they have acquired and to brothers property acquired from their father and to Deborah Wheeler certain property which after her death goes to nephews, John H. and Josiah H. Wheeler. After death of wife to nieces, Elizabeth Kittery, Caroline Harding, nephew, Josiah Harding. Ex.: Ann Harding, wife. May 25, 1820. Probated Sept. 11, 1820.

SHAW, JANE—Gives to her daughter, Hannah Hartley and to granddaughters, Nancy and Jane Shaw, daughters of son Thomas, and to son John remainder of property. Ex.: John Shaw. Jan.17, 1821. Probated Dec. 11, 1820.

WHITE, MARY—Gives to son, William White; to children of John White, deceased, William G., Lucinda, Mary, Elizabeth, Sallie Glover, Robey White and Anna White; to daughter, Nancy Balthorpe; to daughter, Mary Floyd; remainder to granddaughters, Winnie Balthorp, Eliza Floyd, Eliza J. White, Mary M. White and to great-grandchildren, Mary Jane Glass, Robert William Glass. Ex.: William White, son, and Lee White, grandson. July 15, 1820. Probated Dec. 11, 1820.

WHIPS, GEORGE—Gives to his two sisters, Rebecca and Elizabeth. Witnesses: Thomas Laws, Joshua Whipp, P. Payton. Oct. 21, 1820. Probated Dec. 11, 1820.

HAWS, PETER—Gives to his wife, Hannah; to son, Benjamin and Peter Omar; to sons, John and Benjamin; to daughter, Peggy Ebby, Sallie Maple, after death of Sally Maple, her share to her children, Polly Mellott, Elizabeth Finley, Sybella Thorn, Hannah Seabolt, John Haws, Benjamin Haws and Rebeca Omar. Ex.: Benjamin Haws, Hiram Mellott. July 19, 1819. Probated Feb. 12, 1821.

REYNOLDS, CHARLES—Gives to his wife, Margaret, after her death, among children; to his granddaughter, Sarah Noor, and to son, Thomas Reynolds and grandchildren; children of daughter, Sarah Godman; to his daughter, Elizabeth Williams; son, John and to son, Abraham; daughter, Esther; to John Noor and his wife, Mary; to Jacob Godman and his wife Sarah; to Basil Williams. Ex.: Margaret Reynolds. Oct. 30, 1820. Probated Mar. 12, 1821.

PRESTON, WILLIAM—Gives for use of Hancock and William C. Preston, sons; the remainder, Henrietta, Maria, Caroline, Josephine, Hancock, William and Susanna, and to his wife, Caroline. Ex.: Caroline Preston, wife, James A. Pierce, Dennis Fitzhugh, Joseph Cabell Breckinridge, Barnet Payton, James McDowell, Sr. Jan. 3, 1821. Probated Feb. 7, 1821.

YEWELL, LEVY—Gives to sister, Pasty Forman and her children, ½ of property; remainder, Benjamin Pope, Martin Yewell, Joel Yager, Julius Withit and Joshua Christley. Dec. 27, 1820. Probated May 14, 1821.

PENDERGASS ,MARY—Gives to daughter, Margaret A.; to daughter, Louisa Brown. James Brown, guardian. Ex.: John Murphy. Mar. 13, 1821. Probated May 14, 1821.

DORSEY, JOSHUA—Gives to his granddaughter, Caroline Mary Chiles, to daughter-in-law, Matilda Dorsey; to granddaughter, Matilda Dorsey Hite; to daughter, Sarah Ann Dorsey; to daughter, Matilda Dorsey; to son, Columbus Dorsey; to son, Reasin Hammond Dorsey; to Elbert Talbot; gives freedom to negro man, Daniel; residue to children, Nimrod, Corrilla, Reazin Hammond Dorsey, Eliza Chew Booker, Ruth Maria Dorsey, Sarah Ann Dorsey and Matilda Dorsey. Ex.: Nimrod Dorsey, Columbus Dorsey, sons. Dec. 6. 1820. Probated May 14, 1821.

HARRISON, JOHN—To his wife, Mary Ann; John Harrison to hold one-fifth of estate for Sophia Jones New, his sister; to sons, Benjamin, Charles, John and James. Ex.: John, Charles, Benjamin, James Harrison, sons. June 19, 1821. Probated Aug. 13, 1821.

RICE, EDMUND S.—To his wife, Mary at her death to son by adoption, John; freedom to colored girl, Catherine. Ex.: Henry Churchill, John Speed, Jacob Lytle. Dec. 10, 1813. Probated Aug. 13, 1821.

McKUNE, TERRECE—Gives to wife, Mary, entire property except $150.00 to Terrece M. Lisher; gives to Hugh Quinn, John McKune. Sept. 6, 1821. Probated Oct. 11, 1821.

HARDING, ANN—Gives to Sarah Ann Wrenn; to niece, Malinda W. Wrenn and to Hezekiah Magruder; to nephew, Josiah Harding Magruder; remainder to nephews and nieces, Hezekiah Magruder, Josiah Harding Magruder, Verlinda W. Wrenn, sons and daughters of Daniel Magruder. Ex.: Hezekiah Magruder, Josiah H. Magruder. Oct. 15, 1821. Probated Nov. 12, 1821.

BANKS, JOHN—Gives to his wife, Mary; to his sons, Clement and John and daughter, Rachel; to children, Patsy, Runah, Polly, Elias Butler. Ex.: John Stowers, Samuel Stores. Sept. 16, 1821. Probated Nov. 12, 1821.

POMEROY, GEORGE A. K.—Gives to his wife, Jane; to daughter, Ann Duncan; Margaret Lynes; Isabella M. Cully, wife of James; son, James. Ex.: James Pomeroy, son, Jane Pomeroy, wife. Oct. 19, 1821. Probated Nov. 12, 1821.

CHAPMAN, SAMUEL—Gives to his wife, Mary and children, William and Elizabeth. Ex.: Mary Chapman, wife. Nov. 6, 1821. Probated Nov. 13, 1821.

GLASS, SARAH—Gives to nieces, Sarah Ann Bower and Mary Vance Bower; remainder to sister, Mary Vance and brother, Joseph Glass. Ex.: Robert B. Vance, Joseph Glass, Samuel Glass. May 8, 1821. Probated Dec. 10, 1821.

MORRIS, RICHARD—Gives to son, James Maury; Edward Garland, son-in-law; daughters, Martha and Maria and Martha Garland, and to Edward Garland, Edwin Gales Winston; to daughters, Elizabeth and Clarissa. April 2, 1820. Probated Dec. 10, 1821.

EDWARDS, WILLIAM—Gives to wife during her widowhood or life, his estate, at her death to his children. Ex.: Lydia Edwards, wife, John Edwards, Henry Rudy. Sept. 22, 1821. Probated Jan. 14, 1822.

MARRSEE, JOHN—Gives to his wife ,Agnes; to son, Andrew; to daughters, Mary McClasson, Elizabeth Ross, Anes Wailor; to son, John, Alexander Nathan, Rachel Marrs, (Marrsee) Allen; daughter, Sarah; Andrew; son-in-law, Reuben Ross. Exrs.: John Marsee, Alexander Marrsee. Proved Dec. 10, 1821. Probated Jan. 14, 1822.

GARDNER, SILAS P.—Gives to his wife, Phoebe Gardner, all his property. Oct. 30, 1821. Probated Feb. 11, 1822.

LITER, ELIZABETH—Gives to her sons, Jonah and Johnathan; to her daughters, Barbara and Sallie and to daughter, Mary and son. Ex.: Johnathan Liter. Oct. 21, 1821. Probated March 11, 1822.

VEGALON, HENRY—Gives to his wife, Jane, and daughter, Louisa. Ex.: Jane Vegalon, wife. April 9, 1819. Probated Jan. 14, 1822.

PHILLIPS, JENKIN—Gives to sons, Thomas and Richard; children of deceased son, Samuel and children of daughter, Hannah Duberty; children of daughter, Katherine Hunter; to Ann Hamilton, his daughter; to daughter, Lydia Clark; to daughter, Susan Riley; to granddaughter, daughter of Eleanor Hamilton, deceased; to granddaughter, Hannah Hunter; to granddaughter, Mary; to grandson, Jenkin Phillips, and freedom to negro, Nell; remainder to legal heirs. Ex.: Thomas Phillips and Richard Phillips, sons. Nov. 29, 1819. Probated Feb. 11, 1822.

LEWIS, GEORGE—Gives to wife, Diana Lewis, all his property. Ex.: Diana Lewis, wife. Dec. 26, 1821. Probated Jan. 15, 1822.

ROGAN, JOHN—Gives to his friend, Thomas Worrall (Wornall) and his heirs. Ex.: Thomas Worrall. Feb. 6, 1822. Probated Mar. 11, 1822.

OFFAND, JOHN M.—Gives to wife, Henrietta Offand, and after her death to his children. Ex.: Henrietta Offand, wife, James Pryor, Fortunatus Cosby and William McKeever. Nov. 23, 1818. Probated Mar. 11, 1822.

HAMPTON, EPHRIAM—Gives to his wife for life, after her death to his children. Oc. 25, 1821. Probated Mar. 11, 1822.

PENDEGRASS, MARGARET ANN, of Cuba—Gives to Vincent Gray in trust for her father, Garret Elliott Pendegrass; to half sister, Louisa, and freedom to negro, Letitia. Ex.: Garrett Elliott Pendegrass, father and Vincent Gray. Jan. 16, 1822. Probated Apr. 8, 1822.

FENLY, RICHARD—Gives to sons, George Fenley and John H. Fenley; to Jacob Lytle; to daughter, Amelia Fowler; to daughter, Ann

Lytle, and to Malinda Hawley, wife of Hezekiah. Ex.: Jacob Lytel,
Hezekiah Hawley. Feb. 11, 1818. Probated April 8, 1822.

VENARSELLAY, ANDREW LECOQ—Gives to wife, Teresa Lecoq
Venarselley and to children, Venise Lecoq and to Just Lecoq Venarselley. Ex.: Teresa Lecoq Venarselley, wife, and Just Lecoq Venarsellay, son. Apr. 28, 1819. Probated May 13, 1822.

MILLS, SAMUEL—Gives to son, Jonathan; to daughters, Sallie and
Sidney Lee, and to his mother, Mary. Ex.: Jonathan Mills, son.
June 27, 1821. Probated June 10, 1822.

WINCHESTER, REBECCA—Gives to daughter, Lavina, wife of Francis Snowden; to Olivea Veach; to grandchildren, Frances Ann Veach,
Rebecca Elizabeth Veach; to daughter, Polly Dorsey Bowles; to
daughter Louisa Winchester; to son, William Chambers Winchester; to son-in-law, Francis Snowden; son, Benj. Winchester; remainder among children Lavina Snowden; Olivia Veach; Amanda
Hall; Polly D. Bowles; Louisa Winchester and son William C.
Winchester. Ex.: Francis Snowden, Josiah Bowles, Alexander
Veach. Mar. 11, 1822. Probated June 10, 1822.

EARICKSON, MARY—To her two nieces, Elizabeth and Susanna Earickson; and to her sister, Ann Eastin; and to her brother, James
Earickson. Ex.: James Earickson. Nov. 30, 1811. Probated Nov.
11, 1822.

EASTIN, ANN—Gives to her four nieces, Nancy Sneed, Catherine W.
Hite, Harriet Funk and Rebecca Hite. Nov. 7, 1820. Probated
Nov. 11, 1822.

AUGUSTUS, SPRINGER—Leaves to wife, Nancy Augustus, after her
death to children of brothers, John, David, Jacob and James. Ex.:
James Augustus, Abraham Keller, Samuel Gray. Probated Nov.
11, 1822.

USHER, DIANA PYE—Leaves to adopted daughter her property. Witnesses: Nicholas Clark and Amelia Clark. Nov. 14, 1822.

CRANE, JOHN H.—Gives to Madam Sarah Smith, widow of Rev.
John Smith; to William D. Sohen of Boston; to William Smith and
to Nathaniel Coffin and his wife, Mary Porter Coffin. Ex.: Chaun-
cey Whittelsey. March 10, 1820. Probated Nov. 11, 1822.

WAGGENER, JAMES—Gives to his wife, Elizabeth and three children,
George, Mary and Elizabeth. Witnesses: Ben W. Johnson and William Lewis. July 27, 1822. Probated Oct. 15, 1822.

REAUGH, JOHN—Leaves to his wife, Margaret for life, and after her
death to daughters, Nelly Johnson, Harriet Black, Sarah Haines;
granddaughters, Pauline Susanna Dyer Reaugh, Aseneth Catherine,
Langham Reugh; and to son, Samuel Reaugh; also ground for Christian Church. Ex.: Isaac Spriggin, George Smith, Margaret Reaugh,
wife. Mar. 10, 1822. Probated Sept. 9, 1822.

LEWELLEN, SAMUEL—Gives to his wife, Patty Lewellen; to his
children, Nancy Speig, Thomas B. Lewellen, Catherine Biggs, Mary

Everett and Samuel R. Lewellen. Ex.: Patty Lewellen, wife, and David McCallister. Probated Dec. 9, 1822.

COLEMAN, BETTY—Gives to grandson for use of granddaugther, Hure Malinda, grandson, Philip Rootes Thompson; to grandson, Robert Coleman Thompson; to granddaughter, Mildred Ann Thompson; to grandson, Francis Thornton Thompson; great-grandson, John Thompson Strother; great-grandson, Frank Strother; great-grandson, Robert Coleman Thompson; grandson, William L. Thompson; to Mrs. Jennie Ebert and her children; to grandson, John Thompson. Ex.: John Peay, William Lightfoot Thompson, grandson. Aug. , 1820. Probated Dec. 10, 1822.

BRISCOE, ROBERT—Gives to his wife, Mary and to his daughters, Ruth, Elizabeth and Mary. July 15, 1822. Probated Aug. 12, 1822.

FITZHUGH, D.—Gives to his wife, Fanny Fitzhugh; to son Clark and to daughter Lucy Ann. Dec. 7, 1821. Probated Aug. 12, 1822.

TRIGG, WILLIAM—Gives to his wife, Ann Trigg, to daughter, Nancy Noel; to son, William Trigg; at death of wife, property to be divided among Daniel Trigg, Thomas Trigg, William Trigg, Nancy Noel and grandson, James Duerson; also mentions Miss Offner Carny. Ex.: Daniel Trigg, William Trigg and Thomas Trigg, sons. Jan. 24, 1818. Probated Aug. 12, 1822.

PRYOR, JAMES—Gives to James Gilly; to brother, Robert L. Pryor; to Nathe Pryor; to Robert McClelland; to sisters, Jane B. Gilly and Eliza Oldham. Ex.: John B. Gilly. Dec. 25, 1814. Probated Aug. 13, 1822.

FRY, SUSAN—Gives to her sister, Rebecca Whipps; to daughter, Polly Frey; and to son, William Fry. Ex.: Denton Whipps. Aug. 16, 1822. Probated Sept. 9, 1822.

DELANEY, WILLIAM—Gives one-half his property to Catholic Church. Aug. 20, 1822. Probated Sept. 10, 1822.

MARRS, AGNES—Gives to son, Andrew and to children, John, Alexander Nathan, Mary McClaslen, Elizabeth Ross, Nancy Nailer, Allen Marrs, Rachel Marrs and Sarah Sherley. Ex.: Andrew Marrs, son. Sept. 13, 1822   Probated Oct. 14, 1822.

SHUTT, FREDERICK—Gives to his son, William. Ex.: John H. Miller. Aug. 12, 1822. Probated Oct. 8, 1822.

RICE, JOHN—Gives to Richard Stinson. Ex.: Richard Stinson. May 21, 1822. Probated Dec. 11, 1822.

TOMPKINS, ROBERT—Gives to wife and children, William and Benjamin. Ex.: William Tompkins, Benjamin Tompkins, sons. Feb. 13, 1821. Probated Jan. 13, 1823.

SHIPP, EDMUND—Gives to brother, Ewell Shipp, all his property. Ex.: John Gwafthmey, Daniel S. Howell. Dec. 11, 1816. Probated Jan. 13, 1823.

FIELDS, RUBEN—Gives his wife, Mary Myrtle Field all his property. April 22, 1822. Probated Jan. 14, 1823.

WOOLFOLK, WILLIAM—Gives to his wife, Nancy and to children, James M.; to daughter, Sophia; to son, George; to daughter, Fanny; to son, William; to son, Francis; to daughter, Mary B. Kendall. Ex.: William, Francis, James Woolfolk, sons and Amos Kendall, son-in-law. Aug. 8, 1822. Probated Jan. 14, 1823.

TYLER, EDWARD—Gives to his wife, Rebecca; to Benjamin Gawthorn, in case of wife's death; to brothers and sisters. Ex.: Levi Tyler, Isaac Tyler. Nov. 23, 1822. Probated Jan. 15, 1823.

JEYERLIHNER, NIKLAUS— Gives to wife, Elizabeth. Sept. 4, 1822. Probated Nov. 6, 1822 in Indiana; Kentucky January 18, 1823. Witnesses: Aloyse Bachmanne, John Buehlen.

KEEN, THOMAS S. V.—To his wife, Julia Keen and to son, James Lawes Keen and to daughter, Louisa Keen. Wts.: Joseph Franklyn, E. Sheridan, Luther Owings. Apr. 6, 1822. Probated Jan. 18, 1823.

OLDHAM, SAMUEL—To his wife, Ann Oldham; to son, William; to son, Conway; son, Harry's wife; to daughter, Sarah Merriwether; to daughter, Nancy Taylor; to daughter, Patsy; to daughter, Winny Mercer; daughter, Elizabeth, wife of Levi Tyler; to daughter, Amelia, wife of Charles L. Harrison; to Mary E. Powers in trust. Ex.: Conway Oldham, son, Levi Tyler, son-in-law. Sept. 4, 1820. Probated Feb. 10, 1823.

SMITH, DANIEL—Gives to his wife, Ann E. F. Smith, his property. Ex.: William S. Vernon. Feb. 1, 1823. Probated Mar. 11, 1823.

SPARKS, WILLIAM—Gives to his wife, Morning Sparks; to son, Hampton ;to son, Ephriam; to son, David; to daughters, Fanny and Nancy. Ex.: Hampton Sparks, son, Roland Hampton, son-in-law. Nov. 18, 1822. Probated April 14, 1823.

GARRET, SILAS—Gives to son, Anderson W.; son, Regin W.; to wife, Judith, and to children, Peter B., Susan W., and Betsy Ann. Ex.: George Setson, William Markwell. April 1, 1823. Probated April 14, 1823.

LAMPTON, MARK—Gives to wife, Susanne Harrison Lampton; to daughter, Minerva Stone; to son, Edmund S. Lampton; to daughter, Fanny M. Lampton. Ex.: Ephriam S. Stone, William Lampton. Mar. 1, 1823. Apr. 14, 1823.

FONTAINE, AARON—Gives to daughter, Barbara Cosby; to sons, Alexander M., Henry Fontaine, Aaron; daughter, Emeline. Ex.: Worden Pope, Alfred Thrustin, Charles M. Thrustin. Mar. 18, 1823. Probated Apr. 16, 1823.

GROGHAN, WILLIAM—To his wife, Lucy; to son, John; to son, William; to son, George; to daughter, Ann H.; to daughter, Eliza C.; to son, Nicholas; to son, Charles; to William Clark. Ex.: Lucy Groghan, wife, John Groghan, George Groghan, William Groghan, Nicholas Groghan and Charles Groghan, sons. Aug. 27, 1822. Probated May 12, 1823.

FARNSLEY JAMES—Gives to sons, David, Joshua, James, Alexander, Gabriel, Joseph; to daughters, Mary Earickson and Sarah Farnsley. Ex.: Joseph B. Gatewood, John Jones, Steven Jones. Oct. 7, 1817. Probated May 12, 1823.

BURTON, JEREMIAH—Gives to his wife, Polly; to Pelina, Davis, Simeon, John, Elliott, Charles, Jeremiah and William. Ex.: Polly Burton, wife. Mar. 5, 1822. Probated May 12, 1823.

LINCOLN COUNTY
(Formed 1780)

Note: Some estates from Books A and B have been published in the Register of the Kentucky Historical Society.

ALLEN, JAMES—Bk. B, pg. 255—Son, Hartwell; dau., Lucy Giles; wife, Rebecca; chdn., James, Churchnell, Thomas, Rebecca, Gabriel, Ludwell, when of age. Son, Hartwell, Extr. Written July 25, 1804. Probated Oct. 1804.

CLOYD, JAMES—Bk. B, pg. 242—Wife; Aggy Nash; to Polly and Nancy Nash, Thomas and Tramp Nash, chdn. of sister, Peggy; Charles Lockridge son of sister Polly; Polly Hood, dau. of sister Polly; James and John Lockridge; oldest dau. of Nancy Robertson, dau. of sister Polly. Extr.: Wm. Logan, son of Benj., deceased. Written April, 1804. Probated May 14, 1804.

CRAIG, SAMUEL—Bk. B, pg. 268—Division of Estate—To Zachariah Tucker and wife, Polly, formerly Craig; Pleasant Tucker and wife, Sally, formerly Craig; Isham Gilbert and wife, Ann, formerly Craig; Samuel Craig ;John Craig. July 9, 1804.

BYARS, JEREMIAH—Bk. B, pg. 170—Division—To widow, Elizabeth and three chdn.; Nancy Smith, wife of Jesse; son, Edmund Byers; son, John. Nov. 18, 1796.

BARNETT, JOHN, JR.—Bk. B, pg. 272—Chdn. of half-sister, Polly Moore, wife of Elisha Moore; to Anna Barnett, dau. of Robt. Barnett; to Wm. McNeely of Montgomery Co., Va., and to his dau., Polly for their service and love for them; my little child recognized by me called Green Barnett; to Jos. Hall; Green Barnett to share alike with chdn. of Joseph Hall and Ann Hall his wife, "my sister"; chdn. of bro., Jas. Barnett and wife. Written April 8, 1805.

BLAIN, ISAAC—Bk. C, pg. 126—Three eldest chdn, viz: James, George and Polly Blain; to wife, Ann and youngest chdn. Extrs.: wife and Walter Anderson. Written Nov. 23, 1807. Probated Dec. 18, 1807.

BALDOCK, LEVI—Bk. D, pg. 89—To wife, Ann; youngest chdn., Levi, James, William and Elizabeth; property previously given Reubin and Tabby. Extr.: son, Reubin. Written July 13, 1790. Probated Oct. 17, 1808.

BENEDICT, JOHN—Bk. D, pg. 385—Oldest son, John; son, Jacob; wife, Mary Magdalin; sons, Benjamin and Anthony; to Susanna Veach; Cataron Silvers, Hannah Winfree. Extrs.: John and Jacob Benedict and Wm. Silvers. Written Nov. 7, 1809. Probated Jan. 15, 1810.

COOK, SUSANNAH—Bk. C, pg. 120—To sons, Adam, David, John, Henry and William; and Christopher Hammon; g. dau., Genny, dau. of son Wm.; daus., Christen Hammon; sons, Jacob and Valentine. Wm. Shanks, Extr. October 12, 1807.

DUDGEON, JOHN—Bk. B, pg. 274—To wife, Mary; sons, Wm. and John, land in Campbell Co., rest to other son and daus.; sons-in-law, Armstrong Kerr and John Rogers; dau., Polly Dugean, Peggy Dugean and son, Sublett Dugean; to Polly, Patsy and Sublett and Jno. Rogers. April 10, 1804.

DICKERSON, WILLIAM—Bk. D, pg. 362—"Of Orange Co., Va." Property previously given sons, Wiley, Thos. and John; to wife until youngest child comes of age; balance to sons and daus., "my last children." Extrs.: Bernis and Brightberry Brown. Written Aug. 19, 1800. Probated March 20, 1809.

FORD, WILLIAM—Bk. C, pg. 1—Wife, Sarah; son, Wm. Bob Ford; Jas. Tinsley; Chas. Ford; Daniel McElroy. Dated 1801.

GILBERT, JOHN WEBSTER—Bk. D, pg. 373—To wife, Mary; two sons, John and Isham; wife and her sons, John and Samuel Craig; all my chdn. (not named); dau. Rachel and her husband, James Gilbert have had equal part with chdn. in Shelby; to James Clement; four youngest chdn. Extrs.: sons, John, Isham and Sebert Crutcher. Written Nov. 4, 1807. Probated Oct. 16, 1809.

GIBSON, JOHN—Bk. D, pg. 389—Wife, Catherine; sons, Richard, James, John; dau., Polly. Written Dec. 21, 1809. Probated June 18, 1810.

HENDERSON, CHRISTOPHER—Bk. D, pg. 9—Inventory—Susannah Henderson, dower. John Henderson, Admr. 1808—pg. 169—James Wall, husband to Susannah, widow of Christopher Henderson, deceased.

HUNTSMAN, JOSIAH—Division—Bk. C, pg. 113—To Wm. Huntsman; Polly Huntsman, now Rutherford; George Huntsman; Benjamin Huntsman; Sally Huntsman. Aug. 3, 1805.

JOSTLING, JOHN—Bk. D, pg. 99—Division July 20, 1797—Son, J. Jostling, receipt, also receipt from Wm. Jostling, son Daniel Jostling and John Whittle; son, Wm Jostling receipt for parts of Lucy and James Jostling, etc. (pg. 101); also receipt from dau., Molly

Evans; Samuel Shackleford, Sr., receipt; and son, John Joslin; Wm. Jostling's receipt for his brother, Benjamin Jostling and Jesse Evans, (pg. 104).

MOODY, WM.—Resident of Kentucky who died in Pittsylvania Co., Va., Oct. 22, 1794. To wife, Judith Moody of Ky.; sister, Mary Moody when she married; mother, Elizabeth Moody; two daus., Elizabeth Buford Moody and Mary Moody. Father-in-law, Wm. Buford, Extr. Written Oct. 23, 1794. Proved May 9, 1797, Lincoln Co.

MONTGOMERY, WILLIAM—Division—Bk. C, pg. 108—James Montgomery, Robert Montgomery „John Montgomery, William and Nancy, Thomas Montgomery, Alexander and Polly Smith Montgomery. Jan. 13, 1807.

McCORMACK, DANIEL—Bk. D, pg. 378—To wife, Ann; chdn. of Peggy Estis when of age ;son, William; dau./ Nancy Martin; son, Daniel. Extr.: son, Daniel. Written Sept. 21, 1809. Probated Nov. 20, 1809. Wt.: John McCormack.

OVERTON, CLOUGH—Bk. D, pg. 392—Bro., Richard Overton, land 2000 acres; 1800 acres, etc.; 3 sisters, Mary, Betsy and Sary Overton, 300 acres; bro., John Overton, 1200 acres; bros., James and George Overton, 200 acres; bros., Wm. and Tom Overton; father, John Overton, 1000 acres; brothers and sisters, 55,000 acres, 15,000 acres; to Betsey Poage, 500 acres, etc., etc. Friend, Waller Overton, etc., Extr. July 16, 1782—Jan. 21, 1783.

ROBERTSON, HANNAH—Bk. D, pg. 50—Division, 1793—To Pat. Shields; Thos. M. Murry, gdn. for four chdn. of Catherine Murray, and gdn. for two chdn. of E. Ruddle. Son, Luke Robertson, Extr. Moses Payne and Isaac Ruddle gave receipts.

SLOAN, MARAGRET—Bk. B, pg. 15—To son, Thomas; three daus., Margaret, Betsy and Ann Sloan. Written Aug. 14, 1791. Probated Nov. 15, 1791. Wt.: Agnes Sloan.

SMITH, HENRY—Bk. B.—Division—Henry and Christopher Smith, Extrs. Sept. 1789. Widow, Bellsarah; Henry Smith, Jr., (gdn.); Chloe Dial's legacy pd. to her husband, John Dial; Elizabeth, (gdn.) Liberty Smith (gdn.); (his mother, Margaret).

SUTHERLAND, WM.—Bk. B—To son, Fendels; son, Wm.; son, Owen; son, George wife, Mary daus., Theny Hawkins, Milly Goldsmith, Susan Harper, Polly Jones daus., Jenny and Nancy when eighteen. No probate date. Written June 22, 1803.

THURMONS, JOHN—Bk. D, pg. 79—Wife, Molly; chdn., not named. Sons, Bennett, John, Jr. and Pierce and Wm. Wade, Extrs. Written Jan. 11, 1808. Probated Sept. 1808.

WALLIS, SAMUEL—Bk. B, pg. 127—"Old age." Son, Andrew ;son-in-law, Henry Pauling and wife, Elizabeth (dau.); son, Caleb. Codicil division to be made between all chdn. (not named). March 24, 1794. Probated Aug. 18, 1795.

MADISON COUNTY
(Formed from Lincoln County, 1785)

INDEX TO WILL BOOK A.

*—left will. dow.—dower

Names appearing in this index are not included in General Index

Howard, Hanah (dow)
*Hawkins, Nathan
Harris, Benj.
Harris, James
*Hamilton, William
Hill, Joshua
*Hawkins, Joseph
*Hart, William (Index signed John Hart)
*Huggins, Wm.
Haland, John
Hathman, Jonathan
*Harris, Thos.
*Harrison, James
*Hawkins, Abraham
*Hawkins, John
*Hagard, Edward
Hawkins, Joseph
Harry, Chas.
Ham, Wm.
*Hill, David
Ham, Elizabeth (dow)
Hawkins, Philip
Hawkins, Nancy (dow)
Harris, John
Hill, Joshua

*Irvine, Christopher
*Irvine, David

Jones, James
*Johnson, Barnod
Jamison, John
*Jone, Mosias
Jarvis, John
Jamison, Samuel
James, John

Kincaid, John
Knight, John
Kavanaugh, Philemon
Kavanaugh, Ann (dow)
Kincaid, Moore
*Kavanaugh, Chas.
Kelly, Samuel
Knightly, Elijah
*Kincaid, John
Kinder, George
Kelly, John

Lynn, John
*Lowry, James
Lee, George
Lee, Wm.
*Lipscomb, Wm.
Laughlin, Henry
*Lewis, Abraham

McNeely, James
McKinney, Joseph
Martin, James
*Mason, Wm.
McMullin, James
*Maxwell, Thomas
Merrett, Joseph
Moore, Benton
*Miller, Abraham
*Martin, James
*Moore, Wm.
*Moody, Andrew
McCreery, Jane
*Maupin, Daniel
Miller, John
McMullin, Wm.
Manion, John
*Morrison ,Hugh
*McWilliams, James
*Miller, John
Massie, Sylvands (Sylvann)
*Moore, Wright
Morrison, Geo. W.
Maxwell, Balzaleel
Maxwell, Nancy (dow)
Moore, Wm.
McDaniel, James
Maxwell, Thos. (widow's dow.)
*McQueen, Joshua
More, Reubin
McClane, Jane (Jas.)
*Morehead, Wm.
Maxwell, Nancy (dow)

*Noaks, Benj.
Noble, David
*Noland, Joshua
Newland, Isaac
Newland, Patsy (dow)

*Owsley, Thos., Sr.
*O'Rear, Jeremiah
*Olehy, Michel
*Oldham, John

Paton, Jane (dow)
Phelps, Geo.
Parks, Allen
Purcell, Benj.
*Province, John
*Portwood, Loyd
*Portwood, Thomas
*Phelps, John, Sr.
Paton, Abraham
Perkins, Dabney

Reynolds, Thomas
*Roberts, Edward
*Robertson, William
*Rice, John
Ross, Thos.
*Rice, Chas.
Richardson, Aaron
*Rabourn, Robt.
*Reese, James
*Robertson, Absalom
*Rikard, Leonard

Shelton, Thos.
*Searcy, Bartlett
*Stephenson, Elizabeth
*Stephenson, Edawrd
*Stapp, James
*Stone, Benj.
*Shackleford, James
*Scrivner, James
Starns, Isaac
Stone, Samuel
*Skidmore, Thomas
Smith, James
Stevens, Nunford
*Smith, Reubin
*Snapp, Nancy
Sampson, Isaac
Smith, Tabitha (dow)
Sanders, Wm.
*Shelton, David
Storker, Thomas (Stalker)
Stephenson, James
*Scott, Mathew
*Stephenson, Thos.
*Smith, James
Seward, John

Turpin, Elizabeth (dow)
*Timberlake, Richard
Thompson, David
*Tevis, Nathaniel
Turner, Edward
*Tatum, Samuel
*Tincher, Wm.
*Tipton, John
Turpin, Wm.
*Taylor, Peter
Taylor, Nancy (dow)
Taylor, Creed (Curd)
Toda, Joseph

*Vanover, John

Wooley, John
*Watson, Jesse

Williams, Isaac
Welch, Thomas
White, David
*Watts, John
*Walding, James
*Woolfscale, Wm.
Wolfscale, Jane (dow)

*Woodruff, John
Williams, Henry
*Walker, Asaph
*Woodruff, John
*Williford, Samuel
Wallace, Michael

Walker, John W.
Wallace, Jane (dow)
Willie, John
*Williford, Joseph
*White, Henry
*West, John

INVENTORIES AND APPRAISEMENTS, WILL BOOK A

Names appearing in this index are not included in General Index

Allen, Rev. Cary H., 1795
Allcoin, Wm., 1798

Broadis, Wm., 1799
Boyles, Wm., 1800
Blockley, Jno., 1790
Burnett, Rowland, 1790
Black, Jas., 1790
Barns, Samuel, 1795

Chaffery, Chas. 1787
Corlew, Bedford, 1799
Carrick, Wm., 1799
Clark, Jas., 1794
Carpenter, Edw., 1794
Cloyd, Samuel, 1796
Campbell, Thos., 1796

Dever, Dennis, 1790
Douglas, Alex., 1792

Estill, Wm., 1798

Fleming, Jas., 1799
Fitzgerald, Jno., 1795

Green, Stephen, 1798
Gillespie, Wm., 1794
Gully, Thos., 1799
Goff, Alex., 1795
Gillespie, Wm., 1798

Hawkins, Catherine, 1798
Harris, Jas., 1798
Hoy, Rowland, 1790
Harris, Benj., 1797

Irvine, Chris., 1789

Jones, Jas., 1794

Knight, Jno., 1793
Kavanaugh, Philemon 1787
Kincaid, Moore, 1795
Kincaid, Jno., 1793

Kavanaugh, Chas., 1797

Linn, John, 1792

Martin, Jas., 1793
Mason, Wm., 1797
McMullin, Jas., 1793
McNeeley, Jas., 1788
Moore, Benton, 1795
Mettitt, Jos., 1793

Noland, Joshua, 1799

Oleky, (Olehy) Michel, 1798

Reynolds, Thos., 1792
Shelton, Thos., 1794
Woodruff, Jas., 1799
Williams, Isaac, 1790
Welch, Thos., 1794
White, David, 1795
Woolfscale, Wm., 1796
Wooley, Jno., 1787

WILLS FROM BOOK A

BATTERTON, SANFORD—Wife, Eliza I. Batterton. Extrs.: wife and David Irvine. Written Feb. 27, 1810. Wts.: Henry Batterton, Robt. A. Sturgis, Ezekiel H. Field. Probated April, 1810.

BLACKWELL, ARMSTEAD—To chdn. viz: Wm., Nancy, Randolph, Zekiel, David, Salley and John; wife, Dicy Chammon. Extrs.: son, Wm .and John Sappington. Written May 5, 1794. Wts.: Green Clay, Geo. Brown, Benj. Blackwell. Probated Oct. 1794.

BRIDGES, GEORGE—"Of Fayette Co." To Nellie (?) Betsey Fox, dau.; to half-bro., Samuel Fox, late immigrant from Hanover Co., (Va.); niece, Rebeccah Farthing, dau. to half-sister, Ann Farthing of James City Co., (Va.); niece Betsey Piggott, dau. to sister, Mary

Piggott of City of Williamsburg; bro., Isham Bridges and he apptd. Extr. Written Sept. 7, 1790. Probated July 3, 1792.

BURGIN, ISAAC—To dau., Nancy; wife, Mary, she with Dennis Burgin, Extrs. Chdn. to be schooled. Written March 10, 1794. Wts.: Leavin Gray, Chas. Burgin. Probated March 6, 1794.

BURNET, ROLAND—Wife, Maragaret; all chdn. (not named). Extrs.: Cornelius Maupine, John Miller, Daniel McGuire, Wm. Chenault. Written Sept. 13, 1789. Wts.: Chas. Colley, Peter Rush. Probated March 2, 1790.

BRAMWELL, JOSEPH—To wife, Esbell. Extrs.: wife and Samuel Walhup. July 23, 1793. Wts.: Jno. Kennedy, Wm. Morrison, Andrew Harris. Probated Jan. 1, 1799.

BLYTHE, WM.—To wife, Ony (?) until son, Jas. comes of age; stepson, David Mortin. Extrs.: Robt. Rodes, Jacob Patton. Written July 18, 1795. Codicil: money left in hands of Mr. Jno. Reed, was surety on David White's estate; interest he has in S. Carolina or in Cumberland; bro. Jas. Blythe to collect debts. Written July 9, 1795. Wts.: Jno. Cloyd, Thos. Cloyd. Probated Aug. 4, 1800.

CLOYD, SAMUEL—"Of Montgomery Co., Va." Wife, Elizabeth and at her death to Nenyan Cloyd's son, Thomas. Extrs.: wife, Joseph Cloyd. Written Feb. 28, 1789. Wts.: G. Cloyd, Jas. Cloyd, Thos. Cloyd. Probated May 5, 1795.

CHIZUM, JAS.—Niece, Sarah K. Williams; Wm. Hogans; Sophia Shawhen; John Wheeler; mother; Thos., Jno., Isaac, Betsy, Rosey and Samuel Williams, sons and daus. of my bro., Jno. Williams; niece, Mary Chambers; sister, Martha Dossey (?), her dau., Delia. Extrs.: Jno. Sappington, Jno. Wheeler. Written March 8, 1795. Wts.: Thos. Tevis, Thos. Shawhan, Jno. Carpenter. Probated May 5, 1795.

COFFEY, NEBUZARDEN—To wife, and all chdn. viz: Joel, Sary, Polly, Fielding, Sail, Nias, Hays, Betsy and Ruth; property divided when youngest child comes of age. Extrs.: Joel Coffey, Jas. Coffey, Fieldin Coffey. Written Oct. 1, 1796. Wts.: Wm. Allin, Cleveland Coffey, Marthy Coffey. Probated March 7, 1797.

CAMPBELL, THOS.—To wife, Ellender; four smallest chdn. when of age; property sold and divided among all chdn. (not named), five youngest chdn.; mentions lease of Drury Willis. Written May 17, 1796. Probated Oct. 4, 1796. Wts.: Benj. Holladay, Jno. Campbell, Geo. Moore.

COULTER, JAS.—To son, James, property adjoining lands of Travis Booton; wife, Alsey; chdn., Jas., Isabella Jackson, Elizabeth Coulter, Anna Freeman, Jane, Nancy, Alsey, Polly and Sally Coulter; previously given married chdn. part of their portion. Extrs.: wife and Wm. Miller. Written Apr. 30, 1806. Wts.: Archd. Woods, Jas. Bratton. Probated July 7, 1806.

DEJARNETT, DANIEL—To wife, Tude; son, James; son, Abijah; Susannah Dejarnett; son, James; dau., Polly Howard; dau., Mildred Hoy; dau., Martha Ford Tully (?); son, John. Extrs.: Thos.

Watts, Jas. Dejarnett. Written Aug. 23, 1807. Wts.: Thos. Watts, Jno. Foster, Nancy Million. Probated Oct. 3, 1808.

DUNCAN, BENJ.—To wife, Elizabeth; son, John; son, Samuel; son, Benjamin; first chdn. (not named); dau., Elizabeth Arnot. Extrs.: Jno. Reed, Sr., son, John. Written Nov. 5, 1796. Wts.: Alex. Gaston, Jno. Black, Alex. Mackey. Probated Dec. 1796.

DOZIER, JAS.—To son, Zachariah; dau., Elizabeth Davis and after death to her dau., Rebeckah Davis; to Rebecca Scott and at death to her son, Jas. Scott; to dau., Sarah Montgomery and at her death to her son, Thos. Montgomery; son, Leonard; Susannah Crews, her husband, Elijah Crews; son, James; son, Thos.; son, John; grandson, John Cash; wife, Martha; five sons. Extrs.: Leonard and Zachariah Dozier. Written Oct. 21, 1790. Wts.: Aaron Lewis, Benj. South, Weldon South. Probated May 3, 1791.

DAUGHERTY, THOS., HRS.—Bk. B, pg. 464—Sarah Daugherty, dower; Salbee (Satbee) Daugherty; Nancy Daugherty; Wm. Miller and Elizabeth, late Daugherty; Stephen Goggin and wife, Mary, late Daugherty. Written July 27, 1818.

ELLIOTT, ROBT.—To wife, Elizabeth; son, Jas.; dau., Aney; dau., Agnes; dau., Rebecah; dau., Margaret; son, John; son, David; dau., Polly; granddau., Elizabeth Hoff (?); granddau., Polly, Margaret's dau. Extr.: Jno. Snoddy. Written April 6, 1802. Wts.: Samuel Wallace, Robt. Caldwell, Jno. Kincaid, Wm. Douglas.

FARRISS, MICHAEL—To wife, Febey; chdn., small, to be made equal with other chdn.; all chdn. (not named); son, Dudly Faris; son, Jorge (George); son, Thomas. Written Oct. 27, 1799. Wts.: Jas. Moore, Robt. Creath. Probated Dec. 3, 1799.

FLETCHER, WM.—To wife, "lot at Boonesborough on which we live"; sons, Jno., Jas., Robt., Wm.; dau., Mary; daus., Betsy and Salley; chdn. named and Mary Fletcher, Jno. Fletcher, Betsey Fletcher, Salley Fletcher, James Fletcher, Robt. Fletcher and Wm. Fletcher. Written May 12, 1790. Wts.: Wm. Orear, Wm. Calk, Jas. French. Probated Aug. 7, 1792.

GASS, DAVID—To wife, Sarah; son, John; son, Wm.; son, Jas.; son, David; dau., Mary Black; dau., Margaret Mitchell; son, Thos., dau., Susannah Harris; dau., Sarah Black; grandson, Jas. Mitchell; son-in-law, Jno. Mitchell; Anney Black; Elloues Black, Jas. Black and David Black, chdn. of dau., Mary. Extrs.: wife, sons, Jas. and John. Written Apr. 14, 1806. Probated May, 1806.

GELLESPIE, DAVID—To wife, Betsey; dau., Patsey Gellespie; to Ephriam Musick and dau., Winny Musick, his wife; Thos. Withered (?), Nancy, his wife; son John; son, David; son, James; dau., Patsey; son, Benjamin; dau., Polly Guthridge; balance of chdn. not named. Wife, Betsey, Ephriam Musick and Joseph Barnette, Extrs. Wts.: Ephriam Musick, Ephriam Sinkens (?) and Patsy Gillaspie. Probated May 8, 1814.

HARRIS, THOMAS—Wife, Maryan; father-in-law, Travis Booton; wife pregnant, if child should die, property divided among all brothers and sisters. Extrs.: Wm. Wood, Wm. Goodloe, Jas. Berry, Jno. Woods, Christopher Harris. Probated April 7, 1806.

HARRISON, JAS.—Wife, Winny; Ben Moore in his debt; son, Elias; Wm. Cooper in his debt; dau., Polly Moore; son, Robert; dau., Charlott. Written Sept. 7, 1806. Wts.: Joseph Williams, Levy Moore, Sally Williams. Probated Oct. 1806.

HAWKINS, JOHN—To son, Philip, land in Garrard C.; four grandsons, Henry Bright, Elijah Hawkins, Philip Hawkins, Geo. Hawkins sons of Weden Hawkins; son, Elijah; most of chdn. had previously received their portions. Extr.: son, Elijah. Written Aug. 20, 1810. Wts.: Joel White, Jno. Black, Geo. Tomlinson. Probated Oct. 1, 1810.

HAWKINS, NATHAN—To dau., Elizabeth Level; dau., Mary Stephenson; dau., Nancy Schooler; son, Nicholas, great Bible, etc., in consideration of trouble he had in moving "me and my family here in yr. 1798, he enabled to pay on land in Bourbon"; wife, Catherine; son, Nathan; dau., Marcy; dau., Margaret Bernet; dau., Elizabeth; dau., Nancy; son, Simon; seven chdn., Elizabeth, Mary Nancy, Simon, Nicholas, Nathan, and Marcy. Written Jan. 14, 1794. Wts.: Leven Cole, Jno. Bone, Geo. Cormack, Thos. Bone, Jas. Partin. Probated Nov. 4, 1794.

HARRIS, CHRISTOPHER—"My first chdn., Dabney, Sarah Martin, Robt., Mourning Jones, Christopher, Mary Jones; wife and other chdn.; negroes divided agreeable to Cornelius Dabney, Sr's. will. Extrs.: Foster Jones and Christopher Harris. son, Overton; son, John; son, Benj.; son, Wm.; son, Barnabus land in Albemarle Co., Va.; sons, Jas. and Samuel; to other sons (not named); three daus., Jane Gentry, Margaret Harris, Isabel Harris; last set of chdn. Extrix.: wife and Extrs.: Jno. Sappington, John Harris. Written Feb. 20, 1794. Wts.: Hartly Sappington, Richard Sappington, Joseph Wells. Probated March 4, 1794.

HOY, WM—Wife, Sarah; dau., Betsey South; son, Rowland, land in Bourbon Co., said land sold Thos. Hoy; Humphrey Tunstall, part of partnership lands with Caleb Calloway; Jas. McMullen; to eight of chdn., viz: Roland, Jones, Docia, Kizia, Wm., Fanna, Celia, Thania. Extrs.: son, Rowland, Jno. South, Richard Tunstall. Written March 15, 1790. Wts.: Wm. Jones, Wm. Holland, Jno. Rush. Probated April 7, 1790.

JOHNSON, BARNED—To wife, Jane; son, Barnabus; debts due from Jas. Devier; Jno. Stalen; Christopher Hand; to Costher Kinder, dau. of dau., Jane Kinder; to Geo. Kinder; son, Robt., debts due from Jno. Davis and David Miller; Jno. Curry; son, William. Written May 18, 1798. Wts.: Wm. McGuier, Peter Kinder, Daniel McMullen. Probated July 3, 1798.

KAVANAUGH, CHAS.—To James Mills Moore and two chdn., Chas. Kavanaugh Moore and Elizabeth Moore; mentions law suit in Culpeper, Va. Extrs.: Wm. and Chas. Kavanaugh, Peter Woods, wife, Ann Kavanaugh, five chdn., Mary, Wm., Chas., Joel, Sara Hann (Sarah Ann, Sarah Lann?), hrs. of eldest son, Philemon, decd. Wts.: Wm. Irvine, Is. Hockaday, Wm. Fox. Written Oct. 13, 1795. Probated Oct. 1796.

KINCAID, JOHN—Wife; son-in-law, Wm. Baird; John and Sarah Barksdel; two chdn. above named; grandson, John, son of Jas. Kincaid, land in Mercer Co., to be disposed of by his father for his education; to Samuel Jamison for education of his son, Joseph when ten yrs. old; two oldest sons, Jno. and Jas., "land whereon I once lived in Washington Co., Va."; two youngest sons, David and Moore, land where "I now live," Moore to have possession at his mother's death, located in Mercer Co.; dau., Ruth; dau., Jean. Extrs.: oldest son, Jno. and wife. Written July 9, 1792. Wts.: Alex. Mackey, Andrew Kincaid. Probated March, 1793.

MASON, WILLIAM—Body to be interred in graveyard of Silver Creek Meeting House; wife, Isabella; dau., Mary (?); son, John; dau., Isabella; son, Jas.; dau.,Jean; wife pregnant; land to which he has claim in Va., in Co. of A____(?); bro., James to dispose of this. Extrix.: wife, Extrs.: bro., John Couchran, Mathew Scott. Wts.: Jno. Couchran, Wm. Balch. Written Oct. 28, 1793. Probated Dec. 3, 1793.

MAXWELL, THOS.—To wife, Agnes; oldest son, Bezald and "Magr." Edmund Terrell, Extrs. To chdn., as they come of age; son, Thos.; son, Robt.; dau., Ann Maxwell, land in Clark Co.; daus., Mary Terrell, Rebeccah Schol, Ann Maxwell; three sons. Written Oct. 7, 1795. Wts.: Jas. Partin, Wm. Morrison, Jas. Dever. Probated Jan. 5, 1795.

MARTIN, JAMES—To son, Azariah, land partly in Clark Co.; son, Christopher, land in Clark; son, David, land in Clark; three sons, Wm., Tyree, Robert, tract bought of Laurence Thompson; son, Wm.; sons, Hudson and Nathan; wife, Sarah; grandson, David, son of son, James, deceased; son-in-law, Pleasant Proffit and his wife, Mary. Extrs.: wife and sons, Wm., Tyree and Robt. Written July 5, 1796. Wts.: Jas. French, Green Clay. Probated March, 1799.

McDANIEL JAS.—To daus., Nancy and Ruth McDaniel; balance divided between chdn. by name: Aaron, Jas., hrs. of dau., Rachel Butler, decd., Polly Walker, two daus., Nancy and Ruth. Extr.: Jno. Bennett Taylor. Written Jan. 3, 1811. Wts.: Lydia Hawkins, Abram Hawkins, Jeremiah Tevis. Probated April 1, 1811.

McKENEY, JOSEPH—Extr.: James Crawford; to well beloved bro., Henry, land in Ky. and N. C., he to pay four sisters; to sisters, Hannah and Elizabeth; brother. Written May 6, 1791. Wts.: Geo. Adams, Jno. Adams, Jas. Barnet. Probated July 5, 1791.

MILLER, ABRAHAM—Nuncupative Will—Died third of July past; to bro., Benj. Milner (Miller?); wife, Mary Milner (Miller?) Recorded Aug. 1798. Wts.: Oswald Townson, Susannah Moore.

MOORE, WM.—To wife, Margaret; son, Right; son, Joseph; son, Wm., property including improvement made by Samuel Kelly; son, Jas., Martin Glenn to satisfy debt due hrs. of Alex. Douglas, decd.; to Wm. Glenn; Hugh Glenn; all chdn., except Jean Glenn, whose share is allowed hrs .of Alex. Douglass; grandau., Betsey Burnsides. Written Sept. 15, 1799. Jas. McCormack and son, Jas., Extrs. Wts.: David Elliot, Joseph Glenn, Lavis (Tavis?) Allen. Probated Oct. 1799.

MOOREHEAD, WM.—Wife, Achsah; her two daus., together with Rebecah Howell; son, John at his death, to Mary Collier and Ashsah E_____?, together with granddau., Rebecah Howell; son, John to collect money in hands of Col. Thos. Humphries in Loudoun Co., Va., his two sisters, Mary and Achsah (or Achsel). Extrs.: Joseph Glenn, Jas. McCormick. Wts.: Samuel Montgomery, Daniel Barycraft, Martin Glenn. Probated Jan. 17, 1802.

MOODY, ANDREW, SR.—Wife, Katy; son, Isaac when 21; son, Andrew. Extrs.: wife and Jas. Anderson. Written Feb. 2, 1800. Wts.: Jno. Moody, Joseph Moody. Recorded July, 1800.

NOLAND, JOSHUA—To wife until youngest child comes of age; dau., Polly. Written Aug. 27, 1798. Wts.: Samuel Hoppers, Wm. Noland. Probated Feb. 4, 1799.

OREAR, JEREMIAH—To wife, Nancy. Three sons, Jno., Benj., Daniel, Extrs. Written March 21, 1793. Wts.: David Roland, Sr., Richard Roland, Jesse Rowland. Probated Jan. 1, 1799.

OWSLEY, THOS.—After death of wife, property to twelve chdn., viz: An Williams, William, Thomàs, Henry, Anthony, Jonathan, Chloe Williams, Verlinda Huchison, Daniel, Mary Bryant, Patience Bledsoe, Elizabeth Gouge (Googe); grandson, Thos. J, Chilton; grandson, Walter Williams; son Anthony's dau., Sarah. Written March 3, 1795. Wts.: Chas. English, Absolom Brown, Feathergill Adams, Robt. Moore. Probated March 7, 1797.

PHELPS, JOHN, SR.—Nuncpative Will—By Jno. Stapp (Stepp?)—Cary Phelps and Stephen Salley; to daus., Nancy Phelps, Rody Phelps, Patsey Phelps, these to have as much as rest of chdn.; son, Cary Phelps, Jno. Phelps, Sarah Sally, Molley Phelps, Betsy Willis, Thos. Phelps, Shadrach Phelps, Magdalin Stapp and Philip Phelps, all to be made equal; wife, Mary. Extrs.: sons, Cary and Stephen Salley. Recorded Aug. 1798. Wts.: Jno. Stapp, Stephen Salle, Cary Phelps.

PROVIANCE, JOHN—Wife, Mary; dau., Sarah, when she marries; son, Wm.; youngest dau., Rebeckah; sons, Alexander and John, preemption on Cumberland (River?); daus., Ann and Mary; son, Wm. (under age); all chdn. not named; bro., Andrew Provin(ce). Extrs.: wife, Aleander Dany, Samuel Woods. Written Feb. 27, 1792. Wts.: Joshua Nichols, Robt. Henderson, Alexander Reed. Probated April 3, 1792.

PORTWOOD, THOS.—To wife, Elizabeth; two sons, Solomon and Thos.; profits for rearing chdn. to be in wife's hands until boys are of age; rest of chdn. Extrs.: wife, Jno. and Peter Woods. Wts.: Jno. Crooke, Agnes Orchard, Thos. Crews. Probated Aug. 28, 1795.

PORTWOOD, LOYD—To son John when of age; my chdn. not named; two girls when of age or marry; wife, Elizabeth. Written April 30, 1792. Wts.: Thos. Portwood, Lude (Loyd?) Portwood. Probated June 5, 1792.

STEPHENSON, EDWARD—Nuncupative Will—To chdn.; dau., Betsey; son, Wm.; wife to keep portion of estate to rear chdn. Admrs.:

John Snoddy, Jas. Stephenson, son, Wm.   Dated Aug. 11, 1792. Probated Aug. 20, 1792.

STEPHENSON, ELIZABETH—To granddau., Jean Stephenson, money out of what son, Jas. has in his hands; balance to Joseph Hunter; grandau., Jean McKnigh; David Maxwell and his chdn., all but Jno. and Elizabeth; Joseph Hunter and David Maxwell.   Written Feb. 8, 1791.   Wts.: Edward Stephenson, Wm. Mitchell.   Probated April, 1792.

STONE, BENJAMIN—To wife, Sarah; son, Dudley when of age; three daus., Elizabeth, Jane, Fanny; three sons, Samuel, Daniel, Dudley; had exchanged place in Guilford Co., N. C., with Burges, his son, for bond on Aaron Lewis for 500 acres, he to have choice of several entries of Lewis' in Ky., and "I have pitched on tract of 1250 acres"; sons, Jno., Samuel, Daniel; daus., Jeane, Fanny; rest of chdn., Burgess, Susanna, Mary, Rebekah.   Extrs.: wife and Aaron Lewis.   Written Jan. 20, 1795.   Wts.: Aaron Lewis, Isaac Lewis, Thos. Lewis, Jno. Lewis, Sarah Lewis.   Probated Aug. 4, 1795.

SHACKELFORD, JAS.—To wife, Sarah; son, John; son, Edward; dau., Sarah Hicks; dau., Betsey Sanders; dau., Ann Beasley; son, Jas. Written March 10, 1795.   Wt.: Thos. Jno. Chilton.   Probated Aug. 4, 1795.

STEPP, JAS—Wife, Luse; chdn. leaves in care of Jno. Stepp and Golston Stepp, Extrs.   Written Feb. 23, 1794.   Wts.: Joseph Stapp (Stepp), Elizabeth Stapp, Thos. Lowhorn.   Probated Nov. 4, 1794.

SEARCY, BARTLETT—"Of Granville, N. C."   Wife, Lucy; when youngest child is fifteen years of age property sold and divided. Extrs.: wife, son, Samuel, Jno. Williams, Esq., Reubin Searcy. Written July 28, 1780.   Wts.: Thos. Searcy, Reubin Searcy, Elizabeth Searcy, Leonard Hays.   Proved Granville, N. C., Nov. 1784, when Lucy Searcy, Reubin Searcy, Samuel Searcy qualified as Extrs.   Probated in Madison, 1795.

TEVIS, NATHANIEL, SR.—To sons, Robt. and Thos. Tevis; dau., Peggy Tevis; two daus., Peggy Tevis and Susannah Wheeler; son, Jeremiah.   Written Aug. 29, 1798.   Wts.: Jno. Sappington, Robt. Reburn, Edward Davis.   Probated Oct. 2, 1798.

THOMPSON, DAVID—Mentions money due from Geo. Adams of Fayette; same from Jno. Mecawl; same from Geo. Smart and Robt. Smart; sister, Marget Thomson living in Glasgow, Scotland; to Catherine Burman, Hugh Burman, David Burman, living in Parish of Delfandan.   Extrs.: David Belingall, Wm. Todd, Andrew Bogie.   Written Jan. 29, 1798.   Wts.: Jas. Bogie, Loftis Pullins, Levin Cole.   Probated March 6, 1798.

TIMBERLAKE, RICHARD—Wife, Sarah; dau., Sarah Butler; sons, Jno. and Philip.   Extrs.: Martin Gentry, Thos. Butler.   Written Feb. 16, 1795.   Wts.: Will Irvine, Jno. Bratton, Stephen Jett.   Probated May 5, 1795.

WATSON, JESSE—Nuncupative will—While sitting at Lick watching for deer, Jno. Anderson going upon same business, had the misfortune to fire on him and wound him; the evening following he made known his will expressing desire to see Jas. Stephenson, and express desire that wife ,Milly have all. Testified to by Evanthas Watson. Wts.: Jas. Barnett, Jas. Anderson. Jas. Stephenson testifies he later saw him and heard him say he desired wife, Milly and his heirs should enjoy what he had equally between them. June 1, 1790. Recorded Aug. 3, 1790.

WATTS, JOHN—Wife, Sarah; seven daus., viz: Esther Sebree, Franky Quinn, Mildred Tomlinsons, Betty Vowter, Anny Merry, Aggatha Turner, Molly Watts. Extrs.: Jessey Vewter, Richard Sebree, wife. Written Feb. 4, 1796. Wts.: Jno. Gess, Stephen Eastin, Jno. Armstrong, Humphrey Magee, Sam Loyd. Probated July 5, 1795.

WALDING, JAS.—To wife, Anne; son, Benjamin; dau., Elizabeth Chisum; son, Jas.; son, Jesse; son, Wm.; all chdn. (not named). Extrs.: Wm. Walding, Jno. Reed, Joel Short. Written Feb. 8, 1796. Wts.: Elijah Evins, Joel Short, Randal Yarber. Probated July 5, 1796.

WHITE, HENRY—To dau., Flurany; wife. Extrs.: Calen White, Jno. Black. Written Aug. 7, 1812. Wts.: Thos. Clayton, Jno. Rateken, Jas. White. Probated Jan. 4, 1813.

WHITE, JOEL—Hrs.—Bk. B—Division—Widow; Yelverton and wife; Thos. Fox and wife; Jno. Crook and wife; Henry White, decd.; Reubin Gentry. Galen White and Durritt White, Admrs.

TAYLOR, HANNAH—Late widow of Jas. Howard, deceased, alloted dower, Nov. 4, 1794.

BLACK, JAMES—Thos. Campbell and wife, Elender, alloted ⅓ of estate of Jas. Black as dower right of said Elender, Nov. 4, 1795.

COOPER, SHERSHAL—Account of gdn. to Wm. Wood. July 2, 1796.

TITUS, JOSEPH—Administrator's settlement on estate of Elizabeth Stephenson, decd. Aug. 2, 1796.

BELL, SAMUEL—Allotment of widow of Samuel Bell, decd., made Wm. Barnett. Dec. 4. 1796.

BURGIN, ISAAC—Sett. with Gdn. and Extr. of Isaac Burgin's orphans, widow of Isaac, Mary Webb. March, 1797.

GILLESPIE, WM.—Sett. with Admr. of Wm. Gillespie, decd. Jno. Hartgrove and Ann Gillespie, Admrs. Aug. 7, 1798.

MASON COUNTY
(Formed from Bourbon County, 1788)

INDEX TO ESTATES TO 1840

Note: Not all listed died in Mason leaving estates, some are executors' accounts and widows who were assigned dowers. When the name appears several times, within a brief period of years, the name is here given only once as these usually pertain to additional court orders regarding decedant's estate.   *Left wills.

Names appearing in this index are not included in General Index

1791
Arms, Wm.
*Allen Nathaniel
Anderson, Abner
1798
Allison, John
Armstrong, James
1809
Anderson, Matthew
Adamson, John
Atkens, Thomas
Applegate, Daniel
1815
Arthur, John
*Asberry, George
Asberry, Mary
Allison, Joseph
1819
Asberry, Squire
Applegate, Ab'ham
*Anderson, Charles
Atchinson, Silas
Atchinson, Ruth
1823
Asberry, Squire
1826
Adamson, Stephen
Allen, Louiza
Allen, Robert
Anno, Benj.
*Arnold, John
1832
Allen, Charles
Anderson, John L.
*Anderson, George
Allen, Samuel
*Armstrong, Johnston
*Anderson, Worsham
Atchinson, John
*Armstrong, Ann
Anderson, Francis B.
Anderson, John S.
Anderson, John W.
Armstrong, Eliza
Anderson, Susan
*Armstrong, John
1837
Adamson, Joseph
Asberry (see White-
head)
Austin, Thos.
*Arthur, Matthew
*Allen, Wm.

*Anno, Wm.
Anderson, Susan,
(now Mannen)
Arnold, Farnattar
Arnold, Lucy
*Anderson, Eliza W.
1791
Bowen, Levi
Berry, Baldwin
*Bailey, Samuel
*Beeson, Mary
Botts, John
Barr, Samuel
1798
Byram, Peter
Burns, Zepheniah
Brooks, Thos.
Bennett, Moses
Brown, Robt.
Botts, Wm.
Brooks, Jonathan
Berkelow, Arthur
Berry, Enock
*Burns, Farens
*Berkelow, Arthur
*Beaseley, Charles
Brown, Lititia
Bennett, Titus
Bryant, George
Barns, Ann
Bennett, Elizabeth
1809
*Bayles, Daniel
Bradford, Wm.
Bell, Rawleigh
Burriss, Benj.
Baker, Graftin
Baker, Wm.
Berry, Enoch
*Bronough, Wm.
*Berry, George
Baker, Abner
1815
Brooks, George
*Boggs, Samuel
Brooks, Humphrey
Barber, Samuel
Boak, David
Berry, Jas. K.
Blockson, Wm.
*Burkham, Telphey
*Barbour, Richard
*Brannegan, Nicholas

1819
Bryarly, Mary
*Berry, Thos.
Blanchard, Wm.
Blannegan, Nicholas
Bayles, Stephen
Berry, Thos.
*Burgess, Cynthia
Bayles, Daniel
*Buskirk, John
*Berry, Wm.
Berry, Joseph, Jr.
*Bullock, Robt.
Brown, Robt.
Brooks, Jonathan
*Bowhe, Robt.
Bennett, Moses
Boyles, Daniel
*Bell, Richard
*Biggers, Macon
Bronough, Wm.
Brown, Maria
Berry, Judith
*Burrows, Benj.
Brown, Jas.
*Bursell, Sarah
*Bell, Rawleigh
Boone, Levi
Brooke, Geo.
Bickley, Joseph
Beasley, Ezekiel
1823
Blan, (Bland) Benj.
*Browner, Ann
Bramhall, Jonathan
Bramhall, Thompson
Bates, Alvin
Boyd, John
Baker, John
Baker, Simon R.
Bickley, Joseph
Bland, Benj.
*Bramhall, Wm.
Beall, (Bell) T. A.
Bell, Chas., Sr.
*Berry, Henry
1826
Branough, Mary
Bland, Micajah
Burges, Thos., Jr.
Bland, Mary (now
White)
Barker, Wm.

Boone, Jacob
*Bullock, Lewis
Burroughs, Eliz'beth
Baker, Elizabeth
Breeze, John
1829
*Baldwin, Henry
*Byram, Wm.
Boone, Mary
Burrows, Wm.
Brown, Wm.
Bayles, Stephen
Ball, Milton
Bullock, Jas. W.
Bland, James
*Barren, Thos. J.
Buchannon, John
Brewer, Rachel
Bryam, Sarah
Booten, Abraham
Barclay, Stephen
*Bledsoe, Benj.
Burke, Thos.
Ball, Wilfred
Brown, Elizabeth
Brown, Mary
Brown—see Waddle
Bennett, Daniel
1839
Bryant, Geo.
Bledsoe, Benj.
Bennett, Daniel (see
  Forman)
*Bickley, Wm.
Ball, Joseph
Byers, James
*Bayless, Benj.
Bean, Benj.
Byars, Anna Maria
Bruce, Richard P.
Barclay, Joseph D.
Brown, Coleman D.
Brotherton, Eliz'b'th
Baker, Hiram
Baker, Frances
Baker, Asa S.
Biggers, Anderson
Brown, Jno.
1840
Baker, Jno.
1791
Cook, Paden
Craig, Absolom
*Collins, Benj.
Campbell, Jas.
Connett, Wm.
Cochran, Robt.
Crabb, John

Colglazer, Abram
Castleman, Stephen
1798
Conwell, Jane
Clarke, Wm.
Cleneay, Wm.
Camron, Abraham
*Carrell, Edward
*Crosby, Wm.
Carrell, Dempsey
Corwine, John
Campbell, John
1809
Calvin, Luther, Jr.
Carrell, Lawson
Curtis, James
Cooper, Duvall
Cash, Nancy
*Cash, Thomas
Clifton, Burdett
Clarke, John
Calvert, Wm.
Culbertson, Samuel
Calvert, Wm.
Clifton, Baldwin
*Curtis, John
Curtis, Nancy
Corwine, Richard
Carty, Chas.
Cleft, (Clift) Mason
Coryell, Joseph
*Cassell, Daniel
Curtis, Ann (Nancy)
1815
Corwine, Nancy
*Cassell, Sanford
Cahill, John
Clift, Henry
Collin, Henry
Cauby, Lydie
Collin, Wm.
Calvert, Wm.
Clift, Linney
*Cape, Jacob
1819
Corwine, Richard
Crichfield, Samuel
*Corwine, Sally
Cooper, Margaret
*Cooke, Littleton(s)
Carter, Moses
Conway, Susan
Cain, Hannah
*Compton, Thos.
1823
Coburn, Mary
*Calvert, Jas.
Conway, Miles

Clarke, Elizabeth
Carrell, Elizabeth
Curtis, George, Jr.
Cox, Joseph
*Chambers, Jas.
Craig, Wm.
Cox, Joseph
*Craig, Lewis
*Cash, Catherine
Curtis, Hiram
1826
*Campbell, Jno.
Cash, John
Collin, Wm.
*Craig, Elijah
Craig, Mary
Chuman, (Cheesman,
  Cheeman), Wm.
Crookshanks, And'w
Cooper, Hugh
Cockrell, Nilley
*Calvin, Luther
Coryell, Cornelius
*Clift, Benj.
1832
Calvert, Zeal
*Cole, Benj.
Craig, Sanders W.
*Coburn, John
*Chansler, John
*Cahill, Lawrence
Cooper, Isaac
Cooper, Catherine
*Cheesman, Polly
Curtis, Elizabeth
*Catlett, Robt.
*Cahill, Ruth
Cundiff, Wm. B.
1834
Coburn, Wilson
Clarke, Jas.
*Chiles, David
Clarke, Septemus
Chamberlain, Wm.
Curtis, Jas.
Case, Jas.
Clift, Newton
*Cooper, James
Calvert, Redmon
Carroll, Jane
Calvert, Fielding G.
Catlett, David
Clarke, Joseph
1837
Chamblain, John
Clarke, Septemus D.
Calvert, Alice
Campbell, Caroline

Cushman, David
Cordry, Hosea
*Chinn, Elijah
Clarke, Walter
1839
*Curtis, Elizabeth
Craig, Jno. L.
Case, Jas.
Cole, Jno.
Critchfield, Wm.
Coburn, Wilson
Clarke, Jane
Clarke, Hiram
Clarke, John
Chamberlain, Jno.
Curtis, Robt.
*Conway, Jno.
Cooper, Alfred
Chinn, Elijah
Chiles, David
Clarke, Walter
Clarke, Jane
Clarke, Mary
Clark—see Morton
Clary, Elizabeth
Craig, Lewis
Coleman, Jas. C.
Clarke, Septimus D.
1791
*Daugherty, John
*Darah, John
Dobyns, Edward
*Dane, John
1798
Dunlary, Anthony
Downing, Ellis
Dawson, George
Downing, Robt.
Duvall, Jno. P.
Daggett, Elmore
*Davis, Nicholas
Duvall, Jno. P.
Dyall, Simon
Daggett, Elizabeth
Drake, Cornelius
*Dye, Wm.
*Davis, Garrard
Downing, Ellis
Drummond, Saml.
Davis, Joseph
Davis, Jno.
Dawson, Sybil
Dawson, Isaac
Drake, Josiah S.
Davidson, Hugh
*Doniphan, Joseph
Drummond, Saml.

Drake, Ralph
Daugherty, David A.
Dyal, Simon
Drake, Jno.
1815
Drake, Runey (Rune)
Drake, Jane
*Deaver, Micajah
Dawson, Abraham
Dawson, Sybel
*Downing, Timothy
*Dye, Kenneth
Davis, John
Donaldson, John
Daugherty, John
*Dorsey, Thos.
Drummond, Samuel heirs.
Dye, Phebe
1819
Drummond, Robert
*Dennissan, John
Downing, Jane
*Dye, John
*Drummond, John
1823
Danavan, Wm.
*Deaver, Diana
*Dawson, Sybil
*Durrett, Richard
*Downing, John
Daugherty, Michael
*Duncan, Thos.
Downing, John
1826
Dawson, Robert D.
*Daugherty, Alex
*Duncan, David
Dye, Kenneth
*Drake, Samuel
1829
Denniston, John
*Drake, Phillip
*Dawson, Abraham
Daulton, Mary
Duttan, A. S.
Duke, Margaret
David, Samuel
Dobyns, Chas.
1832
Downing, Nancy
Drake, Samuel
Davis, Samuel
Dye, Thos.
Donovan, Thos.
Dimmett, Jas.
*Drake, Cornelius

Doggett, Richard
David, Michael
Dawson, Lucinda
Dobyns, Samuel
Dimmett, Elizabeth
Dorsey, Wm.
1834
*Duryea, John
David, Elizabeth
Drake, John
Dawson, Abijah
Dawson, Malinda
Dickson, Geo.
Durrett, Paul
Dailey, Thos.
Dennestan, Wm.
Daugherty, Mary
1837
Dye—see Wells
Dillan, Wm.
Davis, Jesse
Dobyns, Chas.
Dye, R. H.
Durrett, Gabrilla
Dye, S. L.
Dye, R. W.
Dye, Geo. W.
Dreshill, Benj. F.
1839
Drake, Jacob
Dobyns, Thos. B.
Duke, Basel
Dickson, Geo.
Dickson, Henry
Dickson, Cynthia A.
Drummond, John
*Drake, Wm.
*Doniphan, Andrew
Downing, Ellis hrs.
Duffy, Jas. H.
*Duvall, Notley
Daugherty, Jas.
*Davis, Thos.
1791
*Edwards, Jacob
Edwards, James
1798
Ellis, Jas.
1809
*Evans, Charles
1819
Elliott, Elizabeth
Edwards, Alexander
Edwards, Elizabeth
*Evans, Wm.
Ewell, Leroy

1832
*Eastin, George
*Evans, Griffith
1840
Early, Thos.
1791
Fox, Wm.
*Fuss, Randolph Jno.
Fox, Arthur
Fuss, John
Figards, Daniel
Fulton, Elisha
1798
*Ficklen, John
Finch, Jno.
Fitzgerald, Bartholomew heirs
1815
Finley, Wm.
Froman, Sol. heirs
Fields, Wm.
*Fristoe, John
*Fowke, Roger
Foster, Joshua
1819
*Farrow, George
*Fleming, Stephen
*Fitzgerald, Benj.
Faw, Wm. H. S.
*Fyffe, Jonothan
Feagan, Edward
*Fletcher, Geo.
*Faw, Nancy
1825
Froman, Solomon
French, James
Ficklin, Judith
Field, Elizabeth
Frazer, Wm.
French, Mason
Finch, Leven
Frazee, Ephriam
Frazee, Susan
1829
*Fulton, Hugh
Franklin, Zepheniah
*Fitzgerald, Moses
*Fulton, Hugh
Forman, Joseph
1832
Forman, Thomas M.
Frazee, Joseph
Ficklin, Thos.
French, Hugh
*Fristoe, Jesse
Fields, James
French, Malinda
Frazee, Hiram

*Forman, Samuel
*Fulton, Jefferson
1834
Fuller, Soloman
Fields, Jas. G.
*French, David
Frazier, Wm.
Forman, Thos. S.
1837
Forman, Ezekiel
Fleming, Stephen
Fields, Greenberry
1839
Ferrin Elizabeth
Forman, Joseph, gdn.
to Danl. Bennett
*Fleming, John
*French, John
1798
*Graham, Elizabeth
*Gallagher, Edward
1809
Glausleriener, John
Gordan, Amos
*Ginn, Benj.
Gray, John
Gray, Rachel
Gibbons, _____
1815
*Gifford, Elisha
Gault, Edward
*Graham, Richard
*Gash, Thos.
1819
Green, Jas.
Ginn, Mary
1823
*Green, Ashsah
*Grant, Jas.
Gill, Edward
Gow, Mary
1826
Ginn, Jas.
*Gaither, Cornelius
Grant, Jas.
*Grant, Geo., Sr.
Grinstead, Wm.
*Gorsuch, Chas.
1829
Grant, Peter
Grinstead, Wm.
Grinstead, Mary A.
Graves, Joseph
Graves, John
*Gates, Wm.
*Gore, Ann
1832
Gill, James

Gibbons, Robt. S.
1834
Graves, Edward
*Gooch, Benj.
Gooch, Chas.
Gooch, Freeman E.
Gibson, Chas.
*Gray, Matthew
Glasscock, Washington
1837
Gates, Wm., Sr.
Green, Robt.
Gash, Bernard P.
Gash, Barnet P.
*Guthrie, Henry
1839
Garrison, Elijah
Gill, Ann
Gibbons, Cloe
1840
Graves, Elijah
1791
*Hains, Joseph
*Hughes, John
Hoken, Pleny
1798
*Hill, Joseph
*Hurst, Henry
Hale, Jas.
*Heflin, Simon
*Hamilton, Alexander
Hill, Asberry
Hickens, Jesse
Holtan, Alex.
Hanes, Sam'l
Hatterbough, Isaac
Hixsan, Nathaniel
Hickman, Isaac
Holladay, Robert
1809
Hillman, Daniel
Harle, Edward
Harras, John
Higgins, Wm.
Higgins, Prescilla
*Hiett, Elisha
Harrah, John
*Heath, John
Howell, Wm.
Hord, Thomas
1815
Helm, Mary
Hampton, Sarah
*Huntingdon, Zelphey
Hunter, John
1819
Holtan, Wm. A.

*Hammond, Chas.
Harrow, Mary Ann
Hord, Ann
Hord, Chas.
Hord, Rhodeus
1823
Hughey, Elizabeth
*Hord, Edward
Hall, Joseph
Harris, Edward
Harris, Edward, Jr.
Harlan, Nathaniel
Hugheys, Jno.
Howison, Jno.
*Hammond, Rosannah
*Hieatt, Stephen
*Hawke, Jas.
1829
Howison, Mary
1829
Hauke, Jas.
*Hixsan, Nathan, Jr.
Hieatt, Nancy
Hughey, Elizabeth
*Hieatt, Mary
Hieatt, Benj.
Hargate, Whitfield
Harrison, Daniel
Howisan, Mary
Howisan, John
*Hubbard, Jas.
Holladay, Joseph
Hieatt, Stephen
*Holton, Wm.
1832
*Hill, E.
Hodges, Wm.
Hays, Patrick
*Harris, Margaret
*Hill, Thos.
Hawes, Lawman L.
*Hamilton, Elizabeth
Hays, Patrick
Hise, Phillip
*Hancock, Geo.
Hieatt, John B.
Hieatt, Mary
1834
Hord, Thos.
Hieatt, I. B.
Hord, Edward
Hyde, John
Hughey, John
1837
Hukill, Oliver
Heiatt, Jno.
Hyde, Margaret

*Hixson, Nat'l
Heath, Nathan
Harrison, Sarah
*Harget, Peter
*Hitt, Susan
Hord, Thos.
Higgins, Jas. R.
*Holton, Enoch
*Heiatt, Kezeah
1839
Howard, Robt.
Hughey, Elizabeth
*Hudnutt, Moses D.
Howard, Sally
Hickman, Elizabeth
Hickman, Sarah
Hargate, Peter
Harrison, Peter
Hickman, Azuba
Hickman, Martha
Hukill, Oliver H.
*Holton, Enoch
Holton, Wm.
*Henry, Jas.
Hargate, Peter, hrs.
Hickman—see Summers
1791
Jones, Thos.
*Jackson, Richard
Johnston, Jno.
*Jones, Michael
Jessup, Edward
Journie, (Jownn) Joseph
*Jackson, John
1809
Jones, James
Jones, Wm.
Jones, Euphemia
*Jackson, Samuel
Johnson, Jas.
Jno, Eli
1815
John, John
John, David
Jenkins, Walter
Jackson, Walter
Johnson, Hiram
1823
Johnson, Wm.
Johnson, Hugh
Jenkens, Elizabeth
1826
*Johnson, Wm.
1829
Johnson, Jno.

1832
January, A. M.
1834
Judd, Jas. R.
Jefferson, Perry
1839
*January, Samuel
*Jones, Samuel
*Jennings, Wm. B.
1791
Karr, Jno.
Kilgour, Samuel
Keith, Isaiah
1798
Kent, Jno.
1809
Killgour, Samuel
*Kelsey, Thos., Sr.
1815
*Key, Jas.
Kilgour, Ann
Key, Payton R.
1819
*Kennard, Joseph
Kopp, Jacob
1823
Kinnard, Wm.
Kinnard, Margaret
*Kilgour, Elizabeth
1826
King, Wm.
Kennard, Wm., hrs.
1832
Kenney, Eleazer
Kirk, Benj.
Kirk, Sarah
Kirk, Geo.
Kercheval, Kranklin
*Kirk, Wm.
1834
Kercheval, Benj.
Kilgore, Thos.
Kennard, Jonathan
Knight, Woodson
1837
Kemper, Joshua
Knight, Allen
Knight, Nelson
Kirk, Geo.
Knight, Amelia
Knight, Elvira
Knight, Letitia
1839
Knight, Allen A.
Kennard, Elizabeth
*Kilgore, Robt.

*Keith, Thos.
Kirk, Thos.
Kilgore, Joseph
Killgore, Mary
Killgore, Sam'l K. S.
1791
*Lee Stephen
Lewis, Isaac
Lyon (Lynn) Jas.
Lawhead, Jas.
Lyon, (Lynn) Jos.
Lee, Richard
Lyle, Ludwick
1798
*Leitch, David
Logan, Martha
*Lewis, George
Lewis, Mary
Loundsdale, Thos.
Litler, (Litter) J. L.
Lee, Lewis
Lee, Ann
Lounsdale, Margaret
Lewis, George
1809
Lynn, Joseph
Littler, Jno. S.
Lawhead, Jas.
1815
Light, Ludwick
*Lee Edward
Lashbrooks, Stephen
Lamb, Pierce
Lee, Henry
Logan, Jno., Sr.
Logan, Mary
*Leitch, David
Lee, Edward
Logan, Jno.
1819
Loyd, Richard D.
Lanthan, Jno. W.
1823
*Lamb, Wm.
Lastly, Benj.
1826
*Lee Stephen
1826
Linthicum, Chas. G.
Logan, John hrs.
Leurty, Jno.
Linthicum, Elizab'th
1829
Linthicum, C. G. hrs.
Lamb, Basil
1832
Lee, Barnett
*Langhorne, Jno. T.

*Lucas, Samuel
Lusty, Mary
*Lyon, Elizabeth
Lacy, Nancy
*Lynn, Andrew
Logan, Alex.
1834
*Lashbrooke, John
Lunsford, Larkin
Linthicum, Lydia
Lacy, Walter
Lucas, Samuel
Lurty, Mary
Littlejohn, John
Luttrell, Simon
Linthicum, Mary
Linthicum, Slingsby
Linthicum, Chas., by
gdn.
1791
Morgan, Daniel
McDowell, Thos.
McIntire, Alexander
Matslar, John
Matslar, widow
McClure, Frances
*Miller, Robert
*Morton, Joseph
Miller, Thos.
Morris, David
1798
*Murphy, Timothy
*Metcalf, John
Musgrove, John
McFadden, John
Marshall, Robert
*Maddox, Notley
McIlvain, Wm.
McClung, Jas.
*Marshall, Thos.
Miller, Robert
Morris, Mary
Maddox, Jno.
*McKinley, James
*McDonald, Mary
*Morris, Mary
*McDowell, Joseph
Moke, Jas.
Machir, Peter
Morton, Robt. H.
Morton, Joseph
McShirley, Wm.
Matshar, Jno.
*Mattocks, Jas.
1809
Moke, Jas.
*McGowen, Hackley
Morrison, Ed.

McShirley, Wm.
McDougal, Francis
Murphy, Timothy
*Marshall, Wm.
Morrison, Motley
Martin, Will (?)
Moore, Jno. B.
McClung, Wm.
Martin, Edmund
Morris, Jasper
Masterson, Jno.
Marshall, Robert S.
McDonald, Francis
Merrill, Joseph
McLaughlin, Geo.
McClure, Sarah
Mitchell, Isaac
*McMichael, Marg't
McGow, Wm.
Mefford, Geo.
Mefford, Malinda
Morris, Wm.
*Moss, Jas. W.
1815
*McAnelly, Hugh
Martin, Wm.
McDonald, Sarah
McGhee, Francis
Machir, John
1819
*Morgan, Chas.
*McIlvain, Harriett
McGinnis, Neal
McIlvain, Mary
*Martin, Susannah
*Mannen, John
*Mitchell, Geo.
1823
McLaughlin, Ann
*Mitchell, Sarah
*Murphy, Wm.
McKinley, George
*Mackey, Andrew K.
*Mitchell, Ignatius
1826
*Marshall, John
Martin, Henry
McNeal, Donimick
*Miles, George
*Martin, Harry
McCardle, Mary
Morton, Geo. B.
McCalla, Purnell
Machir, Clementina
Merrick, John
*Marshall, Eliza G.
1829
Morton, George B.

*Mason, Silas C.
*Machir, Elizabeth
Mitchell, John
Marshall, James K.
*Monohon, John
McKee, Thos.
Murphy, Wm.
*Mitchell, John
1832
  Macher, Henry
  Marshall, Dolly
*McGlasson, Paschal
  Mannen, John
*Moran, Andrew
  Morrison, James
*Murray, David
*Musgrove, Mary
  Morrison, Mary
*Morgan, Daniel
*Mefford, George
  McFerrin, Catherine
  Mitchell, Wm.
  Marshall, Thos.
  Marshall, Francis
1834
  Mannen, James
  Morford, Abraham
  Matthew, Edward R.
  McGlasson, Paschal
  Morris, David, gdn.
  to:
    Waller, John
    Waller, Maria
    Waller, Thos.
    Waller, Charity
    Waller, Achash
1837
  Murray, David
  Machir, Henry
  McAdow, John
  Mitchell, David
  Mefford, George
*McDonald, Wm.
1839
  McDonald, John D.
  Morton, John, gdn.
  to:
    John Clarke
    Hiram Clarke
  Mannen, Susan
*Morton, George
  McAtee, Benj.
1840
  Mackey, James
1798
  Nebbs, George
  Nicholas, John
*Nicholas, Thos.
  Nicholls, Ann (same

    as Ann Barnes)
  Norris, Wm.
1809
  Nicholls, Simon S.
1815
  Nelson, Robert
1819
  Nettleton, Leonard
1823
*Nicholls Margery
  Norris, Jas.
1829
*Nicholson, Thos.
1832
*Nower, Alex.
1834
  Nower, Samuel
1839
  Nicholls, Mary
*Newdegate, Wm. C.
1847
  Neal, Elias
*Newell, Wm.
1791
  Oden, John
1798
  Overfield, Abner
*Ocull, Jas.
  Overfield, Paul
1819
*Outten, Isaac
  Overfield, Mary
*Owins, John
  O'Neal, Arthur J.
  Owens, Nathan
1826
  Owens, Joshua
1829
  Owens, Ludwell
1832
*Owens, Asabel
  Oliver, A.
1837
  O'Neil, Elizabeth
  Owens, Richard
*Owens, William
1839
  Owens, Maximillian
  Oliver, Amos, by
    gdn.
1791
  Phillips, Gabriel
  Pitzer, Christopher
  Philips, Milley
1798
*Phillips, John
  Porter, John
  Porter, Regnol
*Phillips, James

*Phillips, Harriet
*Purcell, George
  Philips, Gabriel hrs.
  Proctor, Jeremiah
*Pottell, Mary
  Pollard, Ben
  Proctor, Wm.
1809
  Phillips, Moses hrs.
1818
*Porter, James
  Perrie, Lititia
*Prather, Rachel
  Porter, Sarah
  Peed, John
  Price, Vizey
1819
*Peddicord, John
1823
*Phillips, George
*Perrine, Henry
*Parker, Richard
  Perrie, Francis
*Paxton, James
*Pepper, Wm.
  Phillips, Sarah
1826
  Putman, Henry
*Padget, Wm. W.
  Pepper, Lucy
  Parker, Richard
*Payne, Wm.
*Parker, Wm.
1829
  Pollet, Elizabeth
  Payne, Duvall
  Payne, Hannah
*Peers, Valentine
*Pickett, John
  Prather, Sarah
  Prather, Thos.
1832
  Poe, Thos.
  Pollett, Robt.
*Parker, Amy
  Peck, Jas.
  Pogue, Robt.
  Prather, Ross
  Prather, Wm. R.
1834
  Poe, Wm.
  Payne, Geo. M.
*Pepper, Elkanah
  (Elixanah)
  Poe. Jesse
  Peck, Jas.
  Pickering, Orange
*Peddicord, John
*Pepper, Wm. H.

Pogue, Jane
*Palmer, Edmond
*Pogue, Robt. C.
1837
*Parker, Winslow
*Phillips, Milley
Pepper, Lucy
Peddicord, Emman'l
*Phillips, Edmond P.
1839
Prather, Wm. R. by gdn.
Paul, Loyed
Paxton, Thos.
Pogue, Edwin P.
Parker, Wm.
*Peck, Susannah
Pollett, Jas.
*Parmer, Parmelia
*Proctor, Wm.
1791
Richards, Reuben
Richards, Elijah
*Reeves, Benj.
*Richards, Lucy
Rust Matthew
Rubbett, Jno.
Richey, David
1798
Rogers, John
*Robinson, Ralph
Rush, Wm.
*Roseberry, Joseph
Ramey, Francis
Reeves, Jas.
1809
Records, Josiah
Reeves, Samuel
Reeves, Elizabeth
Ramey, Jacon hrs.
Ravenscraft, Jno.
1815
Rutter, Lititia
*Runford, Jonathan
Ross, Wm.
*Runyon, Daniel, Sr.
1819
*Rutherford, Robt.
*Rankins, John
Riley, Jas.
Robbins, Rebecca
1823
*Robinson, Richard
Rowland, Joseph
Riggs, James
Ross, Thos.
Riley, Jas.
Riggs, Jenny

1826
*Rees, Daniel, Sr.
1829
Reynolds, Benj.
Reeves, Mary
1832
Reeves, Benj.
Rippey, Dunning
*Rankin, Jno.
Rumford, Elizabeth
Reeves, Susan
1834
*Reed, Jas. Sr.
*Ritchey, David
*Runyon, Jas. M.
1837
Rankins, Wm.
*Reed, Wm.
Rudd, Elizabeth
Rush, Wm. L.
Ruggles, Mary
*Reynolds, Thos.
Richardson, Harrison
Runyon, Jas. M.
Roff, Jonathan
1839
*Rutter, Richard
*Reed, Joseph D.
*Ramey, Deborah
Reeves, Austin S.
*Reed, John H.
Rose, Mary
*Roe, Jacon
Richardson, Jno.
1791
*Smart, John
Sellers, John
*Stevens, John
*Shipley, Samuel
1798
*Standerford, Aquilla
*Sanders, George
*Soward, Richard
*Shockey, Isaac
Somers, Samuel
Somers, George
*Smith, Wm.
Smith, Moses
Shehan, John
Stallcull, Jno.
Scott, John
Sandridge, Jas.
Strong, Gilbert
Smith, Jonathan
Shepherd, George
Small, Henry
Small, Rebecca

1809
Shipley, Samuel
Smith, Samuel
Sandige, Patsey
Sandige, Jas. hrs.
Smith, Margaret
Snyder, Christian
Shelton, Rebecca
Shelton, Wm.
Sidwell, Ruben
Stout, David
Shackleford, Jas.
1815
Stubblefield, Robt.
Sherod, Jas.
Sidwell, Nathan
Sidwell, Reubin
1819
Stephenson, Alice
Stapp, Jas.
Supplee, Jacob
Stout, Jonathan
Summers, Fanny
Stout, Mary J.
Steele, Wm.
Shelton, Fanny D.
Small, Malinda
Stott, Jno.
Stotl, (?) Mary I.
*Stewart, Bevin
1823
Smott, Samuel
Shelton, Thos.
Smith, Gideon
Smott, Lydia
*Shackleford, Jas.
*Shipley, Niah
*Sutherland, Wm.
Shotwell, John
1826
Stewart, Jno.
*Sandige, David
1829
*Stroad, Samuel
Schmidl, Charles
*Stephenson, Thos.
*Shotwell, John S.
Shackleford, Wm. B.
Stout, Rachel
*Samuel, John
*Scott, Samuel
Scudder, Chas. gdn.
*Sidwell, Nathan
Smith, Jas.
1832
Senteney, Jacob
Seybold, Israel
*Samuel, Elizabeth

Shroufe, (Shroofe)
Adam
Shroufe, Hannah
Stephenson, John
Shackleford, Susan
Sandford, Reuben
*Stewart, Soloman
Savage, P. M.
Stout, Mary Jane
Sumrall, John
Shelton, M.
1834
Stewart, Soloman
Sandide, Jas.
Sidwell, Nathan
Staggs, Geo. B.
Stephenson, Nathan
Sunrall, Elizabeth
Scott, Samuel
*Slack, Jacob
*Shepherd, Geo. B.
Senteney, Jno.
Stephenson, Nathaniel
Stroud, Jacob
Sidwell, Nancy
1839
Small, Thos.
*Soward, Thos.
Sandige, Jas.
Smith, Chas. B.
Summers, Wm.
Summers, Ruth
Smith, Henry D.
Shroufe, Sebastian,
gdn. to Van Buskirk
Shipley, Noah
Summers, Jesse, gdn.
to Elizabeth, Sarah, Azuba, and
Martha A. Hickman
Stockwell, Allen M.
Shock, Christian
Smith, Henry D.
Sidwel, Nancy
*Strode, Samuel
*Suit, Nathaniel
Strode, Mary
1840
Shackleford, George
1791
Tandy, Wm.
Thompson, Wm.
*Thomas, Levi
*Thrailkill, Benj.
*Tillett, John

1798
*Thomas, Robt. S.
Thomas, Jacob
Thorn, Robt. S.
Tevis, Peter
*Renneson, Absolom
Thomas, Joseph
1809
Triplett, Wm.
Triplett, Francis
Triplett, Elizabeth
Tilton, Richard
Thompson, Wm. hrs.
Thompson, Joseph
*Thomas, John
Triplett, Wm. hrs.
1815
Tebbs, Samuel
Tevis, Peter
Truford, W. I.
*Tabb, John L.
Tebbs, Sarah
Tebbs, Daniel gdn.
of Tebbs hrs.
Thoroughman, Chas.
*Tevis, Peter
Tebbs, Samuel hrs.
Tilton, Thomas
Thoroman, Williams
1823
True, Benj. hrs.
True, Susan
Taylor, American
*Thompson, Andrew
*Thomas, David
*Treacle, Orphea
1832
Thornton, Samuel
Thompson, And'w F.
Tabb, Edward
1834
*Thomas, Robert
Tiffle, Abijah
1839
Tolle, Presley
Tolle, Thos. N.
*Tebb, Thomas C.
Thompson, Joel W.
True, Jas.
1840
Terhune, Luke
1791
Underwood, Isaac
1840
Underwood, Elizb'th
1798
*Vanschoick, John
Voshell, Daniel

Vansickle, Wm.
1819
VanBuskirk, Jno.
VanCamp, Gerards
VanCamp, Mary
1823
Vanbuskirk, Cath.
VanCamp, Samuel
1829
Vannoy, Frances
1832
VanCamp, Levi
Vanbuskirk, Jas. H.
1840
Varney, Henry
1791
White, Wm.
Wiley, Wm.
*Wood, Ben J.
Wheatley, Francis
Whiteker, Hezekiah
Woodyard, Henry
1798
*Ward, Thos.
*Wilson, John
Watson, John
Worthington, Wm.
Wilson, Jas.
Weaver, Jas.
Weaver, Henry
Wood, George
*Washburn, Jeremiah
*Waters, John
*Whaley, John
*Williams, Chas.
Watson, Jas.
Wilson, Nathaniel
Walker, Jas.
1809
Whaley, Jas.
Whipps, Jas.
Watson, John hrs.
Winters, Martin
*Wiggins, Archibald
*Watson, John
Weisegar, John K.
White, Jas.
1815
Wood, Nancy
*Wood, Ben J.
Wallingsford, Mark
West, Thomas
Wilson, Robt.
Wiley, Walter
*Waller, Thos.
Wood, Andrew
1819
*Watson, Michael

Winters, Jack
Watson, Rebecca renunciation of will of M. Wilson
Wallingford, Mark hrs.
Waugh, John
Watson, Rebecca
Wallingford, Mary
*Ward, Simeon
Winters, Jacob
1823
*Wheeler, John
Wheatley, John
Waugh, John C.
*Walkins, Mary
Wheeler, John
Wallingsford, Jos.
Wilson, Josiah
*Whipps, John
*Watson, Elkanah
Wallingsford, John gdn. to S. Froman's hrs.
1826
Williams ,Henry
White, Mary (late Bland)
Wilson, John A.
1829
Willoughby, David
*Wallingsford, Nich.
Waller, John
*Winters, John
Waller, Elizabeth
*Wyman, Wm. B.
*Willett, Chas.

Wood, David
Ward, Jas.
*Wiggins, Thos.
*Wilson, Michael
*Watson, Zephemiah
1832
*Weaver, Jas.
*White, Jas.
*Wilson, Thos.
Wilson, Susan
*Wood, Daniel
Wells, Wm. R.
1834
*Wilson, Jas. B.
Wright, Thos. B.
*West, Simeon
*Willett, Jas.
Wilson, John
*Williams, Thos.
Wheeler, Lawrence
White, Halsey
Waller—see David Morris
Warder, Walter
Wilson, Miles
Walton, John
Wallingford, Jos.
Walker, Linden
1837
West, Simeon
Waters, Nancy
*Wilson, James
Wheeler, Lawrence
*Worthington, Eliz.
*Weaver, Henry
*Whipps, Wm.
Whitehead, Jno. gdn.

to H. and S. Asberry
*Woodward, Asabel
Worthington, Walter F.
Ward, Chas.
Waddle, G. G.
Waddle, I. W., gdn. to Elizab'th Brown
Wells, Jno. D. gdn. to S. S. Dye and G. W. Dye
Warder, Walter
*Wells, Thos.
1839
Waller, Thos.
Waller, Achsah
Waller, John
Waller, Charity
Waller, Maris
*Walton, John
Walton, Nancy
Waddle, Geo.
Wilson, Priscilla
*Worthington, Wm.
Wilson, John
*Wilkerson, Chas.
*Whaley, Thos.
Wallingsford, Mark C.
Wallingsford, Martha Ann
Wells, Wm.
Worthington, Thos. T.
1839
Yancey, Elizabeth

ANDERSON, GEORGE—Bk. I, pg. 142—To son, Joseph; son, Elias; wife, Sarah; four sons, Horris, Joseph, Elias and Henry; daus., Elizabeth; dau., Isabel Y. Anderson; to Achsa Chanslor; to John Waller's chdn. Extr.: son, Horris. Written Oct. 6, 1832. Probated Nov. 1832. Wts.: Pierce L. Dye, Charles Scudder.

BARKALOW, (BARCALOW) ARTHUR—Bk. A.—Mar. 4, 1800 of Township of Upper Freehold in Co. of Monmouth, Eastern Division of State of N. J. Daughter Sarah Barcalow; son, Derrick Barcalow; son, John; son, William; his uncle, Lefford Pothemus clothes. Six children, namely: Elenor Beard, William, Tobias, John Derrick. James Brewer and son, Derrick and David Barkalow, Extrs. Wts,: Arthur Jefferson, Benjamin Polhamus (Pothemus) and Samuel Emley. Jas. Tapscott, John Lloys and John Emley of Co. of Monmouth, N. J. May, 1802.

CARRELL, DEMPSE—Bk. C.—Advanced in life. Daughter, Nancy Sybold; sons, Daniel, Dempse, Jr., and Sanford Carrell; daus.,

Molly Wheatley, Sally Blincoe, Fanny Bronaugh; son, John Carrell; Wm. H. Carrell, Lawson Carrell, Joseph and Lawson Carrell; gd-dau., Patsy Castleman (to be be paid to her on her marriage of arrival of lawful age); gd-son, Jas. Castleman (to be paid at lawful age); son-in-law, Wm. Bronaugh. March 27, 1806. Oct. 13, 1806.

DOGGETT, ELMOUR, HRS.—Bk. C, pg. 90—Jan. 1810. Mary, Elmour, Elizabeth, Lucinda and Julia Ann Doggett, infant heirs.

ELLIS, JAMES—Nuncupative—Bk. B, pg. 137—Aug. 9, 1799—To Elizabeth Ellis, Jr.; to Esther Ellis; to Macajah Deaver; to _____ Allison; to John Ellis; wife, Elizabeth; Sarah Alison without property being controlled by John Alison. Recorded Sept. 23, 1799. Wts.: John Ellis, Thos. Hayns.

FRISTOE, JOHN—Bk. C.—Dec. 3, 1810—Wife, Jemima (in my old age) all. Hope children and grandchildren will not feel hard. July, 1817. Wts.: Samuel Taylor, James Byers, John Chambers.

FULTON, HUGH—Bk. H, pg. 103—To dau., Nancy Fulton; dau., Mary Pangburn land in Brown Co., Ohio; wife, Margaret. Extrx.: wife, Margaret, and dau., Nancy Fulton. Written Sept. 16, 1829. Probated Feb. 1830. Wts.: Jno. McClung, Richard Mitchell, Jno. Tucker, Geo. H. Crosby.

HITT, SUSAN—Bk. L, pg. 261—To only child, Elizabeth Hitt; father, Aaron Hitt, Extr. Written Jan. 13, 1838. Probated Apr. 1838. Wts.: Wm. S. Allen, Catherine Donovan.

HOLTON, WM.—Bk. H, pg. 509—To wife, Abigail; division made among chdn., hrs. of son, Alexander Holton, decd.; son, Lewis Holton's daus., Sally Sayre and Polly Cave; son, Elijah Holton. Extrs.: sons, John, William and Jesse. Written Dec. 5, 1827. Codicil mentions dau., Rebecca Dowden; Elizabeth Navis; Wm. H. Dowden; Patsy Wood; John Dowden, Jr. Probated Dec. 1831. Wts.: Rice Boulton, Benj. Flinn.

LOUNSDALE, THOS.—Bk. B.—Wife, Margaret; son, James, 200 acres; dau., Elizabeth ,150£ to be put to interest till she is 18; son, James lot of ½ a. in Martinsburg, Berkeley Co., Va., a lot in Harrisonburgh, Rockingham Co., Va. Extrs.: Capt. Thos. Marshall and John Davison. May 3, 1795. June 9, 1806.

MURPHY, TIMOTHY—Bk. B.—Wife, Elizabeth Murphy; son, Henry Corbit Murphy, my part of estate of Jno. Gallan, decd., and also my right to title, interest in any property held by the Gallan family, generally in Harford Co., Md.; dau., Mary Murphy, land of Benjamin Worford, Bracken Co. Son, John Murphey; friend, Elijah Hadan and wife, Elizabeth, Extrs. Jan. 22, 1799 Feb. 25, 1799.

MARSHALL, ROBERT—Bk. C, pg. 191—To M. Marshall, ⅓; to Robert Marshall, ⅓. Robt. Marshall, Admr. Inventory—Bk. B, pg. 104— May, 1800. Settlement—Bk. C, pg. 200—To widow, her dower; to Robert Marshall; to James Curtis; to Simon R. Baker; to Alex. Edwards and Robert Marshall, assignee of John Hurst, representative of Robt. Marshall, decd. June 30, 1812.

MILLER, ROBERT—Bk. A.—Cecil Township, Washington Co., Pa. Chilren, Henry, James, Anna, John (by first wife), Elizabeth, Mary, Robert, Keziah, Martha (second wife). ("John's infirmity") "till youngest is 18." Matthew Ritchie and Graig Ritchie of Washington Co., Pa., Extrs. May, 22, 1794. August 23, 1796.

PORTER, JAMES—Bk. D, pg. 1—Three chdn., John Porter, Elizabeth Porter and Malinda Porter. Extrs.: son, John and Wm. O. Watts. Written Sept. 10, 1813. Probated Dec. 1815. Wts.: Walter Reed, Anne Reed, Wm. O. Watts.

SANDERS, GEO—Bk. B, pg. 38—To son, George when of age; to my beloved Martha Sanders; dau., Maryann Sanders; wife, Susanna now pregnant; dau., Margaret; dau., Kezea Sanders. Extrix.: wife. Written June 4, 1799. Probated Oct. 1799.

SHOTWELL, JOHN'S HRS.—Bk. H, pg. 82—Thos. Fletcher, gdn. to Nathan, John and Parmelia Shotwell, hrs. of John Shotwell, Sr., decd. Sarah Shotwell; William Shotwell. Nov. 11, 1829.

STANDERFORD, AQUILLA—Bk. A.—Daus., Hannah Hawkins, Sarah Hildreth, Mary Smith and Rebecca Bartlett (1 shilling); son, Nathan, 1 shilling; dau., Milcah Little, 750 a.; son, George, 750 a.; son, Elijah, 354 a.; son, Aquilla, 110 a., adjoining Hildreth; son, John; wife, Sarah. Jan. 10, 1799. June 24, 1799. Wts.: John Gaheagan, Squire Hildreth, Samuel Hawkins.

THRALKILLE, BENJAMINE—Bk. A.—**March 27, 1793**—Wife, Ann; eldest sons, John, William and James Thralkille, land in Shenandoah Co., Va.; son, Daniel; wife to rear small children, etc.; dau., Elenor; dau., Lydia; dau., Lucy; dau., Ruth; dau., Nancy; dau., Elizabeth; dau., Margaret.

WARD, THOMAS—Bk. B, pg. 45—To sister, Rebecca Davis. Extr.: Francis Taylor. Written Dec. 1, 1799. Probated Dec. 23, 1799. Wts.: I. Brown, Philip Ebart.

WOOD, BENJAMIN—Bk. A.—**Jan. 20, 1797**—Wife; son, Amos; son-in-law, Philip Baltimore; dau., Keziah Griggs; son, William; dau., Nancy Wood. Other children, Curdalah Wood, Matthew and Ashberry Wood. Son, Aquilla, "lot in town of Williamsburg to be sold." Aaron Houghton and Ruth Wood, Extrs. Wts.: Fr. Joseph Handcock, Cath. Handcock, Jo Henry Symmonds. June 26, 1797.

WALLER, THOMAS—Bk. D.—Wife, Sophia; son, Richard; daus., Sophia Ragsdale, Amy Threlkeld, Polly Threlkeld, Elizabeth Small, Anna Barns, Eleanor Small; son, Cornelius Waller; son, John. Extrs.: Pogue & Bodley. Gd-dau., Ann Threlkeld; daus., Sophia, Aira, Polly, Elizabeth, Anna and Elizabeth to their children. Cornelius and John, Extrs. Feb. 6, 1817. June 1817. Wts.: James Morris, J. S. Morris, Wm. H. Pepper.

WATSON, JOHN—Bk. C, pg. 218—Wife, Rebecca; daus., Pheby Helm and Mary Ann Vickers; son, Wm.; sons, Calvert, Arthur and Hiram. Extrs.: son, Wm. and Benj. Watson. Written Sept. 2, 1812. Probated Oct. 12, 1812. Wts.: Jno. Mannen, Thos. T. Worthington.

NICHOLAS COUNTY
(Formed from Bourbon and Mason, 1799)

INDEX TO WILL BOOK A
1800-1816

Abbreviations: W.—Will, I.—Inventory, S.—Sales, Div.—Division, Set.—Settlement.

Names appearing in this index are not included in General Index

Allen, William—W. and I.
Augustus, Enock—I. and S.
Anderson, Jas.—I. and S.
Anderson, Vincnet—S.

Beard, Wm.—W. and I.
Bell, Robert—W. and I.
Buckner, Robert—W., I. and S.
Boyd, William,—I. and S.
Buchanon, James—I.
Bratton, Joshua—I.
Burdin, Jas.—W. and I.
Barlow, Thos.—W. and I.
Buckner, Saml.—Set.
Baker, Martin Sr.—W., I. ,S.
Baker, Jacob—I., S.
Bradshaw, Geo.—S.

Dailey, Bryan—W. and I.
Dunsmore, Saml.—W. and I.
Dale, Matthew—W.
Downey, Archibald—W .and I.
Deal, Matthew—I.
Deatty, Jno.—I.
Drummonds, Jas.—W. and I.
Davidson, Jno.—W. and I.

Forsythe, Wm.—I.
Foster, Thos.—W., I. and S.
Finley, Michael—I. and S.
Forsythe, Jno.—I. and S.

Glasgow, Jas.—W. and I.
Gressum, Phillimon—I.
Gray, Jas.—W. and I.
Grasamar, Jno.—I. and S.
Gethens, Henry—I. and S.
Glasgow, Jno.—I.

Hellman, Jno.—W.
Harney, Mills—W. and I.
Hartley, Mordacai—I.
Harris, Saml.—I. and S.
Hildreth, Squire—I. and S.
Howerton, Geo.—S.

Howard, Matthews—I.

Jordan, Wm.—I. and S.
Jenkins, Saml.—I.
Jones, Robt.—I. and S.
Jones, Jno.—W. and I.
Johnson, Jonathan—I. and S.

Kimbrough, Nathaniel—I.
Kincart, Samuel—W., I. and S.

Leepers, Jno.—W. and I.

Mitchell, Wm.—I. and S.
Moncrief, Maxa—I.
McClelland, Jane—W.
Munford, Wm.—W. and I.
McCormick, Jas.—I.
Mitcheltree, Jonas—W. and I.
Morgan, John—W. and I.
Myers, Geo.—I.
McDowell, Robert—I.
Mumford, Wm.—I.
Manulty, (McAnulty) Jno.—W., I. and S.

Neale, Robt.—I.

Olliver, Jno.—W., I. and S.

Philips, Michael—W.
Pough, Henry
Porter, Wm.—I. and S.
Prater, Jeremiah—W.
Powell, Thos.—I.
Poe, Benj.
Prater, Jeremiah—Recpt.

Robinson, Alexander—W.
Stewart, Robert—I.
Stewart, Jno.—W. and I.
Snapp, Geo.—W.
Smart, Joseph—I. and S.
Stephenson, James—W.
Stokes, (or Stoker) Hamlet—W.

Sadler, Jno.—W.
Stephenson, Wm.—W.
Smart, Jas.—I.

Tucker, James—I. and S.
Trousdale, Jno.—W. and I.
Trousdale, Wm.—W. and I.
Thompson, Joseph—I.
Thompson, Alexander—W. and I.

Vanhook, Thos.—I.
Vaughn, Thos.—I.

Welch, Michael—W.
Williams, Nathaniel—I. and S.
Wallace, William—I. and S.
Wills, Aaron—W.
Warren, Isaac—I.

INDEX TO WILL BOOK B

1816 to 1829

Names appearing in this index are not included in General Index

Archer, John—W.
Arthur, John—W.
Ardery, James—W.
Alexander, Sarah—I.

Bevens, John—I.
Bevens, David—I.
Byers, David—I.
Brown, Jas.—I. and Set.
Byers, Nancy—I.
Bannister, Nathaniel
Brown, James—I.
Bennington, Neh.
Brown, Samuel—W.
Bartlett, Wm.—S.
Blair, Wm.—W.
Brown's—W.
Brown, Elizabeth—Dower
Brown, Willi—I.
Baker, Jas.—Gdn. Set.
Burnan, Frances—W.
Baker, Nath'l—Set.
Bartlett, Wm.—Set.
Barker—Com. Set.
Baker, Martin—S. and Set.
Baxter, Edmund—W.
Baxter, Fr.
Burns, Jno.—Set. with Gdn.
Brown, Samuel
Burns, Jno.—W.
Brown, Wm.
Byers—Set.
Bartlett, Wm.—S.
Brown, Jas.—W.
Brown, Samuel—Set.

Clarke, Jno.—W.
Caldwell, Robt.—W.
Collier, Jno.—W.
Cunningham, Robt.—W.
Caldwell, Alex.—W.

Criss, (?) Valientine—W.
Collier, Hannah
Clark, H., for Thos. Davidson
Cottrell, Thos.—I.
Clinkingbeard, Jno.
Criswell, E. P.
Campbell, Jas.—W.

Drummon's—W.
Davidson, Thos.—See Clark
Duncan, Jas.—Set.
Duncan, Benj.—S.
Deatly, Jno.—Div.
Deatly, Jemima—Dower
Duncan, Phebe—I.
Dalzell, Alex.—I.
Darneille, Thos.—Set.
Dinsmore, Jno.—I.
Dalzell, Abrm.

Ellis, Benj.—I.
Elliott, Betsey—W.
Ellis, James—W.

Fulton, John—I.
Furlow, Cathn.—W.
Fishback, Jesse, Hrs.
Fleet, Wm.—I.

Geohegan, Jno.—W.
Godman, Wm.—W.
Glasgow, Jane—I.
Grigg, Thos.
Grisham, Jane—I.
Graves, Wm.—D.
Gragg, Saml.
Glenn, Jane—Dower
Griffeth, Saml.
Glenn, Archd.

Hansford, Stephen—W.

Hamilton, Robt.—W.
Howard, Jacob—I.
Ham, Michael—I.
Hanson, Luke—I.
Hamilton, Jno. M.—W.
Howe, Esra—I.
Howe, Saml.—W.
Hurd, Nathan
Henderson, Jesse—Div.
Hughes, Jas.—W.
Hughes, Wm.—I.
Hansford, Stephen—I.
Hall, Lawrence—I.
Huddleston, Wm.—I.
Hughes, Jas.—I.
Hall, Robt., Hrs.
Holear, Jno. F.—W.
Hopkins, Robt.—W.
Harney, Rowland—I.
Hinton, Ezekiel—W.
Haram, Henry—I.
Hen, Danl.—W.
Harden, Cath.—I.
Hamilton, Samuel—I.
Hayden, Lott—Commr's. Rpt.
Hunt, Woldridge—Gdn.
Harden, Jno.
Harney, Hiram—I.
Howarton, R. M. L.—Div.
Hill, Ephriam

Johnston, Will H. J.
Jolly, Martha—W.
Jolly, David—W.
Jones, Will R.
Jones, Jacob—I.
Jolly, Margaret—Gdn. Set.
Ishmael, Benj.—W.
Johnson, Isham—W.
Johnson, Enock—I.

Kennett, Wm.—I.
Kincart, Samuel—Set.
Kelly, Thos.—W.
Kimbrough, Nathl.—Div.
Keney, Jas.—W.
Keats, Thos.—W.
Kincart, Isabella—I.

Leeper, Jno.—I.
Letton, Michl.—Gdn. to R. B.
  Smith's hrs.
Leeper, Susannah—W.
Lane, John R.—I.
Lockridge, Jno.—W.
Leach, Benj.—I.
Laddock, Harry—W.

Mears, Jas.—W.
Maxwell, Gavin—I.
Morgan, David—I.
Martin, John—I.
McAnulty, John—I. and Set.
McIntire, Robt.—I.
Marshall, Archd.—I.
McClintock, Wm.—W.
Mason, Burgess—I.
Myers, Geo.—I.
McCarty, Jas.—I.
McClanahan's Will
McGills, Alex.—W.
Moler, Jos.—W.
McQuown, Lawrence—I.
McCoy, Jno.—I.
Magnor, Jno.—I.
McCurty, Jas.—Set.
Miller, Stephen—I.
McCoy, Mary—I.
McDonald, Cinderela—Gdn.
McCurty, Jas.—S.
McCleary, Sam'l—W.
McIntire, Robt.—Set.
McCormick, Eliz.—I.
McClintock, Dan'l—W.
McGinnis, Jno.
Marshall, Daniel—Set.
McAnulty, Joseph—Set.
McCoy, Jno.—Set.
McCarty's Hrs.
McCune, Robt.—W.
Mathers, Jas.—I.
McKinsey, Jno.—I.
McCune, John—W.
Musick, Thos.

Nesbutt, Nathan
Nesbitt, Thos.—Gdn.
Nelson, Willis—Gdn.

Ockerman, Jos.

Powel, Thos.—W.
Ploughe, Jeremiah—I.
Pawley, Jno.—W.
Potts, Wm.—W.
Payne, Jas.—I.

Richards, Burton G.
Radford, Jno.
Rule, Sarah—I.
Runnels, Jesse—I.
Robinson, Jas.—I.
Rule, Samuel
Ray, Jas.—W.
Ross, Jno.—I.
Reveal, Michael—W.

INDEX TO WILL BOOK C

1830-1839

Names appearing in this index are not included in General Index

Conway, Wm.—W.
Collier, Jas. H.—W.
Collier, Wm.—W.
Collier, Elizabeth H.—W.
Crouch, Jona., Sr.—W:
Craycraft, Eli
Cunningham, Robt.
Cress, Val.
Cull, (or Call) Margaret

Dalzell, Abra.
Dale, Isaac, to Dinali
Dalzell, Thos.—W.
Dykes, Robt.—Div.
Duncan, Phebe
Deatley, Porter
Dudley, Ann
Dougherty, (Doughty?) Thos.—
    Div. 298—Hrs.
Dickerson, Elizabeth to Ann and
    chdn.
Dinsmore, Wm. M.
Dykes, Kitty
Dickerson to Smith

Earp, Simeon, em. of slaves
Evans, Ludwell, Gdn. to W. Hunt
Ellis, Mary—I. and S.
Edwards, Benj.—Agt. for Royses
Endicott, Joseph
Ellis, Richard
Edwards, Hannah to Katty, deed
    Em. (slave)
Edes, Thos.

Foster, Jas.—W.
Fisher, Turner—Gdn. for M. A.
    Smith
Fields, Jas.—Div.
Franklin, Jno.—W.
Fielden, Geo.

Grimes, Davis
Grimes, Geo.—W.
Grimes, Christian
Grimes, Elizabeth—W.
Gray, Isaac
Gray, Jane—Dower
Geohegan to Snap
Graves, Judith
Graves, Joseph H.—W.
Glenn, Moses F., to Squire, deed
    Em. (slave)
Hughes, Jas., Hrs.
Howerton, Henry T.
Hughes, Logan G.—Set. with Wm.
    Hughes, gdn. of Jas. M.

Hughes; with Wm. and Jesse
Hughes, gdn. of Robt. P.
Hughes; with Wm. Hughes,
    gdn. of Wm. Hughes gdn.
    of Jas. Hughes.
Howard, Thos.—W.
Harding, Jno.
Hughes, Wm.—Admr. of Jas.
    Hughes
Hall, Saml.—W.
Hardy, Armistead
Hobb, Wm. C.
Huddleson, Hance—W.
Hughes, Jas.—Set.
Hardy, Gdn. for E. Howerton
Hill, Ephriam
Hopkins, Joslin, gdn. for Owings
    Hrs.
Hopkins Wm.—W.
Holladay Robt.
Holladay Wm.—W.
Holladay, Margaret
Horward, Thos.—Set.
Howard, David, Jno., and Irvine,
    gdn. rpt.
Hadden, Thos.—W.
Howe, Sam'l—Set.
Hardy, Armistead—Set.
Howse, Richard—I.
Hall, Benj.—Set.
Herndon, Jas.—Set.
Hardy's Heirs—Set.
Holloway, Wm.—Set.
Ham, Michael—W.
Holladay, Jno.—Gdn. Rpt.
Huddleson, Wm.—Set.
Howe, Amos P.—Gdn. Caldwell
    hrs.
Hayden, Lott—Set.
Hughe, G. L.—Gdn. Rcpt.
Hopkins, Josiah—I.
Howard, David L.—Rcpt.
Hopkins—Gdn. Owens hrs.
Hopkins, Wm.—Set.
Howard, John—Set.
Hamilton, S. P.—Set.
Howse, Elizabeth—Dower
Howse, John—Set.
Hughes, Jesse, Gdn. Jos. Holla-
    day's hrs.
Hopkins, John G.
Hardy and Boys—Set. with Mc-
    Clintock, Admr.
Howe, Edward—Deed
Howse, Elizabeth—Deed
Hendricks, Levi—S.
Howard, Evan—Set.
Ham, Sam'l—W.

Hendricks, Rebecca—Dower
Hamilton, John—Set.
Hann, Jonas—Set.
Hughes, Toliver—I.
Hawkins, Sam—I.
Huffman, Peter—W.
Hamilton, Elizabeth—I.
Hardy, E. W.—Gdn. Set.

Johnson, Wm.—Set.
Jeffers, Nancy H.—W.
Johnson, Nicholas and Elvira—
Div. slaves
Johnsan, Isham—Set. with Miller
Johnson, Isabella—Gdn. Rpt.

Koopenhendolpher,—Gdn. Set.
Kennedy, Wm.—Set.
Kimbrough, Sam—I.
Kennedy, J. P. and hrs. of Wm.—
Div.
Kimbrough, Robt.—I.
Keets, Thos.—Set. with Dalzelle
Kern, Adam—Deed
Kimes, Jacob—I.
Kennedy, Alfred—Set. Gdn.
Kennedy, John—Set. Gdn.

Lockridge, Robt.—Set.
Lane, Jno.—Set.
Letton, N. W.—Set.
Lilly, Pleasant—I.
Low, Isaac—W.
Lathram, A.—W.
Letton, Michael—I.

Mathers, Jos.—Set.
McKinsey—Set.
Morgan, Joseph—W. and Set.
McClure, John—I.
Mathers, Joseph—I.
Miller, Stephen—Set.
Miller, Wm.—I.
Mayhugh, Bryan—W.
Manson, Sam'l—I.
Mumford, Asher—I.
Miller, Nancy—Dower
Mastin, Peter—Set.
Marshall, Hugh—W.
Mathers, Wm.—Gdn. Peytons
Miller, John—Gdn. S. Miller
Monson, Sam'l—Gdn. E. J. John-
son
McClure, John—Deed
McClure, Nancy—Dower
Magner, Sophia—Set.
Mathers, Thos.—Set.
Millekin, Wm.—Set.

Monson, Sam'l—Set.
McClure, Wm.—Set.
Miles, Amos—I.
Mathers, B., and Hrs.—Div.
Moore, Jno. A.—Deed
Morgan, Jno.—Set. Gdn. Jos.
Holladay
McClintock—Gdn. of Margaret
Patton
McGinness, Jos.—Set.
McClure—Gdn. J. M. McClure

Nesbit, Nathan—Set.
Nesbit, Margery—W.
Nesbit, Sarah—W.

Ogden, Henry—Div.
Ogdon, Lucy C.—Deed

Peyton, Stephen—Dower to wid-
ow
Parker, Thos.—I.
Potts, Wm.—Set.
Peper, (Piper)—Asher Set.
Piper, Sam'l—I.
Piper, Jno.—Set.

Robison, Jas.—Set.
Ribelin, Martin—W.
Royce, Hiram—Set.
Robison, Mary—Dower
Robertson, Sam.—W.
Ritchie, Soloman—I.
Ribelin, Catherine—Dower
Riggens, Jesse—Set.
Royse, Wm.—Set.
Riley, John—I.
Robeson, Mary—W.
Rickey, John—I.
Royce, Catherine—Dower
Roberts, Wm.—I.

Smith, Richard—Div.
Smith, Mary Ann—Set.
Smither, John H.—Deed
Stam, Joshua—Set.
Smith, Nathan—W.
Shulse, Peter—Set.
Smedley, Aaron—Deed
Set. 13th R. K. M.
Sledd, Thos.—Deed
Smith, Jno.—Set.
Smith, Wm.—Set.
Stitt, Mary—Dower
Sturman, Valentine—W.
Schwartywelder, Peter—I.
Squires, Jno. W.—W.
Selley, Major—W.

Smart, Sam'l—I.
Smedley, Aaron—Set.
Shaw, Geo.—Set.
Stodler, Jno.—I.
Shankland, Jno.W.
Scott, Jno. C.
Snapp, Geo.—Set.
Squires, Leonard—W.
Squires, Turley—I.
Squires, Harrison—Set.
Squires, Thomas—Set.
Smith, David—Set.
Squires, Jos.—Set.
Smith, Wm.—I.
Stephenson, Wm.—I.
Sims, Ambrose—I.
Summett, George—W.
Selby, Margaret—W.
Snap, Robt.—Rcpt.
Sears, Jno.—I
Smith, E. G.—Rcpt.

Thompson, Mary—Set.
Thompson, Henry—Set.
Turley, Jno.—I.

Taylor, Joseph—Set.
Tweedy, David—W.
Throckmorton, Thos.—W.
Trigg, Thos.—W.
Trigg, Elizabeth—Dower
Thomas, Rapel, Hrs.
Tarmer, Richard—I.

Victor, Jas.—I.
Vanschoiack, Jerry—I.
Vimont, B. F.—Gdn. Set.

Woods, Joseph—Gdn. Set.
West, Richard—I.
Wood, Angelica—Set.
West, Robt.—Gdn. Nancy Gray
Woods, Joseph—Gdn. Blair's Hrs.
Wilson, Katherine—W.
Wasson, Jos.—Deed
Ward, Elizabeth—Dower
Woods, Joseph—Set.
Wasson, Sam'l—Set.

Young, Jacob—Set.

OLDHAM COUNTY

(Formed from Henry, Jefferson, Shelby Counties, 1823)

Contributed by Hattie M. Scott, Frankfort, Ky.

INDEX TO WILL BOOK 1.

Names appearing in this index are not included in General Index

WILL BOOK 2
(Throug H)

Names appearing in this index are not included in General Index

July 9, 1843–Aug. 21, 1843.
Barnhill ,Joseph_____417
Bryant, Mark_____416

Coons, John_____ 97
Chambers, Margaret_____438
Carpenter, ——————_____(3-143)

Duncan, Ludwell_____ 22
Dysert, John_____ 71
Dawkins, Wm._____ 96
Duerson, Thos._____ 97

Duerson, Mary_____300
DeHaven, Wm. P._____436

Ellison, Winafer_____442

Findley, Thos._____381

Goff, Wm._____ 95

Henshaw, Philip T._____ 7
Howell, John_____360
Hardin, Rowley_____405
(1843-1843)

SHELBY COUNTY
(Formed from Jefferson, 1792)

INDEX TO EARLY ESTATES

WILL BOOK 1
(1794–1805)

See also Volume I for Shelby County Records

Note: Abbreviations: W.—Will; D.—Dower;

Names appearing in this index are not included in General Index

Anderson, John

Bowling, Wm.—W.
Bazan, Jesse
Buchannon, Wm.—W.
Breeding, Richard
Boyles, David
Boyd, Willi
Boyd, Mary—D.
Brown, Jas.—W.
Boswell, Geo.
Butler, Eliza
Briscoi, Jas.—W.
Boyd, Wm., Hrs.

Conley, Jno.—W.
Clarke, Jno.—W.

Daniel, Robt.—W.
Downing, Oliver
Dunn, Jno.

Elam, Richard

Fullenwider, Henry—
　W.
Felty, Jno.
Ford, John—W.

Green, Jonathan—W.
　Glover Jonah
Garrett, Jno. (wife,
　Margaret)
Gassaway, Richard—
　W.
Green, Catherine

Haniel, Phillip
Hogland, Richard
Hill, Hardy—W.
Hansbrough, Monias
　—W.
Hartman, Anthony—
　W.

Jacob, Thomas
Johnston, Phillip
Leatherman, Jno.
Lemasters, Richd.
Lastley, Robt.
Lewis, Jno.
Lambert, Lane—W.
Lawrence, David

Metcalf, Jas.
McClain, Sam'l
Muke, (?) Jesse

McClelland, Daniel—
　(Gdn's Acct.)
McCampbell, Jane—W.
McLure, (McClure)
　Jas.
McClain, John

Newland, Jacob
Newland, Lucy
Newland, Isaac

Owens, Geo.
Owen, Brackett—W.
Perkins, Willi
Pruit, Michael—W.
Potts, Jno.
Pennington, Isaac
Powell, Willi

Robins, Wm.
Reed, Jas.
Redding, Willi

Shannon, Willi—W.
Smith, Jacob
Shields, Patrick
Stout, Jas.
Sled, Willi—W.

Shannon, Thos.—W.
Shuck, Andrew—W.
Squires, Jno.

Thompson, Thomas

Vancleave, Ralph

Wilson, Sam'l—W.
Warford, David
Whitaker, John—W.
Whitaker, Jesse—W.
Williams, Wm.—W.

Walker, Jos.—W.
Williams, Jno.
Williams, Elizabeth—
W.

Young, Nelson

WILL BOOK 2
(1804-1811)

Names appearing in this index are not included in General Index

Ashby, Silas
Adams, Simon

Bell, Henry
Booker, Richard M.—
W.
Bonta, Hendrick—W.
Beadle, Jonathan
Beard, Rebecca—(Gdn
to E. and Sam'l
Booker)
Booker, Parham
Ball, Edward
Bozell, Nancy
Boyd, G. W.—(Gdn.
list rec'd of Dan'l
McClelland)
Brite, Lewis
Beard, Rebecca
Boyd, Wm.—Acct. as
Gdn. to Jno. B.)
Beard, Steph.—(Acct.
as Gdn.)
Boyle, Wm.
Booker, Richard
Black, Chas.—W.
Bradshaw, Wm.
Boyd, Wm. G.—(Acct.
as Gdn.)
Boone, Geo.—W.
Booker, Jno.

Childers, Susannah
Cravenson, Geo.—W.
Cannon, Tubman
Craveton, Rebecca—
W.
Chiles, Walter—W.
Crow, Wm.—(Acct. as
Gdn.
Castleman, Jacob—
(with Abrm. Neal,
Set. as Admrs.)
Carr, Moses

Cooper, Elial
Carr, John
Cardwell, Geo., (with
Nicholas Sharp,
Admrs. of Jno.
Sharp)
Carson, Robt.
Clarke, Jas.
Churchill, Richard
Coburn, Jas.

Dugan, Hugh
Demoree, Sam'l—W.
Daniel, Geo.
Davis, Ezekiel

Elkin, Robt.
Elliott, Robt.—W.
Elliott, Augustine
Ellis, Isaac (and Bal-
lard, Jas.—Set.)
Ellis, Wm. (and Mary
Lee)
Ellis, Jesse

Finley, Wm.—W.
Finley, Sarah
Fulton, Jas.
Fulton, Winny—(Set.
as Admrs.)
Gillespy, Jas.
Gouldman, Robt.
Graves, David—W.
Griffin, Wm.
Gash, Michael
Gash, Thos.
Gash, Elizabeth—Acct.
Grafton, Jas.
Green, Catherine

Hamon, Wm.
Hill, Margaret
Houghland, Jas.
Hill, Margaret

Hornsby, Joseph—W.
Hall, Austin
Hern, Owen

Jones, Richard—W.
Jewil, Wm.
Johnston, Philip

Lewis, John, Hrs.
Link, Jacob—W.
Lucas, Ab.
Lewis, Margaret—(Set.
with Abrm. Lu-
cas)
Lawrence, David—
(Acct. of Thos.
Arbuckle)
Lastly, Alex.
Lee, Wm.
Lee, Dan'l
Lemmon, Jas.
Lacefiel, Patsey
Lewis, John—(widow's
D.)

McCampbell, Sam'l
McClain, Jno.
McWaid, Henry
McKinney, Jno.
McDowell, Chas.
Martin, Jno.
Moore, R. M.
McFalls, David
Martin, Peter
Mitchell, Thos.—Gdn.
Acct.)
Maddox, Wilson
McWaid, Margaret
McDowel, Rachel—
(Set. with)
McQuade, Henry
McFall, Letty—W.
Matthews, Jno.
Merewether, Richard

Mitchell, Thos.—(with Thos. Hanna, Set. with Carter Mitchel)
Mitchell, Thos.—(with Jon. Retcham, Set. with Elias Hogland's Admr.)
Mitchell, Thos.—(with Thomas Hannah, Set. with Jas. McClain, Admr. of Sam'l McLain)
McCrocklin, Jno.
Mitchell, Wm.
Meeks, Jno.
Mitchell, Thos.—(Gdn. Acct. of Ann A. Ridgway, Jno. Ridgway)
Marquiss, Wm.
Miles, Sam'l—W.
McClain, David—W.

Neaves, Jno.

Owen, Katherine—D.
Owen, Abrm.

Postelhwait, Joseph
Pearcy, Jno.
Prewitt, Michael

Perry, Roderick—W.
Payton, Chas
Prewett, Jas. (in Shelby and Hardin)
Peyton, Chas.
Pollard, Henry—W.
Prewett, Nathaniel— (and Long, Wm., Set.)
Pearcy, Geo.

Reid, Jas.
Robinson, Jas.—W.
Radford, Richd.
Robinson, Jno.
Ridgway, Richard
Reed, Caleb
Reddings, Reubin
Rennolds, Sally
Ridgway, Sam'l—Gdn. Set.
Rice, Rowlett—Gdn.
Rennolds, Wm.—Gdn.
Rutlege, Jno.
Ridgway, J. R.—Acct.
Ridgway, Ann—Acct.
Roberts, Geo.—W.
Reed, Susannah
Ridgeway, Richd.

Smith, Nicholas— Admr.

Snider, Peter—W.
Simpson, Joseph—W.
Straughem, Jno.
Simpson, (Sampson) Benj. (wife, Sarah D.)
Simpson, Jas.
Stone, Geo.—W.
Sharpe, Jno.

Talbot, Ezekial
Threlkeld, Thos.—W.
Triplett, Roger
Tarr, Jno.
Talbott, Geo.—Gdn.
Thomas, Hilead

Utterback, Henry— (wife, Patsey, D.)

Vardemon, Peter—W.

Whitaker, Jno.
Williams, Elizabeth
White, Sarah—W.
Whitaker, Isaac— (Extr. of Jno.)
White, Matthew
Williams, Isaiah
Weaver, Benj.
Wood, Jno.—W.

RANDOM COURT RECORDS

JONES, JOSEPH—Will—Bk. 12, pg. 131—"Far advanced in years." Spot of ground in Bourbon Co., on Hinkston's Creek conveyed him by Nicholas Amos, and secured to Ann Jones, his wife, by deed of trust for life and after her death to be divided between son, Abram Jones and dau., Ann Amos. Extrs.: son, Abram and son-in-law, Nicholas Amos. Written Sept. 16, 1836. Probated Jan. 1837. Wts.: Sam. W. White, Leonard D. White, Geo. Pence.

POLLARD, HENRY—Will—Bk. 2, pg. 672—Wife, Rachael; my chdn., son, Elijah Pollard, Rachel Fenley; chdn. of Rebechah Ragsdale, decd. Extrs.: son, Elijah and Thos. Mitchell. Written Aug. 1811. Probated Oct. 1811.

MARTIN, JAS. L.—Will—Bk. 3, pg. 201—Wife, Rebecca; oldest daus. already received property, except Betsey Emily and Elleen; our oldest sons, Thos., Isaiah, James, Wm. and Robt. Written Dec. 4, 1813. Probated Oct. 1814.

MARTIN, JOSEPH—Will—Bk. 6, pg. 52—Wife, Elizabeth; chdn., Geo., David and Mary to be educated; chdn., Jno., Joseph, Elias and Benj.; chdn., Lucy, Geo., David and Mary; son, Jno. who is married;

Sons, Jno. and Joseph, Extrs. Written Nov. 1822. Probated Mar. 1823.

October Court, 1810—Appearing to satisfaction of court that Mary Nash is widow of Thos. Nash, decd., who died intestate, formerly of Cecil Co., Md., and late of Jefferson Co., Ky., that he was the bro. of Samuel Nash, also decd., having died intestate, that said Thos. and Samuel were sons of Thos. Nash, also decd., having died in Cecil Co., Md., and that Harmon Nash of Jefferson Co., Ky., and Noble Nash of Shelby and Elizabeth Johnson, wife of Richard Johnson of State of Ohio are chdn. and hrs. of her late husband, Noble Nash which is ordered certified.

PORTER, JAMES—Will—Bk. 9, pg. 210—Wife, Elizabeth; "all my chdn.," (not named). Written Sept. 15, 1831. Probated Feb. 1832.

PORTER, JNO.—Will—Bk. 6, pps. 61-62—To bro., David; three sons of bro., Samuel Porter, decd.; sister, Jane Porter; sisters, Jane Porter, Jennet Burton, Margaret Boyd. Extrs.: David Porter, Geo. Boyd, Joel Hnadsbrough, Jas. Lutrell. March, 1823.

BULLARD, (BALLARD) REUBIN, HRS.—Agreement with Wm. Bullard (Ballard)—Deed Bk. K, pg. 146—Jan. 1, 1810—Hrs .listed: Wm. Ballard, Wm. Sanders, Reubin Ballard, Geo. Gill, Nancy Ballard, Fanny Ballard, Caty, widow of Reubin.

ELLIOTT, ROBT., HRS.—To Jos. Helm Sr.,—Deed Bk. R, pg. 20—June, 1819—Hrs. listed: Robert McConnell and wife, Sally, late Elliott, Samuel Dickerson and wife, Betsey, late Elliott, by Geo. B. Knight, Commissioner and Elliott Headington, infant son of Joshua Headington and wife, Ann, late Elliott, under 21 yrs., by Geo. B. Knight, Commissioner of Jefferson Co., to Joseph Helm, Sr. of Lincoln Co.

MEREWETHER, JAS. HRS.—To Joseph Helm, Sr.—Deed Bk. R, pg. 23—June, 1819—John B. Booker and wife, Elizabeth, Wm. Merewether, Richard Merewether, Jas. Merewether, Jane Merewether and Judy Booker, hrs of Jas. Merewether, decd. and Ge. B. Knight, Commissionare apptd. by court, deed to Joseph Helm, Sr., of Lincoln Co.

ASHBY, DAVID HRS—To Richard Sharp—Deed Bk. P, pg. 190—May 20, 1818—Hrs. listed: Landen Ashby and Edith Ashby, Washington Ashby and Jane Ashby, Willis Ashby and Polly Ashby, Charlotte Ashby, Vina Ashby Luisa Ashby.

ALLEN, JAMES HRS.—To Richard Vandyke—Deed Bk. Q, pg. 331—Feb. 14, 1820—Hrs. listed: Elizabeth Reason and Josiah Reason, Wm. Allen, Thos. Allen, Mary Allen (widow) and Elenor, Silvester, Susannah and Marquis I. Allen, minor hrs.

NEWLAND, JACOB HRS.—To Wm. G. Boyd—Deed Bk. R, pg. 53—Feb. 24, 1820—Elizabeth Newland and Abner Newland, inft. hrs. of Isaac Newland, decd., by Abner Newland, gdn. of Shelby Co. Whereas Jacob Newland died seized of land in Shelby, Isaac, one of hrs. of Jacob Newland, did bind self to convey land whereon Isaac's mother then lived (May 25, 1814) and said Isaac departed this life without making conveyance, said gdn. makes conveyance for Lucy Jane Newland, Elizabeth Newland, Abner Newland, inft. hrs.

WARREN COUNTY
(Formed from Logan County, 1796)

Contributed by Hattie M. Scott, Frankfort, Ky.

INDEX TO WILL BOOK A

Alexander, Andrew (Inventory, page 5).
Ayers, David (Will). Wife, Polly and children. Page 238.

Beard, Barzilla, deceased, (Inventory). Page 64.
Blackford, Reubin, Sr., (Will).- Wife, Elizabeth, children.
Blasingame, Thos., (Will). Wife and children. (Not named).
Bunch, Calloway, (Will). Wife, Nancy, children.
Bower, Thos., (Inventory).
Barten, Barberster, (Will). Wife, Elizabeth, 6 sons named.

Compton, Varnel, (Inventory).
Curd, Wm., (Inventory). Daniel Curd, Admr.
Carver, Henry, (Inventory).
Chason, Joseph, (Inventory).
Chaplain, W., (Inventory). Elizabeth Chaplain, Admx.
Chapman, Abner, (Inventory).
Cole, Zacheus, (will). Wife, Mary, children named.
Chastin, Joseph, (Inventory). Division to number of children.
Camp, Josias, (Inventory).
Cowles, Edmund, Jr., (Will). One son named.

Dobson, Elias, (Inventory)
Dye, Benjamin, (Will). Wife, Fanny, children not named.
Doyel, (Doyle) Thos., (Will). Wife, Mehuldy, children named.
Doyle, Gregory, (Evidently infant with guardian).

Eubank, William, (Will). Names children and grandchildren.

Ficklin, Joseph, (Will). Wife, Esther, names children.
Finney, William, Sr., (Will). Names children.
Ficklin, Robt. P., (Will). Names wife and other relatives.
Foster, James, (Inventory).

Gillespie, Daniel, deceased, (Inventory). Infant's account.
Grammer, John, Sr., (Will). Wife, Elizabeth, and children.
Goodman, Samuel, (Inventory).
Greer, Isiah, (Will). Wife, Mary, and many children named.

Hale, Mathew, (Inventory).
Hudspeth, Joseph, (Will). Wife, Anna, children named.
Hill, Moses, (Inventory).
Halsey, Elijah, (Inventory).
Hodge, Wm., (Inventory). Alice Hodge, widow, heirs named in sett
Hendricks, James, (Will). Wife, Mary, children, but not named.

Hickerson, Thos., (Inventory). Wife, Mary, Admx.
Howard, Chas., (Inventory).
Hendricks, John, Sr., (Will). Wife, Fanny, children not named.

Jones, Wm. and Eliz. (Named in estate of Daniel Gillispie).
Johnson, John, (Inventory).
Jenny, Abel, (Inventory).

King, Robt., (Inventory).
Key, Simon, (Will). Wife, Eliz., children named.
Kerby, David, (Will). Wife, Elizabeth, number of children named.
    (The vital statistics state that he was born in Franklin County,
    Virginia, and that he died December 17, 1852, aged 95 years, 1
    month, and 25 days).

Lowry, Jas., (Inventory). Jane Lowry, guardian to infant children.
Loyd, Job, (Inventory). Chas. Loyd, Admr.
Landers, Henry, (Inventory).
Lucas, Nathaniel (Will). Wife, Sarah, many children named, refer-
    ence to lands he own in Virginia.
Long, Mary, (Inventory).
Lyle, Manas, (Manaseth), (Inventory).
Lightfoot, Claybourn, (Inventory).
Lewallen, (Llewellyn?) Wm., (Will). Wife, Miriam, children not named.
Lloyd, Chas., (Will). Wife, Catherine, children named.
Lowry, Wyatt, (Will). Names brother only.

McGinnis, Thos. S., (Inventory).
Magnis, Perrygreen, (Will). Wife, Mary, etc.
Madison, Rowland, (Inventory).
Murry, John, (Inventory).
McColey, Daniel, (Will). Leaves all to son.
Morris, Valentine, (Will). Wife, Ruth, and number of children named.
McCurry, John, (Will). Wife Lidy, and many children not named.
Miller, Isaac, (Will). Wife, Margaret and others named.
Marshall, John, (Inventory). Mary, Wm., Gilbert Marshall bought at
    the sale.
Moore, Robt., (Will). Wife, Mary and children named.
Motley, John, (Will). Wife, Elizabeth and many children named.
Mannen, (Kannen) Wm., (Will). Children named .
Moberly, Chas., (Inventiry).
Miller, George, (Will). Wife, Mary, children named.
Moore, George, (Inventory).
Mirrison, John, (Inventory).
Morrow, John, (Inventory).
McFadin, Jonathan, (Inventory).

Nesler, Joseph, (Will). Wife, Jenny, son named.

Philips, Martha, deceased, (Inventory).
Perry, Thos., (Inventory).

Rowlins, (Rollins?) Chas., (Inventory).
Rowland, Daniel, (Inventory).
Roberson, John, (Inventory).
Ross, Wm., (Inventory).
Reatherford, (Rutherford?) John, (Inventory).
Reid, James, (Will). Wife, Anney, many children named.

Robinson, Jeremiah, (Will). Wife, Isabell, many children and in-laws named.

Shipman, Daniel, (Inventory).
Stuart, Chas., (Will). Wife, Elinor, children, reference to other State.
Stice, Chas., (Will). Wife, Caty, children named.
Strother, Robt., (Will). Number of children named.
Stump, Frederick, (Inventory).
Stewart, Wm., (Inventory).
Stoval, Bartholomew, (Will). Wife, Susannah, many heirs named.
Stewart, Wm., (Inventory). Sarah Stewart, Admx., infant orphans mentioned.
Smith, Jacob, (Inventory).
Smith, George, (Will). Wife, Elizabeth, 11 children named.
Stuart, James, Sr., (Will). Wife, Mary, children and in-laws named
Snowden, Jacob, (Inventory).
Simmons, Hannah, (Inventory).
Stewart, Benj., (Inventory).

Tilley, James, (Will). Wife, Martha and children named.
Taylor, Wm. ,(Will). Wife, Rhoda, children and brother.
Tirgert, (Tigert) James, (Will). Wife, Joan, number of children named.
Tiller, Thos. (Inventory).
Turner, Hardin, (Will). Wife, Rachel, many children named.

Venable, Joseph, Sr., (Will). Wife, Lucy, children and others named.

Williams, James, (Inventory).
Williams, John, (Will). Wife, Silvery, and children not named.
Wheatley, Daniel, (Will). Wife, Mary, many children named.
Wright, Winkfield, (Wingfield), (Inventory). Many of same name at the sale.
Wren, Nicholas, (Will). Wife, Elizabeth, sons named.
Whitsitt, Samuel, (Will). Wife, Elizabeth, names many children, (6 sons and 8 daughters).
Whitten, Elijah, (Inventory).

WOODFORD COUNTY

(Formed from Fayette County, 1788)

INVENTORIES AND ESTATES APPRAISED

Names appearing in this index are not included in General Index

Allison, Chas., 1792

Bailey, Samuel, 1791

Cowin, Samuel, 1790
Curry, John, 1795
Cook, Hose, 1792
Cook, Jesse, 1793
Cox, Agnes, (widow of Samuel Cox), dower, 1794

Grinstead, Wm., 1791
Crim, Peter, 1790

Davison, Robt., 1790

Edwards, Uriah, 1792
Egbert, Laurance, 1791

Division between widow, Elizabeth Plough (?); David, Dellancy, Sally, Jas., Lawrence, orphans. Dec. 1791

Fulton, Wm., 1791

Hastings, Wm., 1789
Hatton, Robt., 1792
Hatton, Wm., 1794

Little, Nancy, 1792

Morris, Brinkley, 1791
Moss, Elizabeth (late widow of Edmund Woolridge) dower, 1792

Mastin, Lewis, 1793
McHarg, (Harge) Robt., 1792
McCumpsey, Robt., 1789

Nash, John, 1793

Roberts, Wm., 1791

Sample, John, 1793
Smith, Thos., 1793
Samuel, Giles, acct. as gdn. of Peter and Larkin Samuel, orphans of Jesse Samuel, decd., Jan. 1794

Todd, Robt., 1792

WILLS FROM BOOK A

ALLISON, JOHN—To wife; son, Halber; daus., Sarah and Isabella, in hands of Alexander McClure; division among chdn. when of age. Extrs.: wife, Isabell and David Steele. Written Nov. 3, 1791. Wts.: Jas. Stevenson, Wm. Elliott, Jas. Risk. Probated May, 1792.

BELL, THOS.—To wife, Elizabeth, and at her death division among chdn.; two sons, Robt. and Wm., land near Ky. River and to build their mother suitable house upon said land; money due from Wm. Leigh of Rockfish to be divided among surviving chdn.; grandson, Thos. Montgomery; to Mrs. Elizabeth Bell, widow of Jno. Bell, decd., and at her death to her chdn. Extrs.: wife and son, Thos. Written Sept. 9, 1791. Wts.: Samuel Shannon, Chapman Taylor, Lewis Snell, Wm. Coleson. Probated April, 1793.

GRANT, SAMUEL—"Of Fayette Co." Wife, Lydia; son, Elijah; dau., Elizabeth Grant; my two chdn., Elizabeth and Elijah. Extrix.: wife, Lydia, Extrs.: Elijah Craig, Wm. Grant, Jr., Irael Grant. Son, when 21 yrs. old, dau., when 18 yrs. old or marries to receive portion. Written Aug. 10, 1787. Wts.: Henry Cave, Henry Herndon, Francis Stewart. Probated Sept. 1, 1789.

HOLEMAN, HENRY—"Of Fayette Co., Va." (later Ky.). Wife, Jane; to eldest son, Nicholas; son, Edward; three daus., Rozetta, Elizabeth and Mary; three sons, Wm., Isaac and Jesse £75 for purchase of lands over the Ohio; three sons and four daus., Sarah, Anne, Jane and Martha. Extrs.: son, Edward and David Daret, Richard Rue. Written March 6, 1789. Wts.: Jas. Fisher, Edward Holman, Geo. Holman, Sarah Williams. Probated Sept. 1, 1789.

JANUARY, PETER—"Of Fayette Co., Va." (later Ky.). Aged and infirm; to sons, Samuel and John; son-in-law, Wm. McConnell; if either of two sons die before 21 yrs. of age or marry, then to surviving one; wife, Deborah; sons, James and Ephriam, Samuel and John and dau., Sarah if she should move into district of Ky. Extrs.: sons, Jas. and Ephriam. Written Feb. 26, 1787. Wts.: Caleb Wallace, James C. Frisco, Samuel Walker, Michael Kirkham. Probated July, 1789.

JACK, FRANCES—To dau., Elizabeth Jack; dau., Jane Jack; dau., Frances Jack; son, Samuel; dau., Nancy; son, Patrick. Extrs.: Jno. Watkins and Cave Johnson. Written May 30, 1789. Wts.: Jno. Jones, Geo. Admire. Probated Oct. 6, 1789. H. Marshall as gdn. in acct. with Samuel Patrick and Nancy Jack, Sept. 1791.

JOHNSON, JOSEPH—"Of Fayette Co., Va." (later Ky.) To wife, Mary; son, Benj.; child wife is now pregnant with. Extrix.: wife. Written June 30, 1788. Wts.: Jas. Rentfro, Elijah Creed, Jeremiah Rucker. Date of probate not recorded.

JOHNSON, THOS.—To wife, Elizabeth; eldest son, David, when of age; son, Silas; four daus., Mary, Ann, Betsey, Salley; property at wife's disposal until chdn. come of age. Extrs.: wife, Joseph Hughes, Thos. Reed of Fayette. Written Aug. 24, 1792. Wts.: Daniel Veatch, Jeremiah Veatch, Arthur Ingram. Probated Oct. 1792.

JAMERSON, JAMES—"School Master on South Elkhorn." Wife, Marthiah; friend, Jas. Waugh, School Master; friend, Jas. Bain, School Master. Extrs.: James Waugh, Jas. Bain. Written Feb. 22, 1791. Wts.: Alex. Dunlap, Jno. Underwood, Ann Crow. Probated Nov. 1791.

McBRIDE, JAMES—"Of Antrim Township, Cumberland Co., Pa." Sister, Mary's two sons, James and Henry McBride, land in Antrim Township; sister Jean's chdn., preemption right in Ky.; sister Hannah's chdn. all other claims in Ky. Extr.: Jas. Poe of Cumberland Co., Pa. Written April 3, 1783. Wts.: Joseph McClean, John Maxwell. Probated Nov. 1790.

McNEIL, THOS—To son, Daniel, if he lives to age of 21, and if he dies, property to be divided among surviving daus.; wife, Elizabeth; son, John. Extrs.: wife and bro., Jonathan. Written May 27, 1790. Probated ____ 1790.

PEMBERTON, CHAS.—To wife, Sarah; dau., Delph Gatewood; dau., Elizabeth Edwards; son, Bennet, large Bible, etc.; dau., Nancy Owens; mentions suit brought by Henry Gatewood. Extr.: son, Bennet. Written Jan. 1790. Wts.: Samuel Cox, John Price, Jr., Wm. Trueman. Probated April, 1792.

PROCTOR, JOHN—To wife, Suckey; support of chdn. until youngest child is of age. Extrs.: wife and Jno. Ellis. Written Jan. 23, 1790. Wts.: Richard Young, Jno. Arnold, Sowyel Woolfolk. Probated Feb. 2, 1790.

RICE, GEO.—"Late of Frederick Co., Va., now of Woodford." Father to live in family during his life; land in Ohio purchased of Henry Banks who derived title from John Champ Carter, half of Pierce Holland's land, land purchased of Anderson, land on Cumberland in State, Military land assigned by Jno. Harvies, also land in name of John Slaughter patented in name of Andrew Waggoner and all expenses of Pierce Holens (Nolins?) pd. by him to his bro. John Rice's four sons in payment for land, sd. bro. willed to be sold and money laid out in Western lands; all interest in Western waters to six chdn. (not named) equal division to be made; land in partnership with Robt. Hollingsworth, to four nieces, Mary Rice, Sary Rice, Elizabeth Boyd and Jean Sullivan, wife of Wm. Sullivan;

bro., Edmund Rice; wife, Elizabeth while widow to remain on plantation in Frederick and she bring up chdn. until 21 yrs. old. Extrs.: wife, Andrew Waggoner, Jas. McDonald, Jno. Mitter, Micajah Roach. Written Aug. 4, 1792. Wts.: T. Marshall, Marquis Calmes, Daniel Preston. Probated Oct. 1792.

SEARCY, BARTLETT—"Of Fiat Co., Va., (Fayette? Co. Ky.) To wife, Ann; son, John Morgan Searcy; dau., Elizabeth Searcy, land held in partnership with Col. Marshall to be held for schooling of son and dau., John and Elizabeth. Extrs.: wife, Col. Daniel Boone, W. Flanders Calloway. Written Sept. 17, 1784. Wts.: Andrew Paull, Squire Boone, Jesse Bazan (Bryan?). Codicil: Two chdn., John and Elizabeth; Atty. John Brown to bring suits, to have charge of land assigned by John Brown of Bedford Co., to himself and John Fowler. Dated Jan. 8, 1789. Wt.: Wm. Phillips. Probated Sept. 1790.

TODD, ROBT.—To wife, Jane; son, Wm.; wife pregnant; if chdn. die to Jno. Parker's second dau. Extrs.: wife, Richard Steele, Jno. Parker. Probated Jan. 30, 1792.

THOMPSON, ANTHONY—To dau., Eleanor Thompson; dau., Judith Bell out of land I am to have of Anthony Thornton; son, Robt., certificate on an order to him to receive of Samuel Brockman; to Susanna Thompson; to Betsey Thompson; dau., Susanna under age; son, Henry after his mother's death or he comes of age; wife, Ann. Written May 7, 1794. Wts.: Moses Ogden, John Blanton, Wm. Blanton. Probated Oct. 1794.

WEST, EDWARD—To son, Edward and dau., Betsey Cumins (?), property previously given them; wife, Elizabeth; sons, Wm., John, Thomas, Lewis and James; daus., Polly West, Peggy West and Sally West. Extrs.: sons, Wm. and Thos. Written Dec. 5, 1791. Wts.: Jas. Martin, Adam Johnston. Probated April, 1792.

WOOLRIDGE, EDMUND—To wife; four sons, Edmund, Samuel, Watkins and Powhatan under the age of sixteen years. Extrs.: John Watkins, Henry Watkins, Thos. Woolridge Walthal. Written Apr. 28, 1791. Wts.: Wm. Hill, Thos. Ray, Pageatton Coleman. Probated Sept. 1791.

DEED ABSTRACTS, COURT ORDERS, SUITS

BOURBON COUNTY

RECORDS FROM ORDER BOOKS

October Court, 1798—Jno. Moore, inft. orphan of Thomas Moore, made choice of Barney Giltner and Ct. appointed same gdn. to Barney F. Moore, inft. orphan of deceased. Robt. Wilmot, Secty.

Wm. McClelland appt. gdn. of Andrew and Geo. Moore, orphans of Thomas Moore, decd. Wm. Griffith, Secty.

Rainey Mahan and Elizabeth Mahan, inft. orphans of Jno. Mahan, decd., chose Jno. Clarkson, gdn. and Ct. appointed Jno. Clarkson, gdn. of Wm., Jno. and Agnes Mahan, inft. orphans of Jno. Mahan. Anselm Clarkson, Secty.

On motion of Jno. Clarkson, ordered Charles Smith, Jno. Smith and David Clarkson, or any two, assign Agnes, now wife of said John Clarkson (late Agnes Mahan, widow of Jno. Mahan, decd.) her dower in lands.

Mary Norton, inft. dau. of David Norton, abt. 10 yrs. apprenticed to Jas. Fulton to learn housewifery.

Robt. Edmiston, inft. orphan of Robt. Edmiston, decd., chose Jno. Edmiston gdn. and Ct. apptd. Jno. Edmiston, gdn. of Elizabeth, inft. of said Robt., decd., with Jas. Alexander, Secty.

Deposition of Edward Bradley, aged about 69 yrs., states: In yr. 1776 he in company with Dominick Flanagan came from Boonesborough to McGee's and made improvement which he sold same yr. to Jacob Grotts.

Jas. Park apptd. gdn. to Jno. Park, inft. orphan of Jno. Park, decd. Wm. Griffith, Secty.

November Court, 1798—Letter of Atty. from Joseph Walkins (Watkins?) to Wm. P. Bernard with acknowledgment before Justices of Goochland Co., Va.

Phoebe Ross, Nancy Ross and Mary Ross, inft. orphans of Henry Ross, decd., chose Jno. Love, gdn. and Ct. appointed Jno. Love, gdn. to Elizabeth Ross also orphan of said Henry.

Deposition of David Hughes, aged 41 yrs. to establish land of Chesley Woodward: Became acquainted with place, Spring of '80.

Deposition of Michael Stoner, aged 50 yrs. in the same states: He marked spot in 1775 on what was known as Michael Stoner's path.

January Court, 1799—Letter of Atty. from Wm. Ready, Hannah Dinwiddie, Jno. Bennett and Jno. Bennett, gdn. for Jane Dinwiddie to Jno. Grohogan. Acknowledged in Lincoln Co.

Division of land between Joseph Field, Jno. Field, Thos. Field and Geo. Field, patented in name of Henry Field.

Jas. Congleton apptd. gdn. to Wm., Elizabeth, Mary, John, inft. orphans of Jno. Congleton, decd. Jno. Scott, Secty.

On motion of Chas. Bristol and wife, Margaret, late Margaret Payne, Extrix. of will of Joseph Payne, decd., to summon Waford Payne, another Extr. to show cause for not entering inventory of said decedent's estate.

March Court, 1799—Ordered that Samuel Smith, orphan of Joseph

Smith,, decd., 15 yrs. of age, Christmas last, be bound to Jno.
Keevan to learn trade.

Nathaniel Haydon, inft. orphan of Nehemiah Haydon, decd., 13
yrs. next June, to be bound to Aaron Griffing to learn trade.

Jno. Burns apptd. gdn. to Polly and Joe McMullins, inft. orphans
of Jno. McMullins, decd. Thos. Shannon, Secty.

Benjamin Jones, inft. orphan of Jno. Jones, decd., chose Jno. Jones,
gdn. Jno. Kiser, Secty.

Division of lands of Otwell Worle, decd., among widow and following: Jno. Hinkston, Jno. Worle, Samuel Worle, Jas. Worle,
Robt. Worle. Division made Feb. 1, 1799.

Ordered to settle with Sidney Shannon, late Sidney Haydon,
Admrx. of Nehemiah Haydon, decd.

On motion of Robt. Peery, Secty. for Isbel, now wife of Hugh
McKee, late Isbel Sconce, Extrx. of Thos. Sconce, decd., ordered
to summons Isbel to show why she not give Secty., etc.

April Court, 1799—Jas. Toy (Foy), aged 17 yrs., apprenticed to Geo.
Barnett to learn trade.

On motion of Jno. Jones, Secty. to Elizabeth, now wife of Joseph Williams, but late Elizabeth Hawker, admrx. of Jacob Hawker, decd., to summons said Joseph and Elizabeth to show why
they did not give counter Secty., etc.

Jno. Jacoby, inft. orphan of Francis Jacoby, decd., made choice
of Benj. Hallock for gdn. Frederica Jacoby, Secty.

September Court, 1799—Ruthey Baseman and Catherine Baseman, orphans of Jno. Baseman, decd., made choice of Jno. Owings and
Robert Willmott, gdns., respectively.

Depositions of David Williams, aged abt. 47 yrs., and Joseph
Robinett, aged 48 yrs., to establish land of Wm. Webb.

Deposition of Flanders Calloway, aged 47 yrs., to establish John
Smith's preemption.

Deposition of Isaac Clinkenbeard, aged abt. 41 yrs., to establish
entries of Wm. Clinkenbeard.

Valentine S. Peyton, orphan of Timothy Peyton, decd., chose Bayles
Grigsby, gdn. Archibald Marshall, surety.

Wm. Gosney, Jas. Gosney, Sally Gosney and Richd. Gosney, inft.
orphans of Wm. Gosney, decd., chose Benj. Hailey, gdn. Thos.
Jones, Robt. Collins, sureties.

Benj. Haily, appt. gdn. of Nancy Gosney, Polly Gosney, Fielding Gosney and Agnes Gosney, orphans of Wm. Gosney, decd.
Thos. Jones, Robt. Collins, sureties.

October Court, 1799—John Kennedy's Hrs. Division of Land. On motion of Zachariah Wheat and Nicholas Talbott, ordered that Jno. Boyd and Jas. Duncan, commrs., divide between Zachariah Wheat and Elizabeth; Josiah Ashurst and Rebeckah; Samuel Hatcher and Julia; Eli Kennedy; Joshua Rawlings and Sophia; Nicholas Talbott and Ary, and Washington Kennedy, hrs. of John Kennedy, decd., two tracts of 1000 a. each patented in name of John Kennedy, son of John Kennedy. Eli Kennedy apptd. gdn. of Washington Kennedy. Esther Kennedy, widow of John Kennedy, assigned her dower.

Elizabeth Brush, now wife of Michael Woolery, administratrix of Jas. Brush, decd.

December Court, 1799—Wm. Ellis' Hrs. division of land. On motion of Jas. True and wife, Nancy; Chas. Ellis; Walter Ellis and Polly Ellis, hrs. of Wm. Ellis, decd., commrs. divide land. John Ellis apptd. gdn. of Chas., Walter and Polly Ellis, under 21 yrs.

Robert Jones, orphan, abt. 6 yrs., apprenticed to Thos. Clarke.

January Court, 1800—Depositions to establish entry of John Fleming assignee of Benj. Harris, Jr. Jno. McIntire, of full age, deposeth: abt. yr. 1782 he came out in company with Jno. Fleming from Strode's Station to explore, etc.

Deposition of Daniel Boone to establish land of Thos. Almond.

Jacken Brush, infant orphan of Jas. Brush, decd., chose Jno. Carhagy his gdn. Jonathan Cormack, surety.

March Court, 1800—Deposition of Benj. Dunaway, of lawful age, to establish land of Jno. Davis. Deponent states: in yr. 1799 he made an improvement, and raised corn at Boonesborough in 1779. Joshua Stamper deposeth he came to place in question in 1780 with Jno. Douglas.

April Court, 1800—Deposition of Jacob Sodowsky, of lawful age, to establish land of Abrm. Hite, states: in yr. 1776 he assisted David Williams make improvement to which he objected, as location was too near his brother, Jas. Sodowsky's improvement.

Deposition of Jno. Donaldson, aged 31 yrs., to establish land of John Phelps, states: in spring of 1782 he, in company with Jno. Fleming and Major Thos. Swearingin, started from Strode's Station, etc.

June Court, 1800—Deposition of Wm. Markland, aged 45 yrs., to establish improvement made in yr. 1776 by Jno. Boggs, Jas. Matson, assignee. Deponent states: in yr. 1776 he came in company with John Boggs, Jas. Kelly and others and made improvement at place known as Beave Camp.

Deposition of Michael Cassady to establish land of Thos. Hartly, deposeth: in Dec., 1782, he was in company with Geo. Stockton, Sr., when he made entry for Thos. Hartly.

On motion of Samuel Lyon depositions taken to establish entry

of John Lyon. Wm. Markland, aged 45 yrs. deposeth: in yr.
1776 he, with John Lyon, John Virgin and others, came to the
improvement made by sd. John Lyon. John Virgin deposeth
the same.

Deposition of Simon Kenton to establish land of Jno. Tabb, deposeth: he believed it was in summer of 1781 he was sent by
Col. Trigg to notify Gen. Clarke, then expected to be on his
way down the Ohio, there being an Indian army out on that
route. He marked tree with K. In same summer Loughry was de-
feated by Indians. In fall of 1782 discovered he had more lo-
cations than warrants to cover and gave Wm. Kennedy the location in question which he entered in the name of Martin Pickett and Jno. Tabb.

September Court, 1800—Jno. Peery and Mary Peery, infant orphans
of Robt. Peery, decd., chose Jas. Morrow gdn.; and court apptd.
sd. James, gdn. to Thos., Jas. and Nancy Peery, orphans of sd.
Robert Peery.

Deposition of Jacob Jones, of lawful age, to establish land of
Abrm. Hite, deposeth: in spring of 1794 he settled on plantation where he found mark. Wm. Jones deposeth: in yr. 1794 he
was living with his father, Jacob Jones, etc.

Deposition of Flanders Calloway, aged 48 yrs., to establish land
of Jno. Arnold. In same instrument Oswald Townsend, aged
43 yrs., deposeth: in yr. 1796 the deponant, in company with
Richard Calloway, Nathaniel Hart, Thos. Hartgrove and Samuel
Henderson, came from Boonesborough to lower Blue Licks.

October Court, 1800—Commrs. ordered to set apart to Jno. Ross, one
of hrs. of Henry Ross, decd., his portion of personal estate of
decedant.

Deposition of John Smith, aged abt. 70 yrs., to establish land
of Archibald Bell (Beal) deposeth: he was at place in question
in yr. 1779 with one Jacob Sterns.

December Court, 1800—Deposition of Jno. Martin to establish land
of Isaac Ruddell, deposeth: he was employed to locate land
known as Martin's Cabbins for Reuben Searcy, and he with Geo.
Ruddell marked boundry between Ruddell and Searcy. Jas. Ruddell deposeth: he was with surveyors when land of Geo. Ruddell
was surveyed.

Deposition of Jas. Kelly, aged abt. 50 odd yrs., to establish land
of Samuel Lyon, deposeth: in 1776 he came with Thos. Dickerson
and others to the spring in question and assisted Jno. Lyon, Resin
Virgin, Jno. Virgin and Wm. Markland to cover a cabin, and
was informed regarding claim of one Wm. Hosking, etc.

January Court, 1801—Sarah Morin, infant orphan of Jas. Morin, chose
Wm. Stamps, gdn. Francis Callis, Wm. Hutchison, sureties. Wm.
Stamps appointed gdn. of Joseph, Elizabeth and Margaret Morin,
infant orphans of James Morin, decd.

Joseph Kennedy's Hrs. Division of land. Nathan Kennedy, Rebecca Kennedy, Sophia Kennedy, Joseph Kennedy, Jacob Kennedy, all infant hrs., by Thos. Kennedy, gdn.; David Kennedy, Joseph Hildreth and wife, Elizabeth.

March Court, 1801—Adam Jacoby, infant orphan of Francis L. Jacoby, chose Frederica Jacoby gdn. Ralph Jacoby, surety.

Edward Tucker's Hrs. Division. Widow, Ann Clements; Jno. Tucker; Wm. Tucker; Alexander Tucker; Eleanor Speaks.

April Court, 1801—Joseph Russell, infant orphan of Joseph Russell, aged 12 yrs., apprenticed to Jno. Tillitt.

George Hornback, infant orphan of Simon Hornback, decd., chose Abraham Hornback gdn. Jno. Artman, Wm. Alkire and Geo. McCown, sureties.

Barbara Hornback, infant orphan of Simon Hornback, decd., chose Michael Hornback gdn.

Deposition of David Williams to establish land of David Williams and Jacob Sodowsky. David Williams deposeth: in spring of 1774 he was employed by Benj. Casey to improve land in Ky., this he did in 1776 on now Strode's Creek leading from Boonesborough to Harrod's Lick; was employed in 1780 by Peter Casey to again come to Ky. as agent. He left Benj. Casey, "now deceased," on the So. branch of Patomac when he came out and found him there on his return. By contract with Peter Casey was entitled to one half. Jacob Sodowsky deposeth in same.

Jacob Lair apptd. gdn. to Jacken Brush, infant orphan of Jas. Brush, decd. Michael Woolery, surety.

June Court, 1801—Chas. Smith and Wm. Clarkson, gent., commrs. to settle with admrs. of Jno. Baseman, decd., acct. and with late gdn. to Catherine and Ruth Baseman, orphans of sd. Jno. Baseman.

July Court, 1801—Jacob Allenthorpe, infant orphan, abt. 12 yrs., apprenticed to Aaron Griffing.

September Court, 1801—Will of Joshua Rawlings proved by Jas. Fleming and Jas. Campbell wts., and Sophia Rawlings and Nicholas Talbott, extrs. Sureties, Eli Kennedy, Washington Kennedy and Josiah Ashurst. Other extrs. named were Wm. Forman, Thos. Donnell (Darnall).

Deposition of Jas. Galloway, aged abt. 51 yrs., to establish land of Wm. Davidson. Deposeth: he, with Moses Kirkpatrick, made improvement in 1776 on claim for Adam Coons, he had lived for 14 years about 5 miles from the place.

October Court, 1801—Deposition of David Williams to establish land of Martin Nall, deposeth: in 1775 or 6 he was in company with Peter Higgins and others, and assisted sd. Peter in making improvement, conducted Henry Higgins to place where he built a cabin. Robt. Shanklin deposeth in same.

December Court, 1801—Michael Hornback, Jr., apptd. gdn. to Elizabeth, Rachel, Samuel and Michael Hornback, infant hrs, of James Hornback, decd. Michael Hornback and Ezekiel Hopkins, sureties.

January Court, 1802—Deposition of Patrick Jordon to establish land of Jno. Haggin. Deposeth: in spring of 1799, in company with Thos. Clarke, was on way to Martin's Station; a man named Berry informed him John Haggin was about erecting a station on that place and he had joined sd. Haggin in cutting the logs and was going there to live. In month of Aug. or Sept. preceding, while at Harrodsburg, Jno. Haggin had informed him he would erect station and when he set out he accompanied him part of way. Hugh Shannon deposeth: in fall of 1778 he came to place with Jno. Haggin in order to build for sd. Haggin, himself and others, having thought of living there as soon as station was erected. Patrick Jordon deposeth: in 1776, in company with Jno. Townsend and sd. Jno. Haggin, made improvement.

April Court, 1802—Thos. Darnall and Wm. Furman apptd. gdns. to Susanna, Anne and Lloyd Rawlings, infant orphans of Joshua Rawlings, decd. Jno. Morton and Chas. Lander, sureties.

Jas. A. McClure, infant orphan of Andrew McClure, decd., chose Jno. Boyd and Robt. Trimble gdns. Same apptd. gdns, of Eleanor W. McClure, Mary McClure and Andrew McClure, infant orphans of sd. Andrew McClure, decd., with Geo. McConn, Jno. McKinney, Wm. Hillis and Edward Shropshire, sureties.

Jas. Beard, infant orphan of Mary Beard, abt. 4 yrs., was apprenticed to David Ellis. Rhoda Beard, infant orphan of same, aged 6 yrs., apprenticed to Chas. Hedge. Anne Beard, infant orphan of same, aged abt. 3 yrs., apprenticed to Peter Edwards.

July Court, 1802—James Brush's Hrs. Division of Estate. Polly Brush, Sally Brush, Nancy Brush.

August Court, 1802—Jno. McCormack, infant orphan of Jno. McCormack, decd., chose Wm. McClelland gdn. Security, Willis Field.

Robt. Ellis, infant orphan of Jno. Ellis, decd., chose David Ellis gdn. Securities, Wm. Clarkson, Wm. Ellis.

David Fisher apptd. gdn. to Jacob Ogler, infant orphan of Jacob Ogler, decd. Sureties, Jno. Burger and Peter Schooltz. Samuel Ogler, infant orphan of same, chose David Fisher gdn.

Elizabeth Ward, widow of Benj. Ward, decd., apptd. gdn to Wm., Jas., Susanna, Abraham, Joseph, Malinda Ward, infant orphans of Benj. Ward. David Jamison, surety.

On motion of Ezekiel Mitchell and wife, Elizabeth, late Elizabeth Galloway, commrs. apptd. to allot sd. Elizabeth dower in estate of her late husband, Wm. Galloway.

November Court, 1802—John Mahan's Hrs. Division of estate. Rainey Mahan, Chas. Mahan, Wm. Mahan, Agnes Mahan, Jno. Mahan.

Wm. Phillips, gdn. to Ruth Baseman, hr. of Jno. Baseman, decd., commrs. to settle with sd. Phillips.

January Court, 1803—Deposition of Jas. Ruddell, aged 44 yrs., to establish land of John Logan, deposeth: he resided at Ruddell's Station 1779-1780, recalls improvement in question to be second one from station, etc. John Conway, aged abt. 44 yrs., deposeth: he resided at Ruddell's Station 1779-1780. Depositions taken March, 1802.

Nancy Drummond, infant orphan of Alexander Drummond, decd., aged 6 yrs., 6th of Nov. last, apprenticed to Jno. Currey.

Jas. Galloway, infant orphan of Wm. Galloway, aged 15 yrs., apprenticed to Jno. Curry. Joseph Galloway, infant orphan of Wm. Galloway, aged abt. 13 yrs., apprenticed to same.

Deposition of Augustine Eastin to establish land of Julius Clarkson, deposeth: in yr. 1782 he made entry for Christopher Clark, assnee. for Jas. Parberry.

March Court, 1803—Jno. Godman, infant orphan of Jeremiah Godman, decd., aged 7 yrs., the 27th Sept. apprenticed to Wm. B. Godman.

Commrs. apptd. to set apart to Rebecca Mitchell, late Rebecca Galloway, widow of Wm. Galloway, decd., her dower.

Wm. B. Godman, infant orphan of Jeremiah Godman, decd., aged 16 yrs. 3rd next, apprenticed to Aaron Griffing.

Francis Ray apptd. gdn. to Sarah, Peggy, Jas., Robt., and Elizabeth Turner, infant orphans of Jesse Turner, decd. Sureties, Wm. Henry, Robt. Hamilton.

Jno. Moore apptd. gdn. to Rebecca and Elizabeth Patton, infant orphans of Wm. Patton, decd. Surety, Samuel Dellon.

April Court, 1803—Elijah Hopper apptd. gdn. to Jno. Baseman.

Joshua Hall apptd. gdn. to Prescilla Baseman, infant hr, of Jno. Baseman, decd., in room of Wm. Phillips.

Deposition of Jno. McIntire to establish land of Andrew Swearingen, deposeth: he came to salt spring in 1781. John Donaldson deposeth: he visited entry 1779 and was then abt. 11 yrs. of age. Wm. Wells deposeth: He was first acquainted with location in 1789. Wm. Suduth acquainted with place in 1785.

September Court, 1803—Deposition of Patrick Jordon, aged 54 yrs., to establish James Wright's (Military) survey. In yr. 1775 came with Jno. Floyd, Jacob Baughman, Spottswood Dandridge and Thos. Carpenter to place in question, called for in patent as Jas. Wright's Military survey. Daniel Chambers told him his son, Silas Chambers, had blazed out corner abt. 1784-5. McDowell's Military survey was above Wright's on creek.

Samuel Henderson, Nathaniel Rogers and Wm. Mitchell apptd. commrs. to settle with Thos. Darnell and Wm. Firman accts. as gdn. of estate of Susannah Rawlings, Lloyd Rawlings and Anne Rawlings, infant orphans of Joshua Rawlings, decd.

Ordered Jonathan Davis apptd. gdn. to Polly Collins, infant orphan of Elijah Collins, decd. Jas. McClelland and Isaac Tull, sureties.

Deposition of Jno. Kennedy to establish land of Joseph Penn deposeth: he came out to establish improvements of John Kennedy (son of John) on Kennedy's Creek; met at Thomas' Station and proceeded to location where Joseph Kennedy's improvement was made and from thence to improvement of John Kennedy (son of John). John Kennedy (son of Daniel), abt. 44 yrs., deposeth: in March, 1776, agreed to come out with Thos. Kennedy and at same time John Kennedy (son of John) and Joseph Kennedy made application to deponant with Thos. Kennedy to look out for land for them. Deponant, with Thos. Kennedy, set out on journey, arrived at Boonesborough in April, where deponant met with Michael Stoner with whom he had been long acquainted, both of same occupation having wrought a considerable time in Frederick Town. Stoner knew of no claim on certain land except that of David Gass who had marked trees at a spring, which spring now occupied by Mr. Breckenridge, etc. Edward Wilson, aged abt. 65 yrs., deposeth: in 1782 he surveyed preemption.

October Court, 1803—Deposition of Jno. Kennedy (son of Daniel), aged abt. *54 yrs., to establish Joseph Kennedy's land, deposeth: in 1776 he agreed to come out with Thos. Kennedy, etc. *See foregoing deposition, gives age "abt. 44 yrs."

November Court, 1803—Dicey Anderson, widow of Geo. Anderson, and Reubin Anderson admrs. of Geo. Anderson, decd.

December Court, 1803—Deposition of Jacob Sodowsky to establish land of James Parberry, deposeth: in 1776 he came, in company with David Williams and Jas. Parberry, and they assisted Jas. Parberry build cabin.

January Court, 1804—Deposition of Michael Cassady to establish land of Henry Cox, deposeth: in 1784 he camped with Joshua Bennett. John McIntire and Thos. Jones depose in same instrument.

Wm. Bell and John Bell, infant orphans over 14 yrs., chose Jno. Shawhan gdn. Surety, Wm. Patton.

September Court, 1804—On motion of Jas. Gess and Jno. True, ordered that commrs. divide tract in Bourbon, part of estate of Jno. Gess, decd., among his hrs., to wit: Jno. Gess, Jas. Gess, Nancy Gess, Betsey Cocker, Sally Gess and John True, who intermarried with Jemima Gess and also Thos. Gess, Wm. Gess, Susannah Gess and Polly Gess, last four infant hrs. of Jno. Gess, decd., of whom Sarah Gess is gdn.

October Court, 1804—Deposition of Jno. McIntire to establish land of Thos. Swearingen entry of 1000 acres made in 1782, deposeth: he lived at Strode's Station in yr. 1780 at which time he became acquainted with Plum Lick. Isaac Clinkenbeard states Plum Lick was place of notoriety to hunters from Strode's, he knew it in 1780, trace led from Station to Plum Lick. Jno. Donaldson deposeth: was familiar with place in 1782.

November Court, 1804—Commrs. to allot to Frances Branham, late Frances Sanford, widow of Reubin Sanford, decd., her dower in decedant's estate.

Jane Sanford, infant orphan of Reubin Sanford, chose Wm. B. Branham, gdn. Surety, Jno. M. Hutchinson. Note: Reubin Sanford d. Albemarle Co., Va.

Agnes Mahan, infant orphan of John Mahan, decd., chose Chas. Smith gdn. Nathan Smith, surety. John Mahan, infant orphan of same, chose Chas. Smith gdn. Surety, Soloman Hoggins.

December Court, 1804—Deposition of John Martin, aged 61 yrs., to establish James Wright's Military survey, deposeth: in yr. 1775, he having settled near the plantation where "Col. James Garrard now lives," travelled the old Buffalo road near a spring where "James Wright now lives," and discovered a camp had been made, later in 1775 Jno. Floyd told him he had made a Military survey at the place for one Huggard (Haggard) and others, etc.

Deposition of James Ruddell, aged between 46 and 47 yrs., to establish Isaac Ruddell's preemption, states: in yr. 1783 a certain Thos. Allen, surveyor for Fayette Co., with Joseph Love and Geo. Ruddell, came to make entry of Isaac Ruddell's settlement on Flat Run.

January Court, 1805—Administration of estate of Jno. Jacobs granted Anne Jacobs, widow, and Jackey Hite. Sureties, Geo. Hughes, Jno. Mulherrin.

Deposition of Isaac Ruddell, aged 46 yrs., to establish land of Ephraim Gaither's 2049 acre survey, states he lived at Strode's Station from 1780 to 1785, and was well acquainted with salt spring trace, leading from Boonesborough to lower Blue Licks. Wm. Clinkenbeard, aged 43, deposeth in same, and states he lived at Strode's Station from 1781 to 1784. Joshua Stamper, aged 51, deposeth in same, and states he resided at Strode's Station from 1780 to 1784. Benedict Couchman, aged 49 yrs., in same states he lived at Strode's Station 1780 to 1785. Edward Wilson, aged 66 yrs., states in same, that prior to 1783 he had in his possession several Va. Land Treasury Warrants and had Benedict Couchman assist him in locating said land; he made beginning of Gaither's entry, entered surveys for Peter Henry, Moses Hunter, Duvall Keeves, Anthony Noble, one Byars, Chas. Bryan and David Campbell. He had interest in these but sold to John Wilson, Jesse Enlaw and Geo. Bathe and part of Noble's to Stephen Peyton.

March Court, 1805—John Todd, Sr., apptd. gdn. to Edward Todd, Jane Todd, Polly Todd, to attend to division of tract of Edward Todd, decd., located on Silas Creek.

Administration of estate of Frederick Tarr granted Jno. Gass, Jas. Alexander and Joseph Patton. Surety, Jas. Gass.

Wm. B. Branham apptd. gdn. of Willoughby Sanford and Lucinda Sanford, infant orphans of Reubin Sanford, decd. Surety, Thos. Stark.

April Court, 1805—Wm. D. Jackson apptd. gdn. of Catherine, Samuel, David and Rachel Brown, infant orphans of James Brown, decd. Sureties, David Irvine, Jno. Porter.

Wm. Routt, Jr., apptd. gdn. to Nancy and Thos. Woodyard, infant orphans of Henry Woodyard, decd. Wm. Routt, Sr., surety.

ORDER BOOK A, PAGE 372

The Sheriff, administrator of sundry estates—men who were killed in the "late campaign."

February Court, 1791—

John Spiller	William Miller	Moses Ferguson
Benjamin Ogle	Brinkley Morris	John Liry
Jacob Balm	James Sample	Benjamin Ramph
Charles Low	Alexander Brown	William Reed
Charles Stuard	John Smallwood	Thomas Lucas
Jenkin Philips		

DEPOSITION BOOK A

(Old book found in the basement of the Bourbon County Court House, by Julia S. Ardery, and placed in office of County Clerk.)

Nov. 25, 1816—Deposition of Wm. Steele, taken at home of Jno Nesbitt, north side Hinkson Creek, to establish entry of 400 a and preemption of 1000 a. entered by Wm. Nesbit, states he, deponent, came to Ky. 1775 in co. with Wm. Nesbitt, Joseph Houston and others to the matter of about fourteen, at lower Blue Licks his co. was joined by John Hinkson, John Martin and others who had just come into Ky. That each company sent our parties to explore, and on their return whole co. as well as that of Hinkston and others traveled along the buffalo trace now called Limestone, passing by Millersburg to Lexington until they came to the buffalo road now called Hinkston's trace, turned from Limestone road, that Hinkston's co. took Hinkston's trace and advanced to what is now called Hinkston's Station, that co. in which deponent was, entered Limestone trace until they came to buffalo trail, since called Ruddell's road, encamped on Miller's Run, that co. selected spots for improving and drew lots, deponent drew place on which he has since lived, and Wm. Nesbit improved on the place this day shown, that deponent in said yr. of 1775 assisted Wm. Nesbit in making his improvement, that co. of deponant was visited by co. from Hinkson's Station in 1775, after improvements were made; that John Martin, who established Martin's Station, was one of Hinkson's co. Martin's Station was about seven or eight miles from Wm. Nesbit's improvement, and Hinkson's Station about same distance. Deponent resided in Penn. in 1779 and in 1780 came to Ky., was at Martin's and Ruddle's Stations in 1780, that John Martin and John Haggin knew of improvement in 1779 or 1780, and he believes the following of Hinkson's co. knew of

Nesbit's improvement 1775 and upwards to 1780: P. Logan, Richard Clark, Joseph Cowper, Joseph Houston and Jno. Miller.

Deposition of Henry Thompson states he came to Ky. 1775 in company with Wm. Nesbit, Wm. Steele, Wm. McClintock, Jos. Houston and others to the number of abt. fourteen, that John Hinkson, John Martin, John Haggin and others to the number of abt. fourteen joined his company at Blue Licks, deponent left this country 1775 and did not return until 1784. Question by F. Marshall for self and those claiming under claim of Patty Harris, late Patty Wethers: "Did you not know where improvement was in 1775 or '76?" Deponent states he only heard of it, that the co. divided into companies of three or four persons, that Wm. Steele, Houston and, he believes, Wm. Flennand, Richard Clark improved with Nesbit in 1775, and he heard Wm. Craig, Wm. Houston and Robert Thompson say they worked with Nesbit 1776, heard Nesbit say he intended improving on Thompson's run for his brother, that Nesbit came abt. harvest 1776 to Penn. from Ky., that Wm. Steele made improvement 1775.

Deposition of Wm. McClintock, Nov. 27, 1816, states he came to Ky. 1775, in co. with Wm. Steele, Jos. Houston, Wm. Nesbit and others; he was not in Ky. from 1775 to 1784.

Deposition of David Marshall, Nov. 27, 1816, states he came to Ky. 1783 to Lexington, and came with one James Powers to this part of the country and explored improvements of Wm. Steele and Wm. Nesbit; he understood said Powers was in Ky. 1780 and from Powers and others in neighborhood of said Powers was in old settlement.

Deposition of Wm. Steele, Nov. 29, 1816, states he, in company with Wm. Smith, made a survey of land for Nesbit.

Deposition of Robert Nesbit states he was with Wm. Steele, etc.

Depositions taken to establish Thos. Gist's Military Survey, March 13, 1817—Thos. Rogers, aged abt. 62, settled where he now lives, in Bourbon Co., 1788 or '89, some few yrs. subsequent several men came in search of Gist's survey—John Loverens deposed regarding same. John Frakes, aged abt. 40 yrs., states he settled on Stoner's fork in Bourbon Co., abt. 23 yrs. since. Alexander Barnett, aged 61 yrs., states abt. the yr. 1789 he settled where he resides.

Depositions taken Feb. 8, 1819—To be read in suit in chancery where Humphrey Marshall and others and formerly Thos. Weathers and wife are complts. and hrs. of Samuel Nesbit and others are deftds. Deposition of John Byrd states he came to Ky. in fall of 1779, settled at Ruddle's Station and remained in Station until June 1780; that in Feb., 1780, he went from said station in company with Isaac Ruddle and Wm. Marshall and came to a cabin and remained all night; that Ruddle had a warrant to lay on some land for the father of the deponant, and Ruddle said the cabin was Samuel Nesbit's improvement, and after he returned to the station James Ruddle and others knew of this improvement.

Depositions taken Apr. 15, 16, 1819—To establish preemption of John

Miller on Hinkstons Creek. Cave Johnston, at home of Robt. E. Miller at Millersburg, states he was deputy surveyor of Fayette Co. and made John Miller's original survey in 1783. Deposition of Jas. Feryman in same. Deposition of Wm. Miller states in April, 1775, he, in company with abt. four men, came to Ky., up Licking to lower Blue Licks and traversed the county to find suitable place to improve, that John Miller, Wm. Steele, Wm. Mc-Clintock, Alexander Pollock and others composed the company, that John Miller, Alexander Pollock, John Stear and himself built John Miller's improvement in 1775, and after all the company had improved they went back to Penn., same year, and in 1776 he, John Miller and Alexander Pollock and some others returned to Ky. Further states that when he and his co. landed at lower Blue Licks 1775 they met John Hinkston and his co. of abt. fifteen, that John Martin and Jas. Cooper were of Hinkston's co., that in 1776 John Miller and Alexander Pollock went to John Cooper's, who was another of Hinkston's co., and bought corn which he had raised in 1775. Wm. Steele states in 1775 he and about eight of his co. traveled toward Ky. River and met one David McGee from Boonesborough. Wm. McClintock deposeth he returned to Penn. 1775 and did not come back with others of said co., and not until 1784. Jas. McMillan deposeth he came to Boonesborough March, 1776, his brothers, John and Robert, came to Ky. 1775, he heard Simon Kenton, John Fleming and Jonathan Mc-Millan and one Cooper speak of Miller's improvement, that Wm. McClelland, Wm. Miller and Samuel Nesbit had improved about a mile or mile and quarter from Millersburg.

Depositions taken Apr. 23, 1819—To establish Wm. McClelland's land on waters of Hinkston. Col. Cave Johnson deposeth at the home of Elisha McClelland, that he surveyed said settlement in 1783. Deposition of Henry Swift in same. Deposition of Wm. Miller states he came to Ky. with seven or eight others in 1775 and in 1776 he and his brother, John and Jas. McGran made improvement for Wm. Mc-Clellan. Deposition of Caleb Masterson states he came to Ky. 1779 to Lexington and Bryan's Station and in 1780, he, with others, came from Bryan's Station to lower Blue Licks.

Feb. 28, 1923—Deposition of Charles Smith, now of Christian Co., formerly of Bourbon, taken at Wm. Simpson's Tavern, Bourbon Co., to establish land patented in name of Charles Smith, 3500 a., on Silas run, deposeth he surveyed tract for his father, Charles Smith, decd., in 1785.

SUITS IN CHANCERY—BOURBON COUNTY

(Records filed in book found in basement of Bourbon County Court House by Julia S. Ardery).

Depositions taken in Chancery Suit—To settle disputes between Thos. Respess, John Haggin and John Breckenridge, complainants, vs. Thos. McClanahan, defendant, filed Oct., 1799. Deposition of James Brown, of full age, deposeth he has been acquainted with Cooper's Run since Dec., 1784, and branch on which he lives has been known as West fork. Henry Wilson, Jr., deposeth: he has been acquainted with said run since fall of '80, having traveled

down said run with Capt. Chas. Gatliff and co. to Martin's and
Ruddle's Stations after they were taken by Col. Byrd and the
savages. Thos. Herndon deposeth: he was acquainted with said
fork since 1783. Jas. Garrard deposeth in same, also Patrick
Jordan and Thos. Whitledge. Geo. Finley deposeth: he saw Mary
Cooper, widow of James Cooper, who was killed by the Indians
in Ky., in the State of Penn., with her child, David Cooper, in 1776,
and continued there in Penn. until 1785 when they moved to Ky.
Zachariah Benson and Lewis Marshall, Joseph Case, John Morris
depose in same. Augustine Eastin states in 1783 Jas. Forbush was
pilot for himself and others to survey lands, that he understood
said Forbush had settled in this country 1776, and believes he was
with the first settlers at Bryant's Station. David Cooper, 28 yrs.
of age next July, states in the summer of '82 he was hunting on
Cooper's Run in company with Joshua Mounce and came to a
spring where he believes Mr. Elkin (Samuel) now lives, and he
told deponant that was the head of the N. fork of that run that
was named for his father, James Cooper.

November, 1803—Thos. McClanahan files bill for review of decree.
Lawrence Harrison deposeth: in yr. 1770, in company with Col.
Wm. Lynn, in traveling from Limestone to falls of Ohio, after
crossing Hinkston, they fell upon waters of Cooper's Run, and
that that fork on which they were runs through the plantation
of Thos. Manihon (?), Jr., and where Thos. Strother formerly
lived. Wm. Whitesell deposeth: in yr. 1779 he was first acquainted with Cooper's Run in traveling from Boonesborough to Ruddle's
old Station. John Conway deposeth: he knew Coopers run 1780,
that he was told of said run by Thos. Gilbert, Jas. McBride, Thos.
Stephenson, who were there before, and states at that time he lived
at Bryant's Station. Abijah Woods deposeth: in yr. 1776 he lived
at McGee's Station and that he got information regarding Cooper's
Run from John Townsend and others, then moved to Bryant's Station and there lived four or five years, and frequently traveled
the trace that led from Bryant's Station to Martin's and Ruddle's
Station, passing near where Mr. Strother "now lives." Deposition
taken Aug. 13, 1804. John Ficklin states he became acquainted
with Cooper's Run 1781 or '82, that he lived at Bryant's Station; at
that time; deposition taken Aug., 1804. Jacob Stucker knew
Cooper's Run 1781 or '82, when he lived at Bryant's Station; deposition taken Aug., 1804. Wm. Grant, Sr., states he knew Cooper's
Run 1779, 1780 and 1781, he moved away after 1781 and did not
return until 1787; deposition taken Nov. 18, 1803. John Grant
states he became acquainted with Cooper's Run, 1780, which "now
runs through place of Larkin and Willis Field"; taken Nov. 18,
1804. John Daugherty states he first knew Cooper's Run 1779;
that he, in company with Wm. Whitsell, Samuel Porter and Geo.
Lovelace (Lovelance) and Samuel VanHook, was hunting and
encamped first night above Grant's improvement; taken Feb. 9,
1804.

RANDOM NOTES FROM SUITS FILED IN OFFICE OF
CIRCUIT CLERK

Thos. Jones, Sr., vs. Joseph Kirkpatrick, July 2, 1811, Box 207—Alexander Mitchell departed this life leaving Joseph Kirkpatrick and

Kisiah, late Kisiah Mitchell, Isaac Orchard and Marjorie (alias Marget) his wife, Joseph Mitchell, Jr., John Mitchell, Hannah Mitchell his heirs at law.

Adair-Wigginton Suit, Box 585—1823—Papers filed in suit: Deposition of Robert Nesbit states he came to Ky. in the spring of 1785 and' that John Cook, Sr., lived where his son Isaac Cook "now lives on Flat Run." Henry Timberlake states he came to Ky., 1790 with his father's family. George Redmon's will filed, named brother-in-law, Wm. Bruce; wife, Nancy; sons, Thos., Chas., George, Wm.; daus., Elizabeth, Mary, Margaret, Sarah and John. Extrs.: wife and bro., Wm. Redmon. Written Dec. 31, 1789. Probated Nov. 1790. (Note: From will it seems his wife had daughters of her own). Robert McClelland came to place whereon his brother, Elisha McClelland "now lives" with his father in 1784. Robert Champ's deposition. Benjamin Forsythe's will. Deposition of Mary Timberlake, aged 71 yrs., states that her husband, Richard Timberlake, decd., was half-brother of Benjamin Forsythe and that in 1790 her husband removed his family from Hanover County to Ky.

Patty Harris vs. Pollock, Box 480—In this suit some of the depositions were taken 1805, others in Clark Co., 1811. Joseph McGuer states he came to Ky., 1779. Leonard K. Bradley came 1783. Joseph Procter aged 55 yrs. to Ky., 1778. Nathaniel Bullock came to Ky., 1777, had been captured by the Indians at Blue Licks, 1778, his age abt. 51 yrs. Wm. Suddeth to Ky., 1783 and stopped at McGee's and Strode's Stations. Stephen Boyle to Ky., 1779, settled at Strode's Station, 1780. Jesse Coffee to Ky., 1781, settled at Boonsborough. James Morgan of Farquier Co., Va., surveyor, makes statement. David Linch to Ky., 1779. Wm. Clinkenbeard aged abt. 44 yrs., to Ky., 1779, was at Strode's Station. Roger Clements, (Montgomery Co.), to Ky., 1781, was at McGee's Station. Oswell Townsin to Ky., 1775, settled at Boonsborough. Joseph Berry to Ky., 1782. James Duncan aged 55 yrs. (deposition taken 1805), came to Ky., 1779, was at Boonesborough, returned to old settlement same year and came out to Ky., again in the fall of that yr. and assisted Benedict Couchman and his brother to build the first house at Strode's Station, which was on a fork. That he was to and from Va. several times and when in Ky. he generally resided at Strode's Station, that he moved his family to Ky. in the spring of 1784. Benedict Couchman aged 49 yrs. (1805), came to Ky., 1779. Wm. Cradlebough came to Ky., 1776 and lived with Daniel Boone. James Berry came to Ky., 1779. Benjamin Dunaway to Ky., 1779 and settled at Boonesborough. Zacheriah Easton, deposition. Aquilla White to Ky., 1779, settled at Boonesborough. Frederick Couchman to Ky., 1779, settled at Boonesborough and was at Strode's. Jas. Sodowsky to Ky., 1779. Nicholas Proctor aged 53, (1811), to Ky., 1788, was at Boonesborough and at Strode's. Joshua Stamper aged 58 yrs. (1811). was at Strodes, 1779-1784. Charles Morgan, deposition. Deed filed in suit, 1813, Richard Ratcliff of Fairfax Co., Va., to Humphrey Marshall. Isaac Halbert and Elizabeth mentioned.

Thomas Hrs. vs. Smith Hrs.—Weathers Smith departed this life intestate, leaving Hardage Smith, James W. Smith, Geo. A. Smith, Chas. A. Smith, Lydia Smith, Susanna Rogers, late widow of Chas. Rogers, decd., and Margaret Thomas, late Smith, widow of Benj. Thomas, decd., his chdn. and hrs. at law, some of whom hold the

legal title to said land as hrs. at law of same by voluntary conveyance and each of said hrs. refuse to convey orators: Benj. Franklin Thomas, Geo. Washington Thomas, devisees of Benj. Thomas,
decd., infts. under 21 yrs. by Jas. French their gdn. and Nathaniel
Cotton. Benj. Thomas departed this life about Feb. 1813, leaving will in Montgomery Co., when he divided said land to orators.
Dated May 24, 1814.

Isham Talbott vs Geo. Givens' Hrs.—Alexander Givens, Matthew Givens,
Samuel Givens, Jane Givens, Francis Gray and Lettice Gray, his
wife, late Givens, hrs. of Geo. Givens, decd., Benj. Hendricks,
Robt. Cummings and Samuel McMillan claim title of land claimed
by your orator, Isham Talbott. Dated Dec. 29, 1815.

Samuel Givens Hrs. vs. Jas. Eubank, Box 479, Dec. 3, 1816—Samuel
Lamme and Samuel Givens sold to Jas. Eubank a tract in Washington Co., Ky., on waters of Panther's Creek. Hrs. listed in suit
under date of Nov. 9, 1819: Wm. Craig and Margaret, his wife,
late Givens; John Givens; James Givens; George Givens; Pasty
Givens; Isabella, Elizabeth Ann and Jane Givens, four last being
infants under 21 yrs., by Jas. Givens, their gdn., hrs. of Samuel
Givens. decd.

**Bourbon County Justices for use of Hrs. of Joseph Riley vs. Wm. Mc-
Cann, Admr. for Debt, Box 120**—Hrs. listed: John Riley, Wm. Riley,
John Brown and Euphan, his wife. Aug. 18, 1801.

James Dupuy vs. Samuel Henderson and Others, Box 120—Peter Small
deposeth regarding traces—Question: "In 1780 were you not informed that the trace called Harrod's trace was the oldest trace?"
Answer: "In the year 1780 after returning from Clarke's Campaign, a number of us started from Boon's Station to Lower
Blue Licks to make salt and directed by Col. Boone to go to
Harrod's Lick Trace, which we did, and with difficulty found it,
returned home by McMillan's Trace which we found much the
plainest at that time. James Dupue, Dec .18, 1782—Entered 1000
acres on a Treasury Warrant then in Fayette, now Bourbon, orator states that Samuel Henderson, assign. of Abraham Mitchell
on Dec. 27, 1779, offered a certificate for 400 acres and a preemption of 1000 acres from the Commrs. who sat in Western
country to adjust the titles, etc. Deposition of Edward Bradley—
Taken at house of Andrew Friend, Sept. 8, 1801, states he was
well acquainted with John Pleabe and Stalver in yr. 1782, used
to hunt with him. Deposition of John McGuire, aged 35 yrs., Sept.
8, 1801. Deposition of Samuel Boone, Jr., aged 45 yrs., states
he has been in this county since 1799. Dated Sept. 8, 1801. Deposition of John Pleakand Stalver, Jr.—In the year 1779-80, he
marked a honey locust tree at the spring, and in spring of 1782,
he, in company with Jas. Kill and Edmond Thompkins, came to
the spring and in the fall he made entry for James Dupuy for
1000 acres. Dated May 4, 1801. Ambrose Coffee makes deposition regarding his acquaintance with John Pleakand Stalver,
known him since 1778, and believes in his integrity. Deposition
of Nicholas Anderson—Same as above, known him for 23 years.
Edward Williams states he has known him since 1779 and known
him to be a punctual man of unblemished character, lived in his
neighborhood, etc. John Hayser—Same as above, known him since
1779. Jesse Coper—Same as above, known him since 1776.

John Archer vs. Archer Matthews, Box 120, Feb.-Apr., 1803—John Archer was deputy sheriff under Jas. Henderson, now decd., then sheriff of Greenbrier Co., Va., in 1778–79, was in Ky., 1779. Pltf. Lettice Matthews who intermarried with Joseph D. Kyser, admr. and Thos. and Jno. Stuart, Admrs. of estate of Archer Matthews, decd., and John Anderson vs. John Archer, deputy sheriff of Jas. Henderson.

Markham vs. Wm. L. Todd, Dec. 6, 1822—Amended bill showing Richard Robinet, Joseph Robinet, Joseph Hume and Sarah, late Robinet, only chdn. and hrs. of Joseph Robinet, decd.

Thomas McClanahan Hrs. vs. Admr., Filed May 9, 1834—Bill in Chancery, Box 732—James McClanahan, John McClanahan, Braxton W. Chamblin and wife, Margaret, late McClanahan, Lucy Ann McClanahan, an inft. under 21, by gdn., said Braxton W. Chamblin, Thomas McClanahan and Newman McClanahan, infts. under 21, by gdn., Huball Foster, who show that they together with Elizabeth Foster, late Elizabeth McClanahan, now intermarried with Hubbell Foster, are hrs. and chdn. of Thomas McClanahan, decd., who departed this life in the month of June or July in 1833, possession of slaves and personal estate. Said Hubbell Foster appointed administrator.

Ambrose Young—States four or five yrs. before his father's death he heard him express some uneasiness about his grandchildren, viz: John Charles and Polly Proctor. Deposition of Walter Cave states sometime in yr. 1786 he was going to Va., that pursuant to his departure, Mr. Young informed him he was desirous of his son-in-law, Hezekiah Proctor coming to this country, first because he was anxious about his daughter and second, that Proctor would be an advantage to the neighborhood.

Benj. Bedford vs. Thos. Stark, Box 423—Rubin Rankins states he has known one-eyed John Taylor since yr. 1784, said Taylor lived at Boonesboro mostly in yr. 1784, but in 1785 at Col. John Holders. Deposition of David Jameson, aged 56, taken May, 1813. Deposition of Archibald McNabb, Sr., aged 75, May 10, 1813. Deposition of Josiah McDowell, aged abt. 60, May 10, 1813. Deposition of Jas. Kenney, aged abt. 60, May 10, 1813. Deposition of Moses Thomas who states he resided at Boonesboro in 1779, Strode's Station, winter of 1779 and spring of 1780, taken 1812. Deposition of Jas. Kenney taken 1809, states his residence from 19th day April until June 1776 was at Boonesboro. Samuel J. Dowson, deposition taken 1813, states he is 37 yrs. old. Isaac Clinkenbeard states he came to Ky., 1779, in fall. Chas. Scott, Secty to Gov., signs Treas. Warrant to Thos. Stark. Deposition of Enock Smith, Montgomery Co., was at Boonesboro, states there were about a dozen families at Boonesboro and about 15 or 20 hunters.

Ephriam H. McConnell vs. John Masoner, Box 949—Petition of Fanny Mason, Wm. P. Stone and Chas. F. Spencer to Judge of Bourbon Circuit Court, would show that Fanny Mason has been appointed gdn. of Richard E. Mason, Elizabeth Simpson and Mary H. Spencer, late Mason, intermarried with the co-petitioner, Chas. F. Spencer, who are still infts. under 21 yrs., that Wm. P. Stone has been appointed gdn. of Lewis G. Stone, an inft. under 21 yrs.

McMillen vs. Woodruff, Bill dated Dec. 6, 1838, Box 989—Wm. Brown's will mentions farm purchased of Jesse Huddleston for son, James, for which deed was given; dau., Ruth Anne Smith and husband, James D. Smith, land beginning at Indian Creek Bridge to Ruddle's old dam; to dau., Mary Wilson and son-in-law, Barton S. Wilson, have conveyed brick and log homes in Cynthiana; son, Wm., property in Cynthiana; to other chdn., (not named) land in Ky. and Ill., near 7000 a.; wife, a farm either in Ky. or Ill. Wts.: Thos. W. Buckner, Mat. Stacy: Codicil: reserve out of Ill. land for each of uneducated chdn., viz: Elisha, Rebecca, Eliza, Loyd and Harriett Sarah, when of age, they to be educated. Recorded Morgan Co., Ill. At special term, 28 Oct., 1833, Matthew Stacy and Thos. W. Buckner appeared and proved will. Extrs.: wife, Harriett Brown and Wm. Brown, Jr., sign; recorded in Harrison Co., Ky., July 14, 1840. Deed from Barton S. Wilson and wife, Mary of Cooper Co., Mo., to Wm. Brown, Jr., Extr. of Wm. Brown, decd. of Harrison Co., Ky., Oct. 15, 1839. Deed from John Graham and Elizabeth, heirs of Jared Graham, decd. and Hannah Graham, widow of Jared Graham, to Wm. Brown, lot in Cynthiana, March 13, 1816. Deed dated Aug. 13, 1835, Barton S. Wilson and wife, Mary, of Morgan Co., Ill., to Wm. Brown, Extr. of Wm. Brown. Deposition of Nathaniel Campbell taken in Cynthiana, July 10, 1840, deposeth, he has resided in Cynthian since 1802 or 1803, that Hannah Graham was the widow of Jard Graham and as far back as 1802, she lived in house on ground now occupied by A. F. McMillan, that she had two chdn., John and Elizabeth, etc. Thomas Rankin deposeth in same that he has lived in Cynthiana for more than forty years.

Richard Graves Hrs., vs. Wm. Phillips Hrs., Filed Aug. 31, 1811, Box 315—David Graves, Robt. Graves, Rice Graves, Thos. Graves, John Graves, Sally Graves and Polly Graves, last three infts. under 21 yrs. by David Graves, hrs. of Richard Graves, decd. would show their father died intestate, leaving above hrs. During lifetime he purchased of Wm. Phillips of Louisa Co., Va., 300 acres and Phillips executed bond Mar. 3, 1787, which called for land in Fayette (now Bourbon) as to part in Scott on N. Fork Elkhorn, it being part of patent of 1000 a. dated 1786. Altho their father tried to obtain survey and obtain spot he never did during his life. Said Phillips resided in Va., never executed deed, that the whole tract is covered by prior claims, said Phillips has departed this life, leaving the following chdn., Wm. B. Phillips, Elizabeth Phillips, Cathrine Phillips, Susannah Phillips, Lucy Anderson, late Phillips, who married Francis Anderson and although heirs are over 21 yrs. of age, they refuse to convey.

Ford vs. Porter's Hrs., Box 806, Filed Apr. 1813—Wm. Ford complains of J. L. Hickman, admr. of John Porter, decd., and Lewellen, Lucretia, John and Austin Porter, inft. hrs. of John Porter, decd.

Josiah Ashurst Hrs. vs. Josiah Ashurst Hrs., Suit in Chancery, Box 744, Oct. 9, 1820—Thomas Jones and wife, Patsy, Wm. Jones and wife, Nancy, Sanford Gorham and wife, Polly, Robert Ashurst, John Ashurst, Paulina Ashurst, an inft. under 21 with Washington Kennedy her gdn., Wm. and Rebecca Ashurst, infts. under 21 with Robt. Ashurst gdn. Would show that Josiah Ashurst their ancestor, departed this life intestate, possessed of real estate and slaves and personal property. That oratrix, Polly, Nancy, Polly,

Paulina and Rebecca and orators Robt., John and Wm., together with Josiah Ashurst and Elizabeth are the only chdn of said Josiah Ashurst, decd. Patsy m. Thos. Jones and Nancy m. Wm. Jones and oratrix, Polly m. Sanford Gorham. In division Paulina shown to be wife of Preston Griffing.

Ardery vs. Samuel Nesbit's Hrs., Box 695 Hrs. List—Elizabeth, who m. Samuel McConnell, Rachel, single, Wm. Nesbit, decd., left 2 chdn., Samuel and Elizabeth, both under 21 yrs.

Uriah Humble's Hrs. vs. Uriah Humble's Hrs., Box 809, Petition to Divide Property. Bill Filed Oct. 19, 1833—Orator Jas. H. Humble and oratrix Elizabeth and Catherine Humble would show their ancestor, Uriah Humble, lately departed this life possessed of 230 a. located in Harrison and Bourbon Cos., also negroes and property descended to chdn. who are besides orator and oratrix, Conrod Humble, Sophia Cummings who married Elijah Cummins, Mary Frye who married John Frye, Margaret Humble, inft. under 21 yrs. and Elizabeth, Jane, Chas., Uriah, Thos., Sarah, Jas., Hiram, and Wm. Rankins, chdn. of Delilah Rankins, formerly Delilah Humble, said hrs. being nonresidents.

Henza Darnall's Hrs. Bill Filed for Sale of Property, May 22, 1832,¹ Box 806—Elizabeth Darnall would show that on Aug. 13, 1824, Henza Darnell departed this life, leaving oratrix his widow and Fielding, Harvy, John, Mary, Thos. and Henzy Darnall, his chdn. and hrs. at law, possessed of land in Bourbon to which he had title by deed from Thos. Darnall.

Jas. Whaley's Hrs. vs. George Northcutt and Wife, May Court, 1828, Box 808—Answer of Elinor Nesbit, late Whaley, Daniel Talbot and wife,Ann, late Whaley, Elijah Hayden and Delila, late Whaley, Harriet Night, late Whaley, Barbara Whaley, to bill in Chancery by Geo. Northcutt and wife, Elizabeth, late Whaley. That Elizabeth is the child of Jas. Whaley, decd., and all these defdts. except Eleanor Nesbit are remaining chdn. and as to said Eleanor she is the widow of Jas. Whaley, since his death has married Geo. Northcutt and moved to Mo., where he died leaving her a widow, she having taken out letters of administration upon his estate in Ralls Co., Mo., etc.

Robt. Palmer for Joseph Palmer's Hrs., Box 806, Petition for Sale of Land, Bill Filed May 8, 1834—Would show that complainants, Robt. Palmer, Jr., Catherine Palmer, Wm. Palmer and Elizabeth Palmer, infts. under 21 yrs. by Robt. Palmer, Sr., their next friend, are the Chdn. of Joseph Palmer, Jr., decd., that their grandfather, Joseph Palmer, Sr., died intestate, that by his death there descended to them land located in Clark Co., Ky.

Jas. Duncan vs. Joseph Duncan's Hrs., Box 312, May, 1809—Representatives of Matthew Duncan: Jas. Duncan, Joseph Duncan, John Smith Duncan, Polly M. Duncan and Thos. A. Duncan, inft. hrs. of Joseph Duncan, decd., by Ann Duncan, their mother, sheweth that Mathew Duncan, grandfather, intermarried with their grandmother, Sarah Duncan, and had the following chdn.: Seth Duncan, Sarah Bell, Jane Wilson, Jas. Duncan, Joseph Duncan, and the orators are chdn. of Joseph Duncan, that said Mathew departed this life, leaving said Sarah, who departed this life intestate, leaving her property in the hands of Seth Duncan and Thos. Duncan (since decd. without issue), and said James Duncan, defdt. to this bill, took upon himself administration of her estate. Deposition of Sarah Bell taken at the house of Thos. Dickenson at Glasgow, Barren Co., Ky., to be read as evidence in suit wherein Jas. Duncan and others are defdts. and Labon Ship and hrs. of Joseph Duncan, decd., by Ann Moore, their gdn. are Pltfs., deposeth. Before she moved from Berkeley Co., Va., to Western country, her husband, Wm. Bell, gave a note to her mother, Sarah Duncan, that Wm. Bell died in Martinsburgh, Va., in yr. '94 and that she was supported by her step-son, Wm. Bell as long as she remained in Va. Deposition of Mary M. Laughlin taken in Franklin Co., Pa., deposeth she went to house of Capt. Seth Duncan in Pendleton Co., Ky., about 6 days before death of Sarah Duncan.

CLARK COUNTY

Thomas Winn, Sr. Heirs—Thomas Winn, Sr., made entry on Treasury Warrant 400 acres now in Clark, then in Fayette. After said grant was issued ,about yr. 1790-91-92, Thomas Winn, Sr., departed this life intestate leaving the following chdn. and hrs. at law: William Winn (resident of Ohio), John Winn and Thomas Winn (both of Mo.), Daniel Winn and Lydia Winn, the last since intermarried with Richard Faulkner (both of Ohio), Frankey Winn, since intermarried with Archibald Harris (both of Ohio), Sally Winn, intermarried with William Warren and John Winn.

Adam Winn Hrs.—Adam Winn of Fayette conveyed to William Winn, land (400 a.) which was devised by William Stone, decd., one-third part of legacy devised to heirs (three grandchildren) namely, William Cotton, John Cotton and Gracey Scott and which Adam Winn, decd., purchased from said devisees, and did sell to William Winn the one-third part land from William Stone's heirs. Adam Winn died without children, leaving the following heirs at law: Elizabeth Bradley, wife of Edward Bradley; Catherine Herndon, wife of William Herndon; Mary Cotton, wife of Henry Cotton; Sally Musick, widow or Juharda (?) Musich; and his other brother, George Winn; and George Hancock, Milan Hancock, Harrison Hancock, Synvanus Hancock, Clearcus Hancock, Jno. Hancock, children of Lititia Hancock, decd., sister of Adam Winn, decd.; and Henry C. Clay, Lititia Moran, wife of Edward B. Moran, George Clay, Littleberry Clay, John Clay, Richard Clay, Rachil Clay, Thomas Clay and William Green Clay, chdn. of Nancy Clay, decd., sister of Adam Winn, decd. Orator states that John Winn, since decd., and William Winn obtained from Fayette Co., letters of administration, personal estate of Adam Winn, decd.

FAYETTE COUNTY

DISTRICT COURT DEED BOOK A

Page 1—22 day, 8th mo., 1794—John Hutchinson and wife, Margaret of Philadelphia, Pa., to Samuel Ellison of same place, land in Bourbon County on Morgan's Creek, Stoners Fork, 400 a., preemption obtained in name of Ralph Morgan.

Page 3, March 25, 1796—Samuel Elluson and wife, Rachel of Philadelphia, Pa., to Matthew Anderson, land in Bourbon on Morgan's Creek, Stoner's Fork.

Page 7, Oct. 6, 1794—Peter Skipwith Randolph and wife, Elizabeth of Henrico Co., Va., to John Mosby Shepherd of Richmond, Va., 1000 a. granted by State of Va., July 3, 1774 to Jas. Southall, assee. of John Hickman, located in Fayette Co.

Page 16, June 1, 1796—Peter January and Margaret of Lexington, Ky., to Thos. January of same place, said Peter and Thomas January formerly firm of Peter January and Son, etc.

Page 16, Jan. 1795—Archibald Yancy of county of Elizabeth City, Va., appts. Jno. Duke, Sr., of Louisa Co., Va., atty. to make deeds for land in Ky., on Elkhorn Creek.

Page 18—Archibald Yancey and wife, Mary, of Elizabeth City Co., Va., to Thos. Walsh of Louisa Co., Va., deed land in Fayette.

Page 20, Sept. 14, 1795—Major-General Chas. Scott of Woodford to John and Samuel Postlethwait of Lexington, land in Military boundry N. W. Ohio River, also on Cumberland River in Military boundry, also part of Treasury warrant entered in name of Scott and Moseby, also tracts patents for which either in Va. or sent forward to Alexander Scott, Lancaster Co., Pa.

Page 25, July 23, 1789—Job Johnson of Philadelphia to Wm. Shannon of Northern Liberties in Philadelphia Co., Penn. Whereas by articles of agreement Dec. 12, 1783 between John Philips, John Young, Jr., Moses Bartram, Benj. Say, Wm. C. Butler, Claudius Paul Ragent, Henry Louis Charton, David D. Bartholt, John Dounaldson, John Mitchell, Philip and James Moore, Ramsey and Coxe, Wm. McMurtrie, John Pringle, Jas. Reynolds, John Marie, Wm. Constable, Dominis and Edward Joice, Chas. Young, Peter Whiteside, Jas. Craig, Sr., Wm. Forbes, Chas. Miller, Jas. Butland, Jacob Weaver and Wm. Sykes, all of City of Philadelphia, Penn., and Richard Ellis of Cecil Co., Md., parties of first part secured Treasury warrant from State of Va. for 456000 acres, and John Marie's share amounted to 15000 acres—agreed that Richard Ellis should survey and locate this land near waters of Ohio and lay off in tracts not to exceed 10000 a. each and said Richard Ellis to be entitled to one third of all land; said Richard procured five large tracts in counties of Fayette and Lincoln, land about 30 miles above "Boonesborough the eldest settlement in the Kentucky county;" tract deeded by Jas. Reynolds to Jno. Marie June 29, 1786 and since conveyed to John and Chambers Hart and by them to Job Johnson, and Job Johnson deeds to Wm. Shannon.

Page 40, Feb. 4, 1796—Wm. Farrow and wife, Sarah of Prince William Co., Va., to Simon Luttrell and Thos. Chapman, Extrs. of Wm. Carr, decd., of same Co., and State, to uses as expressed in will of Wm. Carr, decd., deed preemption right in Ky., on waters of Licking granted to Wm. Farrow, also two tracts in Prince William near Dumpries, whereon said Farrow now lives. Wts.: Willoughby Tibbs, Luke Smith, Samuel Howison, Richard Brooke.

Page 45, Aug. 2, 1796—Jacob Rybolt and Barbara of Bourbon Co., deed to Wm. Huston of Fayette, land in Lexington.

Page 51, Sept. 8, 1796—Rice Bullock of Fayette Co., to Ellie Williams of Washington Co., Md., land in district set aside for officers and soldiers of Va. Continental line, on West Fork of Pond River.

Page 53, Oct. 24, 1795—Charles Hill of Hunterdon Co., N. J., appts. Benj. Stout, atty. to sell property in Lexington, Ky.

Page 59, Apr. 13, 1796—Andrew Lewis of Montgomery Co., Va., to Thos Hart, Sr. and Nathl. Shaw of Fayette Co., land in Fayette being part of Military survey of 2000 a. granted Andrew Lewis July 1780, etc.

Sept. 24, 1796—John Rogers of Fayette appoints Beverly Chew of Fredericksburg, Va., atty. to demand two judgments against Thos. Barnett on bond assigned by Messrs. Smith, Young and Hide in district court of Albemarle Co., Va., and agst. Thos. Pollard in Court of Appeals of said State.

Sept. 23, 1796—John Lewis and wife, Rachel, Andrew Lewis and Chas. Lewis, hrs. of Col. Chas. Lewis, deceased ,of Bath Co., Va., to George Winn, Sr. and Adam Winn of Fayette, tract in Fayette containing 800 acres.

Nov. 3, 1796—Percival Butler of Jefferson Co., appts. Jas. Hawkins of Fayette atty. for self and for wife, Milly Butler, formerly Milly Hawkins, one of hrs. of John Hawkins, decd., to make settlement with Extrs. of estate of John Hawkins, late of Hanover Co., Va.

Oct. 14, 1796—John Bradford and wife, Elizabeth, of Fayette Co., to Wm. Chinn and wife, Sarah, formerly Sarah Bryan, Morgan Bryan and James Bryan, hrs. of James Bryan, decd.

Oct. 14, 1796—Joseph Richardson of Caroline Co., Va., to Walker Baylor of Lexington, Ky., land in Green Co., formerly Jefferson Co.

July 13, 1796—Achillis Helm of Fayette Co., Ky., to Simon Triplett of Loudoun Co., Va., consideration of the trouble and expense of said Triplett in getting law passed by Virginia Assembly to carry into effect claim of 3334 acres to which Leonard Helm, father to said Achillis, was entitled in right of his command in the Illinois Regiment and to fulfill contract, deeds 750 a. part of Illinois grant, bound by Wm. Harrod's survey, John Thruston's survey and George Rogers Clark's survey.

Sept. 28, 1796—Samuel Edmonds, Sr. of Fayette to George Laycraft of New York, land in Lexington, Ky.

Nov. 29, 1796—James Bullock and wife, Ann, of Fayette Co., Ky., to Waller Overton, deed for land in Woodford, being part of James Bullock's Military survey of 2000 acres.

Jan. 1, 1796—Thomas Marshall and wife, Mary of Woodford to Joshua Worley, heir of Caleb Worley, decd. of Fayette Co., 162½ a., part of Wm. Peaches Military survey of 2000 a. in Fayette.

Dec. 23, 1796—Henry Garrett, by Geo. Johnson, atty. ,both of Louisa Co., Va., to Richard Booker of Clark Co., Ky., land in Shelby Co.

Nov. 9, 1796—George Johnson of Louisa Co., Va., to Wm. Porter, Jr. of Fayette Co., land located in Madison Co.

State of Ga., Green Co., Aug. 27, 1796—Thos. Daniel of said Co., for love and affection to friend, Reubin Guttery (Guthry?), land on Ky. River in Fayette Co., as will appear by grant to Thos. Daniel by Henry Lee, Esq., Governor of Virginia.

Jan. 21, 1797—Wm. Macbean of Philadelphia, Penn., Geo. Poyzer of Lexington and John Anderson agreement to become. copartners in trade.

Sept. 2, 1796—Archibald Kennedy of Ky., appts. Benj. Turner of Va., his lawful atty. to transact business in Va.

Thos. Herndon Hrs from Thos. Woolfork—Deed Bk. U, pg. 241—Feb. 20, 1821—Widow and seven chdn., viz: Catherine, Mary, Susannah, Martha Eliza, Geo., Thos., Edward James, Wiatt and Frazer.

May 5, 1804—Mary Hawkins to Jno. T. Hawkins, Circuit Court Bk. A, pg. 33. Quit claim to 1115 acres in Albemarle Co., Va.

CIRCUIT COURT DEED BOOK A

March 28, 1803—Cuthbert Banks and wife, Elizabeth, to Innis B. Brent, land in Henderson Co., Ky., all styled "of Fayette Co., Ky."

Page 2—Stephen Collins of Clarke Co., Ky., to John Howrey of Fayette, land in Lexington, Ky.

Page 19, Apr. 1, 1803—Hubbard Taylor of Clark Co., appts. John Hoomes of Caroline Co., Va., atty. to receive 20 pounds due Wm. Blair by power from said Wm. Blair to him, said Hubbard Taylor.

Page 20, Dec. 1802—Thos. Garnett and wife, Rachel of Jessamine Co., Ky., to Thos. Ammon of Bourbon Co., Ky., land in Bourbon on Licking, 900 a.

Page 21, Nov. 18, 1802—Golson Stapp and wife, Rachel of Garrard Co., Ky., to Joseph Rutherford of Fayette, land in Fayette, 150 a.

Page 14, March 30, 1803—Innis B. Brent of Lexington, Ky., to Thos. Young of Mason Co., Ky., land in Henderson Co., Ky.

Page 25, Apr. 11, 1803—John Rector of Fayette to Reubin Anderson of Franklin Co., Ky., land in Ross Co., Ohio.

Page 32, Dec. 2, 1802—Geo. Moore of Aglethorp, Ga., atty. for Richard

Moore of same place, appts. Wm. Ellis of Fayette Co., Ky., to act for him.

Page 39, June 10, 1789—John Coburn and wife, Mary, of Woodford Co., Ky., to Thos. Young of Fayette land in Lexington, Ky.

Page 49, May 12, 1803—Wm. Morton and wife, Sally of Fayette Co., Ky., to Hugh Logan of Lincoln Co., Ky., land in Pulaskia Co., on Fishing Creek.

Page 51,—Wm. H. Harding of Jefferson Co., Va., appts. John Washington of Co. of Frederick, (Va.). Whereas has received power of atty. from Wilson Miles Carey, Extr. of Geo. William Fairfax, Esq., to transact business of estate of said George William Fairfax, decd., by virtue of said power appts. said John Washington. Recorded in Jefferson Co., Va. Wts.: John D. Orr, Abrm. Byrd Page, Eliza B. Fairfax.

Page 53, Feb. 17, 1803—Edmund Bullock deeds Stephen Bullock all claim to land in Nelson Co., Ky., being that part which said Edmund had in the entry of 1200 made in name of his father, Edward Bullock.

Page 54, May 26, 1802—David Morrow of Caroline Co., Va., to Hubbard Taylor of Fayette Co., in trust for Henry Buckner and wife, Elizabeth, to descend to their legal heirs, land located in Fayette Co., Ky.

Page 55, May, 1803—John Fisher, Senr. of Scott Co., Ky., for love and affection for his chdn., viz: Maddox Fisher, Wm. Fisher, Ann Huston, John Fisher and the legal heirs of Susannah McCudy, Thos. Fisher, Clement Fisher—Thos. Fisher and Clement Fisher under 21 yrs. of age—deeds property in consideration of $1.00 and support of himself and Vitator G. Fisher during their lives.

Page 56, May 12, 1803—Wm. H. Harding of Jefferson Co., Va., to Chas. McPheters of Fayette, land located in Fayette Co., Ky.

FLEMING COUNTY

(Formed from Mason County, 1798)

EARLY DEEDS

Note: Dates are those of recording deeds.

Edward Nelson and wife, Jane—Of Bourbon Co. to James Inlaws of Mason Co., land in Mason, on Fleming Creek, part of 1000 a. tract granted sd. Edward Wilson. Apr. 9, 1798.

Robt. Campbell, Sr.—To Jno. Campbell and Robt. Campbell, Jr., land in Fleming Co. June 11, 1798.

Nicholas Hendrickson and wife, Catherine—Of Mason Co., to Edmond Parker of same, land in Mason Co. June, 1798.

Wm. Wilson—Of Bourbon, power of atty. to Michael Cassidy of Fleming. June, 1798.

Wm. Burke—Of Mason, to Wm. Orr of Bourbon, land in Mason. June, 1798.

Wm. Burke and wife, Mary—Of Fleming, to John Garvan of same, land in Fleming. June, 1798.

Indenture—Between Trustees of Flemingsburg, to Cornelius Gooding, sd. trustees deed lot in Flemingsburg agreeable to act of Assembly of Ky., passed Dec. 19, 1796, to establish towns, and agreeable to court of Mason Co., did establish town of Flemingsburg on land of George Stockton. Signed: Wm. Murphy, Michael Cassidy, Adam Bravard, Richard Tilton. June 12, 1798.

Trustees of Flemingsburg—To Richard Morgan of Berkeley Co., Va., lot in Flemingsburg. June 12, 1798.

Wm. Robertson and wife, Peggy—To Thos. Clawson, lot in Flemingsburg. Oct. 8, 1798.

Jacob Myers—Of Lincoln Co., to Jas. Greer of Fleming Co., land in Fleming, by Michael Cassidy, atty. in fact. June 12, 1798.

Mercer Beeson and wife, Catherine—To Thos. Clawson, land in Fleming. Oct. 8, 1798.

John Marshall and wife, Elizabeth—Of Fayette Co., to Micajah Wyatt, of Fleming, land in Fleming. Sept. 10, 1798.

Trustees of Flemingsburg—To Thos. Talmage of Fleming, lot in Flemingsburg. June, 1798.

Lewis Craig—Of Bracken Co., to John Price of Fleming, land in Fleming. July 9, 1798.

Wm. Roberts—Atty. for Joseph Roberts of Culpeper Co., Va., to John Hart of Fleming, land in Fleming, part of 1000 a. tract granted said Roberts by patent. July 9, 1798.

Barnett Fields—Atty. for John Fields of Clark Co., to Noah Dorson of Fleming, land in Fleming, part of Benj. Robert's survey. July 9, 1798.

Lewis Craig and wife, Elizabeth—Of Mason, to Robt. Smith of Fleming, land in Fleming. Sept. 10, 1798.

Division of 35,000 a.—Between hrs. of Major John Mosby, decd. and Lewis Craig, Jr., of Mason. Articles of agreement entered into 1782 between Simon Kenton of Lincoln Co. and John Mosby of Powhatan Co. (Va.), said Kenton received from Mosby warrants for 60,000 a. which sd. Kenton agreed to locate. July 8, 1798.

Jno Hughes and wife, Ann—Of Mason, to Jno. Miller, Sr., land in Fleming. Oct. 8, 1798.

Owen Humphreys and wife, Isabella—Jno. Keith, Geo. Stockton (atty.

for Margaret Keith), Wm. Keith, Isaac Keith by gdn., Jno. Keith, hrs. of Isaiah Keith, late of Mason Co., whereas said Keith became seized of lands in Mason, Fleming, Shelby, Clark and elsewhere, and whereas said Owen Humphrey and Isabella(she being widow of Isaiah), having agreed to relinquish claim to dower due Isabella, in said estate except fifth part, to legatees. Oct. 8, 1798.

John Marshall and wife, Elizabeth—Of Fayette, to John Hopkins of Fleming, land in Fleming. Sept. 10, 1798.

John Allison—Late of Alexandria, Va., now of Wilkes Co., Ga., was granted certificate by Commrs. of Dist. of Ky., Apr., 1780, for improving land on creek now known as Allisons Creek, abt. 7 mi. from Blue Licks, appts. Wm. Allison of Bourbon, atty. to bring suit to recover. Oct. 6, 1798.

Alex. Ramsey, Byram Routt and Basil Hunt—Of Fleming, to Wm. Dawson of Mercer, land in Fleming. Feb. 11, 1799.

Wm. Burke—Of Mason, to Henry Crafton of Bourbon, land in Mason, part of 12,293 a. entered in name of Thos. Perkins which sd. Burke bought of Ezekel Whitman, atty. for Enock Perkins, atty-at-law of said Thos. Perkins. Feb. 11, 1790.

John Hunt, Sr.—Of Montgomery Co., appts. Jno. Hunt, Jr., of Fleming, atty., to recover debts due from Jacob Myers. July 8, 1799.

Joseph Collier—Of Adams, Territory N. W. Ohio River, to Jas. Dale of Fleming, land in Fleming. June 14, 1799.

Daniel Fialds—Extr. of will of Benj. Roberts, decd., of Culpeper Co., Va., to John Callaman of Fleming, whereas said decedant made will leaving lands in Western Waters to certain legatees, and apptd. Daniel Fields, extr., said Daniel by letters of atty. apptd. Jno. Fields to divide said lands, and said Jno. is assigned a tract, he being an heir, located on Fleming Creek, said John Field deeds said Callaman.

Geo. Tanner—Of Fleming, to Jno. Tanner, personal property. Aug. 9, 1799.

Trustees of Flemingsburg—To Hezekiah Lyon of Bourbon, lots in Flemingsburg. March 11, 1799.

John Fields—Of Ohio Co. (Ky.), to Geo. Stockton and Wm. Murphy of Fleming, land on Fleming Creek, patented by Benj. Roberts. June 2, 1799.

Thos. Pearce, Sr., and wife, Elizabeth—Of Fleming, to Wm. Browning, land in Fleming, part of 900 a. survey entered by Joshua Bennett, decd., and patented by Wm. M. Bennett of Berkeley Co., Va. 1799.

John Keith—Of Fleming to Wm. Scott of Bucks Co., Penn., lot in Flemingsburg. Nov. 23, 1799.

Shadrach Nye—Of Sumner Co., Tenn., to Richard Hart of Fleming, land in Fleming. March 25, 1799.

Wm. Bennett—Of Berkeley Co., Va., appts. Geo. Stockton (Stogdon) of Fleming, atty. to convey land located in name of Joshua Bennett, now decd., to Andrew Swearingen and Ralph Morgan, both of Ky. Apr. 1, 1799.

Thos. Dale—Of Loudoun Co., Va., appts. Jno. Keith of Fleming, atty. to convey land patented him by Va. to Geo. Stockton.   Nov. 3, 1799.

John Rust—Of Fauquier Co., Va., appts. Jas. Rust atty. to investigate land office relative to tracts, and receive land located by Triplett, the 1-2 allotted hrs. of Samuel Baley, decd., and all other lands. Feb. 23, 1798.

Jno Kenton—Of Mason Co., trustee for Simon Kenton and wife, Elizabeth, deeds Thos. Hughes land in Fleming. Feb. 12, 1800.

Benj. Kirtly—Hr. to estate of Benj. Roberts, decd., and assignee of Travis Kirtly, decd., hr. of estate of said Roberts, and John Fields, hr. of said Roberts and assignee of Benj. Fields, Aquila Fields, Zacharias Fields, Barnett Fields, Henry Fields, Reubin Fields, John Roberts and Beverly Kirtly, hrs. of said Benj. Roberts, decd., and Geo. Stockton, Jr., assignee of Benj., Joseph, William, Adolajah, Eliah and Abijah Dulany, hrs. of said Benj. Roberts, decd., and Robt. Barnes, Jr., assignee of Benj., Joseph and Geo. Roberts, hrs. of said Benj. Roberts, decd., and Wm. McCormick, assignee of Alcany Dulany, heir of said Benj. Roberts, and Geo. Smoot, assignee of Henry, Benj. and Joseph Fields and Peachy Kirtly, hrs. of aforesaid Benj. Roberts, agree to abide by division of land. 1800.

Mercer Beason and wife, Catherine—Of Fleming, to Archibald and John Hamilton, of same, land in Fleming patented in name of Mercer Beason, hr. at law of Mercer Beason, decd. Jan. 13, 1800.

Ralph Morgan and wife, Mary—Of Montgomery Co., and John Hughs and wife, Ann, of Bourbon Co., to Dav'd Stuart, land in Fleming. Apr. 4, 1800.

Geo. Stockton, Jr.—To Hugh Crawford of Lexington, Ky., land in Fleming. May 2, 1800.

Simon Kenton and wife, Elizabeth—Of North West Territory, Ross. Co., to Abraham Lifgory, land in Fleming. May 24, 1800.

Nancy Hughes, Hugh McKibbon and wife, Susannah, Jesse Roye (Raw) and wife, Mourning, said Nancy, Susannah and Mourning being hrs. of John Hughes, late of Mason Co., decd., to Peter Hysong. Said Hughes left will in which he conveyed to above daughters one-ninth part of remainder of estate. May 13, 1799.

David Campbell—Of Fleming, consideration of moving, etc., appts. Robt. Morrison atty. to recover all due him as admr. of estate of Donald Kennedy, decd., who died at or near falls of Ohio. Sept. 18, 1800.

Jno. Canstant and wife, Elizabeth—Of Fleming, to Jeremiah Thompson of Hampshire Co., Va., land located in Hampshire Co. Nov. 10, 1800.

Joseph Smith—Of Fleming to Wm. Bennington, Jr., of same, all goods in court inventory of estate of Robt. Smith, decd., recorded in Fleming. Jan. 12, 1801.

Robert Armstrong, Jr.—Of Fleming, to Thomas Daugherty, slave. May 2, 1801.

Patrick Queally—Of Bourbon Co., for love and affection to Garland Bradford, of same, but more especially in consideration of whole personal property of which Wm. Bradford of Md., died seized of whom sd. Graland (Garland) is only son and heir, and "I having since intermarried with Sarah Bradford, widow of Said William," and taken into my custody all effects, etc. Oct. 15, 1800.

Jno. Archer—Late of Augusta Ca., Va., decd., made will and apptd. Jno. Poage and Robt. Armstrong extrs., and sd. Poage has departed this life and sd. Armstrong, sole extr., said Robt. Armstrong of Fleming for divers causes, moving, etc., apptd. Jno. Crawford of Augusta Co., atty. as extr. of sd. will. June 26, 1801.

Jno. Kenton—Trustee of Simon Kenton, of Hamilton Co., Territory, N. W. Ohio, to Thos. Hughes, land in Fleming. June 25, 1801.

Lewis Davis—Of Hamilton Co., Territory N. W. Ohio, to Owen Keith and Jno. Keith of Fleming. May 13, 1802.

Daniel Wilson—To James Richards, both of Fleming, lot in Flemingsburg. May 29, 1802.

Margaret Harrison—Extrix. of will of Samuel Harrison, decd., of Berkeley Co., Va., appts. son, Samuel, atty. to negotiate with Gabriel Evans, assignee of Geo. Stockton, concerning tract of 400 a. for conveyance of which sd. Samuel executed bond to sd. Stockton, then to deed sd. Evans. Sept. 24, 1801.

Edward Anderson and wife, Bathsheba—Of Fleming to Jno. Green of Mason, land in Fleming. Sept. 24, 1802.

Marsham Belt—Of Fleming and Thos Belt. of Fayette, Marsham Belt, Jas. Chappell, who married Alice Belt, Jno. Faris, who married Eleanor Belt, of Fleming aforesaid, William of Fayette, Thos. Hutton, who married Polly Belt, Joseph Cross Belt, Dennis Belt, Fielding Belt and Elizabeth Belt by Joseph C. Belt, her gdn., of Fleming, all of Ky., hrs. of Marsham Belt, Sr., late of Fleming Co., decd. Oct. 8, 1802.

Jeremiah Foster—Who intermarried with Joanna Neale (one of the legatees of Joseph Neale, late of Fauquir Co., Va., decd.) and sd. Joanna, and Geo. B. Maddux, who intermarried with Judith Neale (one of the legatees of sd. Joseph Neale, decd.) and sd. Judith, of Fleming Co., to Benjamin Neale of county of Hampshire, Va., whereas sd. Joseph died possessed of 1000 a. patented in name of sd. Joseph located in Bullett Co., Ky., and whereas sd. Joseph left will in Fauquier Vo., Va., devising said tract to five daughters, Sarah, Ann, Polly, Judith and Joanna, parties of first part deed sd. tract. Aug. 4, 1803.

Robt. Gill—Of Fleming to Thos. Cornwell, land in Fleming, entered and patented in name of Jeremiah Powers. Nov. 15, 1803.

Jeremiah Powers—Of Montgomery Co., to Robt. Gill and Jas. Christy of Fleming, land in Fleming. Nov. 15, 1803.

John Brown and Lieurainer, his wife—Of Fleming, to Wm. Secrez of same. Jan., 1804.

Hamilton Reed and Deliverance, his wife—Of Fleming, to Jno. Ross, Sr., of Mason, land in Fleming. March 9, 1804.

Statement—By Wm. Blair that one-third part of mills and farm of which Joseph Goslin died possessed, was all that came into his hands as guardian. Apr., 1824. Farm on which Nathan Goslin now lives." 1825.

Jas Blair—In consideration of moving, etc., emancipates slave. 1819.

David Holt and wife, Elizabeth, Jno. McFarland and wife, Margaret, Andrew Todd and Jno. Todd, infants under 21 yrs. by Mary Todd, gdn., legal representatives of Andrew Todd, decd., deed to Jno. T. Egar and wife, Mary, lots in Flemingsburg. July 14, 1819.

Wade Mosby—Of Powhatan Co., Va., to Joseph Goddard of Fleming, land in Fleming, patented in name of Little Berry Mosby, by Wm. P. Roper, atty. Aug., 1819.

Thos. Bodley and wife, Catherine, Robt. Pogue and wife, Jane—To Henry Bruce, of Fleming, land in Fleming. Jan. 14, 1819.

Elizabeth Little, widow of Henry Little, decd., Samuel Little, Geo. Little, John Jackson and wife, Rachel, late Little, Henry Little, and Abraham Little, hrs. of Henry Little, decd., to Willis D. Lee, land in Fleming. May 1, 1818.

James Thomas, Sr.—Of Fleming, to Asa Thomas, grandson of said James, in consideration of agreement to live with said James and his aged wife, Amia, deed for land adjoining Elijah Thomas, son of said James Thomas. June 1, 1819.

Jno. D. Stockton—Deputy for Jas. Parks, Sheriff, witnesseth whereas execution placed in hands of sd. Stockton issued from office of Fleming Co. Ck. by virtue of judgment in fovar of Robt. Walker, Sr., Samuel Walker, Elizabeth Walker, Jno. Walker and others, hrs. of William Walker, decd., Elizabeth Morrison and Sarah Morrison and others, hrs. of Robt. Morrison, decd., Thos. Bodley, Chapin Austin, Henry Timberlake. Jno. Crenshaw and Reubin Austin, agst. estate of Edward Hord, and Jno. Thomas Wm. Ewell and Smallwood Coghills, amount due hereby delivered. June, 1819.

In Circuit Court of Fleming—Jno. D. Stockton, complainant, and Thos. C. Brown, Thos. Shannon and wife, Margaret, Joseph, Jesse, Eleanor and Isabella Shannon, defendants. commrs. were apptd. to consign defendants lots and to Thos. Brown the lots allotted

Sarah Hackney, late Sarah Shannon, she and her late husband (not named) having heretofore conveyed Dan'l. G. Brown prior to his death which upon his death descended to Thos. Brown, deed to Jno. Stockton.   March 11, 1820.

Isaac Hopkins—Of Fleming, to Nathaniel Graham, land in Fleming, bounded by land of Ezekiel Hopkins, Thos. Newcomb, David Hopkins and Laterman's line.   Oct. 15, 1818.

David Stewart, Jno. Stewart, Chas. Stewart, Robt. Stewart, Elizabeth Stewart, Margaret Stewart and Richie Morrow and Ann Morrow, his wife, sd. David, Jno., Chas. and Elizabeh of Green Co., Ohio, and Robt. Stewart, Ritchie Morrow and Ann, of Fleming, deed to Samuel Stewart of Fleming, land in Fleming.   Deed recorded Highland Co., Ohio.

Jas. Graham and wife, Mary, Jas. Story and wife, Rebecca, Jno. Story and Elijah Story and Martha, wife, Wm. Story and Jane, his wife, Edward Ricketts and Sarah, his wife, and Lewis Story and Ann, his wife, of Fleming, deed tract in Fleming to Joseph Story.   Feb. 26, 1830.

Morton Alexander and Penelope, Henry Renoe and Priscilla, late Alexander, Basil Alexander, Jno. Threlkeld and Cynthia, late Alexander, of Mo., to Benj. Summers.   Whereas William Alexander, late of Fleming Co., died intestate, leaving said Cynthia, who has since intermarried with said John Threlkeld, and other hrs. mentioned, and he died seized of land which has descended to said hrs., said hrs. deed sd. Summers.   Oct. 28, 1830.

Robt. Barr and wife, Mary,—Of Boone Co., Mo., to Lloyd Warfield of Boone Co., Ky., all interest to land in Fleming. surveyed in name of Ralph Morgan and Isaac Barr.   Apr. 18, 1830.

FRANKLIN COUNTY

DEED BOOK A.

Page 2, Nov. 19, 1801—John Barry Darby of Baltimore, Md., son and hr. of Daniel Darby to Wm. Hawkins of same place, tract in Fayette, 2100 a.

Page 4, Oct. 10, 1801—Jonathan Swift of Alexandria Va., merchant, to Wm. Mattocks Rogers of Boston, Suffolk Co., Mass., all interest in tract called Springfield on water of Green River, Hardin Co., Ky.   9200 a.

Page 23, Mar. 10, 1802—Jno. Lewis and Andrew Lewis to Chas. Lewis, land in Woodford Co., Ky., part of tract granted Jno., Andrew and Chas., by Commonwealth of Va.   Patent dated July 14, 1780 as hrs. of Chas. Lewis, decd.   Acknowledged in Bath and Kanawha Cos., Va.

Page 26, Dec. 7, 1802—Jno. Poage and wife, Rachel, of Augusta Co.,

Va., to Jno. Posey of Franklin Co., Ky., land in Fayette, part of Thos. Poag's preemption, assignee of Robt. Todd. Acknowledged in Rockbridge Co., Va.

Page 35, Nov. 18, 1801—Thos. Evans and Mary Ann Morton of Edgefield Dist., S. C., for divers causes, hereunto moving appt. friend, David Clarkson of Albemarle Co., Va., atty., to recover property due as gdns. of Wm. Ragland Morton, Thos. Walker Morton and Jno. Rhodes Morton, located in Ky.

Page 39, Apr. 9, 1803—Geo. Lewis of King George Co., Va., by Gabriel Lewis, atty., to Matthew Patton of Bourbon Co., Ky., land on Deer Creek in Ky.

Page 43, Apr. 15, 1803—Lucas Vanarsdall of Mercer Co., Ky., and wife, Jane, to Lucas Elmondorf of Kingston, Ulster Co., N. Y., land in Shelby and Jefferson Cos., Ky.

Page 51, Jan. 8, 1803—Jonothan Williams of Philadelphia, Pa., power of atty. to Josiah Williams of Woodford Co., Ky.

Page 53—Jonathan Williams, late of Philadelphia, Pa., now of West Point, N .Y. (See above).

Page 57, Mar. 28, 1801—Michael O. Mealy of Baltimore, Md., merchant, to August Jacob Schwartze and Jonas Marean of same, merchants, land in Bourbon Co., Ky.

Page 67, Nov. 19, 1801—Jno. Wigglesworth and wife, Philadelphia, of Spottsylvania Co., Va., deed John Jackson, land in Bourbon Co., Ky.

Page 75, Nov. 11, 1802—John Barry Darby of Baltimore, Co., Md., son of Daniel Darby, deed to Jno. Hunter of Washington Co., Pa., land in Fayette Co., Ky.

Page 78, Nov. 11, 1804—John Barry Darby and wife, Harriet of Baltimore, Md., to Chas. Carnan and Thos. Cradock Walker, both of Baltimore, land in Fayette Co., Ky.

Page 88—Samuel Evans and wife, Hannah of Montgomery Co., Pa., to Joseph Cloud of Philadelphia, Pa., meter and refiner to the mint of the U. S., Alner Cloud, Lydia Offutt, wife of Thos. Offutt and Ann Gary, wife of Everard Gary of Montgomery Co., Md., consideration of 5 shillings, deed to Joseph and Abner Cloud, Lydia Offutt and Ann Gary, three equal fourth parts of all adjoining tracts in Jefferson Co., Ky., in neighborhood of Jno. May and Cos. survey.

Page 95—John Walden and wife, Litianna of Spottsylvania Co., Va., to Jonathan Clark of Jefferson Co., Ky., land in Livingston Co., Ky.

Apr. 15, 1803—Lucas Elmendorf of Kingston, Ulster Co., N. Y., to Lucas Vanarsdall of Harrodsburg, Mercer Co., Ky., land in Shelby and Jefferson Cos., Ky.

March 22, 1802—John Lewis of Fredericksburg, Va., to Mary A Swearengen, Kitty Stubblefield, Geo. Noble, Thos. I. A. Noble and Jno.

L (?) W. Noble, hrs. of Geo. Noble, decd. of Frederick Co., Va., land in Ky., in dist. alloted by Va., for Military warrants, 1000 a.

Mar. 4, 1803—Richard Ridgely, apptd. trustee by chancellor of Md., to sell real estate of Dr. Ephrian Howard, decd. of Anne Arundel. Md., to Stephen Winchester of Spottsylvania Co., Va., land in Shelby Co., Ky.

Page 107, Mar. 11, 1803—Stephen Winchester of Fredreicksburg, Va., to Joshua Howard of Frederick Co., Va., tract above mentioned.

Page 113, July 18,1803—Jno. Smith, late of N. C., died, seized of land in Jessamine and Harrison Cos., Ky., to which lands his widow, Sarah Smith (now Sarah Lee) is entitled to dower, not yet assigned. Wm. Bailey of Wayne Co., Ky., as gdn. of Jas. Smith, under 21 yrs., one of hrs. of Jno. Smith, decd., assigns Sarah Lee remainder of a tract after laying off tract conveyed to Jno. Dougherty.

Page 116, Mar. 9, 1803—Richard C. Anderson and wife, Sally of Jefferson Co., Ky., to Thos. Theweatt of Halifax Co., Va., land in Livingston Co., Ky.

Page 118, May 25, 1802—Dennis Warner and Sarah, late Neale, Henry Daws and Ann, late Neale, which said Sarah and Ann are devisees under will of Joseph Neale, decd. to Benjamin Neale, all their lands devised in said will, recorded in Farquier Co., Va., which was to be divided among five daus. of said Joseph Neale.

Page 124, Aug. 20, 1803—Henry Troutman of Frankfort, Ky., and Daniel Russell of Boston, Mass., articles of agreement regarding two tracts owned by Russell in Mason Co., Ky.

Page 126—Wm. Smith, admr. of Jno. Smith, decd, of Hawkins Co., Tenn., appts. Wm. Bailey of Wayne Co., Ky., atty. to convey to Jno. Doherty of Jefferson Co.

Page 128, July 18, 1803—Wm. Smith, Gideon Smith and Jas. Smith, hrs. of Jno. Smith, decd. to Jno. Dougherty of Jefferson, land in Harrison Co., Wm. Bailey of Wayne Co. acting for Jas. Smith, under 21 yrs.

Page 142, July 1, 1803—Jno. Fowler and wife, Millisent, of Fayette Co., Ky., to Thos. Underwood, Jr., of Richmond Va. 666 a. in dist. set apart for officers and soldiers of Va. Line, So. side of Green River.

Page 147, Mar. 21, 1801—Wm. Mills, Jr., Physician, Louisa Co., Va., appts. Wm. Winslow of Franklin Co., Ky., atty. to recover Ky. Lands.

Page 148, Oct. 17, 1803—Geo. Rowlard of Franklin Co. to Jas. Hawthorn and wife, Milly, late Mily Rowlard of Nelson Co., Ky.

Page 150, Oct. 7, 1803—Geo. Rowland of Franklin Co., Ky., to Amos Anderson and wife, Sally, late Sally Rowland.

Page 156, Oct. 13, 1803—Colby Ship and Sally, his wife of Gallatin Co., Ky., to Philemon Thomas of Mason Co., Ky., land in Floyd Co.

Page 161, Nov. 2, 1803—Otho Beatty and Polly, his wife of Franklin Co., Ky., to Cornelias Beatty of Fayette, lots in Frankfort conveyed said Beatty by Geo. Campbell and wife, Agnes of Woodford Co., Ky.

Page 167, Oct. 10, 1803—Wm. May of Nelson Co., Ky., to Thos. Lewis and wife, Ann of Chesterfield Co., Va., said Ann being extrx. of Jno. May, decd., land in trust for hrs. of Jno. May, decd., located in Breckinridge, formerly Jefferson and Breckinridge, formerly Nelson.

Page 177, Dec. 1803—Robt. Bullock of Louisa Co., Va., power of atty. to bro., Lewis Bullock; whereas mother, Ann Bullock of Louisa is about to give up certain slaves to be divided amongst her chdn., and not convenient for him to be there; atty. to act for him in division.

Page 178, Dec. 7, 1803—Baker Ewing and wife, Lititia of Franklin Co., Ky., to Jno. Smith of Green Co., Ky., land in Green Co.

Page 179, Dec. 5, 1803—Otho Beatty and wife, Polly of Franklin Co., Ky., to Nathanial Rochester of Washington Co., Md., land in Frankfort.

Page 182, Dec. 16, 1803—Jas. Reeves for self and as atty. for extr. of Thos. Reeves, decd. of Henry Co., Ky., to Nathan Cartmill of Bullitt Co., land in Bullitt.

Page 184, July 23, 1802—Wm. Trigg, hr. at law of Stephen Trigg, decd. to Alexander Robinson of Mercer Co., Ky., land in Shelby Co.

Page 185, Apr. 6, 1802—David Jameson and wife, Mary formerly Mary Mennis and Wm. Burt and wife, Frances, late Mennis, which said Mary and Frances intermarried with said David Jameson and Wm. Burt of Culpeper Co., Va., to Philip Slaughter of Culpeper Co.; whereas Holman Mennis was entitled as a Captain for three yrs. in Va. Line to 4000 a. Military land and patents were issued for two tracts of 1000 a. each to Mary and Frances, hrs. of said Holman Mennis, now decd., deed of 1000 a. of said land.

Page 193, Dec. 15, 1787—Elisha Lockland of Washington Co., Md., for divers causes, hereunto moving, appts. Cornelius Gather of Nelson Co., Ky., atty. to convey to Thos. Waller of Washington Co., Pa., all interest in tract in Nelson Co.

Page 195, Aug. 13, 1803—Jno. Craig, Sr., of Boone Co., Ky., together with Robt. Johnson and Elijah Craig as trustees of said Craig of Scott Co. to Geo. Given, Sr. of Lincoln Co., Ky., land in Garrard Co., Ky.

Page 197, May 27, 1813—Nathaniel Richardson, late Sheriff of Franklin Co., Ky., by deputy, Allen Richardson, to John Thompson of Philadelphia Pa.

Page 198, Sept. 3, 1803—Edmon Thomas, Register of Land Office of Ky., to Jno. Martin of Clark Co., land in Madison Co., Ky.

Page 201, Jan. 6, 1804—Jas. Stewart of Philadelphia, Pa., to David

Henly of State of Tenn., whereas said Stewart entitled to 45499¼ a. in Franklin, surveyed by Chas. Morgan in 1784 by warrants from Va., deeds 2-3 parts to said Henly.

Aaron Powell of Bedford Co., Va., appts. Jno. Roberts of Montgomery Co., Ky., atty. to execute deed to land in Lincoln Co., Ky.

Page 426, June 10, 1803—Samuel Estill and wife, Jane, of Madison Co., Ky., to Green Clay, Wm. Irvine and Jos. Barnett of same Co., his interest in lands as partner of bro. Jas. Estill, decd.

Nov. 10, 1804—Jno. Brown and Margaretta of Franklin, to Samuel McKee, land in Pulaski Co., Ky.

Page 434, Aug 7, 1804—James Penn to Robt. Means, both of Richmond, Va., land in Ky., in district set apart for officers and soldiers of Va. Line on Drakes Creek.

Page 207, Nov. 22, 1803—Christopher Greenup of Frankfort, to Wm. Adkin of Garrard, land in Lincoln Co., Ky.

Dec. 15, 1801—Wm. Hunter and Achilles Sneed, atty. for Geo. Graham and Jno. Graham, trustees, in a deed between Jesse Sumns of Alexandria, Va. 1st part; and Walter Jones, Jr., same town, 2nd part; and Geo. Graham of town of Dumfries, State aforesaid and Jno. Graham, 3rd part; and Alexander Henderson of Dumfries, 4th part bearing date July 1800, recorded by Clerk of Ct. of Appeals of Ky., and Alexander Henderson, late of Dumfries, but now of Alexandria.

Page 228, Feb. 21, 1803—Wm. King of Nelson Co., Ky., to Edmund Thomas and Geo. Madison of Franklin Co., land in Jefferson Co.

Page 232, Oct. 26, 1803—Thos. Logwood, by atty., Edmond Lockett, Extr. of Edmond Lockerd, decd. of Va., to Cave Johnson of Boon Co., Ky., land on So. Branch of Licking.

Page 238, Mar. 21, 1803—Wm. Davis and wife, Anne of Woodford to Ballser Snyder of Fayette lot in Frankfort.

Page 241, Dec. 6, 1803—Jno. Smith and wife, Sarah of Green Co., to Baker Ewing of Franklin Co., land in Green.

Page 248 Dec. 7, 1802—Jno. McCoun, Jr., Jno. McGee and wife, Polly, Samuel Adams and wife Jane of whom aforesaid Jno. McCoun and Polly and Jane are hrs. of James McCoun Sr., decd., of Mercer Co. ,Ky., to Jas. Legerwood of same place, land in Mercer, now in Franklin Co.

Page 266, June, 1803—Edmund Thomas of Franklin, to Thos. Corneal of Boone, land in Boone Co., Ky.

Page 265 Jan. 13, 1804—Chas. Ford of Mercer Co., Ky., and Lewis Neill of Philadelphia, Pa., land in Ohio Co., Ky., part of tract claimed by Wm. Montgomery, entered in name of Thos. Crow said land descended from said Crow to his hrs., Thos. Crow, Jno. Crow, Andrew L. Crow and Mary Crow, now Mary Montgomery and said Thos., Jno. and Andrew sold to said Chas. Ford.

Page 270, Feb. 12, 1804—Mann Satterwhite of Fayette Co., Ky., to Noah Sharp of Bedford Co., Va., land in Franklin Co.

Page 272, Nov. 2, 1803—Josua Howard of Md., to Samuel Robinson, son-in-law to said Josua, of same State, deed of gift of land located in Shelby Co., Ky. Acknowledged in Baltimore, Md.

Page 276, Mar. 18, 1804—Humphrey Marshall of Frankfort, to son, Thos. Alexander Marshall, deed of gift of land in Hardin Co., Ky.

Page 278, June 18, 1803—Jno. Cockey Owings of Md. and Thos. Deye Owings of Lexington, Ky., deed to Walter Beall of Nelson Co., Ky.

Page 238—Jas. Roberts of Franklin Co., Ky., to Alexander Parker and Lawson McCullough of Lexington, Ky.

Page 291, June, 1804—Chas. B. Huton of Albemarle Co., Va., to Wm. Huton of Clark Co., Ga., land in Ky., on So. Side Cumberland River.

Page 298, June 1, 1804—Samuel Throgmorton of Franklin Co. ,Ky., to Samuel Forman of Monmouth Co., N. J., land in Franklin Co., Ky.

Page 299, Apr 7, 1803—Bernard Devin of Warren Co., Ky., to Jno. Mulanphy of Franklin, land in Franklin Co.

June 11, 1803—Lewis Hickman and wife, Sarah of Fayette, Richard Laurence Thomson, Laurence Thomson and Kiseah, his wife of Madison Co., Ky., to Jno. Hart of Fayette Co. ,all interest in land-estate of Simpson Hart, decd., which they claim as legatees of said Simpson Hart, also that which said Laurence and Kizeah claim as hrs.-at-law to their son, Nathaniel Hart Thomson, decd., who was one of legatees of said Simpson Hart, decd.

Page 311, Dec. 9, 1803—Bernard McNutt (McNeitt) of township of W. Hanover, Dauphia, Pa., to Jesse McNeitt of same place, land in Fayette, granted by patent to Jacob Myers, assignee of Wm. McNeitt as hr.-at-law of Joseph McNeitt, decd, May 6, 1788.

Page 314, Oct. 6. 1803—John P. Harrison of Stafford Co., Va., to Humphrey Marshall of Frankfort, Ky., land on So. Side Ky. (river). Acknowledged Farquier Co., Va., Sept. 26, 1803, by Whitting Digges, Atty.

Page 317, May 14, 1804—Hester Groveneur, Samuel Groveneur and Thos. Knox, Extrx. and Extrs. of Nicholas Grovernur, late of City of N. Y., merchant, decd., to Lucus Elmendorf of Kingston, Ulster Co., N. Y. Said Nicholas in will empowered Extrs. to dispose of real estate, except lots in 7th Ward of N. Y., and dwellinghouse and apptd. parties of 1st part and brothers-in-law, Peter Kemble and Thos. Bibby, Extrs. and parties of 1st part have proved will, but Peter Kemble and Thos. Bibby have not taken the burden, parties of 1st part deed tracts issued on Treasury Warrants from Va.

Page 323, June 25, 1797—Mary Hassenclever of Philadelphia, widow, in her own right and as Extrx. of will of Jacob Milcher, late of same city, Gent., decd., to Thos. Fisher, Northern Liberties of sd. city 2 undivided fourth pts. (whole in four parts to be divided) in 9000 a. bearing date 22, Apr. 1785 in Campbell Co., Ky. (formerly Fayette) granted unto Jno. Harvie of Richmond, Va., who deeded Isaac Melcher of Philadelphia, Pa., decd., who died seized thereof by last will dated May 22, 1788, recorded in Philadelphia, devised to bros., Adam and Jacob Melcher and sisters, Mary Hassenclever and Elizabeth Shallers, and sd. Jacob Melcher died and appointed sd. Mary Hassencliver, Extrx., who was empowerd to sell decedant's ¼ pt. and she entitled to ¼ pt. by will of bro., Isaac Melcher.

Page 328, Dec. 5, 1796—Jno. Hooper and wife, Ann, of Buckingham Co., Va., to Stephen Thomson Mason of Loudoun Co., Va., Military land warrant issued from Va., Apr. 6, 1784 to sd. Jno. and Ann, she dau. of Jno. Quarles, decd., due in consequence of services for 3 yrs. as Lt. in Va. Line.

Page 335, Oct. 10, 1786—Jas. McConnell and Mary, his wife, of Fayette on Ky. River to Humphrey Marshall, land in Fayette being preemption granted Benj. Hayden.

Page 340—Leven Powell of Loudoun Co., Va., appts. Christopher Greenup of Lincoln Co., atty. ,to transact business in Ky.

Page 344, July 19, 1804—Wm. Fenwick of Franklin Co., Ky., to Wm. Lane of Clarke Co., Ky., land in Franklin.

Samuel Jones—Of Philadelphia, Pa., Minister and Thos. Ewing of same, Merchant, have right to ⅓ part of 113482 a. tract in Nelson Co., Ky., appoint friend, Jas. Lee, Esq., Judge of Court of Common Pleas for Cumberland C., N. J. to transact business regarding said land.

Page 348, Nov. 28, 1796—James Frenchard, late of Philadelphia, Pa., now Bordentown, N. J., Gent., to Rev. Burgiss Allison of Bordentown, ⅓ pt. tract in Nelson Co., Ky., containing 113482 a. granted on two Treasury Warrants issued 1783, 1785 by Va., to Henry Banks and Richard Claiborne in own right and as assignee of Philip Barber for another moiety thereof 1784, which tract was conveyed by Richard Claiborne, atty. to Henry Banks to sd. Jas. Frenchar, 1794, recorded Hardin Co., Ky., also interests of sd. Frenchard and hrs. to hold sd. ⅓ part land granted sd. Burgess Allison and hrs. to use of sd. Allison and sd. Frenchard deeds sd. Allison, excepting persons claiming from Frenchard by leases by article of agreement between sd. Frenchard and David Barbee of Kingdom of Ireland, 1794, it being intended to let sd. Allison into ⅓ of sd. interest of sd. Jas. Frenchard.

Page 352, Nov. 28, 179—Jas. Frenchard, late of Philadelphia, Pa., now of Bordentown, N. J., to David Allison of Philadelphia, land in Nelson Co., Ky.

Page 363, Jan. 11, 1797—David Allison of Philadelphia, Pa., to Wm. Shannon of same place, land in Nelson Co., Ky. (Note: David Allison owned land in other Ky. Cos., as shown by deeds

Page 369, Feb. 23, 1804—Wm. Shannon of Philadelphia, appts. Benj. Brown Cooper of Gloucester Co., N. J., atty.

Page 396, Mar. 12, 1801—Jno. Timmons (Simmons?) of Frederick Co., Va., to Elias Rector of Co., Ross Territory of N. W., deeds land in Henderson Co., Ky.

Page 399, June 23, 1804—Elias Rector of Ross Co., Ohio, to Wm. Rector of same, land in Henderson Co., Ky., in district set apart for officers and soldiers of Va. Line. (Note: Same tract above granted by Jno. Timons to Elias Rector).

Page 403, March 10, 1804—Samuel Robertson the 3rd of State of Md., to Edward Crow, land in Shelby Co., Ky.

Page 412, Feb. 13, 1804—Wm. Tyler and wife, Mary, of Louisa Co., Va., to Zachariah Herndon of Orange Co., Va., all sd. Mary's interest to lands of which her father, Zachariah Herndon, died seized located in Ky.

Feb. 27, 1804—Thos. Herndon and wife, Sarah, of Orange Co., Va., to Zachariah Herndon of Orange, all interest to lands of which Zachariah Herndon, father to sd. Thos, died seized located in Ky.

Page 417—Jno. Herndon of Orange Co., Va., to Zachariah Herndon of Orange all interest to lands of Zachariah Herndon, father to sd. Zachariah and sd. John, of which he died, seized, located in Ky.

Page 419, Feb. 14, 1788—Thos. Alcock of Caroline Co., Va., to Abraham Buford of Mercer Co., Ky., land in Madison Co., Ky., as by patent to sd. Alcock, dated 1786.

Page 422, July 26, 1804—Abraham Maury of Co. of Williamson, Tenn., to Daniel McClain of Scott Co., Ky., sd. Maury having executed bond to Jno. Grant of Campbell Co., Ky., for land in Scott, and since sd. Grant executed bond to sd. McClain, sd. Maury grants sd. McClain sd. tract in Scott Co., Ky.

Dec. 6, 1804—Jno. Dupey of Henry Co., Ky., to George Trimble of Garrard Co., Ky., land in Garrard.

Page 440, Dec. 18, 1804—Jno. Adair, Register of Land Office of Ky., to Abner Baker, Gent., of Garrard Co., Ky., sd. Adair by act of Assembly 1799 to expose for sale, tracts belonging to Jas. Kennedy, non-resident of Ky., in district set apart for officers and soldiers of Va. Line.

Dec. 21, 1804—Christopher Greenup of Franklin to Walter Beall, Sr. of Mason.

Page 446, Jan. 1, 1805—Preston Breckenridge of Fayette and wife, Elizabeth, to Stephen Trigg of Botetourt Co., Va., land in Scott and Woodford Cos., Ky., 1-5 part being Elizabeth's portion as legatee of Stephen Trigg, decd.

July 26, 1800—Baker Ewing and wife, Letitia of Franklin to Robt. Wooldridge of same, land in Franklin Co., Ky.

Oct. 21, 1794—Wm. Logan of Lincoln Co., Ky., to Jno. Daugherty of Jefferson Co., Ky.

Oct. 20, 1804—Geo. Brooke and wife, Judith, to Humphrey Marshall, land in Woodford, part of survey made for John Marshall.

Aug. 29, 1804—Wm. Luttrell of Westmoreland Co., Va., to Chas. Buck of same Co. and State, whereas Jno. Luttrell, late of Orange Co., N. C., did by will, 20th March, 1775 recorded in Orange Co., give to bros., Hugh, Thos., and Wm. Luttrell, ⅓ of tract in which he held interest with Richard Henderson Co., which they purchased of Cherokee Indians on Mississippi River, and whereas sd. Thos. Luttrell above mentioned is dead and Hugh Luttrell from his long absence from the U. S. is supposed dead, whereby land remains to Wm. Lutrell, in consideration of $1.00 and tract in Westmoreland where sd. Wm. resides, sd. Wm. Lutrell and wife, Kisiah deed all property accruing through Jno. Lutrell, decd., or sd. bros.

Page 46—Geo. Madison and Jno. L. Madison, Extrs. of will of Gabriel Madison, decd., for divers causes, hereunto moving appt. Jesse Cravens of Ohio Co., Ky., atty.

Page 470, July 12, 1802—Nimrod Long and wife, Eleanor of Va., to David Moore of Franklin Co., Ky.

March 1, 1805—Jas. Kincaid and wife, Sarah of Madison Co., Ky., to Thos. Hart, Jr., Samuel Brown and Richard Pindall, land in Madison.

Page 480—Wm. Allen and wife, Nancy of Buckingham Co., Va., to Chas. Patterson, (Paterson) Jr., land in Woodford Co., Ky.

Page 484, Apr. 30—R. Patterson to William Greene, whereas sd. Patterson located 10000 a. for Henry Green in name of Thos. Bell and hrs. and sd. Bell having conveyed 5000 a. of sd. land to Ann Green, Wm. Green and Eleanor Smith, wife of Jno. Smith, legatees of sd. Henry Green, etc., sd. Patterson conveys to sd. Wm. Green. (Note: Following deed styles Robt. Patterson of State of Ohio, May 2, 1805.

March 10, 1804—Mary Mason, widow of Stephens Mason of Loudoun Co., Va., and Jno. Thomson Mason of Georgetown, D. C. to Jno. Brown of Frankfort, whereas Stephens Mason by will, April 2, 1803, recorded in Loudoun Co., Va., left all estate to sd. Mary and John T. Mason in following terms: "To beloved wife, Mary and dear bro., Jno. Thompson Mason and hrs,. any family I may have, chdn. to be educated." By virtue of sd. trust, sd. Mary and John T. Mason deed land on Cumberland River, being the same granted Edward Dowse in 1786 and by sd. Dowse to sd. Stephens Thompson Mason, decd.

Page 496, Nov. 1804—Jno. Fowler of Fayette Co., Ky., to Philip Buckner of Bracken Co., Ky., land in Bracken.

Page 506, Nov. 12, 1804—Abraham Hapton of Woodford for divers causes, hereunto moving, appts. Wm. Taylor atty.

Page 511, Dec. 8, 1804—Wm. Duvall of Richmond, Va., to Humphrey Marshall, land in Boone Co., Ky.

Dec. 15, 1804—Elijah Craig and wife, Ann of Gallatin Co., Ky., to Baker Ewing of sd. Co., land at mouth of Ky. River.

Page 518, Apr. 19, 1805—David Foreman by agent, Geo. Horine, both of Mercer Co., Ky., to Geo. Craig of Franklin, land in Gallatin.

Page 520, June 10, 1803—John Berry Darby of Baltimore, Md., to Moses P. Lancaster of same place, sd. Jno. B. Darby, only surviving child of Daniel Darby, land in Fayette Co., Ky.

Page 536—Frederick Harris of Louisa Co., Va., by will, 1799, recorded in Louisa, 1801 (portion of will given), deed dated Jan. 13, 1804 from Richard Harris and Rhoda, Chas. Harris and Mary, George Harris and Mary, Thos. Holladay and Ann Overton (Harris) Holladay, Overton Harris and Jemima of 1st part to Frederick Harris, other part, whereas Frederick Harris, decd., did by will, bequeath Ky. lands to six of his chdn.: Richard, Chas., Geo., Frederick, Ann Harris (now Ann Holladay) and Jemima, wife of Overton Harris, aforesaid these deed to sd. Frederick Harris.

Deek Book D, Page 311, March 31, 1814—John Strode Hrs. Mary Strode, wife of John Strode, deceased, James Duncan and Elizabeth his wife, formerly Elizabeth Strode, James Strode, Mary McMillin, wife of Robert McMillin, deceased, formerly Mary Strode, John Strode, Nancy Brooks, wife of Abijah Brooks, deceased, formerly Nancy Strode, William Lander and Letitia, his wife, formerly Letitia Strode, Stephen Strode, Thomas Lafferty and Eleanor, his wife, formerly Eleanor Strode, heirs of John Strode, deceased, of Clark County, Ky., appoint Jeremiah, their brother and son of 1st named Mary Strode, wife of John Strode, deceased, of Fleming County, their attorney to take charge of all estate in Franklin County, consisting of 2212 acres.
Note: Old family record of Abijah Brooks, Revolutionary soldier, states he was born in Mass., 1759, son of Samuel Brooks (8-12, 1710-1776) who married 4-2, 1747 Abagail Hastings (3-8, 1727-8-1776); in 1791 married Nancy Strode (5-21, 1770, 7-6, 1855) daughter of Captain John Strode of Berkeley County, Va., and Clark County, Ky. Chdn. of Abijah and Nancy (Strode) Brooks of Clark County, Ky.: Samuel and John of Bourbon County, Ky.: Abijah married his first cousin; Robert married Miss Samantha Young of Boone Co., Mo.; Van married Clemency Young, first cousin of Robert's wife; Thomas died young; Polly married Mr. Duncan and lived in Clay Co., Mo.; Nellie married Thomas Duncan of Ky., no issue; Elizabeth married John Ecton; Abagail married David Hopkins; Ann Wire (9-18, 1798-1888) married John Breckenridge (10-7, 1785-1854).

FRANKLIN COUNTY DEPOSITIONS

(Notes made from papers filed in Franklin County Court House by Hattie Scott, Frankfort, Ky.).

Barbour, Philip B. and Frances T. (late Frances T. Johnson of Va.)—Frances one of heirs of Benj. Johnston, deceased, Robt. Johnson. Benj. Johnston departed this life leaving Wm. Johnson, Lucy Barbour, wife of James Barbour and Frances his only children and hrs. at law. (See Robt. Johnston, 325-322).

Bealle, John—Son and devisee of Walter Bealle, decd., 1810. (321 box).

Boyle, Stephen—Dep.—Clark Co., Ky., 1779 at Strode's Sta., in Oct. (Box 412).

Bullock, Nathaniel, May 16, 1811—Aged about 51 yrs., at court house in Paris, states he came to Ky. in 1777 and settled at Boonesborough; taken prisoner by the Indians at Lower Blue Licks, 1778 and returned to Boonesborough, 1779 to 1783; settled where he now lives on north side of Ky. River, near Boone's Station. Born about 1760. (Box 412).

Coghill, Thos., Heirs—John, Thos., Wm., Ewell and Smallwood Coghill, hrs. of Thos. Coghill. Jan. 1, 1815. (Boxes 320-334).

Cury, Archibald—Woodford Quarter Session—Arch. Curry in the fall of 1788, removed his family from Kent Co., Dela. to Ky., leaving behind his son, James Curry, in possession of his land there (crops, 5 negroes, etc.). He, Arch. Curry, owed John Banning and James Curry was to pay him out of crops, etc., but James was running a store and failed, took money for own debts, . . . Banning brought suit, and in 1789 son, James, applied to a certain Seth Catline for money, etc., to pay Banning, . . . Seth Catline and son, James C., came to this county in 1789, and James was killed by 1790 in expedition vs. Maumee Indians, etc., etc. (Suit filed Oct. 12, 1793. (See Curry vs. Catlins, Box 354-356.)

Couchman, Benedict—Deposes in Paris, Sept., 1805, aged about 49, came to Ky. 1779, to Strode's Sta., in 1786. (Box 412.)

Carneal's Heirs—Thos., Thos. D. Carneal, Alice Breckinridge, wife of James Breckinridge, Thos. C. Coleman, inft. son of James Coleman and his wife, Sally, now deceased, lately Sally Carneal, only heirs of said Thos. Carneal, deceased, etc. See Franklin County wills.) (Box 464.)

Cradelbaugh, Wm. — Dep. — Lived with Daniel Boone, 1776-1783. (Box 412.)

Dawson, Henry—Certificate for Military service, 3 years as Lt. in Va. Line. (Boxes 299-319.)

Duncan, James—Aged 55, deposes at house of Morry Langhorn in Paris, Sat. (first) in Sept., 1805, that he 1st came to Ky. in 1779, went to and from Va. number of times, to Ky. 1782 and back to Va., moved his family to Ky. spring of 1784. (Born 1750.) (Box 412.)

Dunn, Thos.—Aged 71 (in 1811), states he came to Ky. in 1776. (Box 412.)

Finley, George—Deposition taken at house of Samuel McMillan in Harrison County, Apr. 28, 1810, of lawful age, said he was prisoner 15 years with the Indians N. W. of Ohio (evidence, etc.) in Morrison vs. Cowgill. (Boxes 325-332.)

Floyd, Geo. R. C.—John Floyd, John Stewart and wife, Mourning Stewart, Jas. D. Breckinridge, Robt. Breckinridge, Henry B. Breckinridge, and Wm. B. Breckinridge, an infant sues by his next best friend, G. R. C. Floyd, 1784. John Floyd, deceased, leaves estate to George, John and Mourning Floyd, his children, and wife, Jane—she, Jane, married again and survived her husband and divided her estate to her children, George, John Floyd and Mourning, James, Robert, Henry and William, (filed 1814. (Box 392.)

Edmonson, John—Son of a sister of Col. Edw. Stevens, Culpepper County, Va. (Letter Aug. 13, 1783. (Hite heirs, Boxes 354-356.)

Ewing, Dr. John—Heirs: Samuel Ewing, James Sims and wife, Mary; John Hall and wife, Sarah; _____ Moore and wife, Elizabeth; Francis Waller Ewing and wife, Hannah; John Ewing, James S. Ewing, Louisa Donaldson, Robt. Harris and wife, Elizabeth; Sarah Ewing, John, Joseph and Edw. Ewing (4 last minors) and sue by Samuel Ewing, their next best friend. June 29, 1787 Henry Banks deed to Joseph Donaldson, Jr., in Jefferson County (now Hardin County, Ky.), Dr. John having died 1802, leaving following heirs: Samuel Ewing, Mary, wife of James Sims, Sarah, wife of John Hall, James Ewing and Elizabeth, wife of Robt. Harris, and John Ewing, his chdn, Elizabeth, wife of _____ Moore; Thos Wallace Ewing and wife, Hannah, and John Ewing, children of his deceased son, Wm. Ewing and Louisa Davidson, dau. of his deceased dau., Anna, wife of Wm. Davidson, his gd. children; John Ewing, son of Dr. John Ewing died Apr., 1816, leaving Sarah Ewing, John, Joseph, and Edward Ewing, his children and heirs at law, etc. (Filed Aug., 1817.) (Boxes 386-390.)

Hite, Abram—Heirs: sons, Abram, Joseph and Isaac. Isaac died 1794 and left Rebecca V. Hite, mar. Chas. Fishback; Eliz. R. Hite died infant, and Jacob Hite; see suits, box 353, 1815, Mar. 8.

Hardin, John—(Deceased.) Extr. Mark Hardin, Martin Hardin, Christopher Irvin and wife, Jane, Washington County, 1803. (Boxes 394-397.)

Hardin, Davis—One heirs of John Hardin, Rosanna Hardin by Martin D. Hardin, her gdn., heir of John Hardin, deceased. Apr., 1807. Barnabas McHenry and wife, Sarah McHenry, heir. Said John Hardin died leaving Mark, Martin, Jane Irvin (wife of Christopher), Martin D. Hardin, of full age, Mark Hardin, Sarah McHenry (wife of Barnabas McHenry), Davis Hardin, Polly Hardin, and Rosannah Hardin, infant children and devisees. Filed Mar. 27, 1801. Boxes 394-399.)

Jolly, John—Son of John Jolly, killed by the Indians. (Box 321.)

Jolly, John, Sr.—Killed 1782 at Battle of Blue Licks. (See McConnell, Jas.)

Jolly, David—Dep.—(Bardstown)—said in 1780 he came with his bro., John Jolly, Sr., and helped him build a house. (Box 321.)

Jolly, John, Jr.—Of Ohio, 1806.

Jolly, David—Of Nicholas County, to appear at Bardstown for dep., May, 1806. (Box 321.)

McConnell, James—At Bardstown, August 14, 1806, says he is bro.-in-law to John Jolly, Sr., deceased, and that John Jolly, Sr., was killed 1782 at Battle of Blue Licks, 1780. (Box 321.)

McClintock, Wm.—Of Paris, deposes that he came to Ky. Apr., 1775, with Joseph Houston, Wm. Steele, James Thomson, Henry Thomson, Wm. Miller, John Miller, Richard Clarke, Wm. Nesbit, Henry Hartley, Wm. Flinn, John Shearer, Patrick Logan, and Alex. Pollock, bro. of James Pollock. (Box 412.)

Madison, James, Heirs—James, Catesby and Susan, only heirs. Susan mar. Robt. G. Scott, res. of Va., Jan. 19, 1788; James Madison, entry, 16000 acres. (Box 355.)

May, John, Heirs—Will—Mother, Agnes May; wife, Ann May; children: John and Polly May, both under 21; my bros., Stephen and David May; sisters, Agnes and Lucy May; my bros., George and Wm. May; wife, Ann, extx. Mar. 5, 1790; Chesterfield Co., Va., Feb. 10, 1791. (Wts.: Chas. Johnston and John Craig.) (Copy May 30, 1808.) (Box 357.)
Ann May, widow, married Thos. Lewis, before July 3, 1797. Polly May married Daniel Epes, before Feb. 21, 1815. (See Franklin Co. records, box 357). (She buried in Frankfort cemetery—see her will). She evidently left no children; her gravestone says: "died July 5, 1853, aged 65 years." (See many deeds in Court of Appeals.)

Mitchell, Joseph Fleming, Heirs—Joseph F. and John A. Mitchell, 2 heirs; also Samuel Mitchell, Alex. J. Mitchell, infants (of age Jan. 9, 1816), by Martha Mitchell, their gdn. Nov., 1799. (Boxes 400-415.) (See Wills of Court of Appeals.)

Marshall, David—Dep.—Aged 57, May, 1811, Bourbon Co. (Boxes 412-411?

Owens, Abraham, Heirs—Thos. Smith and Harriett, his wife, formerly Owens; Daniel Brennan and Elizabeth (Owens), Lucy Owens, James Owens, Nancy Owen, Wm. C. L. Owen, and Susan Owen, heirs and reps. of Abram, deceased. (Box 384.) (See Shelby Co. Wills), etc. Jas. Moon, gd. ad litem.

Price, John, Gent—Aged 44, dep. Wts.; Thos Settle, Clement Bell, July 18, 1804.

Proctor, Joseph—Aged about 55 years, dep. taken Wed., May 5, 1811, at court house in Bourbon Co., said he came to Ky. in 1778, settled at Boonesborough, then lived at Estill Sta.; 1782 settled at McGee's Sta. on No. side of Ky. In 1778 he traveled to Boonesborough Trace to where Millersburg now stands, etc. (Box 412.) (Born about 1756, box 412.)

Proctor, Nicholas—Dep.—Aged about 53 years, at Paris, May 15, 1811., to Ky. in 1778 with his bro., Joseph Proctor. (Box 412.)

Pleakandstaver, (?) John—Mt. Sterling, Sept. 5, 1809, was at Boonesborough 1777.

Richardson, Holt—Military services. (Boxes 299-319.)

Ramsay, Wm.—Of Albemarle County, Va. (Boxes 305-306.)

Ramsey, David—So. Carolina, 1786. No. 398. Heirs: Martha, Henry Lawrence Ramsey, Sabrina Elliott Ramsey, James Ramsey; Nathaniel Ramsey and Wm. Ramsey, minors, by Eleanor Lawrence Ramsey, their next best friend and guardian, and the said Ellenor Lawrence Ramsey, heirs and reps. of Dr. David Ramsey, deceased, citizens and residents of South Carolina, that the deceased' father David Ramsey on Feb. 17, 1786 bought of Anthony D. White, etc., part of 130,000 acres in Ky. (Dec. 12, 1816.)

Spillman, Heirs—Wm. Bowling and wife, Sally (formerly Sally Spillman), James, Thos., Samuel, Spillman devisees and sons of Thos. Spillman, deceased. (Box 411.)

Seddon, John—Stafford Co., Va. John, Thos. and Nancy. (Boxes 299-319.)

Stephens, Adam—Colonel (Military) in Fr. and Indian War, 1763, Berkeley Co., Va., 1789, deed to John Strode, Bourbon Co., 1789.

Steele, Col. Wm.—Aged 48, deposes July 18, 1804, in Adams-Stevens case. (Boxes 320-334.)

Stevens, Colonel Edward—Of Culpepper Co., Va., on June 25, 1779 made agreement with Abram Hite of Hampshire Co., Va., letter from Stevens in Culpepper Co., Mar. 22, 1780., to Isaac Hite, Jr. (Mar. 12, 1782.) (Boxes 355-56.)

Skinner, Alex.—Will—Richmond, Va., Henry Lee of Stratford, Extr., all to Henry Lee, Military lands, etc., Nov. 12, 1788, Henrico Co., Apr. 6, 1789, probated. (Box 357.)

Scott Brothers, George, Elisha, Levi, Elijah—Of Bourbon County, 1798. (Boxes 386-390.) (Their father Baptist Scott's will in Clark Co.) (One or more of them settled in Henry County later.)

Sudduth, Col. Wm.—Deposes at home of Mordecai Gist, Winchester, Ky., Tues., Mar. 24, 1812, that he came to Ky. in 1783, and resided at Myers Station till Dec., then removed to Strode's Station where Charles Morgan and others, Joseph Proctor, etc., tarried; back to Strode's in Dec., 1783. The party in 1783 were Chas. Morgan, Thos. Settle and Joseph Proctor. When first came into the country was with Thos. Brown, Thos. Settle, Caleb Masterson and Joshua Orr. (Boxes 400-415.)

Stamper, Joshua—Deposes Apr., 1811, that he is 58 years old, was at Strode's Sta. in 1779-1784. (Box 412.)

Summit, George—Aged 40, dep. he came to Ky. in 1780. (Box 411.)

FRANKLIN COUNTY CIRCUIT COURT

Lucas Varnawsdall vs. Chas. Lynch and Others, Box 235—Deposition of Jas Guthrie taken May, 1808 in Shelby Co., deposeth he was acquainted with Peter Paul and was in company with him at Falls of the Ohio, 1779 and on the 13th day of May, same year, in company with said Paul and others who left the Falls of the Ohio to go to Monongonhala Country, went with Paul as far as the mouth of Little Miammi, parted about 6th of June, he going to Monongonhala. Question: "Why were you so long going to mouth of Little

Miammi?" Answer: "We were on expedition against Shawnee Indians commanded by Col. Bowman, Paul was bit by snake enroute, didn't see him again in Ky. until 1780." Depostion of Robt. Tylar states he was with Paul on expedition, proceeded up Ohio to mouth of Licking and met Col. Boeman who took command and proceeded to Shawnee Towns, on return, at mouth of Little Miammi, and with said Paul and others proceeded up Ohio to "Wheeland" and from thence with Paul to his father's home in Mononganhala County on creek called Ten Mile. Abraham Whitaker deposeth that he knew Paul on said expedition against Shawnee Indians, that they made one attack on towns, were repulsed and returned to the Ohio, said Paul returned to Ky., 1780 with his father and father's family and settled in Sullervan's Old Station, where he then lived. Jas. Dunbar states he was acquainted with Paul's cabin on Cane Run and he came to Ky., 1780; deposition taken Shelby Co., 1809. Thos. McCarty was acquainted with Boon's Road leading from Louisville to Boone's Station, and helped blaze it, 1781; taken 1809. Abraham Whitaker was acquainted with Boon's Road, 1782. Thos. McCarty in 1779 in company with Peter Paul, Evan Hinton and others helped build cabin. Deposition of Geo. Pumray in same. Jas. A. Sturgis was acquainted with Cane Run, 1780 and with Boon's Trace on road from Lin's Station to Boon's Station, 1781. Jacob Hubbs acquainted with Cane Run, 1780. Robt. Tylar deposeth in Shelby, 1809, states in 1781 Peter Paul was at his home at Boone's Station on Clear Creek when Squire Boone sent for him, states he (Tylar) was in left column in Floyd's defeat commanded by Ravenscraft. Jas. Anderson states he was acquainted with location, 1782. Daniel Sparks was acquainted with Boone's Road, 1781, that he never heard of but one ford on Long Run on Boon's only where women and children were killed, near "where Thos. Sturgeon now lives," about three-quarters of a mile in west direction from ford on Long Run to Floyd Battle Ground. Robt. Tiler deposeth he has known witness, Thos. McCarty, for upwards of 30 years. David White, Sr., knew place in question, 1784, states he was at Detroit when Indians returned from the battles which they and Col. Floyd fought at Long Run and heard Capt. McGee and other whites that were with Indians say the battle they fought with Floyd was on Boon's Road, near the ford of Long Run. Robt. Tiler (Tylar) states in year, 1780, Boone's Road was cut and mile trees cut, 1782. Benj. Opplegate deposeth in same. Wm. Tyler, Sr., states he came to Ky., 1779, and acquainted with Boon's Road, 1781 or '82, Hugh McLawlin killed near it Jan. 18, 1783.

HARRISON COUNTY

(Formed 1793, from Bourbon and Scott Counties)

ORDER BOOK A.

Note: In the following guardians' bonds, orphan children over the age of fourteen years, made choice of guardians; while for orphans under the age of fourteen, were appointed by the court.

Pages 1 and 2, Oct. 1806—Deposition of Nicholas Hart to establish land of Wm. Walker, located on River Creek, deposeth: He knew River

Creek in Aug., 1782, when on his march with Indians to Bryant's Station, at which time he was their prisoner. Jacob Stucker deposeth in same: In July or Aug. he crossed said creek just above where Wm. Beachamp "now lives" and was then informed by Alexander Mac Lean it was called River Creek. Samuel VanHook, 73 years of age the fifteenth of next month, deposeth in same: He was at Bryant's Station when the Commission sat at that place in the winter of 1779 or 1780.

Page 2, Oct. 1806—Deposition of John Morrison states he was acquainted with River Creek in yr. 1780 but did not know of name until 1781 or 1782. Question: Did not the expedition under Clark cross this creek near the mouth where Byrd's road crossed said creek in fall of 1782? Answer: Yes. Deponent states before 1782 he heard the following persons call it River Creek: Jas. McBride (decd. long since), and thinks Jno. Clarke, decd., Bartlett Searcy, decd., Jacob Stucker and Alexander McClain.

Page 3, Oct., 1806—Abraham Venable states he was applied to by Wm. Kennedy to survey Wm. Walker's entry as assignee of Merry Walker.

Pages 26, 27, 28, May, 1806—Deposition of Samuel VanHook to establish land of Thos. Moore and Benj. Johnson on Mill Creek, entered 1780, conflicting with McFall's claim, deposeth: Came back from being a prisoner in Spring of '79, settled at Ruddle's Station, and in year '80 after Christmas moved to Martin's Station and taken prisoner in June following, and returned in four or five years. Wm. McCune deposeth: Saw land in question in company with John Hinkson while living at Ruddle's Station in year 1780. Wm. Anderson became familiar with place in year 1785. Thos. Ravencroft saw same in year 1785.

Page 7, Oct., 1806—Rosannah McCaw and Mary McCaw, inft. orphans of John McCaw, decd., chose Hugh Newall, gdn. Surety: Robt. Brownfield.

Page 20, Feb., 1807—Isabell McDowell, orphan of John McDowell, decd., chose Isaac Miller, gdn., and said Isaac apptd. gdn. to Rebecca McDowell and Thos. McDowell, infant orphans of aforesaid. Surety: Alexander H. Hawkins.

Page 21, Feb., 1807—Jas. Renick, gdn. to Eliza Jones and America Jones, inft. orphans of Uriah Jones, decd. Surety: Samuel Scott.

Page 29, May, 1807—James Kinsler, gdn., to John Hutcherson and Edward Hutcherson, inft. orphans of Edward Hutcherson, decd. Sureties: Abijah North, John McLaughlin.

Page 55, Dec., 1807—Benjamin Hodges apptd. gdn. to Basil Hawkins, inft orphan of Alexander S. H. Hawkins, decd. Surety: Henry Edger.

Page 57, Jan. 1808—Catherine Garten, mother to Benj. Lemmon, inft. orphan of Jacob Lemmon, decd., appeared to show cause why son should not be apprenticed. Continued on motion of Henry Chandler, gdn.

Page 59, Jan. 1808—Chischester Chinn, apptd. gdn. to Thos., Sidney

and David Eads, inft. orphans of Jonothan Eads, decd.   Sureties:
John Miller, Littleton Robinson.

Page 65, Apr. 1808—Joseph Loan, inft. orphan of Isaac Loan, decd.,
chose John Miller gdn.   Surety: Thos. Ravenscroft.

Page 81, Aug. 1808—Wm. Stafford apptd. gdn. to Sally, David, Betsy
and Wm. Sinyard, inft. orphans of John Sinyard, decd.   Surety:
Richard Henderson.

Page 88, Nov. 1808—Depositions to establish Hawes' land on Grays Run.
Joseph Smith, aged 51 yrs. deposeth: Marked lines under direction
of Thos. Allen, then Deputy Surveyor in 1784.   Thos. Allen, aged
51 yrs. deposeth in same.

Page 99, Jan. 1809—Division of land and slaves of John Pickett, decd.,
among Geo. Pickett, Littleton Robinson, John Pickett, Jas. Wilson,
Phil. Samuel, Nicholas Long, Thos. Pickett, Wilson Pickett, Zoel (or
Joel) Wilson.

Page 104, Jan. 1809—Peggy Hamilton, inft. orphan of George Hamilton,
decd., chose Wm. Lowery gdn., and said Wm. apptd. gdn to Dolly,
inft. orphan of said Geo. Hamilton, decd.   Surety: Isaac Miller.
John Wall apptd. gdn. to John and George Hamilton, inft. orphans
of George Hamilton, decd.

Page 117, May, 1809—Samuel Nesbit, inft. orphan of Jeremiah Nesbit,
chose Garret Wall, gdn.   Surety: Wm. Wall.

Page 127, July, 1809—Samuel Dills, inft. orphan of David Dills, chose
Harmon Dills gdn.   Surety: Isaac Dills (Dils, Diltz).

Page 128, Aug. 1809—Nicholas Milnar apptd. gdn. to Miciah Milnar,
Inft. orphan.   Surety: Edmund Dunn.

Page 128, Aug. 1809—Rosannah Rozier, inft. orphan of Michael Rozier,
chose Adam Rozier gdn.   Surety: Reubin Smith.   **Page 130**—Eve
Rozier, inft. orphan of same chose Wm. David gdn.   Surety: Peter
Baker.   **Page 130**—Samuel Bailey apptd. gdn. to Jno. Rozier and
Susannah Rozier, inft. orphans of same.   Surety: John Lee.

Page 131, Aug. 1809—Sally Yarnall, inft. orphan of Jesse Yarnall, chose
Josiah Griffith gdn.   Sureties: Thos. Moore, Benj. Hodges.

Page 136—Aug. 1809—John Clayton and Mary Clayton, inft. orphans
of James Clayton, decd., chose Milly Beading (Reading) and Wm.
Raymon, gdns.   Surety: Moses Random.

Page 139, Oct. 1809—Wm. Ralston apptd. gdn. to Mathew Ralston and
Mary Ralston, inft. orphans of David Ralston, decd.   Surety: Robt.
McKittrick.

Page 141, Nov. 1809—Deposition of Samuel VanHook to establish land
of Wm. Wood. Deponent "76 yrs. old or thereabouts", deposeth:
He was taken prisoner by Indians and British at time Ruddles Station was taken and returned to Bryant's Station from captivity in
yr. 1784 or '5.   Robert Layson, aged 58 deposeth in same.

Page 146, Nov. 1809—Michael Frye, inft. orphan of Jacob Frye, decd., chose Abraham Frye gdn. Surety: Thos. Wilson.

Page 150, Dec. 1809—Ann Angel apptd. gdn. to Nancy and Malinda Angel, inft. orphans of Jno. Angel and Elias Angel, another orphan of same chose Ann Angel gdn. Surety: Benj. Hickman.

Page 158, March, 1810—Wm. Lowery, gdn. to Peggy Hamilton, now wife of Hanson Talbert. Commissioners to settle accts. with Wm. Lowery.

Page 160, April, 1810—Mathew Woods apptd. gdn. to Sarah Seyms, inft. orphan of Nancy Seyme, decd. Surety: Isaac Miller.

Page 162, April 1810—Benj. Coonrad, inft. orphan of Joseph Coonrad, decd., chose Thos. Funnish (?) gdn. Surety: Wm. E. Boswell.

Page 166, May, 1810—Jenny Carrick, inft. orphan of John Carrick, decd., chose John Mallory gdn. Surety: Jacob Salladay (Holladay).

Page 170, July, 1810—George Talbert, inft. orphan of Jno. Talbert, decd., chose Jesse Guthry gdn. Surety: Chas. C. Hutcherson.

Page 174, Aug. 1810—Polly Stevenson, inft. orphan of Joseph Stevenson, decd., chose Wm. Scott gdn.; court apptd. Wm. Scott gdn. to Jas., Margaret and Joseph Scott, inft. orphans of same. Surety: Abijah North.

Page 180, 1810—Alexander Smith Henly Hawkins, inft. orphan of Alexander S. H. Hawkins, decd., chose Thos. Hawkins gdn. Sureties: Benj. Hodges, Archibald Jackson.

Page 184, Nov. 1810—Ordered that Christopher Musselman who intermarried with Winifred Tomley, Admrx. of estate of Epahroditius Tomley, decd., summoned to give surety.

Page 187, Dec. 1810—Jesse Henry, inft. orphan of Watson Henry, decd., chose Wm. Endicutt gdn. Sureties: Wm. Low (?), Moses Endicott.

Page 190, Jan. 1811—Shadrack Sherman, apptd. gdn. to Mary, Wm., and Ann, inft. orphans of Jno. Sherman. Sureties: Wm. Tucker, Abijah North.

Page 191—Jno. Smith apptd. gdn. to Gideon Henson, inft. orphan of Geo. Henson, decd. Surety: Geo. Smith.

Page 202, April, 1811—Wm. Nesbitt, inft. orphan of Jeremiah Nesbitt, decd., chose Peter Barret gdn. Surety: Jeremiah Nesbitt.

April, 1811—Samuel Jamison's children, John, Isaac, and Milton, to be apprenticed.

Page 220, Oct. 1811—Thos. Endicott apptd. gdn. to Emily, Aaron and Sarah Endicott, inft. orphans of Wm. Endicott, decd. Sureties:

Frances Mann, Samuel Endicott. Admn. of estate of Wm. Endicott granted Mary Endicott, Aaron Endicott.

Page 221, Oct. 1811—John Craig and Robert Craig, inft. orphans of Robert Craig, chose their father, Robert Craig gdn., and court appts. said Robert gdn. to Samuel, Agness and Isabella Craig, inft. orphans of same. Sureties: Benj. Hodge, Robert Houston.

Page 225, Oct. 1811—Samuel Reynolds apptd. gdn. to Samuel Colvil and Wm. Colvil, inft. orphans of Jas. Colvil. Surety: Geo. Reading.

Page 226, Nov. 1811—John McCune apptd. Gdn. to Elizabeth Naylor, inft. orphan of Thos. Naylor. Surety: Geo. Reading.

Page 239, Jan. 1812—Reubin Thornley, inft. orphan of Epaphroditius Thornley, chose Chas. Redmon gdn. Surety: Jno. Gale.

Page 242, Jan. 1812—Lewis Day apptd. gdn. to Jno. Hawkins, Alfred Hawkins, Nelly Hawkins, Jenny Hawkins and Miller Hawkins, inft. orphans of Alexander T. H. Hawkins, decd. Surety: Benj. Hodges.

Page 244, April, 1812—Nelson Dills, inft. orphan of David Dills, decd., chose Garrett Wall gdn. Sureties: Jas. Frazier, Isaac Holman.

Page 269, April, 1812—Polly Coleman, inft.orphan of Francis Coleman, decd., chose David Humphreys gdn. Sureties: Lewis Day, Chas. C. Hutcherson.

Page 257, July, 1812—Sarah Hannon and Samuel Hannon, inft. orphans of James M. Hannon, decd., chose Isaac Holman gdn.; court apptd. said Isaac Holman gdn. to Polly, Thos., Maryann and Archimedus Hannon, inft. orphans of same. Surety: Josephus Perrin.

Page 263, Aug., 1812—John Curry apptd. gdn. to Wm. W. C. Dunbar, inft. orphan of Samuel Dunbar, decd. Surety: Robt. Houston.

Page 268, Aug. 1812—Reubin Berry and Rebecca Berry, inft. orphans under 21 yrs. chose Jno. Berry gdn. Surety: John Berry, Sr.

Page 278, Nov. 1812—Reuben George apptd. gdn. to Lucenda George, inft. orphan of Abner George, decd. Sureties: Eli Cleveland, Jacob Coon.

Page 285, Dec. 1812—Elleanor Laywell gdn. to Peggy, Jas. and Susannah Laywell, inft. orphans of Andrew Laywell, decd. Surety: Francis Brower. Geo. Reading apptd. gdn. to Wm., Andrew and Samuel Laywell, inft. orphans of Andrew Laywell. Surety: Richard Henderson.

Page 285, Dec. 1812—Polly, Nancy and David Hopkins, inft. orphans of Thos. Hopkins, decd., chose Jno. Hopkins gdn. Surety: Geo. Henson.

Page 289, Dec. 1812—Covington Coleman, inft. orphan of Francis Coleman, chose David Humphreys gdn. Surety: Isaac Holman.

Page 295, March, 1813—Thos. Jones apptd. gdn. to Thos. Wm., Pamelia, Jas. and John Stevenson, inft. orphans of Wm. Stevenson, decd. Surety: Isaac Miller.

Page 296, March, 1813—Wm. Kinkead and Samuel Kinkead, inft. orphans of John Kinkead, decd., chose Hugh Kinkead gdn. Sureties: John Kinkade, Geo. Smith.

Page 303, April, 1813—Sarah Davis and Wm. Davis, inft. orphans of Joseph Davis, decd., chose Mark Simmons gdn. Surety: Geo. Smiser.

Page 307, May, 1815—Wm. McIlvain, inft. orphan of John McIlvain, decd., chose Wm. McIlvain gdn. and said Wm. was apptd. gdn. to Jane Eliza McIlvain, inft. orphan of said John, decd. Surety: John Craig. John McIlvain, inft. orphan of same chose Peter Barret gdn. Surety: Jas. Kelley.

Page 313, July 1813—Agnes Hudson apptd. gdn. to Jane and Samuel Hudson, inft. orphans of Robert Hudson, decd. Surety: Samuel Taylor.

Page 322, Aug., 1813—John Williams apptd. gdn. to Lambert Slade, inft. orphan of Ezekiel Slade, decd. Surety: Chas. C. Hutcherson.

Page 354, Feb. 1814—John B. Tucker apptd. gdn. to Charlotte Godman and Elizabeth Godman, inft. orphans of Wm. B. Godman. Surety: Wm. Tucker.

Page 357, Feb. 1814—Jas. McClure, inft. orphan of Moses McClure, decd., apprenticed to Richard Hall.

Page 371, May, 1814—Daniel Richardson, inft. orphan of Jonothan Richardson, decd., chose David Richardson gdn. Surety: Jno. Miller.

Page 371—Geo. Hamilton, inft. orphan of John Hamilton, decd., chose Geo. Hamilton gdn. Surety: Wm. Brown. John Hamilton, inft. orphan of same chose John Frazier gdn. Surety: John Elliott.

HARRISON COUNTY DEEDS

Book A, pg. 12, Feb. 13, 1794—John Edmiston of Davidson, territory south of Ohio River, appts. Hugh Fultons of Fayette Co., atty. to deed to Matthew Groves land granted him by State of Va., and located by John Higgins.

Book A, May 6, 1794—George Reading and wife, Nancy, of Harrison Co., to Amos Ragen of Mercer Co., Ky., land located in Lincoln Co., Ky.

Book A, June 3, 1794—John Smith and wife, Mary, of Fayette to John Veatch of Harrison, land located in Harrison Co., Ky.

Book A, pg. 7, 1794—Thos. Logwood of Bedford Co., Va., to Samuel Foster of Harrison, land patented in his, Thos. Logwood's name located in Harrison.   Same to Thos. Veatch, in Harrison, May 20, 1794.

Book A, April, 1794—Jas. Lemmon and wife, Amelia, of Scott Co., Ky., to Jno. Kinkade of Harrison, land located in Harrison Co., Ky.

Book A, pg. 12, March 13, 1794—Jas. Moody of Fayette Co., Ky., to Alexander McClain, land located in Harrison.

Book A, pg. 13, June 25, 1794—Edward Trabue, Extr. of Wm. Trabue of Woodford Co., Ky., deeds land in Harrison Co., Ky., to Chas. Zachry.

Book A, pg. 15, Feb. 9, 1793—David Hogshead of Augusta Co., Va., appts. Robt. McKittrick of Bourbon Co., atty. to divide with Matthew Patterson, a tract surveyed for him in yr. 1785, located in Fayette Co., Ky.

Book A, pg. 17, Dec. 2, 1794—Benj. Holms of Wilkes Co., Ga., deeds to Henry Clay and Benj. Bedford of Bourbon, land located in Harrison on Logans Lick Creek, two miles up creek from Bowman's incampment where his army incamped the 2nd night after he marched from Lexington on his way to Shawney Towns in yr. 1779, including the place where a tree is marked BH.

Book A, pg. 27, Sept. 13, 1794—Robert Rankins, atty. for Jno. Milton of Frederick Co., Va., deeds John Haggin, land located in Harrison.

Book A, pg. 28, Dec. 18, 1794—John Haggin of Mercer Co., Ky., deeds to Robt. Harrison, land located in Harrison.

Book A, pg. 56, Nov. 22, 1794—Josiah Watson of Fairfax, Va., to Samuel McMillen of Harrison, land in Harrison granted said Watson by patent from Va.

Book A, pg. 70, July 17, 1795—John McFall of Harrison Co., Ky., to Henry Coleman and John Hutcherson, gdns. of Elizabeth and Catey Coleman, hrs. at law of John Coleman, decd., land located in Harrison.

Book A, pg. 78, June 17, 1795—Laurence Long of Clarke Co., Ky., to to Jas. Blaine of Lincoln C., Ky., land in Harrison, between N. and S. fork of Licking.

Book A, Dec. 5, 1794—Jas. Powers of Cumberland Co., Pa., to Robert Harrison, land in Harrison County.

Book A, pg. 80, Feb. 24, 1795—Isaac Pierce of Sumner (Summet?) Co., Ohio to Robt. Harrison of Harrison Co., Ky., land located in Mason Co., Ky.

Book A, Feb. 16, 1795—John McLaughlin of Lexington, Ky., and wife, Margaret, to Michael Kookindoisier, land located in Harrison Co., Ky.

Book A, pg. 83, Aug. 25, 1795—Robert Haskins of Chesterfield Co., Va., and Edward Trabue of Woodford, both joint Extrs. in estate of

Wm. Trabue, decd., late of Chesterfield Co., Va., to Wm. McComb of Harrison Co., Ky., land located in Harrison.

Book A, pg. 84, Aug. 27, 1795—Same as above to Jas. Thomas, Jr., of Bourbon Co., land located in Harrison.

Book A, pg. 134, Jan. 7, 1796—Geo. Ruddell of Bourbon Co., Ky., appts. Jno. Mulherrin and John Ruddle attornies to collect debts and answer in suits.

Book A, pg. 143, March 11, 1796—Jas. Trabue and wife, Jane of Charlotte Co., Va., to Elkannah Grinnings of Harrison, land located in Harrison.

Book A, pg. 145, March 26, 1796—Wm. Little and wife, Mary of Fayette Co., Ky., to John Ellison of Harrison Co., Ky., land in Harrison adjoining Robt. Ellison.

Book A, pg. 147, Sept. 12, 1793—Holt Richison of King William Co., Va., for divers causes, hereunto moving appts. Jno .Cook of Bourbon Co., Ky., atty. to deliver deed to Wm. McDowell of Bourbon, land on forks of Licking by virtue of Military warrant.

Book A, pg. 149, Dec. 1, 1795—Thos. Sharpe and Richard Young, attornies for Wm. Wiatt of Fredericksburg, Va., to Jos. Craig of Fayette, land formerly in Fayette but now in Harrison, patented in name of Wm. Wiatt and Joseph Craig.

Book A, pg. 150, Dec. 1795—Joseph Craig, Sr., of Fayette Co., Ky., to Wm. Wiatt and John Anderson of Fredricksburg, Va., land located in Harrison.

Book 3, pg. 1, 1804—Commrs. of District of St. Andre, Mo., province of La., certify that on the second of May, departed this life Lawrence Long, Esqr., inhabitant of Banhomme, in this district, who by will apptd. wife, Priscilla Long gdn. of all estates and sons-in-law, Mr. Richard Coulb and Mr. Ludwell Bacon and oldest son, Gabriel Long, joint Extrs., and said will authorized said Extrs. to sell Ky. land; said Priscilla Long appts. said Extrs. attornies.

Book 3, pg. 2, Nov. 6, 1804—John Coffee of Hancock Co., Ga., deeds to Henry Hall of Harrison, one-fifth of one-third of tract. it being John Smith's, decd., part of survey located in Harrison Co., Ky.

Book 3, pg. 14, Sept. 7, 1804—Geo. Peckett of Harrison Co., to Robert Clarke, Jr. and John Wilkinson, tract in Clark Co., Ky.

Book 3, pg. 18, Apr. 1805—Josiah Watson of Alexandria, Va., by atty. John Taylor, deed to Henry Coleman, land in Harrison Co., Ky.

Book 3, pg. 19, Nov. 8, 1804—Thos. Barbour of Orange Co., Va., deeds to Henry Coleman of Harrison, land located in Harrison Co., Ky., said land patented in name of Richard Barbour and by him devised to Thos., Jas. and Ambrose Barbour and Benj. Johnson.

Book 3, pg. 20, Nov. 3, 1804—Simon Kenton of Green Co., Ohio and John Kenton of Mason Co., Ky., deed to Lindsay Azby of Harrison Co., Ky., land in Harrison.

Book Book 3, pg. 29, March 12, 1805—Thos. Anderson of Garrard Co., Ky., for divers causes, hereunto moving appts. Richard Henderson, atty. to obtain title to lots in Falmouth, Pendleton Co., Ky.

Book 3, pg. 37, Jan. 23, 1806—John Lockhart releases to Wm. Coleman one-half interest in will of Jacob Lockhart, decd., for bringing suits. Pg. 38, same book as above, Charles and James Lockhart of Harrison Co. ,for divers causes, hereunto moving, appt. Wm. Coleman atty. to dispose of lands coming from estate of their father, Jacob Lockhart, decd.

Book 3, pg. 40, Oct. 13, 1808—Philip Huffman and wife, Pegy of Pendleton Co., Ky., deed to Maximillian Robinson of Harrison Co., Ky.

Book 5, pg. 11, Sept. 1816—Humphrey Lyon and wife, Margaret, late Margaret Hinckson, widow of John Hinckson, decd., to Samuel Hinkson and wife, Susannah, said Samuel being son of John Hinckson, decd., and Chas Lair, John Lair, Jr., Wm. Lair, Joseph Lair, Matthias Lair, Betsey Harter, wife of Jacob Harter, late Betsey Smiser, heir to Catherine Smiser, late Catherine Lair, all being heirs of Matthias Lair, decd., deed land located in Harrison Co., Ky.

Book 5, pg. 29, Sept. 1815—Samuel Lewis, John Whitehead, Jonothan Jackson, Elijah Holton and William Ardery, trustees for the town of Maysville in the Co., of Harrison, deed to Samuel Robb of Harrison, land in said Co.

Book 5, pg. 28, Aug. 1816—Whereas Jas. M. Hannon in his lifetime to wit, 12th of Oct. 1807, executed bond to David McFall all right as hr. at law of John McFall, decd., the real estate of decedent's land laid off to Barbara McFall, widow, also interest of Patrick McFall, another of the hrs., held by deed of Patrick McFall. Indenture made Aug. 20, 1816, Margaret Hannon, widow of Jas. M. Hannon, decd., John Hannon, Jas. Hannon, Braxton King and wife, Sally, late Hannon, last three hrs. of Jas. M. Hannon, decd., of lawful age, and Polly Hannon, Samuel Hannon, Hannah Hannon, Thos. Hannon, Mary Ann Hannon and Archemedus Hannon, inft. hrs. of said Jas. M. Hannon, decd., by Isaac Holeman, Jas. Hannon, John Hannon, Commissioners to David McFall, land located in Harrison; patent of John McFall's settlement and preemption.

Book 5, pg. 32, March, 1816—Benj. Adams and wife, Nancy of Fayette Co., Ky., Benj. Grady and wife, Caty of same, Richard Gaines and wife, Sally, James Gaines and wife, Rebecca, heirs of James Adams, decd. of Woodford Co., Ky., deed to Larkin Adams of Fayette Co., Ky., land in Harrison.

Book 5, pg. 104-106, Aug. 7, 1816—James Chambers' hrs. Whereas James Chambers departed this life intestate, leaving Margaret Chambers, widow, Nathaniel Campbell and wife, Jane, Jacob Lindley and wife, Margaret, James Chambers and wife, Sally, deed from hrs. to Martha Chambers one of said hrs.

Book 5, pg. 119, Sept., 1814—Hanson Talbot and wife, Margaret, Geo. Hamilton and wife, Dollethea, and George Hamilton, Commrs. for

John Hamilton now a minor, to Geo. Hamilton, commr. for Geo.
Hamilton, now minor, deed for lots in Cynthiana, Ky.

Book 5, pg. 138, April 4, 1811— John Smith and wife, Betsy of Bourbon
Co., Ky., Jas. Monday and wife, Judith, and John Smith, gdn. for
inft. hrs. of Martha Smith, decd., of Fayette Co., Ky., Samuel
Saunders and wife, Nancy, Lewis Craig and wife, Milly of Gallatin
Co., Ky., deed to Lyons Chambers of Harrison, land in Harrison
entered in name of Samuel Smith.

Book 5, pg. 146, Nov. 14, 1816—Joseph Ward and wife, Margaret, late
Margaret Stevenson, Betsey Stevenson and May Stevenson deed
to Wm. Wright, land in Harrison which descended from their ancestor, Thos. Stevenson.

Book 5, pg. 160, May 1, 1817—Catherine Davis, formerly Catherine
Muse, dau. of Col. George Muse of Nelson Co., Ky., now of King
George Co., Va., deed to Benj. Withers, property devised her by her
father. Proved by oath of Aaron Thornley, aged 67 yrs. that Mrs.
Catherine Davis was dau. of Col. Geo. Muse, formerly of Caroline
Co., Va., and proved by witness who had seen will in Nelson Co.,
Ky., that she was the dau. of said Muse who died in Nelson Co.,
formerly of Caroline Co., Va.

Book 5, pg. 173, Oct. 23, 1816—The undersigned hrs. of Nathaniel Cocke,
late of Richmond Co., Ga., for divers causes hereunto moving appt.
Gen. Wm. Henry of Scott Co., Ky., atty. to transact business in
Ky. Signed: John Cocke, Rebecca Cocke, Eliza R. Bacon, Rebecca
T. Baldwin, Mary Cocke, Augusta Cocke, Rebecca Cocke, gdn. for
Nathaniel Cocke, son of Wm. Cocke, decd.

Book 5, pg. 180, Aug. 30, 1816—Caty Simons, widow of Mark Simons,
decd., Peter Simons and wife, Rachel, Adam Simons and wife,
Phoebe, Thos. Snodgrass and wife, Caty, Robt. Snodgrass and wife,
Christina, Henry David and wife ,Elizabeth, John Hughs and wife,
Sarah of Harrison Co., Ky., excepting Henry David and wife of
Bourbon Co., Ky., deed to Joel Frazer of Harrison, land located
in Harrison.

Book 5, pg. 192,Jan., 1816—Robert Trabue, Jas. Trabue, Wm. B. Scott
and wife, Polly, Judith Trabue, Elizabeth Trabue and Patsy Trabue, hrs. of Jas. Trabue, decd., Judith and Elizabeth being infants
(under 21) by H. Boswell, Commr. of Co. of Harrison and Logan,
deed to Abijah North for land in Harrison Co.

Book 5, pg. 200, June 4, 1817—Jas. Coleman and Esther McMillen,
Extrs. and A. F. McMillin and wife, Mary, Kennedy McMillin and
wife, Peggy, Wm. G. McMillin and wife, Paulina, Polly McMillin and
Marshall McMillin divisees of Samuel McMillin, Sr., decd., of Harrison Co., Ky., deed land in Harrison to Samuel McMillin.

Book 5, pg. 364, Aug. 1817—Boswell Hunt of Fleming Co., Ky., on acct.
of self and as atty. for John Hunt, Reubin Hunt, Absolom Hunt,
Joseph Denton and Dradena Denton, his wife, hrs. of John Hunt,
decd., deed to Joseph Ingles, located in Harrison Co., Ky.

Book 5, pg. 201, June, 1807—John Turner and wife, Sarah of Pendleton Co., Ky., deed lot in Cynthiana, Harrison Co., to Richard W.
Porter.

LINCOLN COUNTY

REVOLUTIONARY SOLDIERS AND PATRIOTS
ORDER BOOK 1781-1783

1781, Page 14—Ordered that Capt. Geo. Adams' Co. be divided.

Jno. Snody recommended as Capt. of Militia.

Capt. Jas. Estill's Co. to be divided into two companies.

Following recommended to his Excellency the Governor of Virginia to serve as officers in militia: Nathaniel Hart as Captain and Christopher Irvine as Ensign.

Page 15—Jno. Logan Lieut. Col. appointed by Governor.

Page 11—Benj. Logan County Lieut. and Hugh McGary Major.

Page 2—Jno. Cowan qualifies as Justice.

Page 3—Following recommended to Governor to serve as militia: Jas. Estill, Geo. Adams, Jno. Daugherty, Samuel McAfee, Captains; Jno. Smith, Jr., Wm. Moore, Benj. Pettitt, Joseph Kinkaid, Jas. Harlan, Jno. Gorden and Stephen Arnold as Lieutenants; Jno. Montgomery, Jas. Brown, James Polly, David Adams, Isaac Hoglin, John Jackson as Ensigns.

The following appointed Constables: Richard Jackson for district in Capt. Logan's Co.; John Miller in Capt. Daugherty's Co.; Anthony Sowdoskie in Capt. Cowan's Co.; Samuel Dennis in Capt. McBride's Co.; James Woods in Capt. Allason's Co.; Wm McBrayers in Capt. McAfee's Co.; John Gritton (or Grillon) in Capt. McGary's Co.

Page 4—The following recommended as militia officers to the Governor: Robert Barnell (Barnett), John Boyles, Captains; Samuel Estill, Benjamin Cooper, Samuel Davis, Lieutenants; Holbert Voris, Samuel Bell, Elisha Clary and Robert Scott, Ensigns.

Page 4—Ordered that the commissions for following persons as Captains be numbered as follows: John Logan, 1; Hugh McGary, 2; Wm. McBride, 3; Samuel Scott, 4; Jno. Allason, 5; Jno. Cowan, 6.

April Court—Commissions produced for Azariah Davis, Lt., and Jas. McKullock, ensign.

Page 7—Samuel Kirkman, Joseph Kincaid, John Martin and Andrew Kincaid recommended to Governor to be appointed Captains in militia: Isaac Hogland, Jno. McClure, Archibald McKinny, Wm. Givens and Jas. Brown as Lieutenants; Jas. Wray, Jno. Erwin, Jno. Smith, Jr., Hugh Morris, Thos. Montgomery, Michael Kirkman and Jno. Logan, ensigns.

Page 9—Following recommended as officers in militia in this county: Thos. Denton, captain; John Smith and Jas. McColough, lieutenants; Clough Overton and Jno. Smith, ensigns.

Jage 9—John Leaveridge proved to the court he was entitled to sett. and preemption on acct. of his coming to county before Jan., 1778 and resided 12 months and he was prevented from laying in his claim on account of "he being in the regular service."

Page 12—John Edwards recommended as one of commissioners of the Peace, Lincoln County.

1782, Page 18—Militia officers recommended to Governor: Gabriel Madison, John Woods, Clough Overton, Isaac Bledsoe, captains; John Kennedy, Robert Bowman, Wm. Young, Jas. Ray, Jno. Smith and Thos. Montgomery, lieutenants; Anthony Sodowskie, Samuel Dennis, John Bryan, David Cook, Absolam Mouse, John McMurtry, Jas. McMullin and Jas. Craig, ensigns.

1783, Page 30—Constables appointed: in district of Capt. Thompson's Co, Jesse Hodges; Joseph Ray in district of Capt. Adams' Co.; Thos. Warren in district of Capt. Wood's Co.; Anthony Rogers in district of Capt. Snoddy's Co.; Joseph Faulkner in district of Capt. Kincaid's Co.; Samuel Shelton in district of Downing's Co.; Edward Loe in district of Capts. Barnet's and Martin's Co.; Wm. Bartlett in Capt. Daughertie's Co. district; John Chadwick in district of Capt. Houston's Co.; John Gritton in district of Capt. Ray's Co.; Abraham Bonta in district of Capt. Irvin's Co.; William Garrett in district of Capt. Kenton's Co.

May Court, 1783—Ordered that following persons be recommended to Governor of Virginia as proper persons to be appointed officers of militia of this county, to wit: John Logan, Esq., Colonel of 1st Battalion; John Logan, Esq., John Edwards, Esq., Lieut. Colonel and George Adams as Major; Gabriel Madison, Colonel to 2nd Battalion; John Smith, Esq., Lieutenant-Colonel; Anthony Crockett, Major, and Samuel Hinch, Gent., Captain in room of Jno. Smith.

August Court—Recommended as Captains in militia: John South, Christopher Irvine, Joseph Kennedy, Wm. Montjoy, Michael Woods, William Whitley.

Gabriel Madison produced commission appointing him Colonel of militia; Anthony Crockett produced commission as Major.

MONTGOMERY COUNTY

(Formed from Clark County, 1796)

DEED BOOK 2

(Deed Book 1 destroyed when Court House burned)

Page 3, Dec. 9, 1800—Smith King to Molly Crump, marriage contract between Smith King and "the widow Crump," property to become common stock during their lives and then divided, respecting Richard Crump, his home not to be interfered with. Signed Smith King and Mary (Molly) Crump. Wts.: John Crump, Richard Crump, Betsy Crump, March 11, 1801.

Page 6, Mar. 12, 1801—Wm. Payne and wife, Malinda of Montgomery Co., Ky., to heirs of John Reed of Fairfax Co., Va., by Moses Thomas, their representative, consideration of relinquishment to claim of 500 a. patented in name of said Payne as assignee of said Reed, and one 200 a. in Montgomery Co.

Page 10, Jan. 14, 1801—Martin Hammon of 96th District and State of South Carolina deeds Mark Mitchell of the Co. of Hawkins, Tenn. Witnesseth that Jas. M. Graham, Wm. Robinson, Wm. Moffett, Commrs. apptd. by court of Montgomery, convey to Mark Mitchell 1400 a. agreeable to bond executed from Martin Hammond, etc.

Page 3, March 7, 1801—Joseph Colville and wife, Rosanna of Livingston Co., Ky., deed Andrew Colville of Washington Co., Va., lot in Mt. Sterling, Ky.

Page 36, 1801—Jas. Bradshaw of Clark Co., Ky., to John Alexander, land in Mt. Sterling.

Page 38, May 4, 1801—Enoch Smith, Wm. Smith, Jeremiah Davis, Duncan Campbell and Jas. Ward, trustees of Mt. Sterling, deed Jas. Ward, property in Montgomery.

Page 40, May 2, 1801—John Worford and wife, Mary of Shelby Co., Ky., deed 100 a. in Montgomery Co., to Jas. Ward and wife, Polly.

Page 85, Feb. 14, 1801—John Troutman of the District of Abbyville, South Carolina, appts. wife, Joanna Troutman of Lincoln Co., Peter Troutman of Montgomery Co. and Peter Bainbridge, Jr. of Garrard Co., all of Ky., attys. to recover debts (except debt due of Wm. John Allen, Esqr. of Bourbon and one from Jacob Troutman of Fayette which he sold to Jas. Ward) and to make sale of property in Lincoln Co. Wts.: Jas. Ward, Michael Troutman.

Page 93, July 14, 1801—Andrew Swearingin and wife, Mary of Montgomery Co., Ky., deed Jacob Warrick, Fleming Co., land in Fleming ,on Licking River.

Page 99, June 8, 1801—Nicholas Merewether of Shelby Co., deeds David Beadell of Montgomery, land in Montgomery patented for Walker Daniel, decd. Wts.: Jacob Trumbo, John Trumbo, John Alkire, A. Simpson, Gam. G. Kennedy.

Page 109, Aug. 3, 1801—Peyton Short of Woodford Co., deeds David Sorrency of Montgomery Co., 200 a. by Alex. Simpson, his atty.

Page 112, Aug. 11, 1801—Andrew Swearengin and wife, Polly of Montgomery Co., deed Robt. Meteer, land located on Flatt Creek in Montgomery, 200 a. part of 1000 a. tract patented by Thos. Swearingen, decd., dated Dec. 2, 1785.

Page 118,—Thos. Jamison of Montgomery Co., deeds to Peter Ringo—

said Jamison claims tract by patent dated 1786, 1000 a. on waters of Hingston and Peter claims 1000 a tract on same by two patents dated May 26, 1790—claims interefer and compromise made.

Page 132, Sept. 26, 1801—Benjamin Okley's heirs have recovered of Miller Okley their legacy and relinquish all claim to father's estate. Signed: Wm. Okley, Thos. Okley, Edmund Okley, Nancy Okley, Fanny Okley, Pleasant Okley.

Page 135, Oct. 18, 1796—Wm. Anderson of Campbell Co., Ky., deeds to John Hildreth of Bourbon, land in Clark Co., part of 10,000 a. survey made for Wm. Davis and conveyed to said Anderson.

Page 144—Wm. Anderson of Montgomery Co., Ky., for divers causes hereunto moving, appts. friend, Francis Hopkins, John McNab, Levi Coryell, Wm. Moffett, John Williams, Chas. Hicklin and Alex. Blair of Montgomery Co., attys. to demand of Wm. Davis of Petersburg, Va., satisfaction for land he, said Anderson, has sold them, which was deeded him by said Davis.

Page 151, Nov. 10, 1801—Wm. Lane, atty. for Geo. Lane ,Extr. of Hardage Lane, decd., one part and Jeremiah Davis, both of Montgomery Co., tract in Montgomery bounded by Temple Smith's 1000 a. tract granted by Va. on Treasury Warrant to Jas. Hardage Lane, 1780.

Page 164, 1801—Agreement between Geo. Hinton of Shanandoah Co., Va. and Arthur Connolly of Montgomery.

Pages 170-171, Jan. 12, 1802—Geo. Turner, inft. orphan of Joseph Turner, decd., 10 yrs. old the 31st of July last to be apprenticed to Wm. Turner. Sudduth Turner, aged 8 yrs .the 19th June last, inft. orphan of Joseph Turner, decd., to be apprenticed to Wm. Turner. Jas. Turner, inft. orphan of Joseph Turner, decd., aged 6 yrs. the 15th of Oct. past, to be apprenticed to Wm. Turner.

Page 213—Abraham Alfree, 16 yrs and 10 mos. the 1st day of March, 1802, apprenticed to Levi Wheeler until 21.

Page 216, Mar. 12, 1802—Samuel Carter of Ohio Co., Ky., deeds to Jas. Alexander of Montgomery Co., Ky., land on head water of Greenbrier out of 500 a. survey made in the name of Wm. Childs.

Page 220, Oct. 10, 1801—Henry Powling of Garrard Co., Ky., to Daniel Turney of Bourbon Co., Ky., 400 a. tract in Montgomery.

Page 228, Feb. 11, 1802—Edm. Terrel of Garrard Co., Ky., deeds to Isaac Conyers of Montgomery 547 a. in Montgomery.

Page 229,—Wm. Taylor and wife, Nancy of Nicholas Co., Ky., deed to Jno. Trumbo of Montgomery 100 a. in Montgomery.

Page 253, Oct. 6, 1801—Abraham Carter of Franklin Co., Ky., agent for Wm. Carter of Spottsylvania Co., Va., deeds Hutson Hammon of Montgomery 283 a. on Grassy Lick Creek in Montgomery.

Page 263, June 17, 1802—Andrew McNab of Bourbon Co., deed of mortgage, in order to secure to John McNab of Montgomery Co., title to place in Bourbon whereon he now lives in Bourbon.

Page 270, Mar. 24, 1802—Greenberry Magers and wife, Sarah of Frederick Co., Md., deed to Jacob Swope of Lincoln Co., Ky., land in Montgomery adjoining Benedict Swope's 800 a. survey.

Page 270, Nov. 27, 1807—Joseph Barsdale of S. Carolina, Co. of Abbeville, deeds to Walter Carr and Lawrence Young, Jr., of Fayette Co., Ky., land in Montgomery on waters of Licking.

Page 287, Sept. 17, 1802—Ezekiel Hayden of Jessamine Co., Ky., deeds to Jacob Sorrency of Montgomery 200 a. in Montgomery.

Page 303, Mar. 13, 1802—Ben Ashby and wife, Jane of Virginia deed to Wm. Sudduth of Clark Co., one half of tract surveyed for said Ashby by said Sudduth.

Page 320, Nov. 1, 1802—Robert Forrest, aged 3 yrs., Nov. next apprenticed to Benj. Hensley.

Page 322, 1802—Richard Moore, Oglethorpe Co., Ga., appts. Geo. Moore, atty. to sell Ky. lands.

Sept. 28, 1802—Hayden Edwards and wife, Susannah of Franklin Co., Ky., deed to Richard Colliver of Montgomery, land located in Montgomery.

Page 341, Jan. 21, 1803—Wm. Caldwell of Montgomery Co., for divers causes hereunto moving, and for love and affection to son, Joseph Caldwell, deeds property.

Page 344—Daniel McGary and Jas. Elliott and Jas. Hill bound to Jacob Coons, John Mitchell, Aaron Hall and Benj. Smith, Gent. Justices, Jan. 24, 1803, consideration that whereas agreeable to petition of Assembly authorizing said McGary and Jas. Elliott (Jas. McGraham or any two) to dispose of land for benefit of widow and orphans of John Elliott, decd., agree to discharge duties, etc.

Page 352, 1803—Robt. Rankin of Logan Co., Ky., to Wiles Cook of Montgomery Co., land on State Creek in Montgomery.

Page 357, Feb. 8, 1803—Wm. Farrow of Montgomery Co., atty. for Wm. Farrow of Prince William Co., Va., deeds land on Grassy Lick Creek in Montgomery to John Tatmon.

Page 39, Feb. 25, 1803—John Six and Mary, his wife, deed to Farinoe Hawkins, land located on Flat Creek in Montgomery Co.

Page 393, Aug. 25, 1802—Thos. Duley, Sr., and wife, Mary of Scott Co., deed to David Waits of Henry Co., Ky., land in Montgomery.

Page 403, Feb. 12, 1803—Geo. Fleming of Allegany Co., Pa., by Anthony Reynolds, atty., deeds to Wm. Caldwell of Montgomery 327 a. conveyed from the heirs of John Fleming, decd., to said George Fleming.

Page 407, Mar. 28, 1803—Joseph Simpson, 4 yrs. old the 16 of April, next, apprenticed to John Sexton.

Page 458, Recorded May 28, 1802—Rawleigh Morgan and wife, Lydia, Thos. Swearingen and wife, Margary, Azariah Thornborough and wife, Drusilla of Jefferson Co., Va., and Andrew Swearingen and wife, Mary of Ky., hrs. of Thomas Swearingen, decd., deed to Wm. Wright of Bourbon Co., Ky., land in Montgomery, it being part of 1000 a. entered in the name of Van Swearingen, decd., 21, Dec., 1782. Wives acknowledge deed which was recorded Berkeley Co., Va., see pg. 411.

Page 435, June 27, 1803—Valentine Stone of Montgomery Co., deeds to Philadelphia Ratcliff of same county for love and affection of a brother to a sister, the land whereon she now lives.

Page 27, Jan. 1803—John Nitherton of Jefferson Co., Ky., and Joseph Robinson of Madison Co., Va., deed to Abrm. Murray of Madison Co., Va., land located in Montgomery Co., Ky. Deed proved by oaths of Humphrey Hame, Wm. Yates and Ambrose Clark in Madison Co., Va.

Page 509, Aug. 25, 1803—Willis Green of Lincoln Co., Ky., deeds to Andrew Cartmell of Montgomery land in Montgomery on Prickley Ash Creek.

Page 512, Sept. 2, 1800—John Finley and Michael Finlay of Fleming Co., Ky., deed to Wm. Ramsey of Montgomery, land located in Montgomery.

Page 517, June 2, 1803—Joseph Proctor of Madison Co., Ky., deeds Philip Hammon and Geo. Cooper of Montgomery, land in Montgomery.

Page 520, Aug. 22, 1803—Wm. Bridges, son of George Bridges, hath bound himself apprentice to Robert Morrow of Montgomery.

Page 521, Aug. 22, 1803—Richard Reynolds, orphan of Job Reynolds, decd., 16 yrs. old the 25th of Dec. next, apprenticed himself to Joseph House.

Page 523, Aug. 22, 1803—Asa Canterbery, orphan, aged 16 yrs. apprenticed himself to Zebulon Cantrill.

Page 525, 1803—Francis Wyatt, son of Francis Wyatt, apprenticed himself to Robt. Morrow.

SCOTT COUNTY

RECORDS FROM DEED BOOKS

Note: Spaces indicate burned portions of records.

B, Page 100, March, 1808—Jno. Scott, late of Orange County, Va., decd., devised unto_____Zachariah Herndon by his dau._____

Jones mentioning particularly by_____Thos. Herndon, Zachariah Hern_____Tyler, Joseph Herndon, Benj. Herndon_____Boswell Herndon and Scott Herndon. Atty. to sue to recover property. Note: See Virginia Magazine, Vol. 12, p. 110.

B, Page 374, Sept. 21, 1816—Polly McCracken, Patsey (Cyrus)_____ McCracken, Geo. McCracken and Virgil McCracken, infant chdn. of Virgil McCracken, decd., by Commrs. deed land on Elkhorn to Thos. Peak.

B, Page 193, Dec. 7 18(12)—Abraham Kirtley (Jno. Kirtley) state of Va. Simeon Kirtley of_____(Elijah) Kirtly of Rockcastle Co., Louisa Kirtly_____Polly Ann Kirtly and Dempsey Carroll of _____(Wm.) Kirtley of Boone Co., Sophia Kirtley, Wm. Craig, Jas. Gano of Scott Co., Jas. Kirtley (Jas. Gaines), Gabriel Gaines, Josiah Pitts listed in deed for lots in Georgetown, Ky.

B, Page 193 _____ 1812—Jno. Pickett's Hrs.: Thos. (Pickett), Jno. Pickett and wife, Sally, George Pickett_____Pickett, Hetta, his wife, Jas. Wilson_____(Littleton) Robinson and Fanny his wife, of the one part_____of Ky. to Philip Samuel and wife, Elizabeth_____and wife, Catherine, deed to Wm. Nicholas Long, Philip, Samuel and Zachariah Wilson of other part. Deed signed: Thos. Pickett, Susan Pickett, L. Robinson, Fanny Robinson, Geo. Pickett, Peggy Pickett, Jas. Wilson—widow relinquishes dower rights.

B, Page 346, Dec., 1815—Samuel Spencer's Hrs._____(Hugh Dickey and) wife, late Margaret Spencer, widow of (Samuel Spencer) late of Scott Co., Ky., and said Hugh (Dickey) of Clermont Co., Ohio_____(Samuel Walker) and Hannah, his wife, late Hannah Spencer, one of hrs. of_____decd., Wm. Dickey and wife, Margaret, late Spencer, another hr. of sd. Samuel Spencer, decd., all of Ohio, and Geo. Johnson and wife, Sarah, late Spencer, another heir of sd. Samuel of territory of Indiana, to Jno. and Andrew Spencer of Scott County. Signed: Geo. Johnson, Sarah Johnson, Samuel B. Walker, Hannah Walker, Wm. Dickey, Hugh Dickey, Margaret Dickey.

B, Page 181, July 1813—David Tilford's Hrs.: Alex Tilford, Jr., David F. Begham and wife, Sarah, Susannah Tilford and Jane E. Tilford, last two mentioned under 21 yrs., by commr. deed to Wm. Tilford, in pursuance of decree in chancery court, sd. Tilford complt. and sd. David Tilford, decd., deft.

H, Page 23—Jno. Bellis and wife, America, deed hrs. of Henry Bellis —whereas Henry Bellis departed this life without having devised certain land leaving Jno., Henry, David, Betsy, Hannah, Mary, Susannah,_____ and Rebecca, and whereas sd. David has departed this life, etc.

G, page 94, Nov. 21, 1831—Thos. Drake's Hrs.: Jas. P. Drake and Catherine, wife, of Ind., Jno. Brockman and Frankey, wife, Richard W. Pack and Polly, wife, Geo. Chisham and Winifred, wife, Henry B. Drake and Barbara, wife of Scott Co., hrs. of Thos. Drake, decd., deed Thos. Wolfe land in Scott Co., Ky.

G, Page 148, Jan. 1, 1824—Wm. Cox's Hrs.: Jasmine Cox, Daniel Cox,

Jas. Cox, Jas. Glenn and wife, Nancy, late Nancy Cox, Wm. *Bailey and wife, Julia, late Julia Cox, Wm. Cox, Benj. Menefee and wife, Betsey, late Betsey Cox, Jno. Cox, Nathanial Cox, Patsy Cox and Hannah Miller, late Hannah Cox, hrs. of Wm. Cox, decd., of Scott Co., deed to Jno. Estill. Signed: Jas. Cox, Anna Cox, Wm. Cox, Nancy Cox, B(enj. Menifee), Elizabeth Menifee, John Cox, Polly Cox, Wm. Bailey, Julianne Bailey, Jas. H. Glenn, Nancy Glenn, Hannah Miller.
*In body of deed "Causey."

G, Page 169, Nov. 9, 1825—Coleman Cook's Hrs. deed to Joseph M. and Jno. M. Gregg of Bracken Co., Ky. Signed: Joseph Cook, Ruth Cook, Geo. Cook, Wm. Cook, Aaron Cook, Benj. Cook, Lucinda (Lucy) Cook intermarried with Ira Balding, all of Cos. Harrison and Scott.

G, Page 268, Feb. 10, 1826—James Power's Hrs.: Joseph Powers, Hatima (?) Power, Julia Power, Edward Power, Wm. Power and Alex Power, Jas. Power of Perry Co., Pa., and Chas Williams, Jas. Perry, Nancy Wilson, Joseph_____Nancy Campbell, Marreitt Williams and Peggy Moore and James_____, Scott Co., Ky., consideration of $10.00 pd. by each of parties of 2nd part, relinquish all interest in tract of 1000 acres patented in name of their father, James Power (Powers) located in Scott Co., Ky. Note: Name spelled both Power and Powers in body of deed.

DEED BOOK G.

Page 539, Dec. C., 1820—Wm. Alexander's hrs. to Wm. T. Cole. W. T. Philips and wife, Margaret (Peggy); Wm. Alexander; D. A. Shannon and wife, Nancy Shannon; Ann S. Alexander; Jas. H. Alexander.

Page 35, May 5, 1823—Daniel Barnhill hrs. to Marklin Lyson. Joseph Guffy and wife, Alice; Clemency Barnhill; Jane Mulinix, late Jane Barnhill; James Barnhill; Anna Fields, late Anna Barnhill; Clemency Barnhill, (widow), adult hrs., and Alexander Curry, Samuel Barnhill and Jno. Price, Commrs. appointed to convey on behalf of _____ for Samuel Barnhill and Amelia Barnhill, infant hrs. of Daniel Barnhill, decd., land in Scott Co.

Page 36, 1836—Leo Tarlton and Mary Ann, his wife of Scott and W. S. Breckridge and Deborah, his wife of Fayette Co., of 1st part and Francis Otwell of Scott, land on which Otwell resides which they may have inherited from Stephen Trigg or other persons.

Page 22, Aug. 23, 1823—Sidney Burbridge of Scott Co. to Galloway's hrs., viz: Richd. Lambert; Margaret Galloway; John Galloway; ____ Galloway; Jas. Galloway; Mary _____, deed for land in Scott Co.

Page 77, same book, Aug. 22, 1823—A list showing names of Ruth Lambert, Samuel Galloway, Nancy Galloway,, Amy Galloway, Rebecca Galloway, Elizabeth Galloway to be added to list of heirs in above record.

March, 1824—Col. Abrm. Buford (wife, Martha), land on Millers Run to Jas. Beatty's hrs., viz: John Wilson, Jonathan Newton, Henry and Sarah Ann Miller, devisees of Jas. Beatty, decd.

Page 282, Sept. 8, 1824—Thos. Hutchraft of Bourbon Co., Ky., 1st pt. and Jemima Boston of 2nd pt. and Fielding E. Dickey, 3rd pt., marriage contract between Thos. Hutchcraft and Jemima Boston.

Page 202, Oct. 10, 1823—Archibald Curry's hrs. from Wm. Sutton of Harrison Co., viz: Jas. R. Curry; Archibald Yell, atty. for Jas. Yell; Alex. Curry; Wm. McHatton and Jno. Curry, deed for land in Scott. (Note: Page 203, Archibald Yell is styled of Bedford Co., Tenn. Archibald Curry, deceased, referred to as formerly of Scott Co. This deed to Milton and Jabez Risk, hrs.).

October 18, 1823—Wm. Tilford and wife, Mary of Indiana and Thos. T. Crittenden and wife, Mary of Cincinnati, Ohio, deed Jno. V. Webb Scott Co., land in Scott, part of Audley Paul's Military Survey, which land was sold by Jno. Grant to Alexander Tilford.

Page 205, Apr. 24, 1824—Sodowitch Davis of Scott Co., deeds to Benj. Marshall of Caldwell Co., all interest in land formerly owned by Jno. Davis, decd., a portion of which descended to said Sodowitch, being same on which Jno. Davis died, also tract in Owen Co., tract on Big Eagle Creek.

Page 409, Sept. 24, 1824—Wm. Dickey, Sr. of Fayette Co., Ind., by Wm. Dickey, (son), atty., to Sinclair hrs., viz: Thos. G. Sinclair, Elizabeth _____ Sinclair, Sally Ann Sinclair, Wm. Payne Sinclair, Jas. Augurd Sinclair, hrs. at law of Armistead Sinclair, decd., all of Ky. land located in Scott.

Page 321—Ambrose Powell of Scott, last will: "having concluded to order my situation in life from single to married, and it is my will to bequeath to my loved sons and daughters the balance of my estate after providing for intended wife, Nancy Cavender, hereafter Nancy Powell." To grandson, Kellis Powell; sons and daus., viz: Elijah, Polly, Reubin, Fielding, Willis, Sally Crofford and Milly, formerly wife of Honor Powell, her chdn. to inherit her portion. Extrs.: son, Reubin and Jas. D. Offutt. October 30, 1824. Agreement with Nancy Cavender of Fayette Co., Ky., dated Oct. 20, 1824.

Book I, Apr. 28, 1804—Wm. Lytle hrs. to Wm. Barlow. Hugh Emison, Mary Emison, Ash Emison, Mary Emison, deed Wm. Barlow all claim to three tracts as hrs. of Wm. Lytle.

Page 28, Aug. 26, 1822—Leonard Hall's hrs. to Macajah Harlow. Anderson Harlow and wife, Naomi, hrs. of Leonard Hall, Sr., decd. of Barren Co., Ky., to Macajh Harlow. Naomi Harlow being dau. of said Lenoard Hall.

Book A, pps. 257-8, July 23, 1811—Jas. Eldridge and others to Jas. Eldridge; Susannah Davis; Jas. Stewart and wife, Sarah; Sarah Stewart; Asa Stewart; Judith Davis; Chas. Stewart and wife, Nancy; Nancy Davis, Stewart Nevil and Lucy Nevil; _____ hrs. of Henry Co., Ky., deed land in Scott.

B, 117—Toliver Craig and Lucy Johnson, marriage contract, dated Mar. 5, 1809.

WOODFORD COUNTY

Book A, pg. ___, Sept. 16, 1789—Adam Stephens of Berkely Co., Va., to John Strode of Bourbon Co., consideration of £1,000, 2,000 acres in Woodford.

Book A, pg. 90, June 10, 1780—John May of Dinwiddie Co., Va., from Richard Cave of Fayette C., consideration £100, 200 acres in Fayette.

Book A, pg. 116, Mar. 2, 1790—Wm. Mercer of Fredericksburgh, Spottsylvania Co., Va., deeds Robt. Alexander, late of Henrico Co., Va., in consideration of £2,000, 2,000 acres in Ky., formerly Fincastle Co., on waters of Elkhorn Creek.

Book B, pg. 4—This day came Coston Beacham, late of Delaware and listed his negroes—July, 1791.

Book B, pg. 14—Andrew Hair of Mercer Co., to John Duncan and Andrew Holmes of Cumberland Co., Pa., merchants, deed of mortgage. Feb. 14, 1791.

Book B, pg. 18—Wm. Elliott and Elizabeth, his wife of Va., Extr. and Extrix. of will of John Filson, decd., for causes and hereunto moving appt. atty. to recover from one John Coleman, money due them as Extrs. 1791.

Book A, pg. 132—Whereas sundry slaves have lately been recovered by decree of high court of chancery in an appeal, Novell vs. Smithers and others from the Co. of Essex (Va.), which decree remains to be carried into execution, whole interest in said slaves so recovered is in some one or all parties to this instrument, whereas, "we are residents of Ky., we, Mary Noell, John Hiett and wife, Ann, Wm. Hiett and wife, Tabitha, Wm. Smither and wife, Esther, Wm. Haggard and wife, Rose and Molley Noel, we hereunto moving, appt. Thos. Gist of Co. Madison, atty. to receive of said Smithers and others slaves bequeathed us by will of Joseph Noell, decd."

Book A, pg. 136—Jno. Allison of Woodford, for divers causes hereunto moving, appts. friend, James McCord of Co. of Washington, So. Carolina, to make deed to 191 acres in said Co., adjoining land of Jas. McCord and Lee Taylor. July, 1790.

Book A, June 15, 1790—Wm. Fenwick, late of the State of Md., took oath respecting importation of slaves into state. July, 1790. Joseph Fenwick, late of Md., same.

Book A, pg. 163, Apr. 28, 1790—Oved McCracken of Allegany Co., Md., appts. John Williams of Woodford Co., atty. to adjust dispute to possession of 1000 acres granted said Williams and himself by patent.

Book A, Apr. 28, 1790—Zachariah Taylor and wife, Alice of Fayette Co., deed Hancock Lee of Fauquier Co., Va., 440 acres.

Book A, Oct. 10, 1789—Wm. Turpin of Cumberland Co., Va., appts. bro, Horatio Turpin of District of Ky., atty. to recover land.

Book A, pg. May 27, 1790—Robt. Holton, late of Md., took oath respecting importation of slaves.

Book A, May 27, 1790—Robert Fenwick, late of Md., took oath respecting importation of slaves.

Book A, May 27, 1790—Ann James, late of Md., took oath respecting importation of slaves.

Book A, Sept. 21,1790—Peter Holes of Buckingham Co., Va., appts, Thos. Mosley of Woodford Co., atty. to recover property due him.

Book A, Feb. 1795—Laban Shipp and wife, Elizabeth of Bourbon, deed Geo. G. Fauntleroy Boswell of Woodford, in consideration of moving and £275, land containing 257 acres in Woodford.

Book A, Apri. 2, 1789—Jno. Miles of Russell Co., Va., deeds Margaret Miles, Jacob Stucker, John Stucker and Henry Stucker of Fayette Co., tract of 400 acres in Fayette Co., Ky.

Book A, June 23, 1789—John May of Dinwiddie Co., Va., deeds Jas. McConnell of Fayette Co., Ky., 400 acres in Fayette as settlement right.

Book A, Oct. 4, 1790—Audley Paul and wife, Jean of Botetourt Co., Va., deed Laban Shipp of Bourbon Co., 600 acres of land in Woodford.

Book A, Sept. 19, 1790—Prettyman Merry and wife, Catherine of Orange Co., Va., deed Rhodes Thompson of Woodford, land located in Woodford, part of tract whereon James Suggate, decd. of Fayette lived and by his will descended to said dau., Catherine Merry, 300 acres.

Book A, Apr. 12, 1791—Jno. David Woelper of Philadelphia, Pa., deeds to Jno. Taylor of Fayette Co., Ky., 2,000 acres in Woodford.

Book B, Feb. 14, 1791—Andrew Hair of Mercer Co., Ky., deed of mortg. to John Duncan and Andrew Holmes of Cumberland Co., Pa.

Book B, Oct. 4, 1791—Wm. Lewis of Botetourt Co., Va., deeds Nathaniel Sanders of Woodford, tract in Woodford, 604½ acres.

Book B, March 17, 1790—Elizabeth Cunningham, Jas. Cunningham, Thos. Whiteing and wife, Ann, deed Edward Elley of Culpeper Co., (Va.), all their shares, being 3-7 of 1091 acres located in Fayette Co., Ky., divided to them by will of Mrs. Ann Cunningham, late of Spottsylvania Co. (Va.), decd., said land granted said Ann by patent Aug. 4, 1786.

Book B, Oct. 15, 1789—Richard Young of Woodford, deed to Wm. Strowther of Culpeper Co., Va., 302 acres on Ky. River.

Book B, July 10, 1791—Wm. Brockman and wife, Elizabeth, of Albemarle Co., Va., deed tract to Elijah Craig of Woodford, 175 acres (Va.)

Book B, Jan. 2, 1792—Robt. Sayers and wife, Jean, of Wythe Co. (Va.), to Aquilla Gilbert, of Fayette, tract in Woodford, 200 acres.

Book B, Jan. 3, 1792—Simon Hancock of Woodford appts. friend, Samuel Hancock, gent., of Bedford Co., Va., to recover debts due.

Book B, March 6, 1792—Wm. Hubbell of Woodford, for divers causes he hereunto moving appts. friend, Asa Hubbell, of New York, atty. to recover debts due him in Penn., N. Y., N. J., Conn., R. I., Mass., N. H., Vermont and Cannady.

Book B, Oct. 13, 1791—Henry Stoner of Paxton Township, Donpin (Donphin) Co., Penn., appts. Jno. Colglaizer of Huntington Township, Westmoreland Co., Penn., atty. to recover of Wm. Hubble all debts delivered him in trust by Jno. Stoner, son of above named Henry Stoner, in a boat on Ohio River, 1791, shortly after being in conflict with Indians, said John Stoner being mortally wounded, when Wm. Hubble, Daniel Light and others were present.

Book B, Dec. 21, 1791—Henry Daugherty of Mercer Co., deed to John Finley of Augusta Co., Va., land in Woodford, 320 acres.

Book B, July 10, 1791—Wm. Brockman and wife, Elizabeth, of Albemarle Co., Va., deed Elijah Kirkley of Woodford, land in Woodford, being part of old Military survey of John Wares, 432 acres.

Book B, Aug. 19, 1791—John Strode and Mary, his wife, of Bourbon Co., deed Samuel Cox of Woodford part of a Military survey granted Gen. Adam Stephen.

Book B, Dec. 7, 1791—Anthony Rucker of Amherst Co., Va., claiming lands in dist. of Ky., appts. James Rucker, his friend, his atty.

July 10, 1785—Commonwealth of Va., to Wm. McConnell 1000 acres in Fayette. Signed, Patrick Henry.

Book B, Dec. 11, 1790—General Chas. Scott of Woodford to Jno. Hoomes of Co. of Caroline (Va.), gent. land in Woodford on Ky. River.

Book B, Feb. 28, 1792—Jas. Wilkinson and wife, Ann, to Demcy Hatton, Robt. Hatton, Thos. Hatton, John Hatton, Wm. Tart Hatton and Elizabeth Hatton, hrs. of Robt. Hatton, decd., all of Woodford, three lots in Frankfort, (Ky.).

Book B, Apr. 16, 1792—Abraham Haptonstall of Greenbrier Co. (Va.), deed to Jacob Coplinger of Woodford Co. (Ky.), Mary, wife of Abrm. Haptonstall, shown by following deed.

Book B, March Court, 1793—Joseph Rearden and wife, Ann, and Extrs. of will of Bartlett Searcy, decd., appt. Richard Searcy of Madison Co. (Ky.), atty. to recover land in Clark Co. on Howards Creek, entered by said Bartlett Searcy in his lifetime given by law to Richard Searcy and deeds issued to Robt. Burton of

Greenville Co., N. C., and conveyed to said Bartlett, decd., and now claimed by Jas. Speed of Mercer Co. (Ky.).

Book B, Jan. 29, 1793—Jas. Wilkinson of Territory N. W. Ohio River deeds Benj. Sebastian of Jefferson Co., Ky.

Book B, Oct. 4, 1792—Edmund Ship of Caroline Co., Va., deed of gift to three youngest chdn. of Richard Ship, Sr., of aforesaid Co., viz: Emly Grant Ship, Edmund Ship and Anderson Ship, some personal property, and delivered into hands of Richard Ship, Sr., and wife, Elizabeth, father and mother of chdn., until youngest chd., Anderson, comes of age of 21 yrs.

Book B, Apr. 25, 1792—John Brisco of Berkeley Co., Va., requests as gdn. of Hezekiah Brisco, infant under 21, act to establish town at present place where court of Woodford now holds on, on lands of sd. Hezekiah Brisco, and that 100 acres be vested in Trustees and sold for benefit of said Hezekiah and that 2 acres be given gratis for erection of public bldgs. on present place known as Falling Spring.

Book B, Feb. 4, 1793—Benj. Watkins of Powhatan, Va., for divers causes hereunto moving appts. Jno. Dupey of Woodford atty.

Book B, Apr. 2, 1793—Geo. Taylor, eldest son of Edmund Taylor, deeds Wm. McCuddy land in Woodford, part of said Eumund Taylor's 3000 acre survey, old Military tract.

Oct. 1, 1795—Bartholomew Dupey of Woodford appts. James Dupey, Jr., and Peter Dupey, Jr., of Nottoway Co., Va., also Joseph Dupey of Woodford, attys. to attend business in State of Va.

Oct. 29, 1792—Jno. Brisco and wife, Eleanor, of Berkely Co., Va., deed John Cooke 500 acres in Woodford.

March 15, 1793—Lawrence Long and Prescellah of Amherst Co., Va., deed Geo. Muter (Murter) 400 acres in Woodford.

March 23, 1793—Eliasas Langham of Fluvanna, Va., appts. Ransaur Langham, of same place, to transact business in Ky.

Nov. 5, 1793—Edward Trabue of Woodford appts. Col. Robt. Haskins Sr., of Chesterfield Co., Va., to convey by deeds tracts of land of estate of Edward Trabue, decd., for him as extr. of estate.

Sept. 9, 1793—Alexander McRoberts of Richmond, Va., appts. Thos Mosley of Ky. atty. to sell 600 acres by virtue of 3 Military Warrants surveyed Aug., 1785, in district set aside for officers and soldiers of Va. line, located on Russels Creek.

May, 1794—Andrew Warnock of Pendleton Co., S. C., hr. at law to Jas. Warnock, decd., for reasons and hereunto moving, appt. Samuel Warnock of Co. and State aforesaid, atty. to recover land to which he is entitled as hr. to Jas. Warnock, decd., preemption of 1000 acres in Woodford Co.

Dec. Court, 1792—Jas. Wilkenson, Brigadier Gen. in 1st U. S. Legion, commanding troops in and abt. Fort Washington in City of Ham-

ilton, in N. W. Territory, sends greetings; appts. Hon. Harry Innis of Ky. atty. to use, lease or devise all or part of tracts in Ky.
of which sd. Jas. now stands siezed.

June 10, 1794—Thomas Marshall, Sr., to Ann Maria Marshall, dau. of
sd. Thos. and wife of Humphrey Marshall, deed of gift, 400 a. in
Harden Co. Same deeds land in Nelson Co., Ky.

July, 1794—Ann Gilmon, wife (widow) of Jas. Gilmon, decd., and Jno.
Gilmon, decd., and his wife, Margaret, and Alexander Gilmon, son
of Jas. and wife, Ester, and Jean Gilmon, wife of Jas. Gilmon ,all of Woodford, for divers causes, hereunto moving appt.
friend, Jas. Gilmon, son of aforesaid Jas. Gilmon, decd., atty to
convey land in Augusta Co., Va., unto Jno. Edward Long.

Oct. 4, 1794—Humphrey Marshall of Woodford appts. Melchesadeck
Spragins of Hallifax, Va., atty. to convey tract lying on Cherry
Stone in Pittsylvania Co., of abt. 1010 acres conveyed by Jas.
McCrow.

May 23, 1794—Hancock Lee and wife, Winifred of Fauquier Co., Va.,
to Jno. Lee of Woodford 440 acres in Woodford.

Feb. 18, 1794—Lewis Craig and wife, Elizabeth, of Mason Co. (Ky.),
to Jno. Hoomes of Caroline Co., Va., 300 acres in Woodford.

Feb. 2, 1794—Kinder Ferguson, Jacob Storm, Ann Ferguson, Andrew
Ferguson, hrs. of Andrew Ferguson, decd., late of Montgomery Co.,
Va., for divers reasons, hereunto moving appt. Arthur Ferguson of
Woodford atty. to convey to Wm. Ferguson of Franklin Co.
(Ky.), tracts in Montgomery Co., Va.

May 21, 1794—Richard E. Beall and wife, Margaret, of Fauquier Co.,
Va., deed to Geo. Blackbourn of Woodford, part of survey made
for said Beall.

Nov. 20, 1793—Jno. Cooke of Berkeley Co., Va., of 1st part and Catherine Burton Cook, of another part, and Geo. Muter and Jas.
Hughs of Woodford Co., Ky., another part; whereas sd. Catherine
Burton Cook, then Catherine Burton Nourse, was entitled to sum
of 500 pounds sterling by deed of gift from aunt, Catherine Burton of Kingdom of England, and sometime in yr. 1778 a marriage
abt. to be solemnized between sd. Jno. Cook and sd. Catherine Burton Nourse, now Catherine Burton Cook, it was agreed between
sd. Cook and Jas. Nourse, father of Catherine, that sd. Jno. Cook
should marry sd. Catherine Nourse and receive with her a marriage portion upon consideration that he settle upon her a por-
tionable part of his estate the 500 pounds sterling, and whereas
marriage was solemnized in yr. aforesaid, and sd. Cook did receive said 500 pounds sterling but never carried marriage agreement into effect, and whereas in yr. 1784 sd. Jas Nourse departed
this life leaving 10. chdn. having devised his estate, consisting
of other things of 1000 acres at Piedmont, in Berkeley Co., Va.,
to be equally divided between them, if any died before 21 years
of age his part to be divided among surviving chdn. and wherein
99 2-3 a. were assigned to sd. Catherine B. Cook, and whereas Jno.
erine B. Cook, and whereas Jno. Cook in 1791 having disposed of
Nourse, one of the sons died under 21, 10 1-3 a. assigned to Cath-

all property except his negroes, 7 of these he was about to send
to Ky., and 500 a. in Ky. and 1-9 pt of claim of sd. Jas. Nourse
in Ky. and being desirous to remove his family to Ky. but having no lands in sd. state in which he thought he could settle with
safety from Indians, and knowing certain Jno. Briscoe was desirous
of purchasing the 110 a. of land so devised to sd. Catherine B. Cook
he agreed if she consent to said sale of 110 a. for 500 a. in Woodford, being part of sd. Jno. Briscoe's preemption, that he could
convey to trustees for her sole use during life or to chdn. after
her decease, or if chdn. not living to her hrs. sd. 500 a. and negroes, and whereas sd. Catherine B. Cook did agree and whereas
sd. Jno. Cook did dispose of same to Jno. Briscoe for sd. 500 a.
and 80 pounds, and agreement never carried into effect, and sd.
Jno. Cook has since disposed of negroes except 7 he sent to Ky.
in 1791, indenture witnesseth Jno. Cook grants to Geo. Muter
and Jas. Hughs tracts and negroes in trust for said Catherine
Burton Cook for her natural life and after her death to such of
her chdn. as might be living.

Oct. 7, 1794—This day came Drury Mahan, late of N. C. and entered
his slaves.

Dec. 5, 1793—Abram Murray (Munay?) in Fluvanna Co., Va., appts.
Jno. Grant and Metcalfe Degeaffemnot of Ky. atty. to transact
business.

Feb. 21, 1793—Horatio Turpin of Powhatan, Va., for divers causes,
hereunto moving appts. Thos. Turpin, Jr., of Co. and State named
to convey Ky. lands.

March 3, 1794—Ann McCoull, Extrix. of Neil McCoull, decd., of Fredericksburg, Va., and Benj. Craig of Woodford—sd. Neil McCoull
in lifetime possessed tract in Ky. and being so possessed departed
life leaving will, appt. his niece, said Ann McCoull, Jas. Somerville, David Blair and Henry Mitchell, Extrs. to dispose of estate
and lay out same in interest of his sons, and sd. Jas. Somerville,
David Blair and Henry Mitchell, refused to qualify, sd. Ann hath
taken burdon of execution and in consideration of 500 pounds,
deeds Benj. Craig 1-2 tract of 2000 acres. Following wts. came
before Fountaine Maury, Mayor of Corporation of Fredericksburg: Jno. McCoull, Beverly Chew, Joseph Craig. Chas. Mason.

Aug. 21, 1794—Jno. Alfred Head of Culpeper Co., Va., appts. bro.,
Hadley Head of Ky., atty. to settle disputes abt. Ky. lands.

May 10, 1794—Archilaus A. Strange of Fluvanna Co., Va., to Tunstall Quarles of Ky., land in Woodford.

RANDOM COURT RECORDS

Bourbon County, Deed Book C, Page 317—Lotspeich, J. C. and Jacoby,
Frederica, settlement—We, Christopher Lotspeich of Va., in America, formerly of Frankinthal in Germany, and Frederica Jacoby,

widow of John Francis Lucus Jacoby, late of Bourbon Co., and State of Va., district Ky., called formerly Joanna Frederica Lotspeich of Frankenthal aforesaid, which said John Christopher Lotspeich and Frederica Jacoby are two of the six children of Catherine Elizabetha Wilhelmina Lotspeich (in the will after mentioned called Catherine Lotspeich) by Conrad Lotspeich, her husband, and Legatee named in the last will of Ralph Landenberg, formerly of Castto Street, parish of St. Martin in Fields within the Liberty of Westminster in Co. of Middlesex, wine merchant, but lately residing at Salisbury in the Co. of Wilts, deceased, Greetings: Whereas, said Ralph Landenberg in will dated about 7th of April, 1784, did bequeath to six children of his late deceased sister, Lotspeich, one-fifth of remaining estate and appointed John Widder of Norwich, gent., Mary Blydesteyer (Blydesteryn) of Harp Lane in London, widow, by name and addition of Mrs. Mary Blydesteryn, widow, and Isaac Blydesteryn of Harp Lane near Tower Street, London, by name and addition of Mr. Isaac Blydesteryn, executors; Whereas, said Ralph Landenberg departed this life without revoking said will, and said John Widder, Mary Blydesteryn and Isaac Blydesteryn have proved same by Prerogative Court of Archbishop of Canterbury and taken upon selves execution thereof—money to Ann Landenberg, wife of Testator, and accounts approved by John Christopher Lotspeich and Frederica, they paid their share as two of the six children of Catherine Lotspeich, deceased, and they relieve said executors of all claims. November Court, 1795.

Culpeper County, Va., Book K, Page 284, Aug. 3, 1780—Read et al. to Canaday—consideration of fifty thousand pounds Hanerson Read, Jas. Pendleton, Thos. Spilman, Jno. Conner, Jr., Joseph Duncan, Wm. Dulaney, Wm. Pendleton, Francis Morgan, Wm. Clark, Jas. Hufman, Geo. Clark, Thos. Brown, Jno. Jones and Lewis Corbin agree to acquit him of any obligation from any personal service either in the Continental Army, State Service for Regulars, or Military Service, except attending musters, for and during the term of twenty-two years from date. (Contributed by Jas. W. Wigginton, Decato, California.) Note: Several of the above moved to Ky.

Linville, Thos—Will—(Robertson Co., Ky.)—**Book 1, Page 4**—To wife, Sarah J., while she remains widow, after which to heirs, viz: Armaliza Linville, Sarah Eleanor Linville, Nancy Thomas Linville, Phoebe Elizabeth Linville, Mary V. M. Linville, Lewis Nelson Linville, Jas. M. Linville. Written May 9, 1868. Wts.: Jas. M. Linville, Edward Mitchell, Executors; Joseph B. Insko, Elijah T. Mastin. Proved May 15, 1868.

Nelson, Edward, Heirs—(Bourbon Co., Ky.)—**Deed Book O, Page 25, July 27, 1818**—Deed recorded in Bourbon County, Kentucky—Moses Nelson, John Nelson and Dicy, his wife, William Boston and Lydia, his wife, William F. Lock and Rebecca, his wife, John Bentley and Elizabeth, his wife, Joseph Peyton, Cinia Nelson and Margaret Nelson of the one part, to Josias Berryman, said Moses, John, Lydia Boston, Rebecca Lock and Elizabeth Bentley, all chdn. of Edward Nelson, deceased, and as such have claim to 2-3 part, together with *Cinia Nelson, widow of William Nelson, deceased, of a preemption of 1000 acres in Bourbon County, Harrods Creek, patented by Benj. Estill, heir at law, which 2-3

has been decreed to said heirs by Bourbon Circuit Court in suit
brought by them vs. Green Clay, and aforesaid heirs deed to said
Josias Berryman tract of 197 a. Recorded April 8, 1819.
*Cinia an abbreviation of Dulcinia, known also as "Jancy."

Louisa County, Va., Deed Book I, Page 159, Nov. 18, 1795—David Arnett, David Bibb, Richard Graves, James Arnett, Charles Brown,
Nancy Richardson, Peter Poindexter, John Poindexter, John Arnett, Thomas Ammon, Arch. Moon, of counties of Fayette, Lincoln, Bourbon and Madison, State of Ky., appt. Wm. Arnett atty.
to receive legacies from Samuel Magghee, decd., to Susannah
Arnett, wife to James Arnett, decd., or to her chdn. any claims
left by said Samuel Magghee, deceased, by his will.

Albemarle County, Va., Order Book 1798-1800, Page 1—Jacob Powers
and Ann, his wife, relict of William Crosthwait, deceased; Shelton
Crosthwait, heir at law of said William Crosthwait, deceased;
Thomas Crosthwait, William Crosthwait, Perry Crosthwait and
Ann Brown Crosthwait, children of said William Crosthwait, de-
ceased, by Shelton Crosthwait, their guardian—suit against George
Divers, administrator of William Crosthwait, deceased. Dated
March, 1798.

Note: Jacob and Ann Powers and above hrs. of Wm. Henry
Crosthwait moved to Harrison Co., Ky.

Ardery, James—Will—(Nicholas Co., Ky.)—Book B, Page 243—To
dou., Polly; dau., Doreas; son, Robert; wife, Catherine; two youngest daughters when of age. Written June 16, 1818. Probated
Dec., 1824. Wts.: Wm. Maxwells, Alexander Ardery, W. Maxwell, Jr. Son, Robert Ardery, executor.

Blair, William B., (Nicholas Co., Ky.)—Will Book B, Page 149—To
wife, Nancy, until eldest son, Alexander Wallace, comes of age;
two sons, Alexander and Joseph Emmerson; brothers, James B.
Blair and Alexander Blair, Jr., all interest in father's estate.
Extrs.: John Hill, Sr., Joseph Woods. Written Dec. 20, 1822.
Probated Jan., 1823. Wts.: B. Traven Hall, Jno. B. Clark.

Darnall, Chas (Fleming Co., Ky.)—Will Book C, Page 390—To wife,
Martha, she to give each child who marries property; chdn., Eleanor Stewart, Isaac Darnall, Thos. Darnall, Elizabeth McIntire,
granddau., Mary Jane Casady, Henry I. Darnall, Sarah Jane Armstrong, Wm. H. Darnall, Jno. S. Darnall, advancements made some
of aforesaid chdn., to such chdn. of dau., Eleanor Stewart as are
now born or may be born, Robt. and Eleanor Stewart to manage
said share; to Henry I. Darnall in trust for granddau., Mary Jane
Casady; son-in-law, Duskin W. McIntire; grandson, Chas. Darnall
Stewart; son, John S. Darnall schooling. Extrs.: friend, T. W.
Andrews and son, Thomas. Written Nov. 16, 1832. Wts.: T. W.
Andrews, Benj. Branard. Probated April 4, 1833.

Hopkins, David, (Fleming Co., Ky.)—Inventory, Feb. 3, 1934.—Produced by Isaac Cassary, Admr. Met at house of Mary Hopkins
to divide lands of Johnson Phillips and slaves of David Hopkins,
decd. Nov. 18, 1832.

Mary Collins to Jas. Sweeney's Hrs., Fayette Co., Ct. Ct. Bk. B., pg. 520, Oct. 1805—Justices certify that Mary Collins of Woodford Co., wife of Joel Collins of Co aforesaid, relinquishes to heirs of Jas. Sweeney all title of dower in 400 a. granted by Va. to Joseph Collins, assee .of Josiah Collins, located in Montgomery Co., on Red River, and conveyed by said Joel Collins, Dec. 4, 1798 to said Jas. Sweeney, now deceased, Oct. 8, 1805.

Philip Grimes, Fayette Co., Will Bk. B. pg. 53—Written Feb. 20,1805. Proved August, 1809. Names: Valinda Grimes, widow of son, John, she formerly widow of Bates; son, James; dau., Mary Payne, decd.; son, Avory Grimes; son, Benjamin; son, Chas.; son, Stephen; heirs of son, Philip; grandchild, Polly Grimes, dau. of son Chas. Extrs.: sons, Chas. and James.

Deed Bk. S, pg. 157, Thos. Darnall Hrs.—From Elizabeth Darnall, widow of Thos. Darnall, Sr. Archibald Darnall, Nancy Parks, Susannah Howard, Rebecca Wycoff, Thomas Darnall, Jr., Bowton Darnall, heirs of Hensa Darnall, deceased and John Darnall. Oct. 3, 1825.

Deed Bk. O, pg. 175, Levi Darnall Hrs.—From Phineas Badders and wife, Rebecca of Montgomery Co., Ky. Hannah Darnall, relict of Levi Darnall, decd., Sarah Darnall, Wm. Darnall, Nathan Darnall, Jas. Darnall and Levi Darnall, hrs. of said Darnall deed for land, being portion where Isaac Darnall, Sr., formerly lived and on which Hannah, widow, now lives. June 15, 1819.

HARRIS NOTES

William Harris, Mercer Co., Ky., Will Bk. 1, pg. 143—Written May 8, 1792. To wife, Henrietta two daus., Ann and Bradbourn, property when of age; property to be divided among "all my children" (not named). Extrx.: wife, Henrietta; Extr.: Geo. Thompson. Wts.: Jas. Taylor, Jr., Wm. Clark, Zach. Field, Geo. Thompson, Jr., and G. Thompson. Probated July, 1793.

Louisa Co., Va., Deed Book 2, pg. 298, Apr. 24. 1759—Wm. Harris and wife, Hennerettah, of parish of Fredericksville, Louisa, deed to Martin Baker of Hanover, for good causes, thereunto moving, part of tract granted by patent March 24, 1725 unto William Harris, and by said William given said Wm. Harris, his son, in will recorded in Hanover Co., (prior to 1734). William Harris, Sr., of Hanover, married Temperance Overton, whose tombstone, standing until a few years ago, bore the following inscription: "Here lyes the body of Temperance Harris, Deceased the 19 of Feb., 1710. W. H."

In Valentine Papers—William Harris and wife, Henrietta, acknowledge deed to Isaac Winston, Henrico Co., Va., May 7, 1764.

Louisa Co., Va., Deed Bk. H, pg. 427, Sept. 1784—Wm. Harris and wife, Henrietta, of Fredericksville Parish, Louisa Co., deed 882 a. to John Boswell.

Louisa Co.,Va., Deed Bk. I, April 3, 1793—Wm. Harris and wife, Henrietta of Fluvanna Co., Va., deed to Thos. Barret of Henrico Co., 248⅔ a. in Louisa.

Louisa Co., Deed Bk. A, pg 484, 1752—John Harris and wife, Patience, Amelia Co., Va., and Wm. Harris, and wife, Elizabeth, Hanover Co., deed tract to Cleavers Duke. Note: It seems possible William

Harris, Jr., married first Elizabeth and second (prior to 1764), Henrietta.

Ky. Land Office—Va. Surveys, Bk. 11, pg. 87—Wm. B. Harris and Jas. Overton's Hrs., assee. of Wm. Stewart, assee. of David Tanner, assee of Emanuel Kelly, assee of Chas. Patterson, 1800 a., part of 2000 a. entry, part of Treasury Warrant, 10694, located in Mercer Co., on Kentucky River, adjoining Isaac Winston's survey of 1600 acres on East side, bounded by lines of Winston and Ann Poage, Jan. 24, 1789. Richmond Harris assigns one-half of land in within plat mentioned to James Overton, Jr., and desires to register grant accordingly. Feb. 25, 1789. Signed Richmond Harris. Note: Richmond Harris was the son of Frederick Harris of Louisa Co., Va., see Franklin Co. Deeds.

Overton Harris, Mercer Co., Ky., Bk. 2, pg. 342-343—Appraisement of estate, Apr. 2, 1803.

Louisa Co., Va., Deed Bk. G, pg. 422—Frederick Harris of Louisa, appts. son, Richard Harris, his atty. in fact to convey his Ky. lands, Mar. 4, 1794.

Richmond Harris to John Overton, Fayette Co., Ky., Dt. Ct. Bk. B, pg. 98, Sept. 5, 1798—Richmond Harris of Louisa Co., Va., by attorney, Richard Harris, deeds John Overton of Fayette Co., Ky., 250 a. located in Mercer Co., on South side of Ky. River, consideration of $500.00.

Madison Co., Ky., Bk. E, pg. 371—Edward Harris of Newbern (New Bern), N. Carolina to James Harris, land in Madison on Muddy Creek, 750 acres granted said Edward Harris by patent Jan. 21, 1797. Dated Aug. 20, 1798.

Louisa Co., Va., Deed Bk. A, pg. 367, 1750—One Edward Harris and wife, Ann, deed Wm. Watkins part of patent granted Wm. Harris, decd., "father of said Edward" patent bearing date March 24, 1725.

Louisa Co., Va., Deed Bk. A, pg. 256, 1746—David Harris deeds part of above mentioned tract issued Wm. Harris, decd. ,to Israel Snoad.

Bourbon Co., Ky., Deed Bk. O, pg. 226, July 19, 1819—Samuel Rash to Claiborne Harris. Samuel Rash and wife, Polly of Bourbon Co., Ky., to Claiborne Harris. Whereas said Samuel Rash intermarried with said Polly Harris, daughter of John Harris of Clark Co., Ky., decd., and whereas said John Harris died seized of tract in Clark Co., and whereas said tract was allotted widow of John Harris and afterward divided among chdn. by order of court, and whereas said Polly is entitled to 1-7 part, said Samuel and Polly Rash deed to Clabourn Harris said tract. Claiborne Harris married Nancy Sutherland in Clark Co., Ky., May 16, 1816.

Note: The name Claborne Harris appears in North Carolina at an early date—see N. C. Archives, Vol. 22, pps. 165, 376 and the name Clayborn Rice appears in the early records of Goochland Co., Va.—see William and Mary Quarterly, Vol. 15, pg. 30, also Virginia Magazine, Vol. 23, pg. 81, which would seem to bear out the tradition that Robert Harris, father of Col. Wm. Harris of Hanover Co., Va., married Mary (Claborne) Rice, widow, and daughter of Col. William Claiborne of Virginia.

MARRIAGES, VITAL STATISTICS, CHURCH, BIBLE AND GRAVEYARD RECORDS

BATH COUNTY MARRIAGES

The following marriages, copied from the marriage book of certificates returned by the clergy, contain many names difficult to decipher and many mispelled names. The spelling of all names in the following list is given as it appears in the original.

Goulsber Green to Jenna Michel, Sept. 7, 1811.
Jas. Michel to Ona Green, Sept. 17, 1811.
John Set to Elizabeth Srout, Apr. 21, 1811.
John Minner (Minnear) to Jerusha McCarty, Apr. 15, 1811.
Adam U. Grayham to Elizabeth Warren, Oct. 31, 1811.
Peter McCollough to Levina Menis, July 17, 1811.
Christian Shutts to Phebe Richards, Dec. 15, 1811.
Grifen Baevent to Phebe Cantrel, Dec. 31, 1811.
Wm Boyed to Lonizy Coffer, Jan. 9, 1811.
Jones Friend to Sarah Butler, Feb. 26, 1811.
Wm. Warden to Katherin Davis, Apr. 16, 1812.
Jonothan Coughren to Susan (Sarah?) Moyers, Apr. 16, 1812.
John Douglas to Margaret Miller, Dec. 16, 1812.
Richard Lynam to Sarah Hunt, Feb. 16, 1812.
George McClain to Caty Roberts, May 30, 1811 (In Nicholas Co.,
    Ky., license from Bath).
Thos. Coshow to Sally Arnett, July 23, 1812.
John Atkinson to Sarah Coshow   Aug. 13, 1812.
Thos. Swinney to Elizabeth Wishart, June 16, 1812.
Robt. Drain to Fanny Mulberry Dec. 31, 1811.
Lewis Spencer to Frances Sorrel, Apr. 5, 1812.
Jas. Richards to Polly Barns, June 11, 1812.
John Turner of Bath Co., to Lucy Yarborough of Fleming Co.,
    June 11, 1812.
Jas. Harrison to Jemima Brown, Nov. 26, 1812.
Hiram Hollidays to Agnes Lemon, Sept. 11, 1812.
Geo. Kile to Peggy Lynch, Sept. 11, 1812.
Wyett Cantrell to Sally England, Aug. 14, 1811.
Jno. Traylor, to Saley Trayler, July 18, 1811.
Jacob Walters, to Polly W. Kinney, Oct. 15, 1812.
Walter Bracken to Dorothy Hornback, Oct. 30, 1812.
John N. Dannel to Rosey Hulse, March 8, 1812.
Obe Parris to Sarah Franklin, Sept. 24, 1812.
Stephen Grimes to Parmelia Boman, July 23, 1812.
Henry Mannon to Nancy Adams, Aug. 30, 1812.
John Mannon to Susannah Sheubert, Oct. 4, 1812.
Reubin Eastin to Polly Mannon, Oct. 9, 1812.
Nelson Rice to Martha Cartmeal, Apr. 25, 1813.
Wm. Manly to Nancy Davis, Apr. 28, 1813.
Wm. D. Morris to Clarinda Brown, Sept. 9, 1812.
Henry Long to Betsey Warfield, Oct. 12, 1812.
Jno. McClain to Patsey Jones, Jan. 21, 1813.
Jno. Woodland, Jr. to Ruthy McGehe, Sept. 21, 1813.
Mathias Griffing to Phebe Shoots, May 11, 1813.
Jno. Jones to Susan Ausburn, Jan. 12, 1813.

Ruben Staten to Susan Hall, Aug. 14, 1813.
Jno .Forgeson to Sarah Kanaday, Sept. 5, 1813.
Isaac Estell to Pegy Trumbo, Jan. 7, 1813.
Wm. Low to Betsey Smith, Feb. 17, 1813.
Israel Thorp to Aves Johnson, March 5, 1813.
Reubin Cassity to Elizabeth Brow, Jan. 12, 1813.
Jno. McCuller to Sally Staten, June 17, 1813.
William Crouch to Polly Beshaw, Jan. 13, 1814.
Jas. Moffett to Nancy Ratliff, Apr. 11, 1811.
John Dunaway to Esther Kinder, March 20, 1814.

DATED 1813

Following list of Leonard Turley:
Alexander Caldwell to Hanah B. Sample.
Benj. Shanklin to Pegy Furgarson.
Jno. Crooks to Esther Cannon.
Henry Shutts to Winnefred Utterback.
Daniel Young to Sally Smart.
Sam Delay to Polly Utterback.
Wm. Gray to Betsey Franklin.
Wm. T. Cincaid to Betsey Mace.
Jas. Baker to Nancy Squires.
Rheubin Hughes to Elizabeth McCulley.
Jas. Fugate to Sarah McGinnis.
Geo. Burk to Ann Stoops.
Wm. Stephenson to Anna Williams.
Jacob Mace to Caty Moler.
Sam'l Workman to Betsey Ockerman.
Jas. McKee to Polly McQuady.
Isaac Perkins to Elizabeth Moore.
David Gray to Elizabeth Morris.
Wm. Gray to Margaret Campbell.
Jonothan Pratts to Sally Wilson.
Jno. Jolly to Polly Berden.
Wm. Turley to Betsey Rively.

Nelson Branch to Elizabeth Robertson, Jan. 27, 1814.
Samuel Jones to Mary Ann Rolls, Apr. 7, 1814.
Solomon Steel to Martha Moor, Nov. 14, 1813.
Jno. McClain to Phebe McCarty, Feb. 15, 1814.
Christopher Mynes (Myres?) to Elizabeth Alfrey Apr. 21, 1814.
Solomon Cox to Ann Lexton (Lenton?), Apr. 28, 1814.
Elig. Atchison to Poly Rogers, May 12, 1814.
Jas. Thomas to Caty McVey, Apr. 17, 1814.
Sam'l Jackson to Sarah Thomas, June 27, 1814.
Thos. Miller to Polly Welch, March 22, 1814.
Wm. Poor to Elener Poor, Apr. 16, 1814.
Nicholas Burnes to Sarah Evans, Dec. 19, 1811.
Christopher Coons to Polly Myers, Nov. 29, 1811.
Sam'l Mitchell to Nancy Florah, Apr. 19, 1811.
Jno. Six to Elizabeth Burns, March 15, 1812.
Henry Jackson to Ruthy Freeland ,Feb. 29, 1812.
Hodlman Rice to Margaret Corbin, June 30, 1814.
Achellas Farmer to Mary Miller, Sept. 1, 1814.
Jas. Adams (Adamas?) to Elizabeth Gray, Sept. 1, 1814.
Isick Manly to Sarah Childers, April 30, 1814.
Jno. Thomas to Rebecca Viz, May 3, 1814.

Wm. Bright to Sibellen Rogers, Oct. 25, 1814.
Samuel McClure to Jane Hendricks, Feb. 20, 1814.
Robert Downs to Polly Ingram, Dec. 29, 1814.
Thos. Ellis to Jane Patrick, Nov. 18, 1814.
Solomon Painter to Polly Adams, Sept. 22, 1814.
Lewis Love to Polly Shoat (Chout), Dec. 25, 1814.
Jno. Owings to Hetty Plat, Feb. 6, 1814.
Jas. Perutt to _____ Shultz, March, 1814.
Wm. Epperson to Hetty Forsithe, Apr. 7, 1814.
Creed Glover to A. W. Choat, June 28, 1814.
Joel Parker to Rhoday Maxey, March 30, 1814.
Abner McNab to Hester Cassity, Aug. 7, 1814.
Isaac Ingram to Polly Lawson, Nov. 3, 1814.
Jno. Ruder to Lucinda Cartmeal, Jan. 7, 1815.
Thos. Fortune to Mary Sailor, Feb. 2, 1815.
Lewis Templemon to Charlotte Gregory, Feb. 23, 1815.
Frances Hopkins, to Celia Mulberry, Feb. 28, 1813.
Ignatius Davis to Sally Rice, March 20, 1815.
Jno. Six to Jean McVey, March 26, 1815
John Adams to Polly Painter, June 6, 1815.
Draper Chipman to Polly Amos, May 10, 1815.
Francis Roberts, Jr. to Peggy Baker, June 8, 1815.
Jas. Ferrel to Sally Mappin, July 21, 1814.
Henry Rice to Anne Darnell, May 30, 1814.
Richard Ross to Catherine McClese, Aug. 29, 1814.
Thos. McClure to Villinda McIlhenny, Jan. 5, 1815.
Rich'd Lamasters to Polly Smith, Apr. 9, 1815.
Richard House to Nancy Hensly, Apr. 13, 1815.
Robert Stone to Sarah Whaley, Sept. 18, 1814.
Robt. Barber to Lidia Richart, March 2, 1815.
Wm. Hopkins to Betsey Brinson, Sept. 9, 1815.
Jas. McVey to Susan (Sarah?) Sroutt, July 29, 1815.
Isaac Ross to Elizabeth Denton, Sept. 28, 1815.
John Hawkins to Jane Rogen, Nov. 21, 1815.

Chas. Harper, Minister of the Baptist Church returns:
Jno. Spencer to Phebe Turner, Aug. 25, 1814.
Jno. Craig to Nancy Cob, Sept. 27, 1814.
Chas. Clayton to Dorothy Barnes, Dec. 8, 1814.
Jas. Lonsdale to Hetty Warren, Nov. 6, 1814.
Wm. Barns to Febe Stickler, March 2, 1815.
Jacob Bumbgamer to Nancy Linch, Oct., 1815.
Joseph Jone to Milly Yarbrough, Feb. 15, 1816.

Lee Lyman to Elizabeth Dunkin, Nov. 16, 1815.
Chas. Lynam to Winney Green, Jan. 14, 1816.
Jno. Pinatt to Anna Masey (Maxey?), Oct. 9, 1814.
Ezekiel McAuty to Marget Pevler, Dec. 29, 1814.
Jas. Clark to Comfort Engname (England?), Feb. 2, 1815.
John Fisher to Nancy Movinston, Nov. 20, 1815.
Levi Goodan to Garner Grouvh, Dec. 3, 1815.
Wm. Kinkead to Polly Small, Jan. 10, 1815.
Robert Powell to Sealy Murphy, Jan. 8, 1815.
Mathew Houston to Agnes McClure, Oct. 12, 1815.
David Davis to Polly Lankester, Sept. 17, 1815.
Robt. Smily to Polly Blackburn, March 21, 1816.
James Milly to Sebey Hanks, Feb. 23, 1816.

Geo. Gates to Sally Chipman, Jan. 2, 1816.
Henry Saunders to Patsey I. Rolston, Jan. 23, 1816.
Coleman Ratliff to Peggy Roberson, March 30, 1815.
Thos. Young to Elizabeth Young, May 18, 1815.
Wm. Leach to Judeth Chatain, Oct. 11, 1816.
Benj. Jones to Polly Jones, April 16, 1816.
Thos. Arnold to Betsy Hughs, Apr. 18, 1816.
Henry Kiphart to Polly Thompson, May 5, 1816.
Jonothan Foster to Mary Hopkins, May 11, 1815.
Thos. Perris to Polly Warren, July 2, 1813.
Thos. Wimberly to Sophiah Barns, Oct. 18, 1815.
Jas. Turner to Rebecca Cooper, Jan. 2, 1816.
David Bradshaw to Rebecah Searscey, Nov., 1815.
David Howard to Peggy Font, March 7, 1815.
Jno. Evans to Ann Becraft, July 4, 1816.
Wm. Brown to Polly Brown, Oct. 8, 1816.
Jas. Gornel to Rebecca Hyten, May 13, 1816.
Sam'l Williams to Patsy Hughart, Oct. 22, 1816.
Jesse Bailey to Caty Evans, Nov. 23, 1816.
Willis Collins to Elleanor Power, Dec. 25, 1816.
Jas. Jones to Dicey Gregory, Dec. 28, 1816.
Wm. White to Tabitha Jacks, Jan. 9, 1816.
Andrew Rusel to Nancy Cracraft, Feb. 8, 1816.
Elijah B. Hall to Sally Graham, March 4, 1816.
Archible Botts to Peggy Waid, Sept. 8, 1816.
Wm. Vize to Hanah Naylor, Oct. 31, 1816.
Augustus Byram to Sally Toulson, Dec. 1, 1816.
Stephen Cassity to Peggy Brown, Feb. 11, 1816.
Joseph Mynes (Myres?) to Rachel Alfrey, Oct. 21, 1816.
Jarrord Harmon to Mary Shrout, Dec. 1, 1816.
Jno. Carpenter to Fanny Jones, Sept. 1, 1816.
David Foster to Mrs. Susannah Rogers, Jan. 19, 1817.
Adam Cooper to Margaret Spoon, March 17, 1816.
Andrew Gray to Margaret Cooper, Feb. 8, 1816.
Thos. C. Owings to Mary Bryan, March 17, 1816.
Barney Johnson to Betty Trumbo, Oct. 15, 1816.
David Hyneman to Martha Lonsdale, Jan. 2, 1817.
Jas. Bruce to Han. Jones, Jan. 21, 1817.
John Doleman to Maria Lacnaw, June 9, 1817.
Peter Hopkins to Mary Mulberry, April 24, 1817.
Frederick Howard to Janey Grant, May 8, 1817.
Jasper Clayton to Malinda Boyd, March 28, 1817.
Joslin Hopkins to Betsy Boyd, March 13, 1817.
Thos. Garvel to Sarah Butcher, March 13, 1817.
Wm. Thomas to Hannah Butcher, March 25, 1817.
Wm. Leach to Judith Chatain, April 11, 1816.
Wm. Campbell to Nancy Coshow, June 30, 1816.
Cadwalder Jones to Betsey Rogers, Sept. 12, 1816.
Thos. Arnold to Betsey Hughes, April 18, 1816.
Benj Jones, Jr. to Polly Jones, April 16, 1816.
John Vanlandingham to Nancy Vanlangham (Vanlandingham),
       1816 or 1817, 17th of Nov.
John Parris to Ann Galasby, Sept. 18, 1817.
Wm. Bright to Elizabeth Chandler, Aug. 20, 1816.
Thos. Moore to Sally Miller, Aug. 29, 1816.
Jno. Utterback to Debby Fernand, Dec. 26, 1816.
Lenay Brooks to Ellen Roberts, Jan. 5, 1817.
Jacob Myner (Myres?) to Lucy Corbin, Oct. 19, 1817.

Daniel McDonald to Elizabeth Power, Oct. 24, 1817.
Henry Hopkins to Catherine Clayton, Oct. 26, 1817.
Wm. Griffin to Ann Jackson, Dec. 1, 1817.
Isaac Busby to Lucy England, Oct. 16, 1817.
Jeremiah Bromgane to Martha Linville, Oct. 9, 1817.
Jas. Linville to Polly Honaker, June 19, 1817.
Charles Williams to Sarah Mynes, Aug. 14, 1817.
John Maler to Ann Ockerman, Nov. 7, 1816.

FLEMING COUNTY MARRIAGES

(Formed from Mason County, 1798)

Spelling is as it appears in original.

Robt. Alexander-Elanor Royce, 1800. Jno. Alexander-Catherine
Gilbert, 1799. Wm. Allen-Anna Jackson, 1804. Purnal Argo-Margaret
Hogan, 1805. Wm. Armstrong-Jurtony Lafarge, 1805. Jacob Arney-
Nancy Truitt, 1805. Wm. Alexander-Synthe Williams, 1805. Jacob
Applegate-Hannah Rowan (Roman), 1800. Jeremiah Atchison-Adah
Wright, 1806. Thompson Arnold-Susan Holland, 1807. Joseph Alex-
ander-Fanny Hambrick, 1808. Chas. Anderson-Rachel Dorsey, 1809.
Geo. Anderson-Elizabeth Shannon, 1809. Zacheus Alexander-Mary Cay-
ton, 1809. Richard Applegate-Catherine Proctor, 1809. Alex. Arm-
strong-Jane Cochran, 1810. James Ackles-Elizabeth Secrest, 1803. Jno.
Alexander-Delila Williams, 1803. Cabal Asberry-Nany Leybold, 1813.
Jno. Arnold-Sarah Ross, 1812. Henry Asberry-Patsy Hixson 1813. Henry
Atchison-Nancy Crain, 1816. Geo. Adams-Jane McIntire, 1818. Peter
Aker-Elizabeth Faris, 1817. Jno. Adams-Sophia Haden, 1817. Thos.
D. Anderson-Amilia Dorsey, 1819. Rolly Asberry-Melinda Threlkeld,
1820. Henry S. Allen-Elizabeth Sullivan, 1821. Willis Alexander-Fran-
ces Pogo, 1821. Jno. Ansley-Lydia Johnson, 1821. Alex. Armstrong-
Margaret Ocby, 1822. Thos. Asberry-Sally Truitt, 1823. Simeon Allen-
Mary Shackleford, 1821. Jno. W. Anderson-Pamelia A. Mathews, 1824.
Ebenezer Atkins-Susannah Flannagan, 1824. Geo. F. Allen-Patsy Ann
Taylor, 1825. Wm. Alexander-Elizabeth Rice, 1825. Jno. Atchison-
Mrs. Harriet Lannden, 1825. Thos. Atchison-Elizabeth Croachwait,
1826. Nelson Asberry-Libby Allen, 1825. Jas. Alexander-Penelope
Threlkeld, 1826.

Edward Bird-Ann Trimble-, 1798. Isaac Butcher-Elizabeth Clark,
1799. Jas. Barnes-Phoebe Strother, 1800. Gabriel Builderback-Rachel
Ferguson, 1799. Am Builderback-Mary McCalliston, 1799. Chas. Bur-
res-Elizabeth Plummer, 1799. Owen Batman-Patience Havens, 1800.
Marsham Belt-Margaret Norman, 1800. Jas. Bridges-Nancy Bennett,
1804. Thos. Berry-Joanna Clift, 1804. Skinner Bonfield-Elizabeth
Edgar, 1804. Elisha Berry-Mary Goddard, 1805. Jno. Burk-Caty Sous-
ley, 1805. Jas. Bradshaw-Ann Wilson, 1800. Geo. Bulas-Priscilly Plum-
mer, 1805. Jno. Benton-Nancy Wishard, 1806. Asa Brown-Irma Alex-
ander, 1805. Wm. Bennett-Polly Quinn, 1807. Shadrick Bateman-
Catherine Rumnson, 1806. Jno. Bales-Elizabeth Dummet, 1807. Wm.
Brendin-Isabella Afennegeo, 1807. Henry Burress-Mary White, 1808.
R. Breen-Ann Goas, 1807. Chas. Burress-Nancy Wire, 1809. Basil
Barnes-Prescilla Williams, 1808. Lewis Bridges-Elizabeth Kelley, 1808.
Elisha Brown-Mary Alexander, 1809. Jno. Breese-Elizabeth Carpenter,
1807. Jno. Bateman-Polly Knash, 1809. Tobias Brandy-Thankful Mc-
Garland, 1809. Jas. Bowl-Elizabeth Crail, 1809. Henry Bloomfield-

176   KENTUCKY RECORDS, VOLUME II

Catherine Dummit, 1809.   Mathew Brackin-Jane George, 1809.   Geo.
Baird-Elizabeth Hart, 1810.   Jos. Bridges-Nancy Fitch, 1810.   Wm. Bur-
rogues-Mary Radenour, 1810.   Jas. Buchannon-Polly Overby, 1810.
David Brown-Prescilla Randle, 1810.   Chas. Burton-Kenah Jones, 1811.
Wm. Bateman-Mary Walker, 1811.   Thos. Bateman-Mary Tillet, 1802.
Benj. Burress-Elizabeth Mahan, 1802.   Mashach Browning-Elizabeth
Vantrecese, 1803.   Horatio Burress-Rachel Truitt, 1803.   Samuel Beck-
Elizabeth Morrison, 1803.   Jno. Burress-Jane Myers, 1811.   Chas. Baker-
Elizabeth Davis, 1811.   Jno. Bowman-Elizabeth Bridges, 1812.   Wm.
Bridges-Priscilla Kelley, 1812.   Peter Bashaw-Elenor Jones, 1812.
Jacob Beckner-Jane Gordon, 1813.   Alling Boge-Marth Leforge, 1813.
Basil Burress-Sophia Rawlings, 1813.   Henry Burress-Hannah Harmon,
1813.   Cary Boyd-Sarah Proctor, 1813.   David Brown-Evelina Simpson,
1814.   Jeremiah Browning-Susanna Hesler, 1814.   Richard Berne-Sarah
McCabe, 1814.   Thos. Berne-Patsy Morehead, 1814.   Gibson Baker-Ann
Hookes, 1815.   Dillen Bridges-Lydia Havens, 1814.   Jno. Boyd-Nancy
Price, 1815.   Wm. Blair-Elizabeth Laforge, 1815.   Wm. Burns-Isabella
Harden, 1815.   Hervy Bell-Elizabeth Baker, 1815.   Benj. Bowman-
Prudence Wallingford, 1816.   Isaac Burress-Margaret McKinney, 1816.
Jno. Basket-Mary Weaver, 1816.   Wm. Burress-Rachel Rawlings, 1816.
Benj-Beabout-Charity Latherman, 1817.   Jno. Burke, Jr.-May Sousley,
1817.   David Baker-Betsy Hooks, 1817.   Jacob Bishop-Mary Bishop,
1816.   Wm. Browning, Jr.-Elizabeth Mooney, 1816.   Jno. Browning-
SallyThomas, 1817.   Benj. Branan-Nancy Warrick, 1818.   Archibald
Bell-Nancy McCarlla, 1818.   Samuel Burnes-Sarah Ferguson, 1818.
Robt. Burnes-Ruth Hardin, 1819.   Jos. Burke-Martha Gettys, 1819.
Jno. Burke-Mary Ferguson, 1819.   David Bramble-Joannah Maddox,
1819.   Beel Babby-Elizabeth McCoy, 1819.   Thos. Blair-Jenny Patton,
1818.   Lewis Browning-Polly Hart, 1819.   Rawleigh Busby-Polly Oxley,
1819.   Jas. Barkley-Rebecca Hart, 1819.   Jno. Botts-Melinda Ficklin,
1820.   Wm. Bennington-Rebecca Kelly, 1820.   David Booth-Louisa
White, 1819.   Wm. Burress-Lucinda Burress, 1820.   Stephen Bark-Mary
Skiley, 1820.   Vincent Babbett-Jane Neal, 1820.   Nathaniel Burress-
Sarah Quinn, 1821.   Nemiah Barnes-Emily Stephens, 1820.   Seth Bur-
riss-Ann Fagan, 1820.   Barton Bunnell-Ann Biddle, 1821.   Geo. Bently-
Catherine Bishop, 1821.   Wm. Breeze-Margaret Triplett, 1821.   Jas.
Briggs-Esthe Hughbanks, 1820.   Chas. Burriss-Rebecca Mark, 1821.
Allen Barber-Rachel Hughbanks, 1822.   Cummins Brown-Elizabeth Mc-
Intyre, 1822.   Henry Bishop-Nancy Sampson, 1822.   Alexander Blair-
Martha Hopkins, 1822.   Hambleton Borham-Margaret Page, 1822.   Wm.
Blair-Polly Davis, 1822.   Richard Blue-Nancy Hiflin, 1823.   Jas. Brown-
Luann Secrese, 1823.   Moses Bridges-Mary Vansant, 1822.   Peter Beck-
ner-Elizabeth Caska, 1823.   Andrew Bright-Martha Farran, 1823.   Jno.
Burgess-Patsy Sampson, 1821.   Jas. Bell-Ruth Shepperd, 1823.   Geo.
Bruce-Sabina Metcalf, 1823.   Stephen Biddle-Nancy Tracy, 1824.   Isah
Bently-Hannah Ann Cord, 1824.   Jas. Burnes-Lucinda Choate, 1825.
Nathan Barnes-Amelia Roper, 1825.   Burell Bell-May Evans, 1825.
Jno. Butly (?)-Hannah Smith, 1825.   Jno. Brammel-Milly Carpenter,
1825.   Thos. Barnes-Melvina Jackson, 1825.   Stephens Burke-Isabel
Craig, 1825.   Sam Barney-Cynthia Choate, 1824.   Jos. Blair-Elizabeth
Crain, 1825.   Hiram Burriss-Eliza Biddle, 1825.   Zadock Burriss- Eliz.
Goas, 1807.
    Edward Choat-Hannah Frasuer, 1799.   Barthalmew Carrel-Fran-
ces Clark, 1799.   Samuel Christy-Polly Day, 1805.   Jas. Collins-Peggy
Wood, 1805.   Zadock Clavel-Elizabeth Eaton, 1805.   Robt. Carnahan-
Rebeccah Tarvin, 1806.   Jas. Cochran-Jane McFene, 1806.   Simon Car-
penter-Sally Dawkins, 1806.   Lewis Crane-Elizabeth Crane, 1806.   Wm.
Cooper-Patty Orr, 1807.   Jas. Cristy-Betsy Deaver, 1808.   Jno. Cassity-

Elizabeth Brown, 1807. Elias Crim-Polly Hush, 1808. Jno. Collins-
Permelia Tribby, 1808. Jacob Crinnan-Mary Plank, 1808. Thos. Cun-
ningham-Lucy Watts, 1808. Chas. Cooper-Elizabeth Filson, 1809. Wm.
Cline-Nancy Filson, 1809. Jas. Colbert-Pollyan Moss, 1809. Wm. Car-
Elizabeth Steel, 1809. Alexander Crawford-Rebecca Alexander, 1809.
Edwin Callahan-Sarah Harper, 1810. Jno. Crinnan-Jane Summerville,
1811. Utley Coneless-Reller Collins, 1811. Jno. Constant-Sarah Hol-
lard, 1810. Henry Crafton-Margaret Craig, 1810. Wm. P. Hume-
Elizabeth Frances Hurchcraft, 1811. Isaac Hellecross-Nancy Inlowe,
1812. Anderson Callehan-Patty River, 1811. Naaman Chapman-Rachel
Willson, 1800. Wm. Chapman-Naomi Brownig, 1803. Samuel Crane-
Hannah Newcomb, 1804. Wm. Crane-Sarah Crane, 1811. Wm. Con-
stant-Rhoda Plank, 1811. Jas. Carter-Jane Wilson,1812. Samuel Cobb
Sally Sailor, 1812. Jas. Cockeran-Elizabeth Moss, 1811. Armon Crav-
ens-Elizabeth Daukins, 1813. Isiah Crawford-Sarah Hillard, 1814. Jon-
athan Cochran-Sarah Crawford. David Crafton-Jane Morrison, 1814.
Jacob Crawford-Elizabeth Jackson, 1814. Wm. Cross-Elizabeth Steph-
ens, 1814. Dan'l Cox-Rachel Truitt, 1814. Jno. Codes- Rebeccah
Knight, 1813. Jno. Cochran-Rachel Reed, 1813. Asher Cox-Elizabeth
Rose, 1813. Jno. Callerman-Anneroh Barnes, 1813. Geo. Cornwell-
Jane Brown, 1815. Simon Carpenter-Ann Fee, 1815. Jas. Craig-Ra-
chel Crofton, 1315. Nelson Clift-Elizabeth Hooke, 1815. Wm. Calvert-
Hety Higdon, 1815. David Craig-Merity Nancy (Nancy Merity),1816.
Jas. Culberson-Sally Weaver, 1816. Henry Conrad-Delilah Williams, 1816.
Jno. Calvert-Sarah Ann Jones, 1816. Jas. Cape-Elizabeth White, 1816.
Jno. Cooper-Pasy Ramsey, 1817. J. H. Cooper-Mary Crofton, 1817.
Asher Cox-Elizabeth Davis, 1817. Bazil Calvert-Elizabeth Jackson, 1814.
Allen Cushey-Rachel Vantrease, 1815. Carret Cord-Ruthey Ann Shock-
ey, 1817. Jno. Carter-Elizabeth Parker, 1817. Jno. B. Clarke-Martha
Terhune, 1818. Isaac Carr-Ann Hellicoss, 1817. Wm. Collins-Eliza-
beth Beckner, 1818. Jas. Curry-Margarett Doggett, 1818. Isaac Cass-
ity-Sally Myers, 1818. Geo. Cord-Polly Blair, 1819. Frederick Cluck-
Betsy Biddle, 1819. Jas. Coe-Elizabeth Todd, 1819. Jas. Cave-Belinda
Stockton, 1818. Thos. Collins-Mary Procter, 1818. Phillip Cord-Nancy
Groves, 1819. Geo. Craven-Fanny Dackin, 1820. Miles Conway-Ann
Mae Keath, 1820. Mathias Christman-Lucy Sapp, 1819. Jno. Chin-
Nancy McIntyre, 1820. Jas. Cox. Elizabeth Williams, 1820. Thos. Cay-
wood-Elizabeth Allen, 18___. Elias Combs- Ailsey Alexander, 1820. Thos.
Collins-Delilah Sampson, 1821. Francis Cassidy-Jane Inlow, 1821. Jno.
Crawford-Fanny Mills, 1821. Thos. Croswaite-Susanna Powers, 1821
Mathias Collins-Polly Taylor, 1821. Jno. Conway-Phoebe Plank, 1820.
Jas. Caldwell-Caty Peed, 1821. Uriah Callerman-Elenor McKinney,
1821. Stockly Coulter-Hester Lukins, 1821. Jas. Collins-Polly Overby,
1821. Wm. Callahan-Elizabeth Hellicoss, 1822. Rowland Carr-Julian
Goodhue, 1822. Wm. Cron-Jane Porter, 1822. Jos. Christy-Ann Gouch-
man, 1821. Jas. Collins-Sally Elliott, 1822. Thos. Campbell-Elizabeth
Eaton, 1822. Wm. Carpenter-Mary Jones, 1822.
     Jas. Demoss-Sarah Burress, 1798. Uriah Dale-Mary Gardner, 1799.
Jas. Davis-Polly McKee, 1799. Jos. Donohu-Elizabeth Williams, 1799.
Jesse Davis-Elenor Williams, 1804. Wm. Dugan-Sally Arrick, 1804.
Abio Dillin-Judith Newcomb, 1804. Jno. Dale-Jane Dennis, 1805. Wm.
Davis-Rachel Barnes, 1805. Chas. Day-Mary Rawlins, 1806. Wm. Day-
Mary Simms, 1806. Wm. Dudley-Samantha Barnes, 1807. Eli Dillon-
Catherine Hillicass, 1807. Isaac Dunaway-Sarah Pentland, 1807. Anthony
Delaney-Polly Holloway, 1807. John Deaver-Nancy Hash, 1809. Waton
Duncan-Amelia Asberry, 1808. Mathias Davis-Rebecca Greeg, 1808.
Henry Dunlap-Mary Palmer, 1809. Barnett Duwitt-Arcada Jackson,
1806. Henry Dallase-Malinda Mils, 1808. Nathaniel Davis-Nancy Davis,

1808.   Thomas Downing-Susanna Clemins, 1809.   George Davis-Sarah
Day, 1810.   Thomas Downing-Sunset Clensing, 1810.   Marlin Duncan-
Maryann Henry, 1810.   John Doyle-Patsey Cord, 1811.   Anderw
Daugherty-Nancy   Mangey,   1811.   William   Dedman-Mary   Orr.
Charles Duncan-Jemimah Foster, 1809.   Edward Dyel-Jane Hanes,
1801.   Gany Davis- Mary Filson, 1812.   Freeman Day-Catherine Wil-
liams, 1811.   Wm. Davis-Drusilla Fauquier, 1813.   David Dunneth-Sarah
Moore, 1813.   Jno. Dixon-Elizabeth Ward, 1814.   Jno. Downing-Lewrey
Browning, 1813.   Lewis Day-Kitty McIntire, 1815.   Jno. Detero-Betty
Randall, 1815.   Wm. Davis-Mary Cline, 1815.   Chas. Dayley-Mary Eaton, 1816.   Ackley Day-Sarah Oxley, 1816.   Thos. Dixon-Leydia Ward,
1816.   Stephen Donaldson-Mary Smoot, 1816.   Bazil Davis-Mary Maddox, 1817.   Jno. Daley-Lucy Buckley, 1815.   Wm. Davis-Lydia Hopper, 1817.   Jno. Dorsey-Nancy Spence, 1817.   Thos. Drennin-Polly Trim-
ble, 1817.   Ambrose Day-Joanna Moss, 1816.   Jno. Dillon-Elizabeth Van-
trease, 1818.   Robt. Davis-Phebe Atkins, 1818.   Jas. Dailie-Elizabeth
Beard, 1818.   Jacob Day-Mary White, 1818.   Henry Durrett-Rebecca
Whie, 1819.   Wm. Dulin-Priscilla Botts, 1819.   Josiah Detra-Nannah Asberry, 1818.   Amos Dillon-Letty Palmer, 1819.   Wesley Denton-
Margaret Ross, 1818.   Joshua Davis-Sarah Humphreys, 1818.   Isaac
Darnall-Cynthia Givens, 1819.   Elisha Price-Jane Harper, 1820.   Jno.
Gallatin-Mary Pollet, 1820.   Jacob Richards-Elizabeth Case, 1820.
Moses Dalrymple-Curdilla Johnson, 1819.   Jno. Davis-Gracey Sweet,
1820.   Jas. Dixon-Jane Dixon, 1820.   Samuel Davis-Jane Potet, 1820.
Isiah Dillon-Elenor Daugherty, 1819.   Richard Doggett-Hannah Sulli-
van, 1820.   Jno. Dalzell-Kisiah Nichols, 1821.   Jno. Daugherty-Fanny
Threlkeld, 1820.   Otho Davis-Nancy Creamer, 1821.   Abner Davis-Pris-
cella Kirk, 1821.   Jno. Dearing-Margaret McRoberts, 1821.   Wm. Dun-
Barbary Callerman, 1821.   Joshua Dorsey-Nancy Williams, 1821.   Lewis
Dearing-Ruth McCoy, 1821.   Thompson Day-Mary Lyons, 1821.   Jas.
Davis-Elizabeth Thompson, 1822.   Samuel Drake-Mary Williams, 1822.
Washington Dobyns-Rebecca Coulter, 1822.   Elijah Dunn, Nellie Caller-
man, 1820.   Asa Dailey-Elizabeth Saunders, 1822.   Lewis Demoss-Mary
Cox, 1822.   Elias Dowell-Nancy Triplett, 1823.   Lewis Denton-Malinda
Alexander, 1823.   Gerrard Davis-Emelia Day, 1823.   Austin Deatley-
Sally Pollett, 1823.   Jno. Denton-Sarah Pritchet, 1823.

Jesse   England-Hannah Mersham, 1800.   Jas. Eubank-Patty Carmer, 1804.   Jas. Elliott-Nancy Muse, 1805.   Samuel Evans-Jemima
Wright, 1804.   David Eubanks-Ann Watts, 1807.   Jno. Estil-Anne Kel-
lian, 1809.   Abraham Enox-Julian Logan, 1810.   Jas. Ellis-Auldra Patton, 1810.   Wm. English-Martha Gorden, 1810.   Jno. Early-Elizabeth
Warring, 1810.   Thos. Early-Catherine Perine, 1803.   Wm. Eals-Polly
Bishop, 1803.   Thos. Ellett, Jr.-Elizabeth Lever, 1813.   Isaac Evans-De-
lilah Foxworthy, 1814.   Daniel Ellett-Sarah Ellett, 1813.   Samuel El-
lett-Catherine Secrest, 1814.   St. Clair Emmons-Alice Bowen, 1814.
Wm. Eaton-Mary Hunt, 1815.   Squire Evans-Bathemy Allison, 1816.
Edward Elliott, Jr.-Hannah Cornwall, 1816.   Wm. Emmons-Betsy Ham,
1816.   Jas. Early-Elizabeth Tully, 1818.   Asa English-Mary Jones,
1816.   Scioto Evans-Jane Clancy, 1818.   St. Clair Eakins-Julian
Spencer, 1819.   Joshua Esham-Harriett McDaniell, 1819.   Thos.
Elliott-Emily Randall, 1818.   Lachem Evans-Fanny Alexander,
1818.   Samuel Early-Mary Williams, 1820.   Jos. Eaton-Susannah Allen-
der, 1820.   Gabriel Evans-Margaret James, 1821.   Jesse Emmons-Mary-
ann Davis, 1822.   Carson Evans-Fanny Mills, 1822.   David R. Estill-
Harriett Weaver, 1822.   Geo. Emmons-Patsy Wilson, 1825.   Zacheus
Evans-Margaret Payne, 1826.   Jesse Evans-Hannah Pitts, 1826.   Jas.
Estill-Mariah Wright, 1826.   Andrew Early-Fanny Summers, 1826.

JESSAMINE COUNTY VITAL STATISTICS
(Formed from Fayette, 1798)

Filed in State Historical Society.

Notes made by Miss Hattie Scott.

Alcock, M.—(see Frances Young).
Andrew, James—(see Eliz. Hamilton).

Baughn, Joseph—aged 56, married, born Hanover Co., Va., son of Richard and Jerriah (?) Baughn, died May 16, 1852.
Bourn, John—aged 74, married, born Culpepper Co., Va., died Mar. 1,
   1852.
Brock, W.—aged 58, born Va., son of J. and C. Brock, died Apr. 22,
   1854.
Bryant, W. T.—aged 66, born Fayette Co., son of D. Bryant, died July
   22, 1854.
Bryant, D.—aged 67, married, farmers' wife, born in Maysville, dau.
   of E. and T. Cravens, died Oct. 17, 1854.
Bruner, C.—aged 80, widow, born Va., dau. of J. Bruner, died June
   14, 1854.
Bourne, E.—aged 84 widower, born Va., son of J. and M. Bourne,
   died Oct. 12, 1854.
Barr, Thos.—(see Sarah Wallace).
Barr, _____—(see Mary Trisler).
Burey, (Berry?) Thos.—(see Frances Robinson).

Collins, Lewis—aged 72, widower, born Va., son of John Collins, died
   Mar. 21, 1852.
Collins, John—(see Lewis Collins).
Craven, E and T.—(see D. Bryant).
Cornelius, M.—aged 68, widower, born Va., son of John and M. Cor-
   nelius, died Nov. 15, 1854.
Cornelius, John—(see M. Cornelius).
Creath, Jacob—aged 75 married, born Va., son of W. and J. Creath,
   died Mar. 15, 1854. .
Collins, Lewis and Sarah E.—(see Polly Lancaster).
Colley, William (?)—aged 68, widower, born S. C., died May 16, 1852.
Chrisman, Margaret A.—aged 44, born Rockingham Co., Va., dau. of
   Conner and Elizabeth Custer, died May 16, 1852.
Custer, Conner and Eliz.—(see M. Chrisman).
Carlisle, Robert—aged 70, widower, born Jessamine Co., son of J. and
   E. Carlisle ,died July 20, 1855.
Champion, Sally—aged 76, widow, dau. of J. and S. Champion, died Nov.
   15, 1855.
Carter, C. E.—aged 86, born in Va., died Feb. 7, 1859.

Davenport, Nancy—aged 65, widow*, born Woodford Co., dau. of John
   and Winny Williams, died Clay Co., Mo., Aug. 5, 1852. *of Fortunatus Davenport.
Douglas, E—aged 60, farmer's wife, born Va., dau. of W. and P. Miller,
   died Sept. 3, 1854.

Elkin, D. and B.—(see Marium Prewitt).
Elmore, James—aged 88, widower, born Va., son of _____, died Dec.
   31, 1852.

Francis, Wm.—(see Susannah Foster).
Foster, Susannah—aged 87, born Va., dau. Wm. Francis, died July 10, 1859.

Goss (Gess?) Jane—aged 70, single, dau. H. and E. Goss, died Oct. 28, 1854.
Gass?—(see Fayette Co. for Gess, Gass—same).

Hawkins, Ann—aged 65, widow, dau. of J. and Jane Wilmore, died Aug. 11, 1855.
Hampton, A.—aged 57, son of John Hampton, died May 11, 1854.
Hager, Wm.—aged 55, widower, born Madison Co., Ky., son of W. and H. Hager, died July 15, 1854.   ✝
Harris, Wm. and Jane—(see West, Sarah).
Hawkins, Mary—aged 53, married, born Jessamine Co., dau. of Margaret and Edmond Singleton, died Jessamine Co., May 13, 1852.
Holloway, James H.—aged 18, born Jessamine Co., son of Samuel and Jane T. Holloway, died Charlotte Co., Va., Sept. 16, 1852.
Holloway, Samuel and Jane—(see Jas. Holloway).
Hamilton, Elizabeth—aged 78, farmer's wife, born Frederick Co., Md., dau. of James Andrew, died Mar. 13, 1852.
Hamilton, Robert—aged 90, widower, born in Scotland, died Nov. 8, 1859.
Hill, Sarah—aged 90, widow, born Va., died Oct. 28, ____.

Johnson, Benj. D.—aged 72, son of Samuel and A. Johnson, born in Md., died Aug. __, 1857.
Johnson, Samuel and A.—(see Benj. Johnson).
Jacobs, Joseph W.—aged 73, son of Geo. Jacobs, died Aug. 30, 1855.

Knight, E.—aged 88, widow, born Va., dau. of W. and P. Williams, died Oct. 10, 1854.

Lancaster, Polly—aged 36, dau. of Lewis and Sarah E. Collins, died Mar. 29, 1852.

McNutt, Samuel—aged 71, hatter, born Va., widower, son of F. and B, McNutt, died June 7, 1859.
Major Sarah—aged 62, widow, born Md., dau. of C. and S. Masoner, died Dec. 18, 1854.
Masoner, C. and S.—(see Sarah Major).
Miller, W. and P.—(see E. Douglas).
Mosby, Frances—aged 70, dau of Geo. Smith, died Apr. 5, 1859.

Neal, George—aged 70, son of George Neal, died Mar. 12, 1854.

Perron, W.—aged 74, married, born Va., son of M. and A. Perron, died Apr. 4, 1854.
Prewitt, Marian R.—aged 58, widow, dau. of D. and B. Elkin?, died Aug. 1, 1855.

Robinson, Frances—aged 75, dau. Thos. Burey, born Va., died Sept. 15, 1859.

Stipe, Martha—aged 60, widow, born Va., dau. of J. and M. Sale, died July 1, __59?.
Sale, J. and M.—(see Martha Stipe).
Smith, Geo.—(see Frances Mosby).

Singleton, Edmond and Margaret—(see Mary Hawkins).
Sodowsky, E.—aged 78, born Va., son of Jacob Sowdosky, died Aug. 20, 1854.
Smith, J. and M.—(see Mary Young).

Trisler, Mary—aged 70, widow, born Md., dau. of _____ Barr, died Nov. 6, 1852.
Todhunter, John—aged 70, widower, born Jessamine Co., son of John and M. Todhunter, died Nov. 10, 1854.

Wilmore, J. and Jane—(see Ann Hawkins).
Williams, W. and P.—(see E. Knight).
Williams, John and Winny—(see Nancy Davenport).
Walters, Mary E.—aged 73, born Owen Co., dau. of John and M. Scripto, married J. Walters, died Jessamine Co., Aug., 1852.
Walter, Richard—aged 74, married, son of D. and M. Walters, died Aug. 18, 1855.
Wallace, Sarah—aged 72, married, born Md., dau. of Thos. and Mary Barr, died Sept. 16, 1852.
West, Charles—aged 52, married, son of Richard West, born Jessamine Co., died Sept. 1, 1859.
West, Richard—(see above).
West, Sarah—aged 50, born Jessamine Co., dau. Wm. and Jane Harris, died June 2, 1852.

Young, Mary—aged 79, widow, born Va., dau. of J. and M. Smith, died Nov. 25, 1854.
Young, Frances—aged 80, widow, born Va., dau. of M. and M. Alcock, died Aug. 5, 1854.

OLDHAM COUNTY VITAL STATISTICS

Some items taken at random from Vital Statistics filed in State Historical Society archives under Oldham County; for the most part of persons past 50 years of age.

Adcock, Joshua—age 77; born Buckingham, Va.; died Nov. 10, 1852.

Branch, Anderson and Barbary; see Nancy Minnis.
Bennett, Eliz.—age 58; born Mercer County, Ky.; dau. Wm. and C. Coons; died May 31, 1858.
Bennett, Evaline—age 66; born Virginia; died June 15, 1856.
Button, Frances—married; age 64; born Virginia; died Aug. __, 1855.
Bowen, Ruth G.—age 64; born Virginia; died Feb. 2, 1856.
Berry, John W.—age 90, widower; born King George County, Virginia; son Thos and Betsy Berry; died Apr. 13, 1852.
Barnhill, Wm.—age 67, married; born Orange County, N. C.; son Robt. and Rachel Barnhill; died Dec. 13, 1852.
Buckner, Samuel—age 86, widower; born Caroline County, Virginia; son Philip and Tabitha Buckner; died Feb. 2, 1852. (Philip and Tabitha Buckner lived and died in Bracken County, Ky., see his will, naming son Samuel, 1817).
Buckner, Coleman—age 53; born Jefferson County, Kentucky; son Samuel and Susan; died Jan. 10, 1852.

Black—see Sarah Sparks.
Boulware,—see Mary E. Prewitt.

Crenshaw, Wm. A.—age 56; born Halifax County, Virginia; son Lewis
    and Sarah Crenshaw; died Sept. 10, 1852.
Coons, Wm. and C.—see Eliza Bennett.
Compton, Wm.—age 49; born London, England; died Aug. 12, 1856.
Carter, Josph—age 63; died Jan. 1, 1856.
Carpenter, A.—age 60; born Virginia; died 1855.
Crider, Peter—age 76, 2nd wife; born North Carolina; son L. and M.
    Crider; died May 2, 1858.
Cornwell—see Jane Wright.

Edds, (Eads?) Drury—age 46, married; born Louisa County, Virginia;
    son William and _____ Edds; died Oct. 8, 1852.

Flint, John—age 85; 2nd wife; died Dec. 10, 1860.

Gathright, Jesse—age 22, in college in Virgina, single; son of John Gath-
    right, resident of Oldham; died in Virginia, Mar. 20, 1858.
Gouner, (Gonner) Jacob—age 75, widower; born in Virginia; died Jan.
    27, 1852.

Hall, Mary—age 70, married; born in Maryland; died Dec. 20, 1852.

Kemper, Joel—see Nay.

Maddox, John—age 65; born in Virginia; son John and E. Maddox; died
    Aug. 1, 1860.
Milner, Marcus—age 76, married; born in Virginia; died Mar. 10, 1858.
Morgan, Nicholas—see Mary Rigby.
McGhee, Rice—age 53, widower; born in Virginia; son John and Ma-
    nerva; died Oct. 10, 1852.
Minnis, Nancy—age 46; born Louisa County, Virginia; daughter Ander-
    son and Marbary Branch; died Nov. 28, 1852.
Mahan, John—see Eliz. Westerfield.

Nay, Elizabeth—age 60, widow; born Maryland; daughter Joel and Ann
    Kemper; died Apr. 29, 1852.
Nay, (Ney?) Jas.—age 66 born Mercer County, Ky.; died Mar. 6, 1856.

O'Bryan, Henry C.—age 60; born in Virginia; son P. and J. (I?) O'Bry-
    an; died July 27, 1858.
Overstreet, M. R.—age 75, married; son M. and K. Overstreet, born in
    Fayette County, Kentucky; died July 18, 1858.
Overstreet, Jeff—age 52, widower; born in Garrard County, Kentucky;
    son Gabriel and Lucy Overstreet; died Dec. 19, 1852.
Overstreet, Samuel and Martha—Lost slave, 1852.

Potts, Thos.—age 73; died Apr. 20, 1856.
Parker, Nancy—age 70, married; born in Maryland; daughter Edm. and
    Agnes Woolfolk; died Sept. 18, 1852.
Prewitt, Mary E.—age 41 yrs. 8 mos.; born Shelby County, Kentucky;
    daughter J. Boulware; died Apr. 19, 1856.

Rigby, Mary A.—age 45; born Fayette County, Kentucky; daughter
    Nicholas Morgan; died Feb. 1, 1858.

Ritter, Hiram—age 47; born Oldham County; son John R.; died Mar. 15, 1856.

Sparks, Sarah—age 73; daughter John and Mary Blak; born North Carolina; died July 19, 1858.

Shrader, Wm.—age 81; born Pennsylvania; died 1855.

Spear, Susan—age 41; daughter J. Hinkley; died 1855.

Spear, Andrew and Eliz.—see Taylor, Mary.

Thomas, Middleton—age 62; born Virginia; son Latamore and Margaret Thomas; died June 2, 1852.

Taylor, Mary—age 49, married; born Shelby County, Kentucky; daughter Andrew and Eliz Speer; died Sept. 22, 1852.

Vincent, D.—age 92, widower; born Virginia; died June 20, 1855.

Westerfield, Eliz.—age 71 years, 4 mos., single (?); born Mercer County, Kentucky; daughter John Mahan; died Nov. 24, 1856. (Should be widow, no doubt).

Wilhite, Stafford—age 78, (B?); born Madison County, Virginia; son Z. Wilhite; died Aug. 5, 1859.

Wright, Jane—age 72, widow; born Virginia, died in Henry County, Kentucky; daughter _____ Cornwell; died Oct. 4, 1858.

Woolfolk, Thos. J—age 53; born Jefferson County; son of Edmund and Agnes Woolfolk; died Nov. 27, 1852.

Woolfolk, Thos. and Adeline—Lost a slave, by death, 1852.

Woolfolk, Edmund and Agnes—Parents of Nancy Parker, see above.

WARREN COUNTY VITAL STATISTICS

Few items from the death "Vital Statistics" of Warren County, on file in archives of State Historical Society, Frankfort, Ky. Contributed by Hattie M. Scott, Frankfort, Ky.

Billingsley, Elizabeth—aged 81 years, widow, born in Pa., dau. of Wm. and P. Parker, died July 3, 1855.

Briggs, Margaret—born in Va., dau. of N. and _____ Calla, died Nov. 28, 1860.

Cherry, Frances—aged 69, widow, born in Edgcomb, N. C., dau. of Jas. and Sally Taylor, died Nov. 17, 1852.

Collier, Bartlett S.—aged 53, resident of Edmondson County, Ky., born in Lincoln Co., N. C., son of Bartlett and Elizabeth Collier, died July 15, 1852.

Dishman, Nancy—98, born in Va., dau. of _____ Miller, died 7-8, '60.

Drake, Tarlton—aged 81, born in Powhatan County, Va., son of James and Mary Drake, died June 16, 1852.

Galaway, Thos—aged 71, son of M. and _____ Galaway, born in Md., died Apr. 1, 1860.

Grider, John—aged 64, born in Garrard County, Ky., son of Henry and Elizabeth Grider, died July 27, 1852.

Higginbotham, James—63, widower, born in Amherst County, Va., son of James and Rachel Higginbotham, died Aug. 15, 1852.

Hareld, Reubin—56, widower, born in Va., son of J. and L. H. Hareld, died Sept. 30, 1860.

Kelly, Elizabeth—aged 66, widow, born in Va., dau. of James and _____ Ashby, died Oct. 25, 1852.

Kerby, Jesse, Sr.—aged 95 years, 1 mo. and 25 days, born 1757 in Franklin Co., Va., son of David and Elizabeth Kerby, died Dec. 17, 1852. (David Kerby, father of this Jesse, died 1811, and left will naming the above Jesse, and many other children, the daus. all being married.)

Mayhew, Walter—77, born in Prince George Co., Md., son of John and Elizabeth Mayhew, died Aug. 15, 1852.

Miller, Benj.—aged 65, born Richmond, Va., son of Jacob and Margaret Miller, died May 20, 1852.

Nash, Wm.—born near Richmond, Va., died Sept., 1852, aged 75 years.

Neely, James—53, born Logan County, Ky., son of David and Eliz. Neely, died Jan. 24, 1852.

Stahl, Magdalene—87, widow, born Huntington Co., Pa., dau. of Henry and _____ Vizziard, died Aug. 8, 1852.

Sulser, Winny—aged 64, widow, born in S. C., dau. of W. and _____ Rackley, died June 22, 1855.

Taylor, Emily C.—aged 60, widow, born Notaway Co., Va., dau. Booker and Nancy Ransey, died Dec. 27, 1852.

Upton, Mary Ann—aged 61, born N. C., ,dau. Joseph and Sarah Taylor, died Aug. 31, 1852.

Watkins, Jos.—73, born Va., son Joseph and Elizabeth W., died Aug. 1, 1852.

Westbrook, Elijah—aged 63, born Charlotte, Va., son Amos and Elizabeth Westbrook, died June 26, 1852.

Wren, Joseph—aged 60, born North Carolina, son of S. and _____ Wren, died Feb. 29, 1855.

CHURCH RECORDS

PARIS PRESBYTERIAN CHURCH RECORDS
June 28, 1820-Aug. 22, 1824.

Sabbath, Aug. 6, 1820—The holy ordinance of baptism was administered to Mary Hall's son, Samuel Wallace and Polly Davises' daughter, Sally Elizabeth.

Same, Aug. 25, 1820—Mrs. Mary Mill's son, Benjamin and Mrs. Ford's son, William.

Same, Aug. 28, 1820—Mrs. Lucy Hall's son, James Laugherly.

Sept. 3, 1820—Benjamin Peers dismissed by certificate| Aug. 27, 1820.

Sept. 3, 1820—Elizabeth Brown, consort of John G. Brown, depd. this life, 13, Sept., 1820.

Sept. 3, 1820—Edward Peers dismissed by certificate 14, Sept., 1820.

Nov. 2, 1820—Recd. Elijah Wright and wife, Nancy, also Letitia Irvin, single.

Mar. 25, 1821—Mr. Andrew Finley and wife, Jane, dismissed by certificate.

May 5, 1821—Baptism administered to chdn. of Elijah Wright, viz: Thomas, Phoebe and William.

May 9, 1821—Mrs. Elizabeth Clark admitted to Church.

May 12, 1821—Baptism administered to Lewis Thornton's dau., Mary Mills.

May 14, 1821—Baptism administered to inft. chdn. of Robert and Elizabeth Clark, viz: Lucinda, John, Robert by Revd. McFarland.

June 3, 1821—Baptism administered to William Alexander's sons, William, Wilson, John, Robert.

June 3, 1821—Mrs. Elizabeth Clark, wife of Robt. Clark depd. this life on sabbath last, 24, June, 1821.

June 24, 1821—Baptism administered to Patsy Mitchell's three daus., Julia Ann, Mary and Martha. Also Thos. P. Smith's dau., Elizabeth Markham.

July 22, 1821—Baptism administered Mrs. Susannah Warfield's daus., Susannah, Rebeccah and Robert Hoar's dau., Hannah.

July 29, 1821—Wm. Mitchell, Jr., had his dau., Rebecca Jean baptized.

Aug. 6, 1821—John Cradock and wife, Sally members in communion, also their infant chdn. as baptized members, dismissed by certificate.

Oct. 4, 1821—Mr. James Alexander, ruling elder, depd. this life, Wed., 3rd, Oct., 1821.

Dr. Thos. Barbee, ruling elder in Presbyterian Church, depd. this life, Sat., 13, Oct., 1821.

Dec. 2, 1821—Ebenezer Sharpe, elder in Presbyterian Church on Market St. in Lexington, recd. by congregation.

Jan. 2, 1822—Mathew Cuthbert admitted to membership.

Jan. 2, 1822—Samuel Taylor, young man, admitted by certificate from church in Columbus, Ohio.

Jan. 5, 1822—Joseph March, young man, admitted by certificate from church in Delaware, Ohio.

Jan. 27, 1822—Baptism administered Ebinezer Sharpe and wife's son, James McChord, also to the dau. of Mrs. Susannah E. Garrard, Ellener Orr.

March 30, 1822—Baptism administered to dau. of Mrs. Lucy Hall, Elizabeth Kinkaid.

April 21, 1822—Baptism administered to Mrs. Alcia Barbee's dau., Alice Thomas.

May 9, 1822—Baptism administered John McFarland, son of Benj. Mills and wife. Same to James Henry, son of Mrs. Sally Suttle.

June 2, 1822—In April or May, 1822, Ralph Letton and wife, Sarah, dismissed by certificate.

June 19, 1822—Mathew Culbert dismissed by certificate, he removing to Philadelphia.

June 29,1822—Baptized Patsey, dau. of Wm. Mitchell, Jr., and wife, Nancy. Prudence Lilly admitted to membership.

June 30,1822—Robert Hoare dismissed by certificate, he removing to Indiana.

July 14, 1822—Mr. Wilson Alexander and wife, Margaret, admitted by certificate from Woodford Church.

Same time, Mr. James Ward and wife, Martha, by certificate from Mount Pleasant Church.

July 14, 1822—William Russell, son of Jas. and Martha Ward, baptized.

Aug. 11, 1822—Baptized Mrs. Jean Johnson's dau., Elizabeth Ann and son, Benjamin Emmit.

Aug. 25, 1822—Sons and daus. of Mrs. Headon baptized, viz: John, Robt., Harrison, Jesse and Julia Ann and Mary Ann.

Aug. 25, 1822—Jean Richards admited. Mr. John Curry, elder, granted certificate for self and family.

Sept. 21, 1822—Baptism administered two sons of Dr. J. Berry and wife, Jean, viz: James Jones and John Smith.

Sept. 23, 1822—Rebeccah Allen, widow, dismissed by certificate, she removing to Millersburg.

Sept. 23, 1822—Michael Bowyer and wife, Mary, Mrs. Eliza Maria Owings, Miss Jane Miller and Andrew Ross admitted. Mrs. Eliza Owings and her son, Thomas, baptized Jan. 28, 1823. Samuel J. Galloway and wife, Elizabeth, she producing extract from session proceedings of New Market Church, Ohio. Mary Rannells admited.

April 6, 1823—John G. Brown and wife, Mary, had their dau., Mary Todd, baptized. Also Mrs. Sally Ford had her dau., Sarah, baptized. William McConnell, ruling elder in the Paris Church departed this life on Saturday, April 9th, 1823, aged about eighty years, (pg. 70). Note: The above Wm. McConnell married 1768 in Penn., Rosannah Kennedy and their dau., Elizabeth, married John Ardery.

July 13, 1823—Baptism administered to infants; Thomas P. Smith's dau., Ann, Wm. Alexander's dau., Lucinda, Elijah Wright's son, Robert Harison, Jean Galloway's son, Wm., Michael Boyer's sons, John, Andrew and Jacob and dau., Eliza and son, Adam.

July 18, 1823—Mr. Wm. McGuffee admitted by certificate from Flemingsburgh session.

July 18, 1823—Mr. James Wilson, presented certificate from Church in Lexington. Miss Lititia C. Oden admitted.

July 20, 1823—Four daus. of Mrs. Mary Fisher baptized, viz: Mary, Eliza, Fanny, Margaret.

Sept. 15, 1823—Mrs. Jean Berry and Geo. W. Ashbridge granted certificates. Mrs. Sarah Ann McCrory, wife of James McCrory, admitted.

Sept. 29, 1823—Mrs. Elizabeth Galloway, consort of Samuel Galloway, admitted.

Oct., 1823—Samuel Galloway produced certificate from New Market.

April 23, 1824—Robt. Allen, David Mitchell and Helena B. Kenny admitted. Archer C. Dickerson applied for membership and baptized.

May 23, 1824—James Winston, son of John G. Brown and wife, Mary, baptized July 4, 1824. Also Sarah Ruth, dau. of Jas. Ward and wife, Martha. Also John Lyle, son of Samuel Galloway and wife, Elizabeth.

July 14, 1824—Samuel R. Alexander admitted, he having been formerly baptized. Mrs. Margaret January, widow of Peter January, depd. this life, Tues., 20th, July, 1824, in 77th yr. Mrs. Mary Ammerman, a baptized person, admitted.

Aug. 2, 1824—Lucinda Frances, dau. of Elijah and Nancy Wright, baptized.

Aug. 22, 1824—Mrs. Nancy Davis granted certificate of dismission. Norah, Ann, Saphinah, dau. of Mrs. Susan Warfield, baptized. Also Susan Garrard's son, James, baptized.

BIBLE RECORDS

ADAIR BIBLE
(In the possession of Mrs. John Towles, Paris, Ky.).

MARRIAGES
Richard Adair and Mary Tarr were married in Bourbon County, Kentucky, January 13th, 1811.

James F. Adair was married to Martha J. Turner, June 4th, 1811.
Robert Farris Adair and Sarah Isabella Dodson, married November 13th, 1854.
Mary Ellen Adair and William Porter Ardery, married September 2nd, 1880.

BIRTHS
Jame F. Adair was born in New Castle, Delaware, 1786.
Richard Adair was born in Delaware, May 16th, 1788.
Mary Adair, wife of Richard Adair, was born October 10th, 1796.
Robert F. Adair, son of Richard and Mary Adair, was born September 4, 1833 in Nicholas County, Kentucky.
Sarah Isabella Dodson was born June 27th, 1839, in the city of Maysville, Kentucky.
Their children:
Mary Ellen Adair was born on Sunday, the 25th day of November, 1855.
Sarah Belle Adair was born Thursday, May 7th, 1857.
Bertie Haden Adair was born November 10th, 1858.
Henrietta Adair was born October the 28th, 1859.
Bertie T. Adair was born April the 27th, 1861, in Fleming County, Kentucky.
Sallie E. Adair was born August 7th, 1864, in Harrison County, Kentucky.
Florence Belle Adair was born October 27th, 1867, in Harrison County, Kentucky.
Robert D. Adair was born July 19th, 1869.
James Curtis Adair was born September 21st, 1871.

DEATHS
Richard Adair died in Nicholas County, November, 1866.
James F. Adair died in Adams County, Illinois, March 8, 188_.
Bertie Haden Adair, died Sunday, December 12th, 1858, aged 4 weeks and three days.
Sarah Belle Adair died October 17th, 1860, aged 3 years, 5 months and eleven days.
Robert Farris Adair died Saturday, May 4th, 1907.
Ella Adair Ardery died Thursday, January 17th, 1918.
William P. Ardery died October 16th, 1916.
Joseph DeJarnette died January 28th, 1918.
Our darling mother, Belle Dodson Adair, died November 8th, on Tuesday at eleven-fifteen o'clock, 1920.
Nettie Adair DeJarnette died April 25th, at two P. M., 1926.
Florence Adair Hedges died October 18th, Tuesday, five A. M., 1927.

BAILEY BIBLE

Bible record of Elisha Bailey, Revolutionary Soldier of Adair Co., Ky., filed with his application for a pension, which was granted.

Elisha Bailey, son of John and Mary Bailey, born Nov. 20, 1763.
Hannah Gay, dau. of Thos. and Peggy Gay, born Mar. 11, 1764.
Elisha Bailey and Hannah Gay married Dec. 19, 1782.

Children:
Thomas T. Bailey, son, born Apr. 3, 1784.

Polly T. Bailey, dau., born Apr. 1, 1786.
John Bailey, son, born July 22, 1788.
Betsey Bailey, dau., born Dec. 31, 1791 (?).
Samuel B. Bailey, son, born Jan. 19, 1796
Hiram Bailey, son, born Aug. 18, 1798
Blane Bailey, son, born July 13, 1803.
Benjamin Bailey, son, born Aug. 25, 1809.
Kitty Bailey, dau., born 1792.

Thomas T. Bailey, son of Elisha and Hannah, married July 12, 1809, to Polly Atkinson (Albemarle Co., Va.).

BATTERTON BIBLE

(In the possession of Mrs. Raymond McMillan)

MARRIAGES

Benjamin Batterton, Senr., and Susannah Guthrie were married March 11, 1790.

L. D. Sims and Anna Batterton were married March 2, 1826.

Elias Batterton and Kitty Ann Smith were married May the 15th, 1834.

Thomas Dinwiddie and Elizabeth Batterton were married April 23rd, 1835.

Benjamin A. Batterton and Mary Jane George were married the 8th of November, 1841 (or 7).

T. J. Shepard and Bettie G. Batterton were married November 12th, 1879.

B. Alfred Batterton and Lizzie H. Boswell were married December 6th, 1882.

John F. McDaniel and Mary S. Batterton were married October 22nd, 1884.

BIRTHS

Benjamin Batterton, born September the 2nd, Anno Domi., 1767.

Susannah Batterton, wife of Benjamin Batterton, was born September 27th day, 1767.

Reuben Batterton was born March the 11th day, 1791.

Anna Batterton was born April the 9th day, 1792.

Sarah Harris Batterton was born December the 5th, 1793.

Elizabeth Batterton was born December the 16th day, 1795.

John Batterton was born December the 22nd day, 1797.

Enoch Batterton was born December the 9th day, 1799.

William Guthrie Batterton was born August the 15th day, 1801.

Henry Batterton was born May the 22nd day, 1803.

Jesse Batterton was born January the 6th day, 1805.

Samuel Batterton was born December the 20th day, 1806.

Elias Batterton was born November the 26th day, 1808.

Benjamin Abbott Batterton was born July the 24th day, 1811.

Elizabeth G. Batterton was born 31st of January, 1854 .

Benjamin A. Batterton was born the 15th of December, 1856.

Mary S. Batterton was born the 2nd of June, 1858.

Benjamin Alfred Batterton, son of B. A. and Lizzie Batterton, was born December 15th, 1883.

George Boswell Batterton, son of B. A. and Lizzie Batterton, was born January 21st, 1885.

Joseph Roy Batterton was born November 18th, 1887.
Mary Elizabeth Batterton was born October 9th, 1890.
Smith Bishop Batterton was born June 24th, 1897.

DEATHS

Jesse Batterton died December the 28th day, 1809.
Benjamin Batterton, Senr., died June the 29th day, 1833.
Sarah Harris King died January the 31st, 1835.
Elizabeth Thomas died June the 16th, 1837.
Henry Batterton died August the 8th, 1838.
Enoch Batterton died August the 20th, 1837.
Nelson Batterton died June the 14th, 1838.
Susannah Batterton died the 11th day of May, 1852.
Benjamin Abbott Batterton died March, 10th day, 1863.
Elizabeth George died March 1st, 1875.

NOTE: Found in the Batterton Bible, old deed as follows: John
Clough to Batterton—Conveyance of Land Warrant, appointed by
father, Ebenezer Clough of City of Boston, Mass., for good will toward
Benjamin Abbott Batterton, natural son of Benjamin Batterton, of
Bourbon County, Ky. "Witness, I have delivered letter signed by my
father, above date," is Dec., 1823, Boston.

BOONE BIBLE
(In the possession of Mrs. Frank C. Reilly, St. Louis, Mo.).

Jonathan Boone was born on the 21st day of November on the
3rd day of the week, about three o'clock in the afternoon, in the year
of our Lord, 1750.
William Power, son of John Power, was born October the 1st day,
in the year of our Lord, 1771.
Thomas Power, son of John and Elizabeth Power, was born March
the 9th day, in the year of our Lord, 1789.
Absolam Power, son of James and Elenor (?) Power, was born
July __ (?), in the year of our Lord, 1789.
Mary Power, daughter of James and Elenor Power was born
November 26th day, in the year of our Lord, 1782.
Jeremiah Power, son of Jas. and Elenor Power, was born November
24th day, in the year of our Lord, 1784.
Rebeckey Power, daughter of James and Elenor Power, was born
May the 15th day, in the year of our Lord, 178 (9?).
Absoliam Power, son of James and Elenor Power, was born July
16th, in the year of our Lord, 1790. (Note: see date given above).
Elenor Power, daughter of James and Elenor Power, was born
March 15th day, in the year of our Lord, 179 (2?).
James Power, son of James and Elenor Power, was born March
6th day, in the year of our Lord, 1795.
George Power, son of James and Elenor Power, was born Feb-
ruary the 18th day, in the year of our Lord, 179 (?), at twenty-five
minutes after twelve———?
Thomas Boone, son of Jonathan Boone, was born November
22nd day, in the year of our Lord, 1774.
Mary Poor, daughter of John Poor and Elizabeth (——?), was
born November 10th day, in the year of our Lord, ———.
Elizabeth (Boone?) was born November 28th day, in the year of
our Lord, 1763 (or 1773).

Elenor Boon, daughter of John Poar and Elizabeth Poar, was born November, 1776.

Rachel Boone, daughter of Jonothan Boone and Susannah Boone, was born January 11th day, in the year of our Lord, 1779.

Jesey (?) Boone, son of Jonathan Boone and Susannah Boone, was born January 6th day, in the year of our Lord, 1779.

Mary Boone, daughter of Jonothan and Susanah Boone, was born November 24th day, in the year of our Lord, 1780.

Elizabeth Poar, daughter of John Poar and Elizabeth Poar, was born the 12th day of March, in the year of our Lord, 1782.

———? Sincler, son of Amos Sincler and Mary Sincler, was born the 11th day, ———, 1770.

———?, son of Amos Sincler and Mary Sincler, was born October 30th, in the year of our Lord, 1772.

Amos Sincler, son of Amos Sincler and Mary Sincler, was born on the 25th day of March, in the year of our Lord, 1775.

———?ry Sincler, daughter of Amos and Mary Sincler, was born 12th of September, in the year of our Lord, 1777.

———?ah Sincler, daughter of Amos and Mary Sincler, was born April 5th, in the year of our Lord, 1781.

BRIDGES BIBLE RECORD

(Owned by Mrs. Hall, Lexington, Ky., 1927)

BIRTHS

Benjamine Bridges, born Nov. 6, 1759.
Susannah, his wife, born Dec. 30, 1769.
Children:
George Bridges, born Oct. 30, 1785.
Benjamin Bridges, born June 27, 1787.
Lucy Bridges, born Oct. 30, 1789.
Betsey Bridges, born Dec. 3, 1791.
Charles Bridges, born Nov. 1, 1793.
Nancy Bridges, born Aug. 4th, 1795.
Rebecca Bridges, born Jan. 8, 1798.
Lucy Bridges, born March 1, 1800.
Rowland Bridges, born Mar. 31, 1802.
Polly Bridges, born June, 1804.
Isham Bridges, born July, 1807.
Susannah Bridges, born Mar. 5th, 1810.
Harrison Bridges, born Nov. 11, 1812.

MARRIAGES

Benjamin Bridges and Susannah were married Dec. 31, 1784.

DEATHS
Rowland Bridges, died Sept. 27, 1820.
Harrison Bridges, died in 1857.

BUCKNER BIBLE

(Data from the Old Buckner Bible, in possession of Mrs. Louise Buckner Pierson, Louisville, Ky.)

BIRTHS

William Buckner, born May 17, 1791.
Nancy (Bridges) Buckner, born Aug. 4, 1795.
H. W. Buckner, born March 3, 1822.
Thomas Buckner, born Oct. 28, 1815.
Leander Buckner, born Nov. 11, 1818.
Emily Pendleton Buckner, born Oct. 11, 1827.
Wm. H. Grainger, born May 4, 1808.
Thomas E. Browne, Jr., born July 22nd, 1824.
Amanthus Shipp, born Dec. 8, 1825.
Adelia Shipp, born Mar. —, 1829.
S. Shipp, born Sept. 7, 1832.
Amelia C. I. Hastings, born Mar. 12, 1827.
William Murdock, was born in Glasslough, Monaghan County, Ireland, in 1816.
Mary E. Bell, wife of Wm. Murdock, was born in Shelbyville, Ky., Apr. 29, 1824.
Wm. Bell Murdock, born Aug. 28, 1847, in Owensboro, Ky.
Joseph Murdock, born Mar. 19, 1849.
Robert John Murdock, born June 21, 1857.
Louis Murdock, born July 30, 1859.
Wm. Bell, born May 4, 1790, near Glasslough, Monaghan County, Ireland.
Mary Allison, was born Jan. 3, 1794.
Louisa E. Ewing, born May 4, 1804.
Edmund Garnet Buckner, born Sept. 8, 1850.

MARRIAGES

Wm. Buckner and Nancy Bridges married May 6th, 1813.
Leander Buckner and Amanthus Shipp married June 23, 1846.
Wm. E. B. Hastings and Amelia C. Shipp married July 27, 1848.
W. H. Grainger and Emily P. Buckner married May 10, 1836.
Adelia M., third daughter of Ewell and Evelina Shipp, was married by Rev. E. P. Humphrey, March 27, 1850, to Thos. Browne, Jr., son of Y. Egerton and Elana B. Browne, at Louisville, Ky.
Mary J. Ewell and James W. Shipp were married May 14, 1856.
Mary E., only daughter of Wm. and Mary E. Murdock, was married to Edmund G. Buckner, Apr. 22, 1872, at Fourth Street Presbyterian Church, in Owensboro, Ky.
Mary Allison was married to Wm. Bell Nov. 17, 1817.
Louisa E. Ewing was married to Wm. Bell Aug. 20, 1837.
Louisa Ewing Buckner and W. W. Pierson were married Feb. 12, 1908.

DEATHS

Thos. W. Buckner, died November 1, 1815.
Mary Allison Bell, died Apr. 14, 1834.
Mrs. Evelina S. Shipp, died Jan. 28, 1850 at 9:15 P. M.
Wm. Henry Buckner, son of Leander and Amanthus Buckner, died Dec. 30, 185—.
Leander Buckner, died Nov. 22, 1855.
Edmund Garnet Shipp, died Aug. 4, 1856.
Emily P. (Buckner) Grainger, died Feb. —, 1877.
James William Shipp, died Nov. 24, 1867.
Samuel Bray Shipp, died Nov. —, 1887.
Wm. Lee Buckner, son of E. G. and Mary E. Buckner, died May 29, 1886, aged 13 years 8 months and 4 days.

Edmund Garnet Buckner, died Aug. 4, 1820.
W. W. Pierson, died Feb. 21, 1912.

BURCH BIBLE

Bible record of John Burch, Barren County, Ky.

John Burch, born Prince George Co., Md., 1758, died Mar. 1, 1834. Elizabeth Burch, widow of John, was 71 years old in Nov. 13, 1850. Married when Elizabeth was 17.

Robert married May 21, 1821. John removed with his father to Charles Co., Md., then to Prince William Co., Va., and later to Farquier and Amherst Cos., Va., died in Barren Co., Ky.

Children:
Robert Burch, born July 11, 1797.
Mary F. Burch, born June 21, 1799.
Landon I. Burch, born August 9, 1801.
Anne Burch, born September 30, 1803.
Fanny P. Burch, born December 19, 1806.
William D. Burch, born October 9, 1809.
John Burch, born February 12, 1816.

CALVERT BIBLE

(Owned by Alfred Marshall Peed, Maysville, Ky.).

James Calvert and Mary Alsey Cheek were married in Culpeper County, Virginia, February 7, 1797.

Births and marriages:
John and Sally Calvert were wedded Dec. 26, 1816.
James and Caroline Peed were betrothed Sept. 2, 1819.
Jesse Calvert and Ann, his wife, married April 24, 1821.
Craven Calvert and Sarah, his wife, were married Nov. 18, 1828.
Sanford Calvert and Frances D. Calvert, his wife, were married Mar. 11, 1829.
Alfred and Mary Peed married Aug. 29, 1833, at Mayslick.
Jesse Calvert was born Sept. 11, 1793.
John Calvert was born Jan. 10, 1798.
Caroline Calvert was born Nov. 9, 1799.
Permelia Calvert was born April 19, 1801.
Sanford Calvert was born April 4, 1803.
Craven Calvert was born Sept. 14, 1805.
James Calvert was born May 15, 1808.
Redman Calvert was born Aug. 6, 1810.
Charles Calvert was born June 30, 1812.
J. M. Calvert was born April 14, 1814.
Mary Calvert was born Feb. 15, 1819.
Ann Wood Calvert, dau. of Craven and Sally Calvert, born Sept. 25, 1829.
Alcy Ann Furman Calvert, dau. of Walter and Permelia C., born July 20, 1836.
Walter Calvert, Jr., born Oct. 11, 1841.

Deaths:

James Calvert, died June 8, 1823, aged 57 years.

Alsey Calvert, died 28th of August, 1828, aged 51 years.

Redmon Calvert, died June 17, 1835, aged 25 years.

Caroline Peed died March 26, 1838, aged 39 years, if lived till Nov. 9, 1838.

Permelia Calvert died Feb. 19, 1852, twenty minutes before 10 at night.

John Calvert died Sept. 17, 1854, aged 56 years, 8 months and 7 days.

JAMES CURTIS' BIBLE

James Curtis was married to Sary Emily Edwards, December 1st, 1796.

Elizabeth Curtis, a daughter of James Curtis, was married to Henry Rains, September 18th, 1817.

Marshall Curtis, a son of James Curtis, was married to Sabina Reed, September 17th, 1822.

Juliann Curtis, daughter of James Curtis, was married to H. M. King, September 24th, 1822.

John M. Curtis, son of James Curtis, was married to Elizabeth Edwards, December 6th, 1836.

Sarelda Curtis, the daughter of James Curtis, was married to Zebulen S. Williamson, 1846.

James A. E. Curtis was married to Miss Genny Collis May 14th, 1874.

James A. E. Curtis married Florence Rains, November 7th, 1883.

Sarah E. Knight was the daughter of Nelson and Cola(?) Knight, married Wm. Dicson 5th of November, 1847 (or 9).

James Curtis was born June 30th, 1770.

Sary Emily Curtis was born April 2, 1780.

Elizabeth Curtis was born September the 18th, 1797.

Marshall Curtis was born November the 18th, 1799.

Juliann Curtis was born December the 2nd, 1801.

Littitia Morris Curtis was born January the 18th, 1804.

Mary Edwards Curtis was born December the 3rd, 1805.

John Monroe Curtis was born January the 31, 1808.

Narcissa Curtis was born February the 13th, 1810.

Sary Emily Curtis was born March the 26th, 1812.

Franky Curtis was born January the 8th, 1814.

Jacob Alexander Edwards Curtis was born January the 15th, 1816.

Parmelia Ellen Curtis was born December the 5th, 1817.

James Curtis was born January 28th, 1820.

Nancy Jane Curtis was born October 27, 1821.

William Nathaniel King was born April 13th, 1827.

William Edwards King was born November the 1st, 1828.

Mary Ellen Curtis, daughter of John M. and Elizabeth Curtis, was born October the 9th, 1837.

Sarah Emily Edwards, daughter of John M. and Elizabeth Curtis, was born January the 2nd, 1840.

Parmelia Ellen Curtis, daughter of John and Elizabeth Curtis, was born March 21, 1842.

Sary Ann Rains was born November 23rd, 1818.

Elizabeth C. Rains was born February 21st, 1821.

James H. Rains was born March 22, 1823.

Sary Ann King was born June 22, 1823.

James E. Curtis, son of Marshall and Sabina Curtis, was born August 2, 1823.

John M. Rains was born 12 of June, 1825.

James Alexander Edwards Curtis was born (son of John and Elizabeth) November 1st, 1844.

George William Rice Baker Curtis, son of same, was born September the 7th, 1848.

Elizabeth (this record too faded to read).

John M. Curtis, died November 19, 1874.

Franky Curtis, died July 3, 1818.

Elizabeth C. Rains, died April 15, 1823.

John M. Rains, died June 20, 1825.

James E. Curtis, died August 10, 1824.

William Alexander Curtis, died August 13, 1826.

Sarah Emily Curtis, died 1828.

James Curtis, died July 27, 1832.

Mary E. King, died March 24, 1836.

Nancy J. Curtis, died April 6, 1836.

Jonny Bullock, died 1874.

Amelia E. Curtis, died March the 24, 1869.

Narcissa Wells, died May 12, 1836.

Sarah E. King, died September, 1836.

Juliann King, died June, 1837.

Elizabeth Rains, died November, 1839.

Mary Ellen Curtis, died June 27, 1840.

Sary Emily Edwards Curtis, died November the 29, 1843.

George W. (or M.) Edwards, died December 25, 1848.

George A. Curtis, died July the —, 1852.

Mary Ann Edwards Davidson, died October 31, 1858.

George W. R. B. Curtis, died July the 3, 1864.

The foregoing records here set forth are true records copied from those appearing in an old family Bible which was once the property of James Edwards, born June 30th, 1770, and which Bible is now in the possession of Mrs. Florence Curtis, of Maysville, Kentucky.

DARNALL-JONES BIBLE
(In possession of Mrs. D. R. Talbert, Calvert, Md.).

John Darnall, born October 7, 1760, died September 14, 1819.

John Darnall and Bathsheba Hurley were married December 12, 1782.

Bathsheba, wife of John Darnall, died May 19th, 1810.

Children of John and Bathsheba Darnall:

Sarah Darnall, born September 19, 1783, died Dec. 12, 1821.

Rachel Darnall, born January 6, 1784.

John Darnall, born June 19, 1788.

Mary Darnall, born January 17, 1790.

Rebecca Darnall, born February 20, 1792.

Isaac Darnall, born January 13, 1796.

Elizabeth Darnall, born June 2, 1798.

Charles Darnall, born January 9, 1801.

Children of Edward Jones who married Sarah Darnall:

William Jones was born July 4, 1807.

Washington Jones was born September 12, 1805, died Dec. 30, 1865.

Mary Susanna Jones, born December, 1810.
Edward Jones, born April 13, 1813, died Feb. 13, 1840.
Thomas Jones, born December 22, 1815.
Charles Jones, born December 29, 1817, died October 30, 1863.
Edward Jones, Sr., died October 24, 1832.
Washington Jones, son of Edward and Sarah Jones, married
    Elizabeth Jane Meekins, September 13, 1831.   Children were:
Sarah Jane Frances, born 1832.
Cecilia Armenia, born 1834.
Mary Susanna, born 1836.
Elizabeth Ann Virginia, born 1838.
Mary Ellen, born 1841.
George Henry Washington, born 1845.
Edward Isaac, born 1847.
Armenia Ataway, born 1850.
Alice Rebecca, born 1852.
Charles Richard Edwin, born 1854.
Mary Ellen Jones married Richard Chapman Billingsley.
NOTE: Sarah Darnall married Edward Jones Jan. 21, 1804,
Prince George Co., Md. Rachel Darnall married John Dodson, Sept.
10, 1803, Prince George Co., Md. Rebecca Darnall married Henry
Dodson (brother of John Dodson above) of Washington, D. C. (See
Dodson Bible).

John Darnall—Will—Prince George Co., Md., Liber T. T. Folio 248
—"I, John Darnall, of Calvert Co., State of Maryland"; to Benj. Tayler of Calvert Co., currency; to Harriot Taylor, furniture, currency,
etc.; to Mary Tayler, furniture, currency, etc.; dau., Elizabeth Darnall,
land to be laid out of tract in Calvert Co., called Mill Mount, in man-
ner not to interfere with Mill or Mill seat; to son, Chas. Darnall,
another part of aforesaid tract; daus., Rebecca Dodson and Rachel
Dodson, tract in City of Washington; to dau., Sarah Jones, all remainder of tract in Calvert, together with all improvements belonging; to daus., Sarah Jones, Rachel Dodson, Rebecca Dodson, Elizabeth
Darnall and to Edward Jones, for use of Mary Davis (James Davis,
husband of Mary), dau., Ann Davis, and to her and "my youngest
son, Chas. Darnall," all residue of Estate. Extrs: Benj. Tollers and
Edward Jones. Written Sept. 1, 1819; probated Sept. 20, 1819. Wts.:
John Soper, Levin Boone, Richard H. Marshall.

Cornelius Hurley's Will—Prince George Co., Md., T. No. 1, 272—
Wife, Mary; dau., Bathsheba Darnall; dau., Rhoda Hurley; son, William; son, Salome (Salem). Probated Dec. 9, 1788.

NOTE: Maryland Records by Brumbaugh, pg. 83, Census of
1776: Cornelius Hurley 46, 19, 11, 3. Mary Hurley, 46, 16, 14, 8.

Cornelius Hurley served during Revolution as member of Grand
Jury. Revolutionary Soldiers by Brumbaugh and Hodges, pps. 32, 33,
35, for years 1780, 1781, 1783—Upper Marlborough. He, no doubt,
rendered military service also.

Deeds—IRM 15, 217—Prince George County, Md.—Thomas Digges,
Garrot Darnall, Francis Osborn and Salem Hurley, Securities to John
Darnall, Sheriff, for which security he deeds Black Oak Thicket, Ma-
gruders Plains, Johns Choice, Covington Edge, Warrings Grove and
negroes. May 28, 1812.

Among the Records at the Land Office, Annapolis, Md.:
John Darnall—Offutts Adventure conveyed by deed of Edward

Jones' Hrs. to Thos. B. Crauford. See, Long Old Fields Last Shift.
John Darnall's "Sylvania," Calvert Co., sold to Charles Graham of Calvert, 1772.

DODSON BIBLE
(In the possession of Mrs. Lillian Dodson, Paris, Ky.)

George Dodson, son of Henry Dodson, and Permelia Elen Curtis, daughter of *James Curtis, were married February 24, 1835.

MARRIAGES
Robert F. Adair and Sarah Isabella Dodson, daughter of George and Pemelia Dodson, married November 13, 1854.
Robert Middleton Dodson and Mary Anne Elstiner, son of George and Permelia Dodson, July 21, 1870.
Almer Dodson and Martha Florence Frost, son of George and Permelia Dodson, May 14, 1890.
Omar Dodson and Mary Elizabeth Steers, son of George and Permelia Dodson, February 14th, 1899.
George Almer Dodson, son of Almar Dodson, married Lillian Ewalt Stolworthy, on March 7th, 1914, at Church of the Advent, Walnut Hills, Cincinnati, Ohio.

BIRTHS
Edwin Titus Dodson, born January 8th, 1836.
Robert Middleton Dodson, born April 21st, 1837.
Sarah Isabella Dodson, born June 27th, 1839.
Omer Dodson, born November 26th, 1841.
James Henry Dodson, born April 1844.
Marion Florence Dodson, born November 13, 1850.
Almer Dodson, born July 9th, 1853.
Rebecca Dodson, born June 23, 1855.
Mary Florence Dodson, daughter of George A., September 15th, 1917.
George Almar Dodson, Jr., son of George A., August 1, 1919.
Lillian Ewalt Dodson, daughter of George A., April 19th, 1923.

DEATHS
Edwin Titus Dodson, died June, 1836.
James Henry Dodson, died January 30, 1845.
Rebecca Dodson, died August 11, 1855.
Permelia Elen Dodson, died January 24th, 1869, Sunday evening at 10 o'clock.
Robert Middleton Dodson, died April 3, 1876, at Cincinnati, at half past 12 o'clock.
George Dodson, our father, at Maysville, (Kentucky), died September 10th, 1890.
Marion Florence Dodson, died at Maysville, June 12th, 1891.
Mary Elizabeth Steers, wife of Omar Dodson, died March 17th, 1912, aged sixty years two months.
Robert F. Adair, husband of Sarah Isabella Dodson, died May 14th, 1907. (See Adair Bible).
Florence Martha, wife of Almer Dodson, died September 27th, 1898.
Mary Elstiner, wife of Robert Middleton Dodson, died 19—.
George Almar Dodson, son of Almar Dodson, died January 27th, 1925.

BIRTHS

Permelia Elen Curtis, wife of George Dodson, born December 5th, 1817.

George Dodson, born August 22nd, 1809.

NOTE: George Dodson, son of Henry and Rebecca (Darnall) Dodson, moved to Maysville, Kentucky, from Washington, D. C. Henry Dodson was a merchant of Washington; his brother, John Dodson, also of Washington, married, September 10, 1803, Rachel Darnall, sister of his wife, Rebecca. John Dodson and Henry Dodson were sons of John Dodson of Maryland. Children of Henry and Rebecca (Darnall) Dodson: George, owner of foregoing Bible; Marion, who was sister of the House of the Good Shepherd of Baltimore, Maryland, and later Louisville, Kentucky, and Ellen. In the obituary of Mrs. Margaret Virginia (Dodson) Wroe, Washington City Times, February 4, 1903, is the following: "Mrs. Margaret Virginia Wroe died of grief Sunday, February 2, 1903, from the death of her husband three weeks ago at 810 13th Street, where they had lived for 63 years, and buried in the quaint, old vault built by her father, John H. Dodson, who gave the land on which the famed Rock Creek Protestant Episcopal Church was built. Mrs. Wroe was daughter of John Henry Dodson, a wealthy land owner and a great deal in that section of Washington City belonged to him, and he, with Dudley Diggs, mostly built the church building of brick. She married William A. Wroe. He was associated with Governor Sheppard in the reconstruction of the city, and became very wealthy." John Henry Dodson was born August 7, 1806, son of John and Rachel (Darnall) Dodson, married 1836 Lucinda Boteler, born Dec. 28, 1813.

NOTE: Journal of Committee of Observation of Frederick Co., Md., 1775-1776, Vol. 11, lists John Dodson.
*See Curtis Bible.

GIBSON FAMILY BIBLE

BIRTHS

Susannah Hart Gibson (called after her grandmother), dau. of Tobias and Louisiana B. Gibson, born 30th May, 1828, at "Spring Hill," residence of Nathaniel Hart, Woodford County, Ky.

Sarah Thompson Gibson, 2nd child, dau. of Tobias and Louisiana Breckinridge Gibson, born May 17, 1830 at home of Ambrose Gibson, Warren County, Miss., 8 o'clock; named for her aunt.

Randal Gibson, son, born Sept. 10th, 1831, at Spring Hill; named after his grandfather, Rev. Randal Gibson.

Wm. Preston Gibson, son, born Oct. 16th, 1833, at home in Terreboune Parish, La.; named for his maternal uncle.

Son, Nathaniel Hart Gibson, born May 22nd, 1835, at "Shawnee Springs,' residence of Col. G. C. Thompson, Ky.; called for his grandsire, Nathaniel Hart.

Son, Claudius Gibson, born Feb. 5th, 1837, Terreboune, La.; named for his maternal uncle.

Son, Tobias Gibson, born Aug. 6th, 1838, in Lexington, Ky.; named for his father.

John McKinley Gibson, born Oct. 3, 1840, in Lexington; named for his paternal great-grandfather, John McKinley.

Son, Robt. Breckinridge Gibson, born Feb. 6, 1845, in Lexington;

named for his cousin, Robt. J. Breckinridge.

Louisiana Breckinridge Hart Gibson, born Jan. 28, 1848, at Oak Forest, on Bayon Black; named for her mother.

MARRIAGES

Tobias Gibson of Jefferson County, Miss., was married to Louisiana Breckinridge Hart, third daughter of Nathaniel and Susanna Preston Hart, of Woodford County, Ky., on 14th day of June, in 1827, by the Rev. Geo. T. Chapman, of Lexington, Ky.

Sarah T. Gibson was married to Josephy A. Humphreys of Woodford County, on June 21, 1853, by Rev. Robt. Black of Lexington.

Wm. Preston Gibson was married to Elodie M. Humphreys, of St. James Parish, La., July, 1855.

Hart Gibson was married to Mary E. Duncan of Lexington, 22nd Sept., 1859, Lexington.

DEATHS

Susannah H. Gibson, died Jan. 20, 1830, at home of Ambrose Gibson, Warren County, Miss., and was buried at Dr. W. Faulks. Removed to and buried at Lexington, Ky. Aged 1 year 7 months 21 days.

Mrs. Susan Preston Hart died at her residence in Woodford County, Ky., aged 33; mother of Louisiana Breckinridge Hart Gibson.

Nathaniel Hart of Woodford County, Ky., father of Louisiana B. H. Gibson. (No date.)

Robert Breckinridge Gibson, buried at Traveler's Rest, 1845, son of Tobias and Louisiana B. H. Gibson, removed and buried at Lexington, June 27, 1857.

Louisiana B. Gibson, wife of Tobias Gibson, died in city of Havana, Cuba, where she had gone for her health, after two years sickness, on Feb. 20, 1851, and buried in Lexington, March 22, in 47th year of her age.

Randal Gibson died at his residence in Warren County, Miss., on April 13, 1836, aged 69 years. Father of Tobias Gibson.

Mrs. Harriett McKinley Gibson died at her residence in Warren County, Miss., on Oct. 6th, 1837, aged 57; mother of Tobias Gibson.

Claudius Gibson died at home of Mrs. S. S. Booth, in Warren County, Miss., on June 4th, 1841. Eldest brother of Tobias Gibson.

Nathaniel Hart, born of Louisiana B. H. Gibson, 1854, Spring Hill, Woodford County, Ky.

Gibson Bible, Philadelphia, Pa., 1826.

GORDON-WALTER BIBLE

Elizabeth Gordon, born Oct. 20, 1782.
*Archibald Gordon, born May, 1774.
Lucy Gordon, born July 23, 1803.
James Gordon, born May 4, 1805.
Price Gordon, born Sept. 20, 1807.
Preston Gordon, born Feb. 18, 1810.
Emily Gordon, born Dec. 7, 1814.
Lucy B. Gordon, born Aug. 17, 1812 (married Geo. Munday).
Mary Gordon, born Oct. 27, 1817.
C. C. Gordon, born June 18, 1820.
Sally and Nancy Gordon, born June 17, 1822.
Lucinda Gordon, born Nov. 7, 1819.

Henry G. Smart, born
Benj. Gordon, born Nov. 7, 1850.
Benj. B. Gordon, born Mar. 3, 1853.
Price Gordon, born Feb. 23, 1856.
Draper S. Gordon, born Dec. 31, 1858.
David Walter, born Mar. 12, 1833.
Antoinette Munday Walter, born Feb. 22, 1834 (wife).
Richard Preston Walter, born Feb. 3, 1864.
Jas. Munday Walter, born Jan. 29, 1865.
Lucy M. Walter, born Apr. 8, 1866.
Reuben P. Walter, born June, 1867.
Mattie Walter, born May 21, 1869.
S. Scott Walter, born Sept. 28, 1872.
Affie Walter, born Aug. 8, 1875.

DEATHS
Elizabeth Gordon, died June 12 1847.
Archibald Gordon, died Mar. 5, 1828.
Lucy Gordon, died ————, 1810.
James Gordon, died Feb. 17, 1852.
Price Gordon, died May 8, 1851.
Emily Gordon, died Aug. 17, 1855.
Mary Gordon, died May 27, 1852.
Benj. Gordon, died May 7, 1852.
Benj. B. Gordon, died Oct. 3, 1854.
Henry T. Smart, died
Lucy B. Munday, died Oct. 15, 1861.
Draper Newton, died Jan. 25, 1864.
P. W. Munday, died Apr. 16, 1863.
J. H. Munday, died June 15, 1864.
Lucinda S. Gordon, died Sept. 14, 1869.
Preston Gordon, died Jan. 18, 1875.
Christopher B. Newton, died Oct. 30, 1876.
Preston Walter, died Jan. 3, 1882.
Reuben P. Walter, died   , 1870
David Walter, died May 31, 1908.
Antoinette M. Walter, died Nov. 18, 1811.

*Son of James and Elizabeth Gordon—Jas. died, Lincoln Co., 1785; see will and deeds of Mercer Co., for heirs.

HUNT BIBLE
(From copy owned by Harvey Rogers, Paris, Ky.)

*John Hunt was born September 19th, 1748, and died May 7th, 1829, of cholera, in Fayette County.
Margaret Wilson Hunt, his wife, was born April 1st, 1757.
Ages of their children:
Nancy Hunt was born January 25, 1775, and married Peter Daniels.
James Hunt was born April 12th, 1777, and died December 8th, 1829.
Wilson Hunt was born December 15th, 1779, and died January 25th, 1840.
Sarah Hunt was born December 15 ,1783, and married Morgan Bryan.
Polly Hunt was born January 1st, 1785.

Jonathan Hunt was born November 18th, 1788, and died May 7th, ——.
Noah Hunt was born October 3rd, 1792, and died July 9th at half past 2 o'clock A. M., 1849.
Peggy Hunt was born January 31st, 1797.
Marriges of Fayette Co., Ky., Book 1, pg. 16: James McClelland to Polly Hunt.

*Col John Hunt, born N. J.; lived during Revolution in N. C. and Ky.

JONES BIBLE

Jones data from the Jones-Stephenson Bible, in possession of Prof. Wm. Bristow Jones, Dept. of English, Georgetown College, Georgetown, Ky. (1930.)

MARRIAGES

Thomas Jones and Nancy were married in the year 1776. Had son, William.
John H. Jones and Mildred were married Nov. 14, 1836.
Thos. W. Jones and Mary E. Jones were married Nov. 13, 1851.
Mollie Jones and John H. Hutchcraft were married Sept. 4, 1856.
John H. Jones and Mrs. Agnes Darnaby were married May, 1858.
Thos. Jones and Albina Dawson were married Feb. __, 1858.
Wm. Stevenson and Peggy were married April 24, 1801.
Thos. Jones and Mary were married Apr. 24, 1810.
Strother Jones and Elizabeth Ann Jones were married Aug. 27, 1812.
Wm. Jones and Mary were married Jan. 27, 1814.
James Mitchell and Elizabeth were married July 13, 1814.
Strother Jones and Nancy S. were married Dec. 30, 1818.
John H. Jones (son of Wm. and Mary) and Mary Ann were married Nov. 11, 1836.

BIRTHS

Wm. Jones was born Anno Domini, 1780, on 9th of May.
Strother Jones was born Sept. 20, 1782.
Peggy Jones was born Jan. 11, 1784.
John H. Jones was born Jan. 20, 1786.
Thos. Jones, Jr., was born Jan. 22, 1788.
Betsey Jones was born Feb., 1791.
Thos. N. Stevenson was born Feb. 28, 1802.
Wm. Stevenson was born Dec. 14, 1803.
Pamela Ann Stevenson was born Jan. 29, 1806.
Jas. Stevenson was born Dec. 29, 1808.
John H. Stevenson was born Jan. 1st, 1812.
Israel T. Jones was born July 1, 1811.
Thos. H. Jones was born Mar. 17, 1813.
Margaret Ann Jones and Wm. Young Jones were born July 3, 1815 (twins).
Wm. Jones was born July 4, 1813.
Abraham Milton Jones was born July 14, 1814.
John Hawkins Jones, son of Wm. and Mary, was born Dec. 22, 1814, at 3 o'clock A. M.
Richard M. Jones was born May 26, 1816.
Thos. H. Jones was born Mar. 30, 1818.
John Milton Jones was born July 20, 1820.

Thos. Wm. Jones was born Jan. 29, 1827, at 8 P. M.
James Wm. Jones was born Nov. 7, 1852.
Ernest Richard Jones was born May 5, 1861.
John H. Mitchell was born May 26, 1817.
Mary H. Jones was born Oct. 8, 1837, at 12 o'clock A. M.
Mollie H. Jones was born Oct. 8, 1837.
Clifton Todd Hutchcraft was born ——— 13, 1858 (7 or 9).
Charlie Sidney Hutchcraft was born ———.

DEATHS

Wm. Stevenson, died Mar. 5, 1812.
Eliz. Ann Jones, died Oct. 27, 1815.
Abraham Milton Jones, died Dec. 25, 1815.
Margaret Helm Stevenson, wife to William and daughter to Thos.
    and Nancy Jones, died Sept. 6, 1823.
Thos. J. Stevenson, died Apr. 16, 1825.
Nancy Jones, consort of Thos. Jones, Sr., died Mar. 6, 1826.
Thos. Jones, Sr., died ———, 1st, 1833.
———? Mitchell Jones, died ——— 21st, 1833.
Mary E. Jones, consort of Thos. W. Jones, died Nov. 15, 1852.
Mary Ann Jones, consort of John H. Jones, died June 25, 1853.
John H. Jones, died Nov. 11, 1881.
Wm. T. Jones, died Dec. 11, 1878.
Agnes E. Jones, died Mar. 13, 1888.
Ernest R. Jones and Mattie Switzer were married Feb. 8, 1881.
Cyrus Wingate and Fannie D. Jones were married Feb. 11, 1904.
Wm. Bristow Jones and Flora Belle Shepard, daughter of Sam-
    uel and George Shepard, were married Aug. 15, 1906.
(Jas. Wm. Jones was born Nov. 7, 1852—see above.)
Grover C. Jones and Louise Moore were married Dec. 23, 1908.
Malcolm Jones, son of G. C. Jones and Louise M. Jones, was born
    Oct. 16, 1909.
Wm. Bristow Jones, born Nov. 28, 1881, at 2 o'clock P. M.
Fannie D. Jones, born May 27, 1883, at 8 A. M.
Grover Cleveland Jones, born Sept. 3, 1884, at 9 P. M.
Fannie and Betty Jones, born Dec. 15, 1888, at 2 A. M.

KENTON BIBLE

William I. Kenton was born Nov. 9, 1841.
Nancy Jane Kenton was born May 13, 1843.
Eldridg Kenton was born April 4, 1845.
Mary Elizabeth Kenton was born May 14, 1847.
Haldy Kenton was born May 5, 1849.
Sariah Margaret Kenton was born June 27, 1853.
Thomas Bruce Kenton was born Oct. 4, 1855.
Lafayette Kenton was born July 9, 1857.
Simon Buell Kenton was born Aug. 13, 1862.
Simon Kenton and Hanner Bishop married Jan. 26, 1841.
W. J. Kenton and Maggie McClanahan married Feb. 13, 1868.
E. B. Wells and Mary E. Kenton married Jan. 6, 1869.
William I. Dennis and Hulday Kenton married April 30, 1873.
Thomas B. Kenton and Elizabeth Thomas married Jan. 17, 1877.
Eldridge Kenton and Nancy Harnett married Oct. 25, 1883.
Simon B. Kenton married Lucie Hampton Nov. 28, 1883.

James William Haffett (or Moffit) was born Jan. 18, 1865.
Simon Moffitt was born Sept. 24, 1869.
Martha Wells was born May 29, 1871.
James Kenton was born Sept. 30, 1877.
Viola Kenton was born July 21, 1884.
John B. Kenton was born Dec. 17, 1886.
Jimmie T. Kenton was born April 26, 1889.
Gracie Kenton was born March 19, 1892.
Cordy Kenton was born March 21, 1894.
Marcus Kenton was born Nov. 24, 1868.
Charles Kenton was born June 29, 1870.
Je Will Kenton was born Feb. 8, 1872.
Eldridge Dennis was born Jan. 23, 1875.
Maggie Dennis was born April 17, 1876.
Walter Dennis was born Nov. 13, 1881.

Sareah Margaret Kenton died Sept. 15, 1854.
Hannah L. Wells died July 27, 1878.
Viola Kenton died Aug. 13, 1904.
Thomas B. Kenton died Jan. 15, 1906.

Riley Wells died Aug. 12, 1903.

LUCKETT BIBLE

Bible records of Samuel Luckett, Barren County, Ky. Wife, Elizabeth, born May 9, 1769.

Samuel Luckett, Sr., born in Maryland, June 12, 1756.

Children:
Samuel, born Mar. 2, 1801.
John, born May 19, 1803.
David, born Sept. 26, 1805.
Nancy, born Jan. 13, 1808.
Anna, born June 17, 1811.

LUCKETT BIBLE
Family of Muhlenburg County, Ky.

H. H. Luckett, was born May 13, 1802.
Jane Mc. D. Luckett, born September 23, 1808.
H. H. Luckett and Jane Mc. D. Robertson were married December 13, 1827.

Children:
John H. Luckett, born October 22, 1828.
David A. Luckett, born November 3, 1831.
Mary Jane Luckett, born July 21, 1834.
Rachel Ann Luckett, born February 25, 1836.
Alfred D. Luckett, born August 1, 1840.
William H. Luckett, born June 27, 1843.
Margaret Kitty Luckett, born April 4, 1846.
Ann Luckett, born March 7, 1849.

MARR BIBLE

Lawrence Marr—His Bible, bought in 1755.
"His children, born unto him and his equal half at Ester, North-
    umberland County, Pennsylvania":
William Marr, born March 13, 1732.
Thomas Marr, born Aug. 6, 1734.
Joseph Marr, born Oct. 30, 1736.
Elmer Marr, born Dec. 3, 1738.
*David Marr, born Dec. 20, 1740.
Daniel Marr, born Aug. 8, 1742.
"The above copied by Enos Marr out of Lawrence Marr's Bible
    in the family of my uncle, Joseph Marr.
            Signed: "ENOS MARR, Oct. 24, 1850."
Children of David Marr and wife, Sarah:
Mary Marr, born Dec. 5, 1764.
Ann Marr, born Feb. 28, 1767.
Elizabeth Marr, born July 4, 1769.
Sarah Marr, born May 25, 1771.
Lawrence Marr, born July 18, 1773.
Eleanor Marr, born April 20, 1775.
Susannah Marr, born June 20, 1777.
Rachel Marr, born May 14, 1780.
Martha Marr, born Sept. 30, 1782.
David Marr, born Aug. 20, 1784.
Margt. Marr, born Aug. 1, 1786.
Judith Marr, born Oct. 7, 1788.
David Marr, born Sept. 10, 1790.
Abraham Dills and wife, Elizabeth (Marr) Dills were married in
    Pennsylvania and immigrated to Harrison County, Kentucky, at
    an early date—see Perrin's History of Bourbon, Scott, Har-
    rison and Nicholas Counties, pg 652.
The foregoing records were taken from the Bibles of Lawrence
    Marr and his son, David Marr.

McBRIDE-ARNOLD-JOHNSON BIBLE AND NOTES
(In the possession of Mrs. E. B. Weitzel, Frankfort, Ky.).

William McBride and Martha Lapsley, his wife, were both born in
Virginia.

William McBride's daughter, Martha McBride, married Stephen
Arnold. The following is from the family Bible but parts are not
legible:
"Died at her residence on Cedar Run, Franklin County, on ____ day,
the 10th ult, at ½ before 12 o'clock, Mrs. Martha Arnold, aged 75 yrs.,
9 mo., 4 days.
"Few such old ladies have lived in this country, few such young
ladies ever have lived. When young her industry, energy, and neatness
found no superior, while her kindness of temper and charitable heart
endeared her with many true friends. She was bereaved of her husband in 1814, who, tho' one of the pioneers of Kentucky, participated
largely in the Indian wars from '85 up to the date of his death, left her
with a large family of helpless children, with but a scant means for their
support. She, though, with the untiring perserverance and good manage-
ment, succeeded in raising her family, in a good circle in society, edu-

cated all of them, and left them a handsome little estate. But far better than this, she left them a good name and the best reasons to hope she has gone to heaven."

The daughter of Martha McBride Arnold, Sarah P. Arnold, name of husband and of all the children we have records of follow:
Sarah P. Arnold, born October 14th, 1796; died Feb. 23rd, 1862.
William Johnson, born October 29, 1791; died March 24th, 1836.
Above two were married March 19th, 1818.
Children:
William P. Johnson (my grandfather), born June 1, 1819; died Jan. 28, 1875; married Mary Elizabeth Cardwell (born Nov. 20, 1831; died July 3, 1919), January 10, 1850.
David A. Johnson and Ola E. Miner were married July 3, 1851.
Jefferson Miner and Eliza Jane Johnson were married Oct. 19, 1854.
Dickson D. Johnson and Mattie Booker were married the 27th of Nov., 1856.
Dickson D. Johnson was born Feb. 13th, 1831.
Eliza Jane Johnson was born Jan. 28th, 1833.
James H. Johnson was born Sept. 21st, 1834.
David A. Johnson was born September 9th, 1826.
Stephen D. Johnson was born August 2, 1824.
John M. Johnson was born April 25, 1821.
Benjamin W. Johnson was born 20th of September, 1828.

Deaths:
John M. Johnson departed this life 4th of March, 1837.
James A. (H.) Johnson died Aug. 26th, 1860.
Mary Elizabeth Johnson died Feb. 22nd, 1863.

Children of William P. Johnson and Mary Elizabeth Cardwell Johnson:
John William Johnson, born Dec. the 27th, 1850; died May 10, 1925. Married Sallie Price Belt Abbott, June 26th, 1883. These are my father and mother.
Sarah Margaret Johnson was born April 13th, 1852.
George Washington Johnson was born February 22nd, 1854.
Eliza Jane Johnson was born March 16th, 1855.
James A. Johnson was born September 30th, 1857.
Lewis Franklin Johnson was born Dec. the 7th, 1859.
Mary Elizabeth Johnson was born May the 13th, 1861.
Lucy Belle Johnson was born July the 26th, 1866.

William McBride was born in Fauquier County, Va. We have no record of birth. Father was Thomas McBride.
Tradition in family says that William McBride was born in the year, 1749.
Have no record of birth or death of Martha Lapsley McBride. However, it is known that Wm. McBride never married but once, that wife being Martha Lapsley.
Martha McBride Arnold, daughter of Wm. McBride, was born in Virginia, April 6, 1773 (we have no record of birth), and died in Franklin County, Kentucky, January 10, 1850.

NOTES BY FLORENCE HELM, JOPLIN, MO., SEPT, 1, 1927

William McBride was born in Fauquier County, Va., died at Blue

Licks, Ky., August 19, 1782. His wife was Martha Lapsley (no record of date or place of marriage).

Lapsley McBride, killed at River Raisin, January, 1813. His wife was Elizabeth Smart. They were married in Franklin Co., Ky., in 1806 (no record of date or place for Lapsley's birth). Lapsley had a brother, William.

Lapsley McBride had several children. One son, James Smart Mc-Bride, was born June 19, 1817. James Smart McBride had a brother, William Lapsley McBride and a sister, Polly. William's son, John, and Polly's son, Silly Robb, visited their uncle, James S. McBride in Missouri at the close of the Civil War.

MILLER BIBLE
(In possession of Harvey Rogers, Paris, Ky.)

John Miller and his wife, Elizabeth, married the 6th of Aug. 1797.
Henry Miller married the 12th of Feb., 1824.
Mitchell Miller and Mary McClelland were married the 4th of Feb., 1847.
John Miller, Senr., was born Jan. 1st, 1775.
Elizabeth Miller, his wife, was born July 18th, 1777.
Abraham Miller was born Jan. 23rd, 1798.
Nancy Miller was born Oct. the 11th, 1799.
Henry Miller was born April the 13th, 1801.
William Miller was born Dec. 16th, 1802.
Samuel Miller was born Oct. 15th, 1804.
Melindy Miller was born Feb. 16th, 1807.
Sally Miller was born Dec. 5th, 1808.
John Miller was born Aug. the 20th, 1810.
Polly Miller was born April the 15th, 1812.
Mitchell Miller was born July 19th, 1814.
Elizabeth Miller was born May 21st, 1825.
William Miller was born Oct. 17th, 1827.
Mary Ann Miller was born April the 14th, 1824.
Mary Elizabeth Miller was born February the 20th, 1848.
Mattie Caroline Miller was born November the 24th, 1849.
John Miller was born July the 4th, 1856.
Elizabeth Miller was born July the 30th, 1834.
Abraham Miller departed this life Oct. 14th, 1814.
Stephen Miller, Senior, departed this life Feb. the 21st, 1824.
Henry Miller departed this life June the 17th, 1828.
Samuel Miller departed this life March the 10th, 1834.
Polly Miller departed this life Sept. the 10th, 1828.
John Miller departed this life Aug. 11th, 1846, aged 71 years 7 months and 11 days.
Elizabeth B. Miller departed this life the 20th of March, 1847, aged 69 years, 8 months and 24 days.
John Miller, son of Mitchell Miller and Mary Miller, departed this life Feb. 10th, 1857.
Mary Ann Miller, wife of Mitchell Miller, departed this life in the morning of the 13th day of Dec., A. D., 1859.
Mitchell Miller, died Dec. 29, 1872.

MOORE-ARDERY BIBLE

Births of my grandfather and grandmother Moore:

John Moore, born Feb. 27, 1752.
Mary (Black) Moore was born Jan. 27, 1753.
Deaths of grandfather and grandmother:
Margaret (Mary) Moore, died Jan. 4, 1817.
John Moore, died April 16, 1830.
My father and mother's family:
Alexander Ardery, born March 21st, 1782.
Sarah Ardery, born July 5th, 1786.
Brothers and sisters:
John M. Ardery, born March 13, 1806.
Margaret Ardery, born June 29, 1808.
James H. Ardery, born Sept. 8th, 1809.
William A. Ardery, born Nov. 28th, 1811.
Mary Ann Ardery, born July 24th, 1814.
Jane Black Ardery, born Dec. 4th, 1816.
Abram A. Ardery, born Sept. 30th, 1819.
Elizabeth Ardery, born Jan. 15th, 1822.
Jason T. Ardery, born March 30th, 1826.
Marriage of father and mother:
Alexander Ardery and Sarah Moore were married March 5, 1805.
Deaths of my father, mother and family:
Alexander Ardery, died Oct. 17th, 1838.
Sarah Ardery, died Jan. 15th, 1848.
Margaret Ardery, died Oct. 22nd, 1808.
Mary Ann Ardery, died Dec. 20th, 1815.
William A. Ardery, died April 19th, 1817.
Jane B. Ardery, died April 11th, 1820.
John M. Ardery, died Jan. 16, 1837.
Jason T. Ardery, died June 7th, 1838.
Abram A. Ardery, died Sept. 24th, 1868.
Elizabeth Talbert, died June 23rd, 1875.
James H. Ardery, died June 26th, 1883.
Samuel D. Ardery, died March 9th, 1907.

Record of James E. Moore, son of uncle William Moore:
James E. Moore born May 29th, 1829.
Lucindy J. Kelly, wife of J. E. Moore, born Sept. 12th, 1830.
Uncle William Moore died May 3rd, 1875.

Record of James D. Patton who married a daughter of uncle, William Moore:
James D. Patton, born Jan. 16th, 1823.
Margaret Moore Patton, born May 16th, 1833.
Their children's births:
William M. Patton, born Oct. 24th, 1865.
John T. Patton, born Feb. 16th, 1867.
Cora A. Patton, born April 12th, 1872.
Austa Patton, born June 12th, 1875.
James D. Patton, died March 18th, 1893.

Record of Samuel J. Moore and family of Highland, Ohio, son of uncle, William Moore:
Samuel J. Moore, born Feb. 13th, 1842.
Salina Goodmancy Moore, born May 22nd, 1846.
Their children's births:
Annie B. Moore, born Oct. 8th, 1866.
Lillian B. Moore, born Jan. 26th, 1868.
Frank M. Moore, born Feb. 8th, 1870.
Elonzo L. Moore, born Dec. 9th, 1871.

Samuel Clay Moore, born April 13th, 1873.
Charles J. Moore, born Feb. 27th, 1876.
Maud V. Moore, born Jan. 29th, 1878.
Liford M. Moore, born Jan. 3rd, 1881.
Silby A. Moore, born Jan. 6, 1883.
Merit E. Moore, born July 7th, 1885.
Salina M. Moore, born May 9th, 1887.
Davis W. Moore, born Sept. 25, 1889.

Record of uncle, Thomas Ardery and family of Indiana:
Thomas Ardery, born in the year 1799.
Martha McKee, wife of Thomas Ardery, born April 11, 1798.
Children of Thomas and Martha Ardery:
Jane W. Ardery, born Oct. 3rd, 1824.
Mary A. Ardery, born Dec. 4th, 1826.
Martha T. Ardery, born April 24th, 1829.
Eliza A. Ardery, born March 29th, 1832.
Nancy M. Ardery, born Jan. 22nd, 1835.
David A. Ardery, born July 8th, 1837.
John W. Ardery, born July 27th, 1840.
Thomas Ardery and Martha McKee were married Oct. 23rd, 1823.
Thomas Ardery died Feb. 17th, 1846.
Martha Ardery died Dec. 17th, 1868.
John W. Ardery died June 29th, 1864.

My brother's family record:
James D. Ardery, born Oct. 27th, 1838.
William Ardery, born March 26th, 1841.
James D. Ardery died in Confederate Army Hospital in Columbus,
    Miss., 1862.

Births of mother's brothers and sisters:
James Moore, born Dec. 24th, 1780.
John Moore, born March 15th, 1782.
William Moore, born March 6th, 1784.
Polly Moore, born Nov. 15th, 1787.
Abram More, born Aug. 24th, 1789.
Peggy Moore, born Oct. 24th, 1793.

NOTE: For earlier record of Ardery family see Ardery Family
    Chart, 1930.

PALMER-WYATT BIBLE

Thomas F. Palmer was born January 20th, 1815.
Sarah Jane Palmer was born May 10th, 1817.
Elizabeth Palmer was born May 12th, 1819.
John Palmer was born March 22nd, 1821.
Joseph Palmer was born May 6th, 1823.
Eliza Jane Palmer was born March 29th, 1825.
Lucy Ann Palmer was born May 6th, 1827.
Agnes F .Palmer was born 1830.
Robert Palmer was born Jan. 30th, 1793.
Nancy Palmer was born Nov. 29th, 1789, and departed this life
    May 29th, 1854.
Joseph Palmer was born May 6th, 1823.
Louisa Wyatt was born April 16th, 1830.

Kate Palmer was born May 9th, 1855.

Mattie Bell Palmer was born January 25th, 1857, 8 P. M.

John J. McClintock was born Feb. 26th, 1849.

Belle Palmer McClintock was born July 18th, 1882, and departed this life Dec. 16, 1900.

Joseph Palmer departed this life March 17th, 1884.

Mattie Bell Palmer departed this life Sept. 17, 1878.

Joseph Palmer and his wife, Louisa, married February 9th, 1854.

Kate Palmer was married on the 10th of Feb., 1874, to John J. McClintock.

D. T. Wyatt, born Dec. 23, 1835, departed this life March 18, 1883.

Mattie W. Witherby, born Dec. 25, 1844, departed this life March 16th, 1885.

George F. Parker was born Nov. 24, 1859, and departed this life November, 1881.

John T. Bowen departed this life July 4, 1879.

F. R. Wyatt was born Feb. 2nd, 1806, departed this life Dec. 27, 1893.

Martha McCauly Rogers, wife of F. R. Wyatt, was born Oct. 2nd, 1808, departed this life Oct. 12, 1889.

Lucy Jane Wyatt, wife of G. W. Bowen, born Feb. 19, 1832, departed this life Aug. 22, 1904.

Susan Rebecca Wyatt, wife of Wm. Lair, was born Dec. 13, 1833, departed this life June 15th, 1874.

Thomas Dudley Wyatt, born Dec. 23, 1835, departed this life March 18, 1883.

Carlomie (Caroline) Wyatt, wife of Chas. Parker, was born May 6, 1838, departed this life Dec. 19, 1859.

George W. Wyatt, born April 3rd, 1840.

Martha Wyatt, wife of J. G. Witherby, born Dec. 25, 1844, departed this life March 16, 1875.

George F. Parker, son of Caroline and Charles Parker, was born Nov. 24, 1839, departed this life Nov. 14, 1881.

Sallie Lula Lair Hedges, born Jan. 10, 1868, daughter of Susan Wyatt and Wm. Lair, Sr.

Ashby Lair, son of Susan Wyatt and Wm. Lair, was born June 12, 1872, departed this life April 14, 1874.

Fleming R. Wyatt and Martha McCauly Rogers were married June 25, 1829.

Joseph Palmer and Louisa Wyatt were married Feb. 9, 1854.

Geo. Bowen and Lucy Wyatt were married, 1843.

Wm. Lair and Susan Wyatt were married Feb. 10, 1859.

J. G. Witherby and Martha Wyatt were married Feb. 17, 1875.

George W. Wyatt and Mollie Bounbarger Eubank were married May 29, 1884.

J. J. McClintock and Kate Palmer were married Feb. 10, 1874.

Callie Bowen and Alexander Kellar were married April 20, 1880.

Ida Bowen and Arthur Kellar were married April 20, 1881.

Belle Bowen and Arthur Newcum were married, 1884.

Lula Lair and F .G. Hedges married Dec. 24, 1904.

Geo. W. Wyatt and Westye Boardman were married August —.

PEED BIBLE
(Owned by Alfred Marshall Peed, Maysville, Ky.)

Alfred Peed was born Sept. 1, 1813, died 1892.

Mary Peed, his wife, was born Feb. 15, 1819, died 1901.

John Peed, born Nov. 9, 1834, died Sept. 9, 1856.
Eliza Jane Peed, born April 24, 1836.
Caroline Peed was born July 20, 1838, died June 20, 1865.
Dorothy Peed was born Aug. 29, 1840.
Mary A. Peed, born May 6, 1843, died July 14, 1921.
J. J. Peed, born Oct. 18, 1845, died Oct. 19, 1914.
J. D. Peed, born Jan. 8, 1848, died Feb. 2, 1907.
Permelia A. Peed, born Dec. 7, 1850, died June 10, 1864.
Alfred M. Peed, born May 3, 1853, died Aug. 29, 1862.
Dorothy Peed, born Jan. 25, 1787 (mother of A. M. Peed).
Joane Peed, born Oct. 13, 1813, died July 12, 1883 (?).
Chas. C. Peed, born July 21, 1856, died July 12, 1858 (?)
Maggie Peed, born July 14, 1859, died Nov. 10th, 1862.
William Peed, born Sept. 30, 1861.
John Peed and *Dorothy were married April 18, 1809.
Alfred Peed and Mary were married Aug. 29, 1835.
Craven Calvert and Sally were married Nov. 18, 1828.
Dorothea A. Peed and J. T. Young.
J. D. Peed and S. (?) A. Jefferson.
J. J. Peed and R. E. Tabb.
J. D. Peed and E. B. Perry (?).
M. H. Peed and J. A. Slack.
W. A. Peed and Mary McIlvain, Jan. 14, 1885.
*Dorothy Marshall.

RENICK BIBLE
(In the possession of Mrs. Jas. Duncan Bell, Paris, Ky.)

BIRTHS
Morris William Renick, born Oct. the 2nd, 1858.
James Scott Renick, born March the 27th, 1860.
Abraham Grant Renick, born Nov. 10th, 1863.
Annie L. Renick, born Aug. 4th, 1866.
Brinkley Messick Renick, born March 29th, 1869.
Gertrude Trimble Renick, born Oct. 8, 1878.

DEATHS
Ann Eliza Renick, died January the 31st, 1839.
Elizabeth Renick, died Aug. 28, 1878.
Julia Fry Renick, wife of Abram Renick, died Nov. 27th, 1903.
William Henry Renick, died Nov. 29, 1912.
Elizabeth Tyndall Renick, daughter of Brinkley Renick, died May 18, 1913.
May McCally Renick, wife of Morris W. Renick, died Jan. 8, 1916.
J. Scott Renick, died in Havana, Cuba, Feb. 14, 1917.
Curtis Pendleton Smith, husband of Annie Renick Smith, born Oct. 21, 1860, died Feb. 20, 1919, at Dallas, Texas, buried at Clintonville, Ky.
George Renick, died February 21, 1839.
Magdalene Renick, died on the 25th of August, 1860.
James Renick, died April 6, 1884.
Sarah Renick departed this life March the 24th, 1854.
Abram Renick, born Jan. 17, 1803, died Aug. 28, 1884.

MARRIAGES
James and Elizabeth Renick married June 13, 1832.

J. Scott Renick and Princie Sutherland Renick married Dec. 23rd, 1881.
Morris W. Renick and May Edna McCallay married Jan. 24, 1889.
Abram Renick and Julia Virginia Fry married Feb. 19, 1890.
Annie E. Renick and Curtis P. Smith married Oct. 21, 1891.
Brinkley M. Renick and Elizabeth Jones married Feb. 6, 1895.
W. W. Renick and Mattie A. Morris married on the 17th of Dec., 1857.
Abram Renick and Bessie McGee Fry married April 5, 1905.
Gertrude Renick and James Duncan Bell married Nov. 7, 1905.

BIRTHS
James Renick, born Nov. 1st, 1793.
*George Renick, born October 6, 1775.
Magdalene Renick, wife of George Renick, born March 31, 1772.
Daughters of John Renick:
Julian Renick, born February the 8th, 1823.
Sarah Renick, born January the 29th, 1834.
William Renick, born July 5, 1893.
Brinkley Coleman Renick, born June 2, 1897.
Felix Renick, born Oct. 29, 1896.
Elizabeth Renick, born March 31st, 1800.
Ann E. Renick, born April 15, 1835.
William H. Renick, born Dec. 5th, 1836.
Mattie A. Morris, wife of W. H. Renick, born Jan. 1st, 1838.
Harry Phelps Renick, born Sept. 28, 1890.
Virginia Renick, born July 7, 1891.
Cordelia Renick, born Sept. 12, 1892.
Willie McCauley Renick, born March 19, 1892.
Robert Willson Renick, born May 31st, 1894.

*NOTE: George Renick was the brother of Felix Renick of Ohio and son of William Renick (1746-1807) of Hampshire and Hardy Cos., Virginia.

ROGERS BIBLE
(In the possession of Harvey Rogers, Paris, Ky.)

Nathaniel Rogers, the son of Thomas Rogers and Elizabeth Annie Carr, was born July 25, 1755.
Frances Rogers, wife of Nathaniel Rogers and mother of W. Rogers, was the daughter of Charles Cobb and Nancy Annie Walton.
Signed May 5, 1859: WARREN ROGERS.

MARRIAGES
Nathaniel Rogers, father of W. Rogers and grandfather of Harvey Addison Rogers, and Miss Frances Cobb were married August the 14th, 1783.
W. Rogers and Miss Annie Cornick were married July the 8th, 1806.
W. Rogers was married a second time to Miss Kate M. Skillman, on the 24th of July, 1817.
Hervey Addison Rogers was married to Miss Sarah W. Neal on the 8th of February, 1832.
Hervey Addison Rogers was married second time to Miss Elizabeth Jane Moran July 12, 1838.
Miss Annie Susan Rogers, daughter of Hervey A. and Sarah W.

Rogers, was married to Henry Clay Williams September 6, 1853.

BIRTHS
W. Rogers was born July 7, 1784.

Annie Cornick, wife of W. Rogers, was born January 28, 1790.

Hervey Addison Rogers, their third son, was born November 7, 1812.

Sarah W. Neal, wife of H. A. Rogers, was born October 28, 1813.

Elizabeth Jane Rogers, second wife of H. A. Rogers, was born February 24, 1819.

William, eldest son and child of H. A. and S. W. Rogers, was born October 18, 1832.

Annie Susan, eldest daughter of H. A. and S. W. Rogers, was born September 6, 1834.

Kate A., second daughter of H. A. and S. W. Rogers, was born December 24, 1835.

Edward Benjamin, eldest son of H. A. and E. J. Rogers, was born August 8, 1839.

Nathaniel Cobb, second son and child of H. A. and E. J. Rogers, was born April 24, 1841.

Sarah Jane, eldest daughter of H. A. and E. J. Rogers, was born October 1, 1843.

Bettie Gano, second daughter of H. A. and E. J. Rogers, was born April 6, 1846.

Nancy Annie, third daughter of H. A. and E. J. Rogers, was born April 21, 1848.

Hervey Allen, third son of H. A. and E. J. Rogers, was born February 26, 1850.

Purviance, fourth son of H. A. and E. J. Rogers, was born Feb. 8, 1853.

Warren Moran, fourth son of H. A. and E. J. Rogers, was born November 27, 1855.

Mary Eliza, fourth daughter of H. A. and E. J. Rogers, was born June 27, 1858.

Louis Ray Rogers, sixth son of H. A. and E. Jane Rogers, was born the 4th of November, 1864.

Louis Ray Rogers, died Feb. 25, 1928. Louis Ray Rogers married Iva Dee Allen April, 1894.

Iva Dee Allen Rogers was born August 12, 1872, died April 10, 1929.

DEATHS
Frances Rogers, mother of W. Rogers and grandmother of Hervey A. Rogers, died September 20, 1790.

Nathaniel Rogers, father of W. Rogers and grandfather of H. A. Rogers, died December 22, 1804.

Annie Rogers, wife of W. Rogers and mother of H. A., died December 21, 1816.

Kate A. Rogers, daughter of H. A. and S. W. Rogers, died November 6, 1836.

Sarah W. Rogers, wife of H. A. Rogers, died January 17, 1837.

Annie Susan Williams, daughter of H. A. and S. W. Rogers, died August 5th, 1854.

Purviance Rogers, died July 8th, 1860.

William Rogers, father of H. A. Rogers, departed this life Saturday evening, the 15th day of February, 1862, aged 77 years 7 months and 8 days. He died as he had lived, full of faith, and he came to his grave in full age as a shock of corn cometh in his season.

NOTE: Nathaniel Rogers was born in the State of, Virginia. He was a Revolutionary soldier and member of the Constitutional Convention of Kentucky, 1790, from Bourbon County, having removed from Campbell County, Virginia in 1798. He was the son of Thos. Rogers (1725-86) of Charlotte County, Virginia, and wife, Elizabeth Ann Carr; he was a great grandson of John Rogers the 5th president of Harvard College.

WILLIAM SCOTT BIBLE
(In the possession of Mrs. Clay Ward of Paris, Ky.)

Benjamin Bibb and Mary Scott were married December, in the year of our Lord Jesus Christ, 1814.

John Tindsley and Jane Scott were married February 16th, in the year of our Lord Jesus Christ, 1815.

John Rogers and Martha Scott were married September the 10th, in the year 1818 (?).

Joseph Carr and Margaret Scott were married July the 29th, in 1819.

James Tinsley and Elizabeth Scott were married February the 24th, 1820.

Lulbearry (?) Carr was born September 30th, 1931.

T. S. (?) Carr was born February 6th, 1834.

Narcessa Carr was born April 13, 1836.

Amelius Carr was born July 6, 1841.

M. S. Carr departed this life November the 27th, in the year 1862, aged 42 years and 8 months.

William Scott was born on March 25th, in the year of our Lord and Savior Jesus Christ, 1765.

Margaret Scott, his wife, was born in the year of our Lord and Savior Jesus Christ, 1762.

Mary Scott, daughter of the above couple, was born in June, the 13th, 1792.

Jane Scott was born March the 9th, 1794.

Martha Scott was born August 25th, 1797.

Elizabeth Scott was born on June the 10th, 1799.

Margaret Scott was born in February, the 22nd, 1801.

Margaret Ann Rogers was born in June, the 13th, 1819.

J. C. Carr was born in November, the 10th, 1850 (?).

Mary Elizabeth Carr was born the 24th day of September, 1820.

Margaret Eliza Tinsley was born December the 16th, 1820.

Telitha Jane Rogers was born December the 25th, 1820.

Robert Tinsley was born the 3rd of March, 1822.

William S. Carr was born March the 17th, 1822.

Joseph B. Rogers was born the 22nd of December, 1823.

Margaret Ann Bibb was born in October, 27th, 1814.

William S. Bibb and Martha Jane Bibb were born December the 15th, 1815.

Dulcina Bibb was born July the 27th, 1817.

William S. Tinsley was born in March, the 10th, 1824.

William S. Rogers was born October the 29th, 1824.

Ransom Hardery Tinsley was born February 12th, 1826.

Nathaniel Carr was born in June, 8th day, 1824.

John G. Rogers was born 23rd day of March, 1827.

James S. Tinsley was born the 23rd day of Oct., 1827.

Margaret Ann(?) Carr was born October the 8th, 1826.

Margaret Ann Rogers departed this life August the 3rd, in the year of our Lord Jesus Christ, 1819, aged 7 weeks and one day.

Benjamin Bibb departed this life September the 9th, 1821.

Nancy Bibb departed this life April the 28th, 1822.

Martha Jane Carr was born January, 1830.

Martha A. Rogers was born March 6th, 1830.

Margaret Scott departed this life January the 2nd, 1842, aged 79 years and 21 days.

Nathaniel Carr departed this life July, the 23rd day, 1854, aged 30 years and 46 days.

Nancy C. Carr departed this life March, the 6th day, year 1855.

Nathaniel J. Carr departed this life the 14th day of April, 1855, aged 4 months and 19 days.

Narcissa Carr departed this life July the 4th, in the year 1854, aged 18 years and 2 months and 22 days.

Mary E. Rasco departed this life March, the —— of May, 1866, aged 26 years, 6 months and 2 days.

Margaret A. Bibb departed this life May 12th, 1827.

John G. Rogers departed this life Sept. 3rd, 1828.

Jessa Clay Carr departed this life June, the 39th day, in the year 1854, aged 7 months and 17 days.

Thomas D. Carr departed this life October the 29th, in the year 1856, aged 22 years 8 months and 24 days.

Joseph Carr departed this life February (?) the 18th, in the year 1857, aged 64 years.

William Scott departed this life December 26th, 1857, aged 94 years and 9——.

NOTE: Wm. Scott first resided in Fayette Co., Ky., later moved to Trigg Co., Ky.

SHELY BIBLE

(Contributed by Mrs. Charles McMillan, Paris, Ky.).

David Shely, born May 27, 1750, died in Jessamine County Dec. 13, 1823.

Mary Hurst, his wife, born Feb. 7, 1758, died in Jessamine Co., Nov. 1, 1849.   Children:

Milley, born July 24, 1777, married a man named Smith.

Polly, born Apr. 20, 1779.

William, born Oct. 27, 1781, died March 6, 1829.

Nancy, born Nov. 8, 1782, died Aug. 9, 1794.

Sally, born July 28, 1785, died Aug. 9, 1794.

David, born Feb. 3, 1787.

Elizabeth, born Feb. 6, 1789.

Margaret, born Feb. 28, 1791, died 1851, married Henry Ball (Danville?).

John, born June 2, 1793, died Jan. 9, 1850; wife's name was Webber.

Elinore, born Feb. 8, 1795, married John Stapleton.

Rebecca, born March 29, 1797, married James Hurst.

Matilda, born Sept. 7, 1798, died March 4, 1831, married Charles West.

Fanny, born Sept. 21, 1799, died March 22, 1847, married Samuel Miller.

Washington F., born May 24, 1802, died Jan. 1, 1941, married Katherine H. Willoughby.

SMITH BIBLE
(Contributed by Mrs. Walter Shropshire, Paris Ky.).

Thomas Porter Smith was born Jan. 1, 1793 on Monday.
Thomas Porter Smith and Frances R. Oden were married Dec., 1814.

Their children, all born in Paris, Ky.
William Oden, born June 9, 1816; died June 2, 1853.
Mary Markham, born June 3, 1818; died Sept. 16, 1818.
Thomas Porter, born July 3, 1819; died Oct. 9, 1841.
Elizabeth Markham, born May 17, 1821; died 1849.
Ann, born Mar. 28, 1823; died May 24, 1847.
John Smith, born Feb. 9, 1825; died Oct. 2, 1826.
Charles Smith, born Feb. 1, 1827; died Aug., 1836.
McFarland Smith, born May 16, 1829; died Feb. 8, 1885.
Frances Oden, born Mar. 23, 1832; died 1884.
Robert Oden ,born April 30, 1835; died April 28, 1892.
Thomas Porter Smith died Nov. 12, 1868.

NOTE: Thomas P. Smith was the son of John Smith, born Feb. 2, 1759, died Aug. 22, 1832, on Aug. 28, 1788 married Nancy Porter, born April 23, 1776, died June 27, 1832. John Smith was son of Chas. Smith, Va., April 15, 1735, died Oct. 26, 1821, Ky., married Patsy Jones, born Culpeper Co., Va., Jan., 1742, died Ky., Sept. 14, 1817. References: Bourne Collection of Manuscripts, Smith Bible, in possession of Mrs. R. P. Smith, Meridian, Miss.

SPEARS-WORNALL BIBLE
(In possession of William P. Wornall, Paris, Ky.).

MARRIAGES
Solomon Spears and Margaret Kerfoot were married December 12th, 1811.
Joseph Morin and Sophia Edwards were married Oct. 14th, 1811.
John K. Spears and Emily Morin were married January 21st, 1836.
William K. Griffith and Margaret K. Spears were married July 5th, 1855.
Joseph Ewalt and Sophia Spears were married December 18, 1856.
W. H. Clay and Emma Spears were married November 3rd, 1869.
Noah Spears and Georgia Chiles were married October 27th, 1875.
Thomas P. Wornall and Catherine K. Spears were married October 27th, 1875.
Joseph M. Spears and Anne Menzies were married Oct. 7th, 1885.
Solomon Spears and Rebecca Keller were married April, 1890.
James W. Bedford and Kate S. Wornall married Jan. 24th, 1900.
William P. Wornall and Elizabeth Woodford married April 11th, 1901.

BIRTHS
Solomon Spears was born March 1st, 1790.

Margaret Spears, wife of Solomon Spears, was born September 20th, 1796.

John K. Spears was born December 15th, 1812.

Emily Spears, wife of John K. Spears, was born June 1st, 1820.

Margaret K. Spears, daughter of John K. and Emily Spears, was born October 24th, 1836.

Sophia M. Spears was born September 6th, 1838.

Infant, born August 1840, not named.

Solomon Spears, son of John K. and Emily Spears, was born November 1st, 1841.

Joseph M. Spears was born July 5th, 1844.

Joseph Morin was born 1787, November.

Sophia Morin, wife of Joseph Morin, was born 25th July, 1793.

Jacob Spears was born April 24th, 1845.

Noah Spears was born March 15th, 1847.

Emily Spears, daughter of John K. and Emily Spears, was born May 5th, 1850.

Catherine K. Spears, daughter of same, was born August 2nd, 1852.

John Spears Clay, son of William H. Clay and Emma Clay, was born September 19th, 1870.

Thomas P. Wornall, son of Elizabeth and Perry Wornall, born Dec. 13th, 1847.

DEATHS

Solomon Spears departed this life August 21st, 1830, aged 21 years.

Margaret Spears, wife of Solomon Spears, departed this life June 30th, 1833, aged 36 years, 9 months and 10 days.

Infant, not named, died in August, 1840, aged 4 days.

Jacob Spears, son of John K. and Emily Spears, died May 31st, 1848, aged 3 years 1 month and 7 days.

John K. Spears departed this life April 11th, 1854, aged 42 years 4 months and 4 days.

Sophia Ewalt, wife of Joseph Ewalt, departed this life August the 27, '57, aged 18 years 11 months and 21 days.

Emily, wife of John K. Spears, died Sept. 10, 1887, aged 67 years 3 months 10 days.

Emma Spears, wife of W. H. Clay, died Dec. 14th, 1918, aged 68 years 8 months.

Joseph Morin, died November 13th, 1869, aged 82 years.

John Spears Clay, son of William H. Clay and Emma Clay, died February 21st, 1871, aged 5 months and 2 days.

Frances P. Clay, son of Wm. H. Clay and Emma Clay, died June 11th, 1880, aged 5 years 8 months 6 days.

Noah Spears, son of J. K. and Emily Spears, departed this life Oct. 10th, 1881, aged 34 years 6 months and 25 days.

Sophia Morin, wife of Joseph Morin, died June 22nd, 1883, aged 89 years 1 month.

MEMORANDUMS

Wm. Henry Clay, son of William H. Clay and Emma Clay, was born Oct. 11th, A. D., 1871.

Francis P. Clay, son of Wm. H. Clay and Emma Clay, was born January 5th, A. D., 1875.

Eddie C. Spears, daughter of Noah and Georgia Spears, was born Sept. 25th, A. D., 1877.

Wm. P. Wornall, son of Thomas P. and Catherine Wornall, was born March 2nd, A. D., 1879.

John K. Spears, son of Noah and Georgia Spears, was born October 22nd, A. D., 1879.

Mathew Martin Clay, son of William H. and Emma Clay, was born August 16th, 1881.

Noah Spears. son of Noah Spears and Georgia Spears, was born Nov. 8th, 1887.

John Menzies Spears was born Sept. 12, 1886, son of J. M. and Ann M. Spears.

Joe M. Spears, son of Joe M. and Annie Spears, born Aug. 21, 1889.

Noah Spears Clay, son of W. H. Clay and Emma, born Aug., 1880.

Roby W. Clay, son of W. H. Clay and Emma, born October, 1887.

Margaret K. Griffith, daughter—John K. and Emily Spears, died Jan. 29th, 1918, aged 82 years.

DEATHS

Wm. Henry, son of W. H. Clay and Emma, died July 19th, 1889, aged 17 years 9 months 8 days.

Samuella Menzies, daughter of Joe M. and Annie Spears, born Dec. 27, 1890.

Elizabeth, daughter of Solomon and Rebeca Spears, born June 27th, 1891.

BIRTHS

William P. Wornall, son of William P. and Elizabeth Woodford Wornall, born June 24th, 1904.

Thomas Wornall, son of William P. and Elizabeth Woodford Wornall, born May 31st, 1908.

Ben Woodford Wornall, son of William P. and Elizabeth Woodford Wornall, born June 13th, 1909.

DEATHS

Thomas P. Wornall departed this life Nov. 23rd, 1891, aged 44 years.

J. M. Spears departed this life Nov. 21st, 1893.

Noah Spears Clay, son of W. H. and E. S. Clay, departed this life May 2nd, 1895.

Thomas Wornall, son of W. P. and Elizabeth Woodford Wornall, departed this life June 27th, 1908, aged 4 weeks.

BIRTHS

S. Parker Wornall, born March 11th, 1912, son of W. P. and Elizabeth Woodford Wornall.

DEATHS

J. William Bedford, son of Coleman Bedford, died July 27th, 1916; September, age 81 years.

STANIFORD BIBLE

(Contributed by Mrs. Harry Linville, Paris, Ky.).

Then was born Aquila Staniford, son of William Staniford and Christian, his wife, Aug 25, 1740.

Then was born Sarah Clark, daughter of John Clark and Hannah, his wife, June 10, 1744.

Then were married Aquila Staniford and Sarah, his wife, December 27, 1764.

Then was born Hannah Staniford, daughter of Aquila Staniford and wife, December 4, 1765.

Then was born Milcah, January 21, 1767.

Then was born Nathen, July 8, 1768.

Then was born George, July 8, 1776.

Then was born Sarah, April 28, 1773.

Then was born Mary, ———— 31, 1775.

Then was born Rebecah, August 9, 1776, and departed this life September 11, 1780.

Then was born Elijah, January 13, 1778.

Then was born Aquila, June 3, 1780.

Then was born Rebecah, July 27, 1782.

Then was born Cassandrew, November 7, 1789.

Then was born John Staniford, January 27, 1786.

Then was born Sophia Staniford ,his wife, July 4, 1800.

Sophia Staniford, wife of John Staniford, departed this life October 13, 1855.

John Staniford departed this life Nov. 29, 1866.

Squire Ann Hildreth was born Sept. 10, 1815.

George Staniford, born July 8, 1770.

Mary McCarty, born September 23, 1785.

George Staniford and Mary McCarty were married July 16, 1804.

Sarah Staniford, first daughter, born September 15, 1806.

Abraham Staniford, first son, born born April 8, 1808.

Elizabeth Staniford, second daughter, born August 13, 1809.

Mary E. Staniford, third daughter, born May 22, 1811.

Cassandrew Staniford, fourth daughter, born October 22, 1812.

George Staniford, second son, born Aug. 7, 1814.

Aquilla Staniford, third son, born November 18, 1815.

Mahaly Staniford, fifth daughter, born Aug. 23, 1817.

Hannah Staniford, sixth daughter, born Feb. 9, 1819.

Susanna Staniford, seventh daughter, born April 8, 1822.

Aquilla Staniford, born November 18, 1815; Fanny Faulkner, born March 1, 1813—were married August 4, 1842.

Elija H. Staniford, born January 17, 1839.

John F. Staniford, born May 16, 1841.

George Wesley Staniford, born May 5, 1843.

Aquilla Staniford, born October 7, 1845.

Mary Elizabeth Staniford, born July 29, 1848.

Francis Marion Staniford, born March 18, 1853.

Ann Eliza Staniford, born November 25, 1854.

STERETT (STERRETT) BIBLE

(In possession of Mrs. Sally DeHaven Moorman, Cloverport, Ky.).

MARRIAGES

John Sterett and Sally DeHaven, his wife, were married October 14, 1806.

Charles V. Lander and Rachel P. Sterett, his wife, were married Aug. 18, 1824.

Wm. Sterett, and Elizabeth E. Dorsey, his wife, were married May Feb. 11, 1827.

Richard Polk and Martha Sterett, his wife, were married May 1, 1834.

John H. Sterett and Dora Barthes were married in Mead Co., Ky., Sept. 9, 1872.

BIRTHS

John Sterett was born Oct. 17, 1779.
Sally DeHaven was born Nov. 27, 1781.
Wm. Sterett was born Aug. 30, 1803.
Rebecca Sterett was born Dec. 3, 1805.
Martha Sterett, born Aug. 24, 1808.
Sallie Sterett born May 8, 1811.
Eliza Sterett, born Nov. 8, 1813.
Peggy Sterett, born May 26, 1816.
Baird Sterett born at the rising of the sun on Jan. 31, 1819.
Martha Mary Polk, born Nov. 2, 1834.

DEATHS

Martha Sterett departed this life Mar. 17, 1818.
Martha Polk, died Nov. 20, 1834. (29th?)
Chas. V. Lander, died Aug. 5, 1835.
Elizabeth E. Sterett, died Sept. 11, 1838, 2 o'clock.
John Sterett, son of Eliza and Wm. Sterett, died Sept. 16, 1838, (3 P. M.).
Rebecca Sterett, dau. of Wm. and Eliza S., died Sept. 24, 1838.
John Sterett, died Apr. 4, 1831.
Baird Sterett, died Apr. 4, 1885, at the rising of the sun.

TARR BIBLE

(In possession of Charles Tarr, Quincy, Ill.).

Charles Tarr born Aug. 8, 1761 and Marion Richardson born March 4, 1772.

Births:

*Polly Tarr, daughter of Charles and Marion Tarr, was born Oct. 10, A. D., 1796.
James Tarr, born Oct. 30, 1798.
John Tarr, born March 4, 1801.
Nancy Tarr, born April 15, 1804.
Sally Tarr, born June 22, 1806.
Huldah Tarr, born Oct. 14, 1808.
Wm. R. (Richardson?) Tarr, born Jan. 14, 1810.
Mariah Tarr, born May 5, 1812.
Eleanor Tarr, born Oct. 12, 1816.
Elizabeth Tarr, born Oct. 14, 1794.
Azariah and George Tarr, twins, born, May 24, 1815.

*Married Richard Adair. Bourbon Co., Ky.

Note: The above Charles and Marian Tarr came from Snow Hill, Maryland to Bourbon County, Kentucky, where they remained until 1829, when they moved to Adams County, Illinois. There they both died, their wills being a matter of record, his dated May 18th, 1835. His son, John Tarr and daughter, Mary, wife of Richard Adair, remained in Kentucky, the other children accompanied them.

TURNER BIBLE

(In possession of Mrs. Mary I. Davis, Paris, Ky.).

William Turner was born November 6th, 1752.
Martha Ricords Turner was born Aug. 19th, 1762.

Children of William and Martha Turner:
Mary Turner, born August 8th, 1779, married Ellis.
John Turner, born August 12th, 1781.
Nancy Turner, born April 3rd, 1783, married Ross.
Robert Turner, born Jan. 16, 1786.
Betsy Turner, born Feb. 1, 1788, married Orr.
Sally Turner, born March 10th, 1790, married Bowls.
William Turner, born Feb. 17, 1792.
Patsy Turner, born August 22, 1794, married Adair.
Stacy Turner, born May 22, 1797, married Dazey.
Milly Turner, born July 14, 1800, married Tarr.
Charles Turner, born Nov. 16, 1803, married Ward.
Above Charles Turner married Mary Ward in March, 1827. Their
   children were Lucinda and John Turner.

Note: The above Wm. and Martha (Ricords) Turner were among
those at Bryan Station at the time of the siege, and she was among the
women who carried water from the spring. This couple came to Kentucky from the Eastern Shore of Maryland, settled in Bourbon County.
Some descendants moved to Quincy, Ill.

WHITE BIBLE

(In possession of Mr. Chas. R. White, Bourbon Co., Ky.).

Jeremiah White and Nancy Preston were married on the 4th day of
Oct., 1832, by R. T. Dillard.
Preston D. White and Martha L. Stuart were married by Rev.
Thomas P. Dudley, Jan. 8th, 1872.
John G. Stuart and Sally Gaitskill were married Nov. 20th, 1818 by
John Smith, Baptist minister.
Albin D. White and Bettie Herald were married on the 25th day of
Nov. 1868, by Elder John A. Brooks.
Charles W. Gaitskill and Susan F. White were married by Elder
David B. Cooper on the 25th day of October, 1870.
L. Butler Carrington and Nannie P. White were married by Elder
I. Pike Powers, Feb. 26, 1881.

BIRTHS

Nancy White, wife of Jeremiah White, was born the 29th, of Oct.
   1807.
Jeremiah White, Jr., was born the 1st of Nov., 1804.
John G. Stuart was born 1783.
Sallie Stuart was born June 20th, 1798.
Preston D. White was born the 21st of Dec., 1834.
Albin B. White was born the 3rd of Oct., 1839.
Elizabeth White was born the 12th of Sept. 1837.
George W. White was born the 22nd of Feb. 1842.
Susan F. White was born the 21st of Aug. 1844.
Charles R. White was born Oct. 12th, 1872.

Frank Preston White was born the 22nd of June, 1877.

DEATHS

Jeremiah White, Senr., died the 22nd of June, 1836.

Elizabeth White, wife of Jeremiah White, Senr., died the 4th of May, 1848.

John G. Stuart died March, 1853.

Nancy White, Senr., died March 8th, 1882.

Elizabeth White, wife of Jeremiah White, Senr., died May 4th, 1848.

Susan F. Gaitskill died Feb. 8th, 1882.

In another place, Susan F. White died Jan. 8th, 1882.

WIGGINTON BIBLE

(Record furnished by Mr. Jas. W. Wigginton, Decato, California).

Roger Wigginton married Eleanor.

Will recorded Loudoun Co., Va., 1778.

Children:

Mary Davis (John Davis) m (?).

Henry, born Nov. 19, 1755, died Sept. 4, 1842; married Ann Vallandingham, Mar. 2, 1778, Montgomery Co., Md.

William, born _____, married Allison Evans, Feb. 7, 1778.

Benjamin, born _____, married Harriett Scott.

Roger, born _____, married his cousin, Elizabeth Wigginton .

Eleanor, born _____, married _____.

Elizabeth, born _____, married Spencer E. Buchannon, May 16 ,1780.

Children of Henry and Ann Vallandingham Wigginton:

Mary, born Dec. 25, 1778; married Giles Tillett, reported Oct. 25, 1798.

Eleanor or Bettie, born Oct. 11, 1780; married Henry Boyer, Feb. 15, 1825.

Jane, born Oct. 1, 1782; married Jeremiah Northcutt, Oct. 28, 1802, May 7, 1801.

Elizabeth, born May 6, 1784; married Roger Wigginton, her cousin, 1810.

Maragaret or Peggie, born June 13, 1785; married Sam'l Corbin, Nov. 27, 1810.

Nancy, born Nov. 28, 1786; married Charles Hazelrigg, Jan., 1825.

William, born Nov. 16, 1787; married Elizabeth Corbin, Jan. 15, 1811.

Peter, born March 12, 1789; married Nancy or Polly Vallandingham, _____, 1821.

Jamima, born Aug. 11, 1790; married John Foster, Mar. 25, 1812.

James, born Apr. 11, 1792; married Nancy Campbell, _____

Spencer, born June 27, 1793; married Susan Smith _____.

John, twin of Elijah, born Apr. 11, 1795; married Mary Ann Trumbo, _____

Elijah, twin of John, born Apr. 11, 1795; married Nancy or Darnsby, _____

Henry, born Apr. 7, 1797; went to Utah.

DEATHS

Jemima, my daughter, was born the 11th day of Aug., 1790, and

died the 29th day of April, 1823. She being the age of 32
years, 7 months and some days, leaving six helpless children
to me for life.

Nancy Wigginton, wife of Henry Wigginton, Sr., was born the 26th
of July, A. D., 1756 and died the 20th of July, 1833.

Henry Wigginton, Sr., died Feb. the 12th, 1844.

Jane Rice Wigginton, wife of William Wigginton, died Sept. 24th,
1855, aged 64 years.

William Wigginton, died Sept. 22nd, 1869.

CEMETERY RECORDS

OLD BOWLING GREEN CEMETERY
(Warren County)

Dates taken from the old cemetery in Bowling Green, Ky. This
has long since been abandoned, and many stones are not legible, and
many have been taken up and stacked in one corner of graveyard. Only
the oldest ones were copied by Hattie M. Scott (Frankfort, Ky.), July
1st, 1930. Many were removed to the new city cemetery when it was
founded.

Atchison, Cynthia G., wife of Samuel L. Atchison and dau. of Armistead and Lucy Morehead; died Oct. 1st, ____, aged __, 7 mos. and
2 days.

Atchison, Mrs. Maria L., born Nov. (?) 16, 1820, died Sept. 24, 1844.

Atchison, Mrs. Elizabeth, born _____, died 1846.

Atkinson, Robt., died Mar. 22, 1844, aged 66 years.

Atkinson, Sarah, died Sept. 24, 1844, aged 66 years.

Barclay, Philander, born July 16, 1798, died July 7, 1838.

Barclay, Mrs. Elizabeth, wife of Philander W. Barclay, born May 24,
1811, died July 18, 1832.

Barclay, Elizabeth, born Mar. 13, 1786, died Aug. 24, 1818.

Barclay, Hugh, died Oct. 20, 1831 (?) (4?), aged 84 years.

Barclay, Sarah, _____

Barclay, Hugh, born Sept. 6, 1805, died in 22nd year.

Barclay, Jane, wife of S. Barclay, born June 6, 1773, died July 10,
1845 (1815).

Barclay, Samuel, born July 27, 1773, died Sept. 24, 1815.

Barclay, Sarah C., dau. of Samuel and Jane Barclay, born Aug. 16,
1796, died Sept. 27, 1823.

Barclay, Sarah C., wife of S. Barclay, and dau. of Pleasant and Agnes
H. Pollard, born Aug. 16, 1816, died May 3, 1844 (?).

Barclay, Mrs. Louisa B., wife of S. J. (?) Barclay, and dau of _____
and Elizabeth _____.

Barclay, Dr. Joseph W., born Dec. 6, 1800, died Oct. 8, 1830.

Bacon, Elizabeth J., dau. of E. I. and M. B. Bacon, 1821-1844.

Bacon, Edmund I., born Feb. 14, 1792, died Aug. 22, 1844.

Burnam, Emily, wife of A. Burnam, and dau. of L. and E. Horworth,
born Oct. 24, 1806, died Jan. 8, 1835.

Bicknell, Daniel, died Nov. 15, 1817, in 55th or 56th year.

Bicknell, _____, Philadelphia, _____, 1825.

(Covered with big slab and could only see above).
Burnam, Roger Williams, son of John and Sara D. Burnam, born
    Mar. 2, 1893 (?), died of cholera _____ 24, 1849.
    (Evidently the engraver meant to say 1793—H. Scott.   Something
    wrong,see below, evidently the mother).
Burnam, three brothers, sons of John and S. D. Burnam.
Burnam, Sara D., wife of John Burnam, and dau. of John and Sarah
    Hinge (?), born June 10, 1812, died July 22, 1849.
Burnam, Alex., born Sept. 18, 1806, died June 21, 1854, cholera.
Burnam, Bennett, born May 30, 1790, died 1852.
Briggs, Mrs. Elizzie, wife of C. M. Briggs, dau. of A. and S. W. Rogers,
    born Jan. 19, 1824, died Oct. 7, 1848.

Campbell, Mary J., dau. of David Campbell, Nov. 1815, Mar. 3, 1833.
Clary (?) Elizabeth, born Cambridge, N. Y., Feb. 11, 1795, died April
    19, 1856, aged 61 years.
Crawford, Presley, son of Rev. Nelson and Kitty Crawford, born June
    2, 1827, died Jan. 27, 1853.
Crawford, Kitty, wife of Rev. Nelson Crawford, born Apr. 12, 1790,
    died Sept. 7, 1862, 72 years.
Crawford, Reverend Nelson, born July 13, 1793, died Oct. 23, 1862,
    aged 69 years.
Crawford, _____, see Harriet Wright.
Cox, Mary A., dau. of E. J. and M. B. Bacon, wife of Henry H. Cox,
    born Feb. 22, 1825, died Jan. 21, 1846.
Challen, Mrs. Sara E., died Aug. 22, 1820, aged 18 years.
Clark, Mrs. S. E., wife of John B. Clark, born Jan. 17, 1820, died Mar.
    12, 1862.
Clark, John B., born Sept. 25, 1813, died Jan. 17, 1863.
Cook, Margaret P., wife of John Cook, born Oct. 29, 1855, died Aug.
    3, 1844.
Cook, John, born July, 1756, died Oct., 1849.
Clark, Elizabeth, born Mar. 19, 1784, died Oct. 7, 1839.
Clark, Wm., born Aug. 23, 1784, died Dec. 3, 1829.
Court, John, born April 31, 1896 (1796) died Dec. 27, 1870.
Courts, Elizabeth, wife of John Courts and dau. of C. B. (?) and Cath.
    Winn, born Mar. 26, 1822, died _____ ?

Donaldson, Mary, wife of Presley Donaldson, born Oct. 3, 1784, died
    Dec. 22, 1843.
Duncan, James, died Jan. 25, 1839, aged 58 years.

Fox, Mary Ann M., died Jan. 25, 1835, aged 46 years and 2 days.

Graham, Isabella A., wife of Robt. Graham, born Oct. 24, 1771 (4?),
    died Feb. 7, 1846.
Graham. Robt., born Sept. 14, 1761 (64?), died Mar. 8, 1822.
Graham, _____ Eliza, born _____ 2, 1807, died Sept. 12, 1822.
Graham, Clarence, born Mar. 13, 1810, died _____ ?
Grider, Henry, born July 10, 1796, died Sept. 8, 1866.
Grider, Mrs. Rachel, died Nov. 2, 1850.
Grider, Henry, Sr., born May 9, 1755, died Feb. 5, 1843.
Grider, Mrs. Elizabeth, wife of Henry Grider, Sr., born May 22, 1764,
    died Dec. 24, 1845.
Grider, Eliz. F., born June 17, 1786, died April 18, 1847.
Grider, Sally, wife of Martin Grider, born Sept. 8, 1785, died June 1,
    1861.
Graham, W_____ E., born Dec. 25, 1796, died (broken slab).

Graham, Druscilla, wife of W. E. Graham, Sr.

Hall, Prince, died Sept., 1858, in 63rd year.
Hackney, Salley, born Nov. 9, 1775 (73?), died May 19, 1837.
Hackney, Stephen, born Apr. 18, 1778, died Jan. 20, 1854, Christian Church.
Hakoy, (?) Louisa, died May, 1858, aged 45 years.
Herdman, Alfred, died Oct. 10, 1852, born Apr. 9, 1811.
Heflin, Sewell, born in N. C., June 14, 1805 (?) died Feb. 1, 1865, aged 56 years.
Howorth, Polly, died Jan. 31, 1849, aged about 52 years.
Howorth, Elizabeth, wife of Lawrence Howorth, died June 27, 1824, aged 53 years, 4 months, 5 days.
Howorth, Lawrence, died Mar. 21, 1818 (?) aged 48 years.
Howorth, John, born Sept. 19, 1800, died May 4, 1857.
Howorth, Lawrence, born Oct. 7, 1839, died July 25, 1860.
Hines, Jas. D., born Jan. 7, 1805, married Feb. 12, 1821, died Feb. 22, 1846. Pastor of Methodist Church.
Harney, Mrs. Hetty C., wife of Jas. E. (?) Harney, born July 26, 1813, died May 20, 1837.
Howorth—see Emily Burnam.
Helton, N. N., born Jan. 15, 1810, died Mar. 8, 1858.
Helton, Martha J., 1843-1859.

Jones, Franklin, born in Royalston, Ms. (?) Md., or Mass. (?), Aug 9, 1801, died Aug.16, 1846. For 11 years Pres. of Bowling Green Female Seminary.
Jackson, Eliza K., wife of J. S. Jackson, born in Prince Edward Co., Va., Mar. 21, 1805, died June 16, 1850 (56?).
Jones, Francis S., died Dec. 14, 1825, aged 18 (48?) years.
Jones, Esther, died Mar. 10, 1861, aged 83 years.
Jones, Wm. C., died Apr. 28, 1829, aged 34 years.
Jones, Wm. O. (?), died Aug. 28, 1829 (?), aged 41 (?) years.

Keel, John, Esq., died May 14, 1820 (1840?), aged 58 years and 29 days.
Keel, James, died July 9, 1859, aged 78 years.

Lucas, John S., born Sept. 30, 1791, died Apr. 16, 1852.
Lucas, Mrs. Margaret H., born May 23, 1789, died Oct. 1, 1868.
Loving, Juda, born 1811, died Feb. 2, 1860, aged 49 years.
Lapsley, Rev. Joseph, born Oct. 3, 1779, died Sept. 25, 1823, and dau.
Lapsley, Lavinna Ann, born May 9, 1811, died Oct. 1, 1826, and son.
Lapsley, Samuel, born July 3, 1817, died Feb. 1, 1819.

McAlister, Hannah, born Apr. 27, 1844, died Sept. 5, 1846.
McAlister, Wm., born Aug. 4, 1796, died Sept. 28, 1854.
McAlister, Emeline, E., born May 2, 1834, died Oct. 17, 1836.
McAlister, Robt. C., born Aug. 22, 1824, (21?), died Sept. 16, 1853.
McNeale, Geo., born Nov. 2, 1828, died Sept. 7, 1830 (?).
Marshall, Eliz. L., born in Va., Dec. 31, 1794, died Jan. 23, 1852
Marshall, Drusilla, born Mar. 17, 1831, died June 4, 1852.
Martin, Dr. Edw. B., born Mar. 16, 1797, died Jan. 25, 1825 (?).
Martin, Joseph B., son of E. B. and M. D. Martin, born Mar. 18, 1822, died Apr. 19, 1852.
Moss, Jane, wife of Thos. H. Moss, died Jan. 6, 1837, aged 72 years.
Morehead, Armistead, born June 4, 1767, died Aug. 26, 1826.
Morehead, Lucy, born Apr. 25, 1774, died Oct. 27, 1827.
Morehead, Cynthia—see Atchison.

Moore, Geo., born Apr. 15, 1759, died 1812.
Mitchell, Mrs. Sally, late Grider, wife of Asa T. Mitchell, died Nov. 2, 1859, in 67th year.
Mitchell, Asa T., died aged 69 years.
Mitchell, Martin, born Mar. 10, 1785, died Feb. 26, 1854.
Mallory, Mary, wife of Albert Mallory, born Jan. 17, 1835, died June 19, 1862.

Owens, Bettie, died Oct., 1856, aged 18 years and 4 months.
Owens, Perry, died Sept. 6, 1865, about 70 years of age.

Palmer, Susan, _____ _____ 1849 (?).
Payne, Betsey, wife of Wm. Payne, born Oct. 7, 1781, died Sept. 24, 1847.
Payne, Wm. R., born Oct., 1781, died Feb. 27, 1847.
Pollard, Mrs. Emily, wife of Thos. Pollard, dau. of John and Frances Courts, died Aug. __, 1831, aged 24 (?) years.
Parry, John J., born in Philadelphia, died Aug. 19, 1840 (?) aged 23 (?) years.
Potts, John, born Nov. 16, 1782, died May 17, 1847.
Potts, Nancy born May 2, 1776, died Mar. 3, 1859.

Robinson, Wm. native of Wharton, Lancashire, Eng., died Feb. 28, 1851, aged 69 years.
Robinson, Elizabeth, wife of Wm. R., died _____, 84 years.
Reese, Angeline, wife of Isaac Reese, born Sept. 7, 1811, died June 29, 1854.
Reese Isaac, born Sept. 24, 1786, died July 15, 1852.
Reese, Washington L., born Aug. 10, 1830, (1?), died July 22, 1832.
Reese, Harriet, wife of Isaac Reese, born Sept. 17, 1788, died Aug. 18, 1831.
Robinson, Jerry A., died June 18, 1860, aged 61 years, 1 month, 25 days.
Robinson, Jas. M., born Mar. 16, 1828, died May 28, 1856.
Rochester, Wm.—Not legible.

Smith, Wm., born in Culpeper County, Va., Feb. 28, 1772, died Oct. 4, 1861, aged 89 years, 7 months and 14 days.
Smith, Elizabeth, born Culpeper County, Va., Dec., 1789, died Mar., 1867.
Smith, Zacharia, born June 17, 1812 (?), died July 9, 1819 (49?).
Smith, Mrs. Virginia, wife of Zacharia Smith, born Dec. 31, 1820, died Aug. 11, 1847 (?).
Sulser, John, died Sept. 10, 1840, aged 55 years.
Sulser, Winey, wife of John Sulser, died June 21, 1854, aged 63 years and 2 months.
Shanks, Nancy Catherine, died _____ 29, 1832, aged 19 years.

Underwood, Henry M., born Mar. 7, 1794, died Sept. 24, 1863.
Underwood, Eliza M., wife of Joseph R. Underwood, born Aug. 31, 1800, died July 17, 1835.

Winn, C. B., and Cath_____—See Courts.
Work, Samuel, attorney, died Mar. 14, 1818, aged 45 years, 3 months and 7 days.
Wright, Harriett, wife of Isham Murrell, anddau. of Rev. N. L. and K. (?) L. Crawford, born Sept. 11, 1818, died Nov. 5, 1848—see Crawford.
Withers, Robert, brother of Francis Withers of South Carolina, died

1825, aged 4_ (?) years.
Wade, Cynthia W., died Nov. 1849, aged about 17 years.
Wade, Nancy J., died Feb., 1847, near 17 years of age.
(Two orphan sisters).
Wilson, Elizabeth, born 1781, died Apr. 11, 1854.

Yancy, John, born Apr. 4, 1787, died Oct. 6, 1818.
Yancey, Margaret, born 1788, died Mar. 18, 1819, (49?).

OLD CANE RIDGE GRAVEYARD
(Bourbon County, Kentucky)

(Inscriptions copied by Mrs. May Stoner Clay)

In the yard of historic old Cane Ridge Meeting House lie the remains of many early pioneers to Bourbon, and here also is buried the distinguished reformer and minister, Barton W. Stone, under whose ministry the church was established. A tall stone shaft marks his grave inscribed as follows:

"The Church of Christ at Cane Ridge and other generous friends in Kentucky have caused this monument to be erected as a tribute of affection and gratitude to Barton W. Stone, Minister of the gospel of Christ and the distinguished reformer of the nineteenth century. Born Dec. 24, 1772, died Nov. 9, 1844. His remains lie here. This monument erected, 1847."

Rev. James Hicklin, died 1819.
Thomas Stone, born 1807, died 1863.
Polly Wilson, consort of George Wilson, departed life, Aug. 5, 1803, in the 37th year of her age.
John G. Black, born 1812 (?), died 1816, erected by Sylvia Matson, Jane Holton and Alexander Whittenden, Harvey and Thomas Allen.
Elizabeth South, died 1823, aged 23 years.
William Black, died 1883, aged 66 years.
Roger, Fannie, Gracie, infant children of J. M. and A. E. Thomas.
Hezekiah B. Burris, born 1803, died 1870.
Mary, wife of B. Burris, born 1801, died 1867.
John Frakes, born 1778, died 1864.
Cynthia, consort of John Frakes, born 1789, died 1852.
Elizabeth, wife of Hamilton Wilson, born 1797, died 1847.
Ann Rogers Irvin, died 1845, in 47th year of age.
John M. Irvin, born 1790, died 1865.
Sara J., wife of John Irvin, born 1800, died 1858.
Amelia, wife of Hamilton Wilson, born 1791, died 1878, aged 82 yrs.
John T. Miller, M. D., born 1812, died 1854.
John R. Morris, died 1881, in 76th year of his age.
Rebecca, wife of J. R. Morris, born 1809, died 1881.
Sara E. Cole, daughter of J. B. Cole, born 1836, died 1862.
J. B. Neal, born 1806, died 1888.
Lucy, wife of J. B. Neal and daughter of Foster Collins, born 1811, died 1865.
Belinda, wife of Thomas Stone, died 1868, in 60th year of her age.
H. Clay Williams, died 1863.
Charles Thomas Colcord, died 1844.
Mary Wheeler, died 1854, aged 20 years.
John Bristow, born 1818, died 1876.

Louisa Colcord, born 1836, died 1853.
Charles B. Colcord, 1789-1854.
Louisa Colcord, consort of Charles B., died 1844, aged 44 years.
Frank P. Colcord, 1828-1899.
Geo. W. Lytle, 1818-1852.
Patsy Laughlin, consort of John Laughlin, died 1819, 25 years of age.
Caty Lucky, consort of Robert Lucky, died 1821, aged 47 years.
Anne, consort of John M. Proctor, born 1826, died 1851.
Louis Campbell, born 1790, died 1849.
Samuel A. Houston, born 1792, died 1851.
James Houston, born 1769, died 1853.
Nancy, consort of James Houston, born 1765, died 1855.
"Erected by David Jameson to the memory of his father and his mother—his beloved wife, Margaret and daughter, two nieces—buried at or near Cane Ridge. Also, one son in Ohio, one daughter in Mayslick, Ky., one sister in Mo. They all died in the hope of eternal life."
C. C. Rogers, born 1829, died 1880.
Nancy Anne Rogers, wife of Nathaniel P. Rogers, born 1813, died 1846. "Retiring modesty, truth in word and deed, and honesty of purpose ,attributes of the Redeemer, eminently possessed by the deceased. By one who knew her best and loved her most."
Nathaniel P. Rogers, 1807-1863.
Anne Rogers, wife of William Rogers, 1790-1816.
"William Rogers, born Campbell Co., Va., July, 1784; removed to Cane Ridge, Bourbon Co., April, 1798; united with the church of Christ at Cane Ridge, 1807; died Feb. 15, 1862, in the 78th year of life. He was the friend of God."
"Here lies Nathaniel Rogers who was born July 23, 1755. He was a member of the Convention that framed the Constitution of Kentucky, 1799. What is of far more consequence, he was a member of the Church of Christ in the bosom of which he died, Dec. 22, 1801, at the age of 49 and reposes in the midst of his friends he loved so well. His only son (William Rogers) from a sentiment of filial respect consecrates this stone as a memento to his memory."
Nancy Cogswill, wife of James M. Cogswill and daughter of William Rogers, died 1860, aged 60 years.
GRAVES KNOWN TO BE IN THIS CEMETERY BUT NOT FOUND
Capt. John Phelps and wife, and their daughter, Oliphet, wife of Richard Cornick.

CONCORD BURYING GROUND
(Mason County, Ky.)
(Contributed by Mrs. Elizabeth Frisbie)

James Quiett, died July 23, 1858, aged about 79 years.
Ellen, wife of James Quiett, died Feb. 11, 1861, aged about 84 years.
Elisa Ellen, wife G. F. Quiett, born Apr. 10, 1846, died June 13, 1872.
Greenup Quiett, died Oct. 26, 1852, aged 36 yrs. 11 mo. 4 da.

ELIZABETHTOWN CEMETERY
(Hardin County)

The following data was taken at random from the cemetery at Elizabethtown, Ky., by Hattie M. Scott, Frankfort, Ky., July 4, 1930, in an attempt to get all of the very old dates. Some of the stones had disintegrated so they were not legible. Some dates are uncertain when followed by question mark.

Adair, Isaac C.—died Feb. 5, 1827, aged 35 years.
Arnold, Susan—wife of W. J. Arnold, born May 25, 1838, died May 4, 1860.
Arnold, W. J.—died 1860, aged 34 years, 10 months, 11 days.
Arthur, Meredith—born Jan. 4 ,1805, died Sept. 28, 1889.
Arthur, Belindar—born May 20, 1808, died Oct. 4, 1852, aged 44 years.
Arnold, Penelope—wife of George Arnold, born Feb. 11, 1792, died Feb. 14, 1835.
Arnold, Jacob—son of George and Penelope Arnold, 1825-1849.

Barr, Thom.—Jan 18, 180_?, died Oct. 24, 1865.
Brown, Thos.—born Mar. 14, 1812, died Apr. 7, 1855.
Bunnell, Elizabeth H.—wife of A. A. Bunnell, born Jan. 13, 1823, died Oct .1, 1884.
Bunnell, A. A.—born July 17, 1805, died Aug. 16, 1885.
Barrett, Joshua—1831-1851.

Carpenter, Hannah—born Nov. __, 1780, died April __, 1845.
Church____?, Elizabeth—wife of John _____.
Cunningham, Mary Caroline—wife of A. H., dau. of H. G. and E. H. Wintersmith, born Mar. 29, 1816, died Dec. 19, 1842.
Charle, (?) Charlotte _____ ?.
Cully, ____eretta—wife _____?.
Cunningham, Susan Hundley—born Oct. 23, 1783, died Sept. 15, 1868.

Dudley, Thos.—age 3 yrs. son of Thos. Dudley and Eliza Y. Brown.
Davis, Mary—wife of Obed Davis, died Sept. 10, 1842, aged 84 years.

Elliott, Stephen—1823-1856.
Elliott, Frances—wife of Stephen Elliott, 1815-1852.
Elliot, Mary—wife of Stephen Elliott, 1824-1873.
Fairleigh, Lettice—wife of Andrew Fairleigh, died Oct. 10, 1845, aged 67 years.
Fairleigh, Andrew—died March 1, 1829 _____?.
_____, John—_____ died 1818?.

Gardner, James, Sr.—born Oct. 21, 1780, died Apr. 4, 1857.
Gardner, Abraham S.—born 1809, died 1875.
Gardner, Mary E.—wife of Abraham, born 1813, died 1882.
Gardner, Elizabeth Spur—wife of James Gardner, born Jefferson County, Virginia, Aug. 12, 1788, died Mar. 4, 1856.
Gardner, D. H.—born July 28, 1825, died _____ --, 1882.

Haycraft, Samuel—died Oct. 15, 1825, aged 71 years, 1 month, 4 days.
Haycraft, Margaret—wife of Samuel Haycraft, died Apr. 12, 1843, aged 83 years, 3 months, 16 days.
Howard, _____—see Stovall and Wintersmith.
Hastings, _____many—did not copy.
Helm, John—born in Prince William County, Virginia, Nov. 1761, to Kentucky in 1779, _____ Mar. 17, ____, died Apr. 3, 1840.
Helm, Sally—wife of John Helm, died Jan. 19, 1853, in 80th year.
Helm, Lewis—son of John Helm, born Jan. 17, 1808, died Nov. 12, 1838.
Helm, Maj. Henry P.—died 1845, aged 53 years.
Hill, Jonathan—born June 17, 1792, died Feb.20, 1856.—(8?).

Hill, Lucy—wife of Jonathan Hill, born April 27, 1793, died May __, 18__, aged (?) _8 years.

Isler, Jacob—husband of Caroline Wintersmith, born June, 1776, died July 4, 1819.

Joplin, Jas.—born Bedford County, Virginia, Nov. 14, 1807, died May 12, 1900.

Kennys, _____—many_____
Kurtz, Elizabeth H.—died Sept. 25, 1834, aged 40 years ,10 months, 13 days.
Kurtz, Conrad—born Feb. 20, 1807, died Jan. 28, 1879.
Kurtz, Susan—wife, 1816-1870.

Larue, J. Warren—born Dec. 27, 1797, died Jan. 10, 1866.
Larue, Eliza—wife of J. Warren Larue, born Feb. 4, 1804, died 1891.

McQuown, Nancy—wife of R. W. McQuown, died July 13, 1842.
McLean, Frances Elvira—wife of Hector D. McLean, daughter of Chas. G. and Ann Wintersmith, born Apr. 15, 1830, died Aug. 28, 1860.
Morris, Milly—second wife of John Morris, born Sept. 17, 1789, died Oct. 5, 1860.
Morehead, Matilda—wife of H. G. Wintersmith, born Jan. 31, 1793, died Feb. 25, 1826.
Miller, Arkgerthooe—wife of F. Miller, born Sept. 1, 1833, died July 2, 1873.
Matheny, James—died Oct. 5, 1831, aged 82 years. (32?).
Morris, John—born May 27, 1789, died Mar. 6, 1865.
Morris, Mary—wife of John Morris, born Nov. 7, 1796, died Dec. 5, 1834.
Matthis, George—born Mar. 29, 1775, died Aug. 19, 1848, aged 74 years, 4 months, 29 days.
Matthis, Mary A.—wife of George Matthis, died May 24, 1834 (?) in 74 year (?).
Matthis, Mrs. Nanny—wife of Samuel Matthis, and daughter of John and Ann Curd, born Mar. 9, 1804, died June 26, 1834. (Long obituary on stone).

Power, Frances—born 1795, aged 63 years. (Died aged 63 years?).
Park, George—born Jan. 12, 1773, died Mar. 24, 1857 (37?), aged 77 (?) years, 1 month, 24 days.
Park, John—born Oct. 21, 1800, died Nov. 30 1856. (died 1850?).
Park, Alice—wife of George Park, born 1782, died 1856, aged 74 years.
Park, Katherine—wife of John Park, died Sept. 10, 1858, aged 36 years.
Park, Nancy—wife of James Park, died _____?.
Park, James—died May 21, 1823, aged 27 years.
Park, Elizabeth—wife of George Park, born July 26, 1777, died Sept. 9, 1824.

Rogers, Mrs. Jane—wife of G. L. Rogers, died Mar. 22, 1823, aged 27 years, 4 months.
Rogers, Jas. W.—died Dec. 1829, in 26th (?) year.
Redman, Jas. H.—1825-1862.
Redman, Nancy—wife of John Redman, born Feb. 18, 1799, died Oct. 2, 1849, aged 50 years, 8 months, 1 day.

Stovall, Elizabeth Howard—wife of Thos. Stovall, born June 6, 1760, died Mar. 10, 1835.   Mother-in-law of H. G. Wintersmith.

Stevens, Clarissa—born May 28, 1827, died 1891.

Smith, Dr. J. W.—born Aug. 26, 1796, died Sept. 2, 1253.

_____, (?) W_____—1839, aged 32 years.

Shepherd, Rebecca—died Mar. 23, 1871, aged 78 years, 11 months, 8 days.

Strickler, G. W.—born Mar. 6, 1818, died Dec. 30, 1859, 41 years, 3 months, 26 days.

Strickler, Edna—wife of Jacob Strickler, born Oct. 30, 1782, died 1851.

Strickler, Nancy—wife of G. W. Strickler, died May 26, 1833, aged 37.

Strickler, _____—see Wilmoth.

Stone, W. D.—died June 6, 1819, aged 32 years.

Strickler, Geo. W.—born Feb. 10, 1796, died May 12, 1877.

Showers, Henry M.—born Nov. 13, 1821, Jefferson County, Virginia, died Aug. 9, 1877.

Showers, Mary—1826-1909, and others.

Thorp, Ann—died Aug. 21, 1847, aged 53 years.

Thorp, Geo.—died Feb. 1828, in 33rd year.

Wathen, Elizabeth—wife of John B. Wathen, born July 19, 1808, died Nov. 6, 1831, aged 23 years.

Wilmoth, Christina J.—born Dec. 27, 1775, died Mar. 22, 1828, aged 62 years, 2 months, 25 days.   Mother of Jacob and Geo. W. Strickler, Sr.

Wathen, Henry—son of C. and G. Wathen, born June 6, 1817, died June 6, 1824.

Warfield, Roderick—born in Ann Arundel County, Maryland, Oct. 16, 1786, to Kentucky 1818, died Jan. 20, 1862.

Warfield, Ann—wife of Roderick Warfield, born June 10, 1792, died Oct. 17, 1866.

Warfield, John Augustus—son of Roderick and Ann Warfield, born Maryland, Nov. 19, 1817, died June 19, 1863.

Warfield, Rachel (Johnston)—1825-1898.

Weller, _____—born in Maryland, died Aug. 21, 1847.

Weller, Susan M. J.—wife of Daniel M. Weller, 1819-1848.

Wintersmith, Elizabeth Hodgen—wife of H. G. Wintersmith, born Jan. 26, 1787, died May 4, 1819.

Wintersmith, Horation Gates—born May 15, 1785, died Jan. 2, 1835. (Small stone has born "85" and large one has born "1786").

Wintersmith, Matilda Morhead—wife of H. G. Wintersmith, born Jan. 31, 1793, died Feb. 25, 1826.

Wintersmith, Mary Caroline—wife of A. H. Cunningham and daughter of H. G. and E. H. Wintersmith, born Mar. 29, 1816, died Dec. 19, 1842.

Wintersmith, Sarah Elizabeth—wife of H. E. English and daughter of H. G. and E. H. Wintersmith, born Mar. 27, 1818, died June 25, 1841.

Wintersmith, Elizabeth Howard—wife of Thos. Stovall, born June6, 1760, died May 10, 1835, mother-in-law of H. G. Wintersmith.

Wintersmith, Virginia—daughter of H. G. and J. C. Wintersmith, born July 15, 1831, died July 8, 1832.

Wintersmith, Eliza Curd—daughter of H. G. and M. W. Wintersmith, born Jan. 25, 1825, died July 11, 1830.

Wintersmith, Matilda—born July 3, 1829, died 1830.

Wintersmith, Horace G.—born Oct. 10, 1811, died July 7, 1854.

Wintersmith, Chas. G.—born in Berkeley County , Virginia, Sept. 17, 1789, died Oct. 1, 1852, aged 63 years.

Wintersmith,—many more of younger generations.

INDEX

Barbee, 134, 185, 186
Barber, 134, 173, 176
Barbour, 49, 50, 137, 149
Barghman, 106
Bark, 176
Barkalow (Barcalow), 79
Barkley (Barcley), 176, 222
Barksdel, 66
Barlow, 160
Barnell (Barnett), 152
Barsdale, 156
Bartholt, 119
Barnett (Barnet, Barnette), 57, 64,
     66, 69, 101, 110, 120, 132, 153
Barney, 176
Barnhill, 159, 181
Barnor, 33
Barns (Barnes), 23, 24, 81, 125,
     171, 173, 174, 175, 176, 177
Barr 128, 179, 181, 228
Barret (Barrett), 145, 147, 169,
     228
Bartlett, 31, 44, 45, 81
Bartram, 119
Barycraft, 67
Baseman, 101, 104, 105, 106
Bashaw, 176
Basey, 19
Basket, 176
Bateman, 175, 176
Bates, 14, 169
Bath Co. Marriages, 171-174
Bath Co. Wills, 10-12
Bathe, 108
Bathes, 219
Batson, 19
Batterton, 62, 189, 190
Batterton Bible, 189-190
Baughn, 179
Baxter, 15, 35
Baylor, 120
Bayse, 19
Beabout, 176
Beacham, 161
Beachamp, 143
Beadell,, 154
Beading (Reading), 144
Beall, 133, 135, 165
Bealle, 137
Bean, 33
Beard, 79, 105, 178
Beasley, 41, 68
Beason, 125
Beatty, 15, 131, 159
Beaty, 42
Beck, 176
Beckner, 176, 177
Beckwith, 49

Becraft, 174
Bedford, 115, 148, 217
Beeson, 123
Beggs, 25, 26
Begham, 158
Belingall, 68
Bell, 34, 40, 69, 97, 99, 107, 117,
     118, 136, 140, 152, 176, 192,
     210, 211
Bell (Beal), 103
Bellis, 158
Belt, 126, 175
Benedict, 58
Benham, 39
Benners, 41
Bennett, 30, 100, 107, 124, 125,
     175, 182
Bennington, 126, 176
Benson 23, 112
Bensten, 33
Bentley, 167, 176
Bently, 176
Benton, 175
Berden, 172
Bernard, 100
Berne, 176
Bernet, 65
Berry, 11, 35, 65, 105, 113, 146,
     175, 181, 186 187
Berryman 167, 168
Berthand, 50
Beshaw, 14, 172
Bever, 17
Bibb, 168, 213, 214
Bibby, 133
Bicknell, 222
Biddle, 18, 176, 177, 222,
Bier, 30
Biddlo, 176
Biggers, 36
Biggs, 54
Billingsley, 183, 196
Bird, 175
Bishop, 44, 47, 176, 178, 202
Black, 26, 42, 54, 64, 65, 69, 182,
     199, 207 226
Blackbourn 165
Blackburn, 173
Blackford, 40
Blackwell, 39, 40, 62
Blain, 24, 54, 148
Blair, 15, 21, 121, 127, 155, 166,
     168, 176 177
Blak, 183
Blanchard, 31
Blanton, 99
Blasingame, 30
Bledsoe, 13, 34, 42, 67, 153

136, 141, 147, 152, 167, 168,
171, 174, 175, 176, 177, 185,
187, 228
Browne, 192
Brownfield 143
Browning, 124, 176, 177, 178
Bruce, 22, 113, 127, 174, 176
Brumbaugh, 196
Brumly, 31
Bruner, 179
Brush, 102, 104, 105
Bryan, 14, 108, 120, 153, 174, 200
Bryant, 67, 179
Bryson, 10
Buckner, 116
Buchannan, 39, 176, 221
Buchner (Buckner), 49
Buck, 136
Buckley, 178
Buckner, 24, 31, 41, 47, 122, 136,
181, 191, 192, 193
Buckner Bible, 191-193
Buehlen, 56
Buel, 13
Buford, 22, 59, 135, 159
Builderback, 175
Bullard (Ballard), 93
Bulas, 175
Bullitt, 47, 48
Bullock, 36, 48, 113, 120, 122, 131,
138, 195
Bumbgamer, 173
Bunion, 19
Bunnell, 176, 228
Burbridge, 159
Burch, 193
Burch Bible, 193
Burey (Berry), 179, 180
Burger, 105
Burgin, 63, 69
Burgess, 176
Burk, 172, 175
Burke, 123, 124, 176
Burman, 68
Burnam, 222, 223
Burne, 42
Burnes, 172, 176
Burnet, 63
Burns, 26, 101, 172, 176
Burnsides, 66
Burres, 175
Burress, 175, 176, 177
Burris, 35, 176, 226
Burrogues, 176
Burt, 131
Burton, 57, 93, 163, 165, 166, 176
Busby, 175, 176
Bush, 42
Bussis, 176

Bustard, 46
Butcher, 10, 174, 175
Butland, 119
Butler, 16, 24, 52, 66, 68, 119, 120,
171
Butly, 176
Button, 181
Byars, 57, 108
Byram, 174
Byers, 80
Byrd, 110, 112
Byrne, 42

Caldwell, 10, 17, 64, 156, 172, 177
Calk, 64
Call, 14
Calla, 183
Callahan, 177
Callaman, 124
Callehan, 177
Callerman, 177, 178
Callis, 48, 103
Calloway, 37, 65, 99, 101, 103
Calmes, 99
Calvert, 21, 177, 194, 210
Calvert Bible, 193-194
Cammack, 39
Campbell, 21, 30, 39, 45, 63, 69
104, 108, 116, 122, 125, 131,
150, 154, 159, 172, 174, 177,
221, 223, 227
Canada, 39
Canaday, 33, 167
Cane Ridge Graveyard, 226-227
Cannon, 10, 14, 172
Canstant, 125
Canterbery, 157
Cantrel, 171
Cantrell, 171
Cantrill, 157
Cape, 177
Car, 177
Cardwell, 205
Carey, 122
Carhagy, 102
Carlisle, 179
Carmer, 178
Carnahan, 23, 176
Carnan, 129
Carneal, 42, 138
Carnwell, 177
Carny, 55
Carpenter, 63, 106, 174, 175, 176,
177, 182, 228
Carr, 34, 119, 156, 177, 211, 213,
214
Carrel, 176
Carrell, 79, 80
Carrick, 145

Carrington, 220
Carroll, 41, 158
Carson, 39
Carter, 15, 23, 49, 98, 155, 177, 179, 182
Cartmeal, 171, 173
Cartmell, 157
Cartmill, 131
Casady (Cassaty), 168
Cassady, 102, 107
Case, 15, 21, 112, 178
Casey, 104
Cash, 64
Caska, 176
Casner, 17
Cassidy, 123, 177
Cassity, 172, 173, 174, 176, 177
Cast, 36
Castleman, 80
Catline, 108
Cave, 80, 97, 115, 161, 177
Cavender, 160
Cayton, 175
Caywood, 177
Cemmons (Cummons), 10
Chadwick, 153
Challen, 223
Chambers, 45, 63, 80, 106, 150
Chamblin, 20, 115
Chammon, 62
Champ, 23, 27, 113
Champion, 179
Chandler, 143, 174
Chanslor, 79
Chanulor, 13
Chaplin, 50
Chapman, 52, 119, 177, 199
Chappell, 126
Charle, 228
Charton, 119
Chatain, 174
Cheatham, 34
Cheek, 193
Chenault, 63
Cherry, 183
Chew, 120, 166
Childers, 172
Childs, 155
Chiles, 30, 40, 52, 215,
Chilton, 67, 68
Chinn, 21, 120, 143
Chipman, 173, 174
Chisham, 158
Chisholm, 33
Chisum, 69
Chizum, 63
Choat, 173, 176
Choate, 176

Chrisman, 179
Christian, 40
Christley, 52
Christman, 177
Christy, 34, 127, 176, 177
Church, 228
Churchill, 48, 52
Church Records, 184-187
Cincaid, 172
Claiborne, 134, 170
Clancy, 178
Clark (see Clarke), 24, 40, 53, 54, 56, 106, 110, 120, 129, 143, 157, 167, 168, 169, 173, 175, 176, 185, 217, 223
Clark Co. Index to Inventories, 38
(Names not included in this Index)
Clark Co. Wills, 32-37
Clark Co. Index to Will Book A, 31-32
(Names not included in this Index)
Clarke (see Clark), 25, 33, 34, 102, 103, 105, 140, 149, 177
Clarkson, 19, 100, 104, 105, 106, 129
Clary, 152, 223
Clawson, 35, 123
Clay, 13, 23, 40, 62, 66, 118, 132, 148, 168, 176, 215, 216, 217, 226
Clayton, 69, 144, 173, 174, 175
Clement, 58
Clements, 104, 113
Clemins, 178
Clendennin, 21
Clensing, 178
Cleveland, 146
Clevenger, 17
Clifft, 175
Clift, 177
Cline, 177, 178
Clinkenbeard, 14, 21, 101, 107, 108, 113, 115
Clore, 50
Cloud, 129
Clough, 190
Cloyd, 57, 63
Cluck, 177
Coats, 34
Cob, 173
Cobb, 177, 211, 212
Cobler, 30
Coburn, 122
Cocker, 107
Cochran, 175, 176, 177
Cockeran (see Cochran, Couchran), 177
Codes, 177

Funstall, 48
Furgarson, 172
Furman, 105

Gaffney, 49
Gaheagan, 81
Gaines, 150, 158
Gaither, 108
Gaitskill, 220, 221
Galasby, 174
Galaway, 183
Gale, 146
Gallan, 80
Gallatin, 178
Galloway, 14, 104, 105, 106, 159, 186, 187
Gano, 30, 33, 40, 41, 42, 158
Gardner, 53, 177, 228
Garland, 53
Garnett, 38, 121
Garrard, 14, 21, 41, 108, 112, 186, 187
Garret, 56
Garrett, 121, 153
Garry, 50
Garten, 143
Garvan, 123
Garvel, 174
Gary, 129
Gass (Goss, Gess), 64, 107, 108, 180
Gaston, 64
Gates, 174
Gatewood, 57, 98
Gather, 131
Gathright, 182
Gatliff, 112
Gawthorn, 56
Gay, 188
Gelaspie, 37
Gellaspe, 34
Gellespie, 64
Gentry, 35, 65, 68, 69
George, 146, 176, 189, 190
Gess (see Gass), 69, 107
Gettys, 176
Gibson, 38, 42, 58, 198, 199
Gibson Bible, 298-299
Gilbert, 57, 58, 112, 163, 175
Giles, 57
Gill, 10, 93, 127
Gillespie, 69
Gilly, 55
Gilmon, 165
Gilson, 40
Giltner, 99
Ginna, 33

Gist, 33, 34, 40, 110, 141
Given, 131
Givens, 19, 114, 152, 178
Glasgow, 14, 15
Glass, 34, 51, 52
Glenn, 66, 67, 159
Glover, 51, 173
Goas, 175, 176
Goddard, 24, 127, 175
Godgell, 10
Godman, 24, 51, 106, 147
Goggin, 64
Goldsmith, 59
Goodan, 173
Goodburn, 48
Goodhue, 177
Gooding, 123
Goodloe, 65
Goosey, 36, 37
Gordan (Gorden, Gordin, Gordon), 33, 34, 152, 176, 178, 199, 200
Gordon-Walter Bible, 199-200
Gornel, 174
Gorham, 116, 117
Goslin, 127
Gosney, 101
Gouchman, 177
Gouge (Googe), 67
Gouner (Gonner), 182
Grady, 150
Graham, 10, 24, 30, 39, 40, 42, 116, 128, 132, 154, 174, 197, 223, 224
Grain 176
Grainger, 192
Grant, 112, 160, 166
Graves, 16, 17, 40, 41, 97, 116, 135, 168, 174
Gray, 53, 54, 63, 114, 172, 174
Grayham, 24, 171
Greamer, 178
Greathouse, 24
Green, 11, 16, 17, 39, 45, 49, 126, 157, 171, 173
Greene (Green), 136
Greenup, 40, 41, 132, 134, 135
Greer, 123
Gregg, 159, 177
Gregory, 173, 174
Grider, 184, 223, 225
Griffin, 175
Griffing, 101, 104, 106, 117, 171
Griffith, 100, 144, 215, 217
Griffy, 17
Griggs, 81
Grigsby, 101
Grimes, 13, 14, 169, 171
Grinnings, 149

Mappin, 11, 173
March, 186
Marean, 129
Marie, 119
Mark, 26, 176
Markham, 18, 23, 115
Markland, 102, 103
Markwell, 56
Marney, 19
Marr, 204
Marr Bible, 204
Marrs, 53, 55
Marrsee, 53
Marshall, 42, 80, 98, 99, 101, 110,
    112, 113, 121, 123, 124, 133,
    134, 136, 140, 160, 165, 196,
    210, 224
Martin, 17, 35, 45, 59, 65, 66, 92,
    99, 103, 108, 109, 110, 111,
    131, 152, 153, 224
Martinie, 38
Masey (Maxey), 173
Mash, 18
Mason, 19, 66, 115, 134, 136, 166
Mason Co. Index to Estates, 69-79
    (Names not included in this Index)
Mason Co. Wills, 79-81
Masoner, 115, 180
Massie, 47
Masterson, 111, 141
Mastin, 14, 167
Matheny, 22, 229
Mathews, 175
Matson, 21, 102
Matthews, 33, 115, 226
Matthis, 229
Maupine, 63
Maury, 53, 135, 166
Maxey, 173
Maxwell (Maxwells), 66, 68, 98,
    168
May, 129, 131, 140, 161, 162
Mays, 19
Mayhew, 184
Mealy, 129
Means, 132
Mecawl ,68
Meekins, 196
Melcher, 134
Mellott, 51
Melvin, 27
Menefee, 11, 159
Menis, 171
Mennis, 131
Menzies, 215, 217
Mercer, 50, 56, 161
Meredith, 26
Merewether, 93, 154

Merity, 177
Merriwether, 48, 56
Merry, 69, 162
Mersham, 178
Metcalf, 176
Metcalfe, 21
Meteer, 154
Metheny, 19
Milcher, 133
Michel, 171
Miles, 39, 162
Mills, 17, 24, 54, 130, 177, 184, 186
Mils, 177
Miller, 17, 18, 26 30 37, 47, 48, 50,
    55, 63, 64, 65, 66, 81, 109, 110,
    111, 119, 123, 140, 143, 144,
    145, 147, 152, 159, 171, 172,
    174, 179, 180, 183, 184, 186,
    206, 214, 226, 229
Miller Bible, 206
Milligan, 15
Million, 64
Milly, 173
Milnar, 144
Milner, 182
Milton, 148
Minner (Minnear), 171
Minnis, 182
Minor, 48, 205
Misner, 45
Mitchell, 10, 14, 16, 20, 23, 24, 25,
    30, 64, 68, 80, 92, 105, 106,
    112, 113, 114, 119, 140, 154,
    156, 166, 167, 172, 185, 186,
    187, 201, 202, 225
Mitter, 99
Moffett, 154, 155, 172
Moffitt, 203
Moler, 172
Monday, 42, 151
Montgomery, 39, 41, 59, 64, 67, 97,
    132, 152, 153
Montgomery Co. Deeds, 153-157
Monthomery (Montgomery), 38
Mountjoy, 20, 153
Moody, 59, 67, 148
Moon, 140, 168
Mooney, 176
Moor, 172
Moore, 18, 19, 20, 25, 30, 33, 48,
    57, 63, 64, 66, 67, 99, 106, 118,
    119, 121, 136, 139, 143, 144,
    152, 156, 159, 172, 174, 178,
    202, 207, 208, 225
Moore-Ardery Bible, 206
Moorehead (see Morehead), 67
Moorman, 218
Moran, 118, 211,

Set, 171
Setson, 56
Settle, 40, 140, 141
Seyms, 145
Sexton, 157
Shackleford, 35, 59, 68, 175
Shaley, 21
Shallers, 134
Shanklin, 104, 172
Shanks, 58, 225
Shannon, 97, 101, 105, 119, 127, 134, 159, 175
Shannonhouse, 47
Shanton, 17
Sharpe, 33, 93, 133 ,149, 185, 186
Sharrah, 20
Shaw, 21, 51, 120
Shawbridge, 46
Shawhen, 63, 107
Shearer, 140
Shelby Co. Index to Estates, 99-92
    (Names not included in this Index)
Shelby Co. Records, 92-94
Shelton, 153
Shelby, 214
Shely Bible, 214-215
Shepard, 189, 202
Shepherd, 119, 230
Sheperd, 30
Sheppard, 198
Shepperd, 176
Sheridan, 56
Sherley, 55
Sherman, 145
Sheubert, 171
Shields, 59
Shiell, 41
Shipp, 14, 40, 46, 55, 118, 130, 162, 164, 192
Shiving, 48
Shoales, 30
Shoat (Chout), 173
Shockey, 177
Shoots, 171
Short, 69, 154
Shortridge, 14, 21
Shotwell, 81
Showers, 230
Shrader, 183
Shropshire, 105, 215
Shrout, 174
Shuford, 21
Shultz, 173
Shutt, 55
Shutts, 171, 172
Silk, 31
Silvers, 58
Simmolt, 17

Simons, 151
Simpson, 17, 24, 111, 115, 154, 156, 176
Simmons, 147
Simms, 177
Sims, 139, 189
Sinclair, 11, 12, 160
Sincler, 191
Singleton, 180, 181
Sinkens, 64
Sinyard, 144
Sites, 22
Six, 156, 172, 173
Skidmore, 49
Skiley, 176
Skillman, 211
Skimerhorn, 50
Skinner, 13, 141
Slack, 22, 210
Slade, 147
Slagle, 19
Slaughter, 13, 41, 98, 131
Sliger, 44, 49
Sloan, 59
Skinner, 141
Small, 81, 114, 173
Smallwood, 109
Smart, 21, 41, .68, 172, 200, 206
Smartwelders, 26
Smelzer, 23
Smily, 173
Smiser, 17, 18, 147, 150
Smith, 14, 17, 19, 20, 22, 23, 24, 26, 34, 39, 40, 42, 47, 50, 54, 56, 57, 59 81, 100, 101, 103, 104, 108, 110, 111, 113, 115, 116, 120, 123, 126, 130, 131, 132, 136, 140, 144, 145, 147, 149, 151, 152, 153, 154, 155, 156, 172, 173, 176, 180, 181, 185, 187, 189, 210, 211, 214, 215, 220, 221, 225, 230
Smith Bible, 215
Smoot, 178
Snapp, 22
Snedekar, 178
Sneed, 41, 54, 132
Snell, 97
Snelling, 12
Snethan, 33
Snodgrass, 23, 151
Snoddy, 64, 68, 153
Snody, 152
Snowden, 45, 54
Snyder, 132
Sowdoskie (Sodowsky, Sandusky), 104, 152, 153
Sodowsky (Sowdoskie, Sandusky),